"THE FANTASY ALMANAC"

Jeff Rovin

A Dutton Paperback

E. P. DUTTON / NEW YORK

BOOK DESIGN: Jos. Trautwein

For information contact: E.P. Dutton, 2 Park Avenue,
New York, N.Y. 10016

Library of Congress Cataloging in Publication Data

Rovin, Jeff.
  The fantasy almanac.
  SUMMARY: An alphabetically arranged review of people,
events, places, and characters significant in folklore,
comic strips, television, and other media of fantasy.
    1. Curiosities and wonders—Dictionaries. [1. Curi-
osities and wonders—Dictionaries] I. Title.
AG243.R63 1979   031   79-11757

ISBN: 0-525-47600-8
Published simultaneously in Canada by Clarke, Irwin & Company Limited, Toronto and Vancouver

10 9 8 7 6 5 4 3 2 1
First Edition

For Ric Meyers:

author, scholar, and good friend

ACKNOWLEDGMENTS

The author would like to thank Ric Estrada, Steve Bissette, Pat Boyette, Mike Snyder, Leo Summers, Rick Veitch, and Tom Yeates for their fine illustrations. A nod, too, to Jim Warren for permission to let Creepy, Eerie, and Vampirella out of the dungeon; to Richard Meyers for short-stopping in the research department; to superagent Jim Trupin; and to Geraldine Duclow of the Free Library of Philadelphia for helping to locate some terribly obscure data. Special thanks to Bill Whitehead who blue-penciled the manuscript with care, enthusiasm, and intelligence, and to the ever-diligent Dave Schow whose digging would do an archaeologist proud!

KEY TO CLASSIFICATIONS

[C]	Comics
[F]	Folklore
[FT]	Fairy Tale
[H]	History
[L]	Literature
[M]	Mythology
[MP]	Motion Pictures
[O]	Occult
[TV]	Television
[U]	Unexplained
[E]	Etcetera

Abrasax

Abrasax [O] A demon whose name derives from the mystical word Abracadabra. Abrasax carries a whip and is pictured as either a king with serpents for legs or a two-legged dragon with the head of a cock. The sum of the seven Greek letters which comprise his name is 365, making him the lord of the 365 virtues, one for every day of the year.

Ackerman, Forrest J. [E] Born November 24, 1916, in Los Angeles, California, to William and Carroll Ackerman. Married to Wendayne Wahrman, "Forry" is the curator of Hollywood's Ackermansion, the world's largest fantasy and science fiction museum. Since 1958 he has been the editor of *Famous Monsters of Filmland* magazine, as well as the head of the fantasy-oriented Ackerman Literary Agency. Ackerman is credited with having coined the term *sci-fi* and, with Wendayne, has edited over one hundred American paperback editions of the adventures of the German science fiction hero Perry Rhodan. see: **Rhodan, Perry.**

Actaeon [M] A celebrated hunter in Greek mythology, Actaeon was the son of Autonoë and her husband, Aristaeus. He was also the grandson of the famous dragon-killer Cadmus of Thebes and the great grandson of King Agenor of Phoenicia. Raised by Chiron the centaur, Actaeon is famous for having stumbled upon the goddess Artemis and her nymphs while they were bathing. Allowing his eyes to lin-

ger, he was noticed by the deity and punished for his imprudence by being transformed into a stag. Panicking, Actaeon fled to Mt. Cithaeron. When he reached the peak, insult was heaped upon injury as the enchanted hunter was attacked and killed by his own fifty dogs. see: **Artemis; Centaur; Nymph.**

Aesop [L] A sixth-century B.C. Greek noted for his moralistic fantasies. Little is known about the historical Aesop. Born in Phrygia in 620, he was apparently deformed. A slave, he served on the island of Samos until being granted his freedom, after which he did a great deal of traveling. Aesop probably would have lived longer had he remained a slave. Visiting Delphi in 560, he accused the residents of overcharging for the use of their oracle. Smarting from the doubtless accuracy of the allegation, they framed Aesop as a thief by placing a gold bowl in his luggage and threw him from a cliff as punishment. Nonetheless, Aesop had a long life during which he authored many fables about animals getting themselves into very human predicaments and learning valuable morals. Among his most famous tales are "The Fox and the Grapes," "The Goose That Laid the Golden Eggs," "The Bat and the Weasels," and "The Lion and the Mouse."

Agib [L] The hero of *The Arabian Nights* tale "Son of a King." The son of King Cassib, proud Agib is at sea when his ship nears the Black Mountain which, a sailor cautions, "attracts to itself all the iron and nails in your ship. This it is that causes the side of the mountain towards the sea to appear of such a dense blackness." Alas, the warning comes too late and the ship falls apart, a victim of the magnetic peak. Agib alone survives, and is able to swim to shore. He is eventually rescued by a metal man in a boat, but that is only the beginning of Agib's adventures. He is subsequently sewn into a sheepskin and carried off by a roc; encounters a black, gold-saddled, winged horse (". . . the handsomest and best-shaped animal I have ever seen . . ."); and faces other wonders before making his way back to Bagdad.

Like many characters in *The Arabian Nights*, the once-smug Agib is humbled by his brush with these denizens of the fantastic. see: **Roc; Scheherezade.**

Agmar [TV] Created by Walter Koenig for "The Infinite Vulcan," an episode in the "Star Trek" cartoon series. Agmar is the leader of the plant beings on Phylos, a world visited by the U.S.S. *Enterprise.* The two-eyed creatures are stalklike, with many legs and a wealth of tendril arms. Intelligent beings, they plan to use clones of Mr. Spock to help regain the long lost glory of their race.

The voice of Agmar was provided by actor James Doohan. see: ***Enterprise*, U.S.S.; Spock, Mr.**

Ahkiyyinni [F] A character from Eskimo folklore. In life, Ahkiyyinni loved to dance. He lived near the Arctic river of Kuvañik and, when he died, he was buried at the top of a nearby hill. A few years later, people sailing down the river spotted his grave and jokingly asked why he wasn't dancing now. In response to their taunt, Ahkiyyinni's skeletal remains pushed from the earth and broke into a feverish jig. Then he removed his shoulder blade and, using his lower arm bone, played it like a drum. The people on the river were terrified, for his gavotte was causing the ground to shake and their boat to rock. They begged him to stop, but with every plea Ahkiyyinni danced even faster. Eventually, the boat overturned and the people drowned.

Ahpuch [M] The Mayan god of death. In itself an evil calling, it was not for this alone that Ahpuch was feared and detested. He also personified all that was wicked and unlucky, and was forever battling the good gods of life and fertility.

In art, Ahpuch is represented as a skull devoid of all flesh.

Aladdin [L] Perhaps the most famous character of *The Arabian Nights*, Aladdin lives in an ancient kingdom of China. The son of the tailor Mustafa, he is so disobedient that his father dies of shame. One day, an African magician promises Aladdin riches in exchange for his assistance. The boy agrees, and the magician sends his charge into a deep cavern to retrieve a lamp. Returning with the artifact, the street-wise Aladdin refuses to hand it over until he is out of the passageway. Outraged, the magician seals him within the pit. After two days, Aladdin happens to rub a brass ring; a genie appears, and Aladdin asks to be freed. When he returns home, he finds his mother starving. Planning to sell the lamp, Aladdin begins to polish it—and out clouds an ugly genie. The djinn gives his master all that he desires. Reformed by his good fortune, Aladdin becomes renowned for his kindness and, a man of property, weds the Princess Badroulboudour.

Meanwhile, the magician hears of Aladdin's success and, while the young man is out hunting, disguises himself as a lampseller. Cajoling the princess into trading him that musty old lamp for a glistening new one, the magician orders the genie to transport the princess and the castle to Africa. Learning what has happened, Aladdin asks the genie of the ring to take him to the palace. Drugging the magician, he retrieves the lamp and returns to China with his castle and his wife. The magician is never heard from again.

When Badroulboudour's father dies, Aladdin becomes sultan and sires a long line of sultans. see: **Djinn; Scheherezade.**

Ahpuch   Quetzlcoatl

Albatross [L] A seabird of good omen. In the 1834 poem "The Rime of the Ancient Mariner" by Samuel Taylor Coleridge (1772–1834), an albatross is shot with a crossbow by the titular seaman. As a result, ill fortune befalls the crew. The seas calm, food runs scarce, and the bird is avenged as:

> *Water, water everywhere,*
> *And all the boards did shrink;*
> *Water, water everywhere,*
> *Nor any drop to drink.*

But the bad times are only just beginning. With the dead albatross hung around the Mariner's neck, he watches as the seas fill with monsters and spirits until Death and Life-in-Death drift by, playing dice for the souls of the crew. As it turns out, Death claims all but the Mariner who goes to Life-in-Death, a grim lady indeed:

> *Her lips were red, her looks were free,*
> *Her locks were yellow as gold;*
> *Her skin was as white as leprosy,*
> *The nightmare Life-in-Death was she,*
> *Who thicks man's blood with cold.*

Rescued and returned to shore, it is thereafter the task of the accursed Mariner to travel from land to land to tell all wanton citizens his woeful tale. And what has the albatross taught him? Quoth the Mariner, "loveth well both man and bird and beast."

Alderley Edge [F] Alderley Edge, in Cheshire, England, is where legend has King Arthur and his Round Table Knights lying asleep with their white horses, waiting to be called to the aid of Great Britain. It is also believed that when a great sea covered this region, a mermaid appeared every Easter. Arthur's Lady of the Lake, perhaps? see: **Arthur, King; Merpeople.**

Alice [L] The protagonist of *Alice in Wonderland* (1865) and *Through the Looking Glass* (1871), novels written by English mathematician and teacher Lewis Carroll (born Charles Lutwidge Dodgson, 1832–1898). In July of 1862, Carroll took three young girls on a picnic and told them a story he called *Alice's Adventures Underground.* He promised one of the girls, Alice Liddell, that he would write the story down. Indeed, it was Ms. Liddell who provided the basis for Carroll's fictional heroine.

In *Alice in Wonderland,* bored with her older sister's company, Alice follows a white rabbit down a hole and thereafter wanders from one bizarre adventure to another. She visits strange lands, meets incredible beasts, and finds herself a delightful pawn in Carroll's satire on human frailties and social intercourse. The odyssey turns out to have been a dream. In a second trek through her imagination, Alice goes *Through the Looking Glass* in her drawing room and has more uncanny adventures—none of which takes the sting from Alice, who remains through it all a very precocious girl! see: **Cheshire Cat; Hatter; Jabberwock; Lobster-Quadrille; Looking Glass Insects; Mock Turtle; Queen of Hearts; Tiger-lily; Tweedledum and Tweedledee; White Rabbit.**

Allerleirauh [FT] In the Grimm Brothers tale that bears her name, Allerleirauh is the daughter of a king. An independent lass, she refuses to marry the man selected by her father. Instead, Allerleirauh runs into the woods, blackens her face and hands with soot, dons a patchwork cloak, and there lives as "The Many-Furred Creature." Discovered by the huntsman of another king, she is mistaken for a mythical beast. As the bemused trapper describes her to his liege, "In the hollow tree there lives a wonderful animal that we don't know, and we have never seen one like it; its skin is made of a thousand pieces of fur. . . ." Taken to the court, "The Many-Furred Creature" intrigues the king, who suspects that there is more

to this beast than fur and filth. Plucking at her hirsute garment, he pulls it
off and reveals her for what she is.
Then, true to fairy tale form, the king
promptly falls in love with Allerleirauh, as does she with him, and
they are married. see: **Grimm, Jakob
and Wilhelm.**

Alley Oop [C] A comic strip character
created by V. T. Hamlin. Hamlin first
became interested in prehistoric life
while working for an oil company in
Texas, where he befriended a paleon-
tologically fluent geologist. Not that
Oop's world was awash with historical
accuracy. Cave people did not coexist
with dinosaurs, and no creature
known to science quite resembles
Oop's pet Dinny, a hybrid diplo-
docus-stegosaur-duck. But the strip,
which first appeared on August 7,
1933, is an artistic marvel with superb
layouts, rampant innocence, and engaging characters. Among the latter
are Alley Oop's girl friend Oola, King
Guz, and Queen Umpateedle. And
when things became dull in the prehistoric land of Moo after six years,
Hamlin simply introduced the twentieth century Dr. Wonmug and his
time machine, which allowed Oop to
make various stops in history. Hamlin
left the strip in 1971, at which time
his assistant, Dave Greave, took over.
A song about Alley Oop was twice recorded in the fifties, by the Hollywood
Argyles, and Dante and the Ever-
greens (also known as the
Dyno-Sores).

Almās, Prince [FT] Hero of the Persian
fairy tale "What the Rose Did to the
Cypress." When his brothers
Tahmāsp and Qamās are killed by
Princess Mihr-afrūz, the Prince
Almās-ruh-baksh, son of Sa-
manlālpōsh, the great King of the
East, goes to avenge them. The task is
easier conceived than executed. En
route, the noble prince is changed
into a deer by the sorceress Latifa;
then is restored to human form and

befriends her sister, the good witch
Jamila, who provides him with enchanted weapons; visits and appeases
the enormous Lion-king (" . . . a wonderfully big lion, which was eighty
yards from nose to tail-tip . . ."); encounters a simurgh; battles the black
giant Chil-maq; slays a monstrous
dragon; and more. Eventually the
bold warrior finds Mihr-afrūz, although his retribution takes the oddest form—the princess repents for
the murders and Almās accepts her as
his bride! Sibling rivalry? see: **Dragon;
Simurgh.**

Alvarson, Airar [L] Son of Alvar and the
hero of Fletcher Pratt's 1948 novel
The Well of the Unicorn. In a country
not unlike Medieval Scandinavia,
Airar is run from his farm, Trangsted
Stead, when he is unable to meet the
high taxes imposed by the cruel military government. Rootless, he joins
the white-haired enchanter Meliboë,
leads a revolution against the dictatorial order, and ends up victorious in
both war and love—the latter represented by the lovely Princess Argyra.
The book's title refers to a wonderful well of peace.

Amalric [L] Created by Lin Carter,
Amalric is a hero who lives on
Thoorana, one of five planets circling
the star Kylix. (Its companion worlds
are Zao, Olymbris, Zephrondus, and
Gulzund.) Amalric is an Immortal, a
seven-foot-tall, gray-eyed, blond-
haired, bronze-skinned superman used
by the gods of Thoorana to slay monsters, overthrow tyrants, and perform
other heroic deeds. His sidekick is the
dwarfish and rather unpleasant magician, Ubonidus.
Amalric's first adventure was "The
Higher Heresies of Ooliman," and it
appeared in the anthology volume
Flashing Swords #1, 1973. see:
Carter, Lin.

Ama-terasu [M] The Japanese goddess of
the sun, born from the left eye of

Ama-terasu

Izanagi. She was the sister of the belligerent sea god Sus-no-o, who was born from Izanagi's nose. Early in her life, Ama-terasu had an argument with her brother; angry and frustrated, she locked herself in a cave and denied light to the universe. None of her fellow gods was able to persuade Ama-terasu to come out—until one clever deity decided to dance for the rest. When Ama-terasu heard the gods' shouts of laughter and excitement, it was too much for her curiosity and she emerged from the cave.

Back on the job, she sent the god Ame-no-wakahiko to rule Japan. Preoccupied with his wife, the daughter of a sorcerer, the emperor forgot to keep Ama-terasu informed of his progress. After eight years she became curious, and sent a pheasant to see what he was up to. But Ame-no-wa-

kahiko, counseled by one of his servants, thought the bird an ill omen and shot it with an arrow. The shaft killed the bird and flew on to heaven. There, it was cursed and flung earthward, stopping only to pierce the ruler's heart. Disappointed, Ama-terasu next sent her trusted grandson Ninigi to rule Japan. To start his reign on the right foot, the goddess gave him jewels, a sacred mirror, and the sword Kusanagi, a blade plucked from the tail of an eight-headed snake. Ninigi succeeded royally on earth, and Ama-terasu's gifts became the emblem of the imperial family he founded. see: **Izanagi.**

Amazons [M] A race of heroic warrior-women in Greek mythology. Their name derives from the fact that they cut off their right breast to better draw their bow—*a* meaning "without," and *mazos* meaning "breast."

The Amazons were the offspring of Artemis and Ares. Their queen was Hippolyta, the daughter of Ares and Otrera, and the male-less race lived on the edge of the Eurasian Black Sea. They perpetuated their number by mating with men from neighboring tribes. Supreme fighters, the Amazons were finally bested by Hercules, whose ninth labor was to fetch the golden girdle of Hippolyta. Upon his arrival, the queen was so smitten by Hercules' magnificence that she ordered her Amazons not to accost him. This did not sit well with Hercules' hate-filled stepmother, the goddess Hera. Wanting the hero to fail, she went among the Amazons and lied that he was planning to abduct their queen—at this point the women waged vicious war against the demigod. Thus, Hercules was forced to slay Hippolyta and many of her women in order to fulfill his mission.

Following the queen's demise, the Amazons were ruled by Hippolyta's sister Antiope. One of the later Amazonian queens, Penthesilea, fought on the side of Troy during the Trojan War. see: **Ares; Hera; Hercules; Theseus.**

Ambrosia [M] The sustenance of the gods of Olympus. By eating this food, the Greek deities retained their immortality. Ambrosia was brought to them each day from the shores of Ocean in the West. Ambrosia also applies to the perfume and unguent used by the gods. The term comes from *ambrotos* which means "immortal."

The drink of Olympus was Nectar, a substance which supplied the gods with their day-to-day strength. see: **Olympus.**

Amulet [O] An artifact in nature or art which possesses mystic powers. Among an amulet's many applications are: warding off disease or a curse, serving as a medium of prayer to facilitate communication with the gods, or bringing good fortune. To be effective, an amulet must always be kept on the user's person and should bear the likeness of the evil influence against which it is being utilized. An amulet is different from a *talisman* in that it protects its bearer passively while a talisman can be employed to work aggressive magic.

Amun [M] One of the greatest of the Egyptian gods. His name means "the concealed one," and he was thought of as the force that sustains the universe. Together with his wife Maut and their son Khuns, they formed the Upper Egyptian Trinity, of which the ram-headed Amun was the chief god.

As the years went by, Amun was identified with other gods to boost his or their importance. Thus did he assume a variety of identities, such as Amun-Num, the spirit of life. However, foremost among these unions was Amun-Ra, which made Amun the god of the sun. Although Ra had long held this position in his own right, his name and function were melded with Amun by priests who wished to elevate the latter.

Amun's wife Maut was thought of as the mother of the gods and the mistress of the sky. She was alternately portrayed with the head of a lioness or a vulture. Egyptians regarded the vulture as the symbol of maternity. see: **Ra.**

Ananta [M] According to the Hindu mythos, Ananta is a thousand-headed cobra representing Eternity. Floating in a sea of milk, it bears Vishnu, the preserver of life, upon its back. This occurs only between the cycles of creation, when Brahma, the creator, is asleep and all else is absorbed within Iswara, the Universal Spirit. After 100 years, Brahma reemerges on a lotus which grows from Vishnu's navel and creation begins anew, lasting for 100 years. (One day in this epic cycle equals 43,200,000 of our own mortal years.)

During the era of creation, the four-handed Vishnu switches mounts, exchanging Ananta for Garuda, a creature that is half-man, half-eagle.

The swan-riding, four-handed, four-headed Brahma and Vishnu, together with the four-handed, three-eyed Siva, the Destroyer, form the Hindu Trinity.

Andersen, Hans Christian [FT] A Danish author of fairy tales. Born in the slums of Odense in 1805, Andersen was the son of a shoemaker; his mother was illiterate. In his early years Andersen received very little education, choosing instead to earn money by acting and singing. Journeying to Copenhagen during his teenage years, he lived modestly while toying with a new field—writing. He wrote in prose, play, and verse form, and sold his first work in 1827, a poem called "The Dying Child." His first novel, *The Improvisatore,* was published eight years later. However, it is for his immortal fairy tales that Andersen is best known. There are 168 in all, and they were written between the years 1835 and 1872—three years before Andersen's death. Among the most famous of these are "The Snow Queen," "The Little Mermaid," "Inchelina" (also known as "Thumbelina"), "The Rose Elf" ("... within every petal of the rose he had a bedchamber ..."), and "The Pixy and the Grocer."

In the 1952 film *Hans Christian Andersen*, the author was played by Danny Kaye. see: **Snow Queen, the; Thumbelina.**

Anderson, Gerry [TV/MP] One of the foremost producers of fantasy fare for television. Born in 1929 in Hampstead, England, Anderson studied to be an architect before signing on as a photographer's assistant. He moved from that position to film editing, sound dubbing, directing for television, and finally packaging entire series for the home screen. His first program was entitled "The Adventures of Twizzle" (1956). It featured marionettes, which were to become the Anderson trademark for many years. Among his subsequent puppet programs were "Supercar" (1959), "Fireball XL-5" (1961), and "Stingray" (1962). In 1969, following the success of his marionette theatrical films *Thunderbirds Are Go* (1966) and *Thunderbirds Six* (1968), Anderson shot a live-action feature entitled *Journey to the Far Side of the Sun.* The producer's experience with puppet-sized sets made the miniature models in this work some of the most convincing the screen had ever seen. But the picture was a financial failure, so Anderson returned to television with the puppet-less series "UFO" (1969), "The Protectors" (1972) and "Space: 1999" (1975). Several episodes of the latter have been edited into a feature film entitled *Destination Moonbase Alpha* (1979), a prelude to Anderson's theatrical comeback. Anderson and his ex-wife, Sylvia, have four children: Gerry Jr., Linda, Dee, and Joy.

Andorians [TV] Inhabitants of the "Star Trek" television galaxy, Andorians are bipedal with blue skin, white hair, and two small antennae jutting from the side of the head. They are extremely violent beings, although their slight bodies and gentle voices disguise this innate hostility.

The Andorians appeared in the live-action episodes "Journey to Babel," "The Gamesters of Triskelion," "Whom Gods Destroy," as well as in the animated adventures "Yesteryear" and "Timetrap."

Angilas [MP] Created by special effects genius Eiji Tsuburaya, this giant quadruped is known as Angilas in its native Japanese screen incarnations and as Angorus in films dubbed for American release.

Angilas' screen debut was in *Gigantis, the Fire Monster* (1955), in which the armored monster battled the featured flame-breather across the length and breadth of Japan. Although slain by Gigantis, Angilas inexplicably returned as a supporting nasty in five other Oriental dramas: *Destroy All Monsters* (1969), *Godzilla's Revenge* (1969), *Godzilla vs. Gigan* (1972), *Godzilla vs. the Cosmic Monster* (1977), and *Godzilla on Monster Island* (1978). see: **Godzilla.**

Antaeus [M] The son of Poseidon and Gaea, Antaeus was a champion wrestler in Greek mythology. A resident of Libya, he lived in a house built from the skulls of his victims.

No one who encountered Antaeus was ever able to defeat him. This was due to both his inherent might and the fact that whenever the brute was thrown to the ground he arose even stronger, drawing strength from the earth—otherwise known as his mother Gaea. He was finally done-in by Hercules who, on his way to retrieve the Golden Apples of the Hesperides, met Antaeus, raised him into the air, and there crushes his evil body to splinters.

In the motion picture *Hercules Unchained* (1959), this classic confrontation was recreated with Steve Reeves as Hercules and Primo Carnera as Antaeus. The film took certain acceptable liberties with the legend, having the wrestler bested when the screen Hercules picks him up and throws him into the ocean. see: **Gaea; Hercules; Poseidon; Reeves, Steve.**

Anthropophagi [F] Although these cannibals were popularized in William Shakespeare's *The Merry Wives of Windsor* (1602) and *Othello* (1604),

belief in the Anthropophagi predates the English playwright. According to legend, they live on a distant island and are of a most hideous appearance. Lacking heads, they have eyes on their shoulders and mouths in their chests. Apart from consuming human flesh, they use bones for tools and employ skulls as drinking vessels.

It is thought that the historical Anthropophagi were actually nothing more than run-of-the-mill cannibals given this monstrous appearance by Europeans who found their diet re-

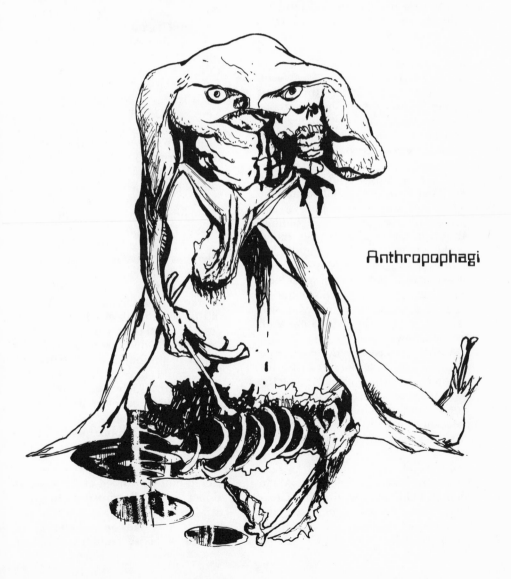

Anthropophagi

volting. Their name comes from the Greek *anthrōpophágos* which means "man-eating."

Antiphates [M] The King of Laestrygonia, a northern land of short nights and human-eating giants. In *The Odyssey*, Antiphates sups on one of Odysseus' scouts, after which thousands of Laestrygonians descend upon the legendary heroes. Hurling huge boulders, the giants destroy eleven of the twelve Greek ships caught within the narrow harbor. Only Odysseus and his crew escape, having had the foresight to anchor their vessel beyond the bottleneck. As for the stranded Greeks, they are all harpooned, reeled ashore, and consumed.

Symbolically, this scene points up a theme that recurs throughout Homer's epic poem, the difference between people as free-thinking individuals and as members of the community. see: **Odysseus.**

Anubis [M] The Egyptian god of the dead, son of the god of evil Set and the goddess of the dead Nephthys, and patron of the art of embalming. Anubis dwelt in Amenti, the underworld, where it was his responsibility to weigh the heart and soul of all newcomers. If they did not meet local standards, their owner was eaten by Ammit, a great monster who was half-lion and half-hippopotamus with crocodile jaws.

Anubis possessed the head of a jackal and was considered to be the guardian of all cemeteries. Among the god's more noteworthy achievements were his part in helping Isis reanimate the slain Osiris, and the grim but not unjustified eating of his wicked father.

Apaukkyit Lok [M] An old man in Burmese mythology. Living in Majoi Shingra Pum not long after the Creation, Apaukkyit Lok decides that he does not like the sundry infirmities which plague the aged. Though he would have lived forever—albeit, as an old man—he elects to regain his youth through magic. Apaukkyit Lok does this a total of nine times, until his impudence finally angers the Lord of the Sun. The all-powerful solar deity deems it unfair that one human be allowed to shed his old age. Thus, the next time Apaukkyit Lok refuses to accept his lot gracefully, the Sun Lord kills him. This is the first death, and the gods decree that thereafter all humans should suffer from it. see: **Luggnagg.**

Aphrodite [M] The Greek goddess of love and beauty. According to one legend, Aphrodite was created in the foam that gathered around the portion of Uranus which, when severed, fell into the sea; a second origin makes her the less spectacular offspring of Zeus and Dione, a daughter of Atlas. Married to the homely Hephaestus, Aphrodite's lovers included the gods Ares, Hermes, Poseidon, and Dionysos as well as the mortals Adonis and Anchises. Among her children were Eros, the god of love; his brother Anteros, the god of unrequited love; Harmonia; Hermaphroditus; and others.

As Aphrodite stirred the gods of Olympus to passion, she inspired the females to jealousy. As a result, the goddess of love was not greatly loved by her fellow Olympiennes. Yet she did possess one item which was coveted by deities and mortals alike, a magic girdle that made its wearer the object of profound desire. (How this belt would have worked for Hermaphroditus is never revealed.)

Aphrodite's counterpart in Roman mythology was Venus. see: **Ares; Dionysos; Eros; Hephaestus; Hermes; Poseidon; Uranus; Zeus.**

Apis [M] The great beast-god of Egypt, a sacred bull worshiped at Memphis in Upper Egypt. Regarded as the reincarnation of Osiris, Apis was a real bull, a holy taurine pampered and housed in lavish comfort. However, the honor was not without strings. Every quarter-century a new beast had to be found with the following distinguishing marks: a black hide, a white spot in the shape of a triangle on its forehead, a knot like a beetle under the tongue, and the figure of a half-moon on its right side. When such a bull was located, the old beast-god was with great ceremony drowned in the Nile and mummified. Twenty-five years later its replacement was similarly dispatched.

Called Hap in the epoch of the pharaohs, Apis is the more familiar Greek form of the name.

Apollo [M] The god of the sun, and of music, poetry, and prophecy in Greek mythology. Apollo was the son of Zeus and Leto, born after nine days of labor on Delos, a floating island until Zeus anchored it so that his paramour could give birth in comfort.

Although he wasn't above a heroic deed or two, and spent much time practicing prophecy at such oracles as Delphi, Apollo's greatest love was music. He invented the flute and the lyre, and the melodies he created were much enjoyed by his fellow immortals. Most of the stories told about Apollo involve music, and highlight his passion for it. To wit, there was the time he skinned the satyr Marsyas alive after beating him in a musical contest evaluated by the Muses. Later, realizing that he had perhaps overreacted, Apollo changed the hideless creature into a river that bears his name. On another occasion, losing to the satyr Pan in a similar competition judged by King Midas, Apollo turned the ears of the potentate into those of an ass.

By the nymph Cyrene, Apollo was the father of Aristaeus. Among his other lovers were the mortal Coronis and the shepherdess Dryope, each of whom bore the god a son.

A popular god, it is thought that Apollo was originally the supreme

deity in portions of Ancient Greece where Zeus was as yet unknown. Later, Apollo's grandeur was diminished slightly by making him Zeus' son. In these early days, Apollo was also known as Phoebus Apollo, the god of light. In Rome, Apollo was worshiped by his noble Greek name. see: **Artemis; Midas; Python; Zeus.**

Appleseed, Johnny [F] A figure in American folklore inspired by the real-life escapades of John Chapman. Born in Boston in 1774, Chapman spent most of his life tending apple orchards. Regarded as a great medicine man by the Indians, he thought nothing of trekking hundreds of miles in the name of his particular ecology; indeed, when he died in 1847, it was from pneumonia caught en route to a clutch of sickly trees. After Chapman's death, his peculiar avocation inspired the figure of Johnny Appleseed. Only slightly more eccentric than his historical counterpart, Johnny crisscrossed the country in ragged clothes, his hair wild and appearance unkempt, planting apple trees and employing supernatural means to cause existing orchards to flourish.

Apsaras [M] To Buddhists, an angel or fairy; to Hindus, a skydancer or nymph located in heaven. Broadly, however, the Apsaras play a variety of roles in both religious and secular matters. Some live in fig trees and bless wedding processions as they pass; others serve as beautiful courtesans of the hereafter who reward those fallen in battle. A few are evil, used by the gods to tender madness to scholars and keep them from becoming too wise or powerful. This last, though, is a subsidiary role. In Tibet, the Apsaras are worshiped as gods.

Apt [L] A deadly native of Edgar Rice Burroughs' Barsoom. A white-furred creature of the northern polar regions, the Apt is seven to nine feet tall, has a head like a hippopotamus, two powerful tusks, large and sensitive eyes, and six limbs—four stocky and powerful legs for moving surely and rapidly on ice, and two arms at the shoulder terminating in pale, hairless hands.

Some Martians consider the Apt sacred; others prize it for the garments that can be cut from its fur. All respect its ferocity. Even when an Apt has fed, it will not think twice about killing for sheer pleasure. see: **Barsoom; Burroughs, Edgar Rice.**

Aquaman [C] A comic book hero created in 1941 by Mort Weisinger and Paul Norris. Aquaman premiered in *More Fun* #73, the son of an oceanologist who had learned how to live underwater. Growing to adulthood, Aquaman became the ruler of the sunken civilization of Atlantis. The Sea Lord is married to the flame-haired Mera, and they have a ward named Aqualad. Aquaman can remain out of water for only brief periods, during which time he occasionally masquerades as surface dweller Arthur Curry. Beneath the waves, Aquaman has the ability to telepathically command sea creatures, from jellyfish to whales. see: **Submariner.**

Aquans [TV] Web-fingered, green-haired subsea-dwellers in the "Star Trek" animated episode "The Ambergris Element." Natives of the planet Argo, the Aquans were once air-breathers. When earthquakes submerged much of their world's land masses, they utilized an advanced medical technique called surgo-op to transform themselves into underwater inhabitants. Humanoid in shape with a prominent dorsal fin, they boast a cancerous hatred for all land-dwellers. Their emotion stems from the barbarity which swept the planet immediately after the eruptions and before the establishment of an underwater civilization.

The young Aquans, recognizing the attitude to be an irrational one, eventually abandon the sea for the land. They promise to stay in touch with their elders and, in so doing, establish an era of peace and sanity on Argo.

Ares [M] The Greek god of war, this son of Zeus and Hera inherited his mother's temper, flavoring it with a fierce bloodlust. Yet, while Ares loved the sight and tang of blood, his enthusiasm waned when the blood being spilled was his own. In fact, when Ares was wounded during the Trojan War, his cry was so loud it equaled that of 10,000 mortal warriors. Lacking strength as well as courage, he was beaten in combat by Hercules and managed to kill Adonis only by transforming himself into a boar.

Though a coward, Ares was exceedingly handsome. The father of Eros, Anteros, and Harmonia by Aphrodite; Ares' other children included Phobos (Terror) and Deimos (Fear) by his sister Eris, Cycnus by Pyrene, and a second Cycnus by Pelopia.

Shunned by his fellow Greek gods, Ares was a more potent figure in Roman mythology where he was known as Mars. The bold and powerful father of Remus and Romulus, he was also known as Mars Silvanus, the god of agriculture; Mars Ultor, who punished the enemies of Rome; and Mars Quirinus, the protector of the state. March, the first month of the Roman year, was named for him. see: **Aphrodite; Eros; Hera; Hercules; Romulus; Zeus.**

Argonauts [M] The legendary heroes who traveled with Jason in his quest for the Golden Fleece. Hand-picked for their bravery, strength, and wisdom, among the distinguished company were Hercules, Castor and Pollux (the brothers of Helen of Troy), Theseus, Orpheus, and many others. They sailed aboard the *Argo*, a great ship expressly built for the long voyage and named after its builder, Argus. Among the many dangers faced by the crew members were the harpies, the sirens, the Symplegades, and fire-breathing bulls. see: **Golden**

Fleece; Harpy; Hercules; Jason; Orpheus; Sirens; Symplegades; Theseus.

Argos [M] The giant watchbeing of the gods. With 100 eyes scattered all over his body, he was the perfect guardian: since his orbs slept in shifts, it was nearly impossible to escape Argos' scrutiny.

Argos' most famous role in mythology involved, alas, his leaving of it. One of Zeus' concubines was Io, daughter of the river god Inachos. To protect the girl from Hera's wrath, the king of the gods transformed her into a cow. But Hera was wise to the deception and, feigning naïveté, asked for the animal as a gift. Since Zeus could hardly refuse without arousing his wife's suspicion, he gave Hera the cow. She, in turn, put it out to pasture under the watchful eyes of Argos. None of this particularly suited Zeus' libido. Accordingly, he assigned Hermes the task of liberating his lover. Up to any challenge, the plucky god disguised himself as a shepherd and whittled a piece of reed into a flute. Approaching Argos, he played drowsy songs, forced all of the giant's eyes asleep, smashed in his skull with a rock, and cut off his head for good measure.

Argos' death upset the queen of the gods almost as much as Io's escape. She honored the fallen servant by placing his eyes on her favorite bird, the peacock. As for Io and Zeus, they were reunited in Egypt where she bore him a son. see: **Hera; Hermes; Zeus.**

Argzoon [L] Savage blue giants created by Michael Moorcock for his exciting Martian trilogy starring adventurer Michael Kane. The hairless Argzoon live in the northern regions of Mars where they are ruled by the evil Queen Horguhl. With their sturdy armor and devilishly pointed ears, the huge warriors present a sinister sight as they charge about the planet riding great Daharas—four-legged, apelike mounts with kangaroo tails. Masters of the underground world called the Caves of Darkness, the Argzoon are kin to the blue Mendishar, a more peaceful breed of giant. see: **Kane, Michael.**

Ariel [L] The "airy spirit" featured in William Shakespeare's last play, *The Tempest* (1611). Imprisoned by the witch Sycorax in a cloven pine tree, the delicate Ariel is released through the magic of Prospero, the exiled Duke of Milan. In return for his liberty, the spirit becomes Prospero's servant.

Ariel's sex is never stated in the play, although what is gender to one whose powers are almost limitless? Possessing the mystic might to carry out almost any mission assigned by Prospero, Ariel also has the ability to adopt any shape. For years of dedicated service, Ariel is rewarded by Prospero with freedom at play's end. see: **Caliban; Prospero, Prince.**

Arquel [L] A warrior hero created by Puerto Rican author Raúl Garcia-Capella (Ray Capella). Arquel is a contemporary of Conan the Barbarian, born in the mythical nation of Argos some twelve thousand years ago. His parents were forced to flee their homeland due to political intrigue; they were later slain by soldiers serving a rebel prince of the nation of Koth. Alone and homeless, young Arquel lived the life of a wanderer, earning his living as a scribe, a minstrel, and an acrobat.

The first of Arquel's many adventures was chronicled in the 1965 short story "Turutal." see: **Conan.**

Artemis [M] The Greek goddess of hunting, chastity and, in later years, of the moon. The daughter of Zeus and Leto, Artemis was born on Delos and is the twin sister of Apollo.

Proud, beautiful, and athletic, Artemis carried around a bow and arrows, as well as darts which brought sudden death to whomever they touched. To be sure, her wrath was swift and terrible: for example, she changed the voyeur Actaeon into a stag and slew Hermes' wife, Chione, when the woman claimed to be more beautiful than the goddess. But not all of her deific expressions were vengeful. When her companion, the nymph Arethusa, was assaulted by the river god Alphaeus, Artemis thoughtfully transformed her into flowing water that she might battle the god on his own terms.

Artemis' one love was Orion, whom she accidentally shafted during an archery contest. The goddess' counterpart in Roman mythology was Diana. see: **Actaeon; Apollo; Hermes; Orion; Zeus.**

Arthur, King [F] A British leader whose factual exploits have assumed legendary proportions.

The earliest account of the historical Arthur comes to us from *Historia Britonum* by Geoffrey of Monmouth (1100–1154). In it, along with other ancient documents, Arturius is described as a brave warrior of the sixth century who leads the Celtic Britons against the Saxons. Later he became a ruler of some note, although details of his political achievements are sketchy. Conversely, the Arthur of folklore is extremely well documented. Born in Tintagel, Cornwall, his mother was Igerne (also known as Igraine and Ygerne) and his father Uther, who assumed the title "Pendragon" or "Leader in Battle" after overcoming petty kings to forge a nation. Arthur became king at age fifteen, appointed by local nobles when he was able to draw a sword from its sheath of stone. When this weapon was subsequently broken in battle, Merlin the magician led Arthur to the eerie Lady of the Lake, who presented him with the immortal Excalibur.

Apart from Arthur and Merlin, the most popular characters in the legend are the Knights of the Round Table.

The Round Table was a gift from King Leodegrance, given when Arthur took the king's daughter Guinevere as his bride. There was seating for 150 knights, and court was held in Camelot. Unfortunately, the glory of the Round Table and of Camelot was short lived, as squabbles soon divided the knights, Sir Lancelot fired Guinevere to infidelity, and Arthur's nephew Modred sought to usurp the throne; it was in dealing with this last unhappy matter that Arthur was fatally wounded. Locked in combat with Modred, he was able to skewer his nephew with a spear—but not before receiving a head wound from his opponent's sword. Brought to a chapel, the king instructed Sir Bedivere to return Excalibur to the Lady of the Lake, while Arthur himself was carried to a barge peopled by wailing maidens dressed in black. It is said that the vessel sailed on to the Isle of Avalon, where Arthur's wound was healed. Legend has it that if ever England has need of Arthur and his knights, they will return.

Among the most famous retellings of the Arthurian legend are Sir Thomas Malory's fifteenth century work *Le Morte D'Arthur*, T. H. White's *The Once and Future King* (1958), and the Alan Jay Lerner-Frederick Lowe musical *Camelot*. see: **Merlin.**

In a departure from Arthur and his England as pure and majestic, American author Mark Twain (1835–1910) used them as vehicles for social commentary in his 1889 novel *A Connecticut Yankee in King Arthur's Court*. In this biting but delightful work, our nameless hero has his soul transmigrated from Hartford, Connecticut to Camelot. There he suffers sundry injustices and triumphs while introducing Arthurian England to modern thought and technology. see: **Alderly Edge; Merlin.**

Asgard [M] In Norse mythology, the home of the gods. This glorious celestial abode, an island floating on Huergelmir, a spring running from Niflheim, was built by the king of the gods, Odin, and his brothers Vili and Ve. Some Norse tales have Asgard composed of the two mansions, Gladsheim and Vingolf, home of the gods and goddesses, respectively; others give them each their own palace made of gold or silver. Asgard was named after the race of the three lordly brothers, the Aesir. see: **Bifrost; Odin.**

Asimov, Isaac [L] Noted author of 200 science, science fiction, and fantasy books. Born in 1920 in Petrovichi, Russia, Asimov was brought to the United States in 1923 and became a citizen in 1928. He received his PhD in chemistry from Columbia University and was for many years Associate Professor of Biochemistry at the Boston University School of Medicine.

Although Asimov writes about science for publications ranging from *The Magazine of Fantasy and Science Fiction* to *Playboy* to *T.V. Guide*, it is as a science fiction author for which he is best known. He sold his first story in October 1938: "Marooned Off Vesta," published in *Amazing Stories.* His first novel was the 70,000 word *Pebble in the Sky* (1950), and among his more popular works are *The Foundation Trilogy* (1951–1953), *I, Robot* (1950), and the novelization of the film *Fantastic Voyage* (1966). His autobiography is entitled *In Memory Yet Green* (1979).

Asimov lives in New York City with his wife, Janet Jeppson.

Asmodeus [O] The king of the Hebrew devils, Asmodeus is the Prince of Wantons and the lord of sensuality, fond of tempting mortals with his swine of luxuriousness. An odd hybrid of many different creatures, the demon has three heads—that of a bull and that of a ram bordering a central human head. He also boasts bat wings,

the thighs of a goat, and duck's feet. Asmodeus is one of what Johann Weyer (1515–1588) catalogued as 7,-405,926 demons of hell, and is best known for having been summoned with fellow devil Zabulon by one Father Urbain Grandier to bewitch a convent of nuns in 1633. see: **Hell; Satan.**

Astaroth

Astaroth [O] A supernatural demon who tempts mortals with idleness and the easy life. Astaroth is portrayed as having the body of a spider capped by three heads—those of a cat and of a frog flanking the head of an old man with pointed ears. Astaroth was also the Phoenician goddess of lasciviousness, equivalent to the Babylonian Ishtar. see: **Hell; Satan.**

Asterix [C] A comic strip hero created by artist Albert Uderzo and writer René Goscinny, Asterix premiered in the October 29, 1959 edition of the European comic weekly *Pilote*. The dwarfish, mustachioed hero of 50 B.C. lives in a small village surrounded by the fortified Roman camps Aquarium, Totorum, Laudanum, and Compendium. How do the antiemperor Gauls manage to hold out against such odds? Asterix possesses super strength which he derives from drinking a magic potion brewed by the local druid Getafix. Asterix's constant companion is the giant Obelix, who eats oceans of wild boar and is a menhir delivery man. Among the other regulars: Cacofonix, the bard, and Vitalstatistix, the chief of the tribe.

Our scrappy hero was the star of his own animated motion picture *Asterix the Gaul*, produced in France in 1967.

Athach [O] In Scotland, the general term for a monster that usually haunts lochs and valleys. Among such creatures are the infamous Rag, a manslaying female demon; Bocan, a fiend which could assume the shape of many monsters; and Direach, a one-legged creature akin to the notorious Fachen. see: **Fachen.**

Athene [M] The Greek goddess of war and peace. Athene was the daughter of Zeus and his first wife Metis, and her birth was unusual even among the annals of mythology. When it was predicted that a child of Metis might one day be greater than Zeus, the Lord of Olympus took the precaution of terminating their relationship by swallowing the pregnant woman whole. But that did not stop Athene. Fully armed and with a rousing yell, she sprang from her father's head to take her place in the hierarchy of the gods.

Athene was the preserver of Athens, alternately cruel and benevolent as she saw fit. When the mortal Arachne challenged her to a weaving contest, the intimidated goddess transformed her into a champion spinner—a spider. She also struck blind the young seer-to-be Tiresias when he happened to stumble upon her bathing. On the other hand, Athene taught mortals how to tame horses and yoke oxen. Also, she invented the trumpet and supervised the building of the Argo. Needless to say, her favorite hero was the bold Odysseus, although she was also partial to Jason, Hercules, Perseus, and Bellerophon.

Athene's counterpart in Roman mythology was Minerva, who was more a goddess of wisdom than of war. see: **Argonauts; Bellerophon; Hercules; Jason; Odysseus; Perseus; Zeus.**

Atlantis [P] The legendary Lost Continent in the Atlantic Ocean, said to have been swallowed by the ocean circa 12,000–10,000 B.C. One of the oldest and most thorough accounts we have of this land comes from the Greek philosopher Plato (427–347 B.C.). In two of his famous dialogues, *Timaeus* and *Critias*, which are based on Egyptian records, he describes Atlantean buildings, topography, history, and customs before going on to say, "There occurred violent earthquakes and floods, and in a single day and night of rain . . . the island of Atlantis . . . was sunk beneath the sea." More recent thinkers have attributed the destruction of Atlantis to glacial activity during the Ice Age.

Allegedly founded by Poseidon, Atlantis was supposed to have been a land of superscience and artistic grandeur, an earthly Paradise. Whether or not it ever really existed is difficult to say, as the geological evidence pro and contra is inconclusive. Regardless, Atlantis remains a symbol of the vast cultural potential inherent in humankind—and the fact that nature couldn't care less. see: **Mu; Poseidon; Ulios.**

Atlas [M] One of the Titans in Greek mythology, Atlas was the son of the Titan Iapetus and the Oceanid Clymene. His brothers were Menoetios,

Prometheus, and Epimetheus. His children were Calypso; the Hyades; and by the Oceanid Pleione the seven Pleiades—Maia, Taygete, Electra, Celaeno, Sterope, Merope, and Alcyone. Several accounts also make him the father by Hespiris of the Hesperides.

Luckless Atlas was one of the Titans who waged war against Zeus and lost. As punishment for his part in the uprising, the Titan was sentenced to stand in the westernmost regions of the earth, there to bear the heavens upon his shoulders. According to some legends, while holding up the sky Atlas was shown the head of Medusa by Perseus, which caused him to become the North African mountains which carry his name.

Prior to this unfortunate meeting with Perseus, Atlas also had a tilt with Hercules over the latter's mission to steal the Golden Apples of the Hesperides. It was a match of skill and wit in which the Titan was soundly thrashed. see: **Hercules; Hesperides; Medusa; Perseus; Prometheus; Titans; Zeus.**

Atom, The [C] The world's smallest superhero. The Atom is scientist Ray Palmer who designed a device which fits in the palms of his red and blue costume and contains matter from a white dwarf star. This invention enables him to shrink to the Atom's standard height of six inches, or become small enough to actually slip between atoms. What's more, the Atom can make himself as light as his namesake or, even when he's the size of an electron, retain his normal 180-pound weight.

Originally the Atom was Al Pratt, a professor at Clinton College, created by artist Ben Flinton and writer B. O'Connor for *All American Comics* #19, October 1940. This Atom drove a sleek orange car called the Atomobile and fought crime in its many forms. However, when the Atom was revived as a comic book feature in 1961 he was given a new identity. Pratt was explained away as the Atom of a world parallel to ours, Earth II, and the dual motemen occasionally share adventures.

Atom Palmer is married to lawyer Jean Loring, and is a member of the crime-busting Justice League of America.

Augeian Stables, The [M] The cleaning in one day of these awesome stables was the sixth labor of Hercules. Owned by King Augeias, the stables housed over three thousand oxen, including twelve pure white bulls sacred to the sun. They were housed at the intersection of the Alpheios and Peneus Rivers, and had not been tended to in years. Surveying the situation, Hercules hit upon a brilliant scheme. Herding the animals outside, he redirected the rivers so that they flushed through the stables. Returning them to their natural boundaries, he then drove the beasts inside and actually managed to complete the chore in under the prescribed time.

But there's a moral here. Augeias had promised to give Hercules 1/10 of the herd if the hero finished the task on time. When the Son of Zeus succeeded, Augeias was so surprised that he reneged on his promise. Hercules accepted the rebuke goodnaturedly—until he was able to join an invasion of Augeias' kingdom and murder the fickle king. see: **Hercules.**

Avenger, The [L] A most unusual crimefighter, created by Paul Ernst in 1936. The star of a short-lived (twenty-four issue) pulp magazine which bore his name, the Avenger is actually adventurer Richard Henry Benson. When Benson's wife, Alicia, and daughter Alice are slain by a crime ring, the shock causes his flesh and hair to turn white, and turns his face into a pliable, puttylike mask. Able to rearrange his features, the sorrow-filled Benson decides to use this power, backed by a superb physique and brilliant mind, to battle the underworld. Assisting Benson in this cause are his aides, Fergus MacMurdie and Algernon Heathcote Smith, as well as the razorlike knife, Ike, and the .22 caliber gun, Mike. Benson conceals these weapons beneath his pants, strapped to the inside of his left and right calf, respectively.

Among the Avenger's righteous escapades are *The Yellow Hoard, The Sky Walker, Frosted Death*, and *Justice, Inc.*—the name of his little anti-evil organization.

Ayesha [L] The immortal queen created in 1887 by English novelist Sir Henry Rider Haggard (1856–1925). When a group of explorers discovers the long-lost African city ruled by Ayesha, the deathless leader recognizes one of the men, Leon Vincey, as the reincarnation of her lover Kallikrates. To say that she sorely misses her inamorato is an understatement: Kallikrates has been dead for several thousand years. Ayesha offers the newcomer immortality if he will but step into a magic flame and share her throne. However, Leon is reluctant to enter the inferno so she goes before him to illustrate how safe it is. Alas, the flame leaves her more seared than seer, as a second exposure to the billowing fires robs Ayesha of her immortality and she dies a brutally withered old woman.

This tale of undying love as recounted in *She* proved so popular that Sir Henry brought her back in *The Return of She* (1905), reincarnated as an Asian princess; *She and Allan* (1921), a story set before Ayesha's demise; and *Wisdom's Daughter* (1923), the tale of Ayesha's origin.

Successful on the screen as well as in print, the saga of *She* was filmed in 1899 by George Melies, in 1908 by Thomas Edison, in 1916, 1917, 1925, 1935 with Helen Gahagan, and in 1965 with Ursula Andress. *The Return of She* was filmed in 1967 under the title *The Vengeance of She*, a sequel to the Andress film.

Baba [F] In Slavonic folklore, a horrible ogress known for cannibalism. With her long nose, emaciated appearance, and disheveled hair, Baba was an odd sight—all the more so when she rode through the air on an iron mortar propelled by a pestle. Also known as Baba Yaga, Baba carried a magic cudgel with which she turned people to stone, and was said to be able to control night and day, as well as the movements of the sun.

Similar to Baba is Berchta of German folklore, a spirit who guarded spinners and was draped in snow. In some tales she is a gentle sort; in others, a hideous cannibal who has large feet, an iron nose, and kidnaps bad children and lazy young men.

Bad One, The [FT] A demon featured in the American Indian fairy tale, "The Ball Carrier and the Bad One." Crossing a swift-running river with the help of a witch's magic glass ball, a young boy enters the hut of the Bad One and tries to steal both gold and a bridge that can extend to any length. Unluckily, the thieving Indian is caught by the Bad One and his demon friends. However, through guile given him by the Great Spirits, the youth is able to escape with his life *and* his prizes, and leads the Bad One on a hectic chase. Reaching the river, he lays down the bridge, causes it to expand, crosses, and leaves it behind. The Bad One follows, and when he is halfway across the boy orders the bridge to resume its normal size. For one blood-freezing moment the demon glowers at the youngster, realizing that he has been tricked, before he plunges into the river and is drowned.

In art, the Bad One is pictured as being a large man with scales and fangs.

Baker, Rick [MP] A young make-up artist who specializes in horror and science fiction films. Born in New York in 1950, Baker began making rubber masks at age thirteen, and was sculpting "Gumby" puppets for Art Clokey's popular stop-motion animation series four years later. Baker's first feature-length film was *Octoman* (1969) for which he designed and built an octopus costume. This was followed by monster make-up for *Schlock* (1972), *It's Alive* (1977), *Star Wars* (1977), and *The Incredible Melting Man* (1978), among others. Perhaps Baker's most famous creation was *King Kong* (1976), for which he both constructed the ape costume and played the giant gorilla when the highly touted life-size robot Kong refused to perform. Baker's contribution to that film went uncredited. Smarting from this rebuke by producer Dino de Laurentiis, Baker went on to play the impotent gorilla Dino in *Kentucky Fried Movie* (1977).

Baker, an Emmy winner for "The Autobiography of Miss Jane Pittman" and a former assistant to Dick Smith, lives in Southern California with his wife, Elaine. see: **King Kong; Smith, Dick.**

Balder [M] The son of Odin and Frigga, Balder was the Norse god of the sun. Beautiful and gentle, he was made invulnerable to all things but mistletoe. His mother thought it was harmless, so why bother? Needless to say, Balder was ultimately vanquished by a dart made of mistletoe, hurled by the blind god Hoder at the urging of evil Loki. Upon Balder's death, his wife Nanna died of a broken heart—

Balder

while Odin and Frigga pleaded with Hel, the goddess of the underworld (and Loki's daughter), to restore life to their son. The grim lass agreed, but only if all things in nature would weep. Hearing the terms, all began to cry, from the forests to the lowest fish in the sea—all but an old giantess who was Loki in disguise. Because of the masquerading god, Balder's life was forfeit. The wrath of the sun god's friends knew no bounds, and Loki, to save his wretched hide, swiftly changed into a salmon. But the gods caught him in a great net where they kept Loki imprisoned until Ragnarok. As for Hoder, the god of winter and dupe of Loki, he was slain by Balder's brother Bali. see: **Loki; Odin.**

Balnibari [L] The fourth incredible country visited by Lemuel Gulliver in *Gulliver's Travels*. During his stay, the English physician was the guest of the great Lord Munodi.

Gulliver was not particularly impressed with this nation. There are many academies of science and art, which Gulliver attributes to the influence of transients from Laputa. Though the forward-looking Balnibarians known as "projectors" pursue

these fields, they do so vainly and let what they *do* have fall to ruin. The result is depression among the general populace. According to Gulliver, "The people in the streets walked fast, looked wild, their eyes fixed, and were generally in rags." Touring Balnibari, Gulliver seems to feel that progress can be more damaging than remaining backward.

The country's main metropolis is Lugado, and its largest port city is Maldonada, which is "about as large as Portsmouth." see: **Gulliver, Lemuel; Laputa.**

Balor [M] A Celtic demon who lived beneath the sea. The grandson of Net, the son of Buarainech, and the husband of Cathlionn, Balor for many years dwelt in harmony with the other gods. But he made the mistake of glancing into his father's house just as a sorcerer was preparing magic potions which affect the eyes. Its fumes poisoned Balor and, thereafter, whatever he looked upon was blighted and died—even the gods. Balor was told that he would be allowed to live, but only if he kept his eyes shut. The poor creature did as he was told and lived in darkness. Then, one day, the god Lugh flung the hot, magic stone Tathlum into Balor's evil eyes. The object flew through the demon's skull and emerged from the other side, killing him. This tale is viewed as a personification of the eternal battle between deadly winter (Balor) and the sun (Tathlum) of the spring (Lugh).

Bandersnatch [L] One of the more amorphous creatures in Lewis Carroll's *Through the Looking Glass*. A beast first mentioned in the poem "Jabberwocky," it is there described as "frumious" and something to shun. Later, it is mentioned by a chess king as being something as difficult to stop as a passing minute. see: **Alice; Jabberwock.**

Banquo [L] A Scottish noble and general in William Shakespeare's *Macbeth* (1606). Returning from a battle against Scottish and Norwegian rebels, Banquo and fellow general Macbeth encounter three witches, who predict that Macbeth will one day be king, but that Banquo will be the father of kings. Macbeth fulfills the first part of the prophecy by murdering King Duncan—and then, when he fears that the second part may also come true, has Banquo's throat cut. But the general will not be stopped by a mere "twenty trenched gashes on his head." At a great feast being held in his memory, Banquo's bloody ghost appears to Macbeth. As the new king is the only one who sees the specter, his ravings lead the assembly to suspect that there is something rotten in the state of their monarch. Macbeth is eventually killed for his various treacheries.

Banshee [O] A ghastly spirit that haunts Irish and Highland Scotch families. Also known as the Bean Si, Bean-Nighe, and the White Lady of Ireland, the banshee attaches itself to a particular family and wails horribly just before and/or upon the death of one of its members. Variations on this motif have her as a singing virgin, a specter who washes the grave clothes of the person about to die, or a shrieking spirit who flies past the moon. As for the origin of the banshee, she can either be someone who has died young in the family or a woman who did not survive childbirth.

The banshee's appearance varies according to geography. Most legends have her sporting long red hair and wearing a gray cloak. Others, especially in Scotland, picture her as possessing only one nostril, one large tooth, and long hanging breasts. To suckle at these breasts is to automatically become her foster child and have a wish granted.

When several banshees gather to-

Banshee

gether, it means that someone great or holy is about to die.

Banth [L] A Martian lion created by Edgar Rice Burroughs. A vicious predator that haunts the dead sea bottom, the Banth has yellow skin and a mighty tail; a trim, supple body; large, awesome jaws; bulging green eyes; a mane of hair around its neck; and ten powerful legs. Its rattling roar is sufficient to root a would-be victim to the spot. Banths roam both alone and in packs. see: **Barsoom; Burroughs, Edgar Rice.**

Baobhan Sith [O] An evil, blood-drinking spirit who usually takes the form of a beautiful girl. How to tell a normal ms. from one of these English vampires? Simple. The latter wear a long green dress to hide the fact that they have hooves instead of feet. The Baobhan Sith are fond of moving about in the form of ravens or crows, and tend to approach their victims in the night as succubi. see: **Incubus.**

Barguest [F] A bogey of Scotland. Able to adopt any form, it generally appears as a long-haired black hound with flaming red eyes. Its appearance invariably precedes the coming of Death. Sometimes every dog in the vicinity will follow Barguest as it scampers into town and runs to the home of the doomed. No matter what shape it takes, Barguest always has fiery eyes, sharp fangs, large claws, and horns on its head. It is occasionally identified with Hedley Kow. see: **Hedley Kow.**

Barsoom [L] The Martian name for their home world in Edgar Rice Burroughs' immortal science fiction series. According to the author, life began on Barsoom in the Valley Dor some twenty-three million years ago. Among the early Martians were sundry fish, birds, and insects. These were followed by large land animals both docile and savage, along with humans boasting dark, white, and yellow skins. Eventually, the white-skinned Orovars came to rule this magnificent planet of five oceans, with the city of Horz the primary center of science and culture. Then, a half-million years ago, the seas began to dry up. The planet became arid and lost much of its air; canals were built to shuttle water from the poles and atmosphere plants were established to keep up the supply of breathable air. Four-armed green giants grew populous and began to rape the globe, making fast enemies of the humans, most of whom had melded into one large red-skinned race. It was into this volatile situation that earthman John Carter was dropped in the first novel about Burroughs' Mars.

Barsoom is the setting of a great many tales. The complete list of titles is as follows: *A Princess of Mars* (1912), *The Gods of Mars* (1913), *The Warlord of Mars* (1914), *Thuvia, Maid of Mars* (1916), *The Chessmen of Mars* (1922), *The Master Mind of Mars*

(1927), *A Fighting Man of Mars* (1930), *Swords of Mars* (1934), *Synthetic Men of Mars* (1939), *Llana of Gathol* (1941), and *John Carter of Mars*—an omnibus volume first published in 1964 and containing the stories "John Carter and the Giant of Mars" (1941) and "The Skeleton Men of Jupiter" (1943).

Peripherally involved in many of the Barsoomian adventures are the worlds Rasoom (Mercury), Cosoom (Venus), Jasoom (Earth), Sasoom (Jupiter), Cluros (Phobos), and Thuria (Deimos). The Jovian name for Barsoom is Garobus. see: **Apt; Banth; Burroughs, Edgar Rice; Calot; Carter, John; Carthoris; Pew Mogel; Ras Thavas; Thark; Therns; White Apes.**

Barugon [MP] A fictitious prehistoric monster with incendiary breath. Created for the 1965 film *Frankenstein Conquers the World,* Barugon emerged from a fissure in the Japanese countryside to battle the titular creature. Able to walk on two or four legs, the beast has huge floppy ears, a horn of bone jutting from its nose, and spines along its back and tail. Although defeated by the giant, disfigured, radioactive Frankenstein, the fire-breather was back in the ring fighting Ghidrah in *Destroy All Monsters* (1969) and joining the filmic fray in *Godzilla vs. the Cosmic Monster* (1977). see: **Ghidrah; Godzilla.**

Basilisk [M] Also known as a cockatrice, this mythical beast of ancient Greece and Europe is widely considered to be the deadliest of all living things. Thought of as the King of the Serpents because of the large comb atop its head, the Basilisk slithers along the ground like a snake, but with the forward half of its body upright. It can kill all other creatures except a weasel. Death comes instantly to anything it looks at, breathes on, or touches, even indirectly. If, for instance, a rider tries to stab a Basilisk, the creature's poison will ooze up the weapon

Basilisk

and kill *both* the attacker and his or her mount. It can only be slain by a crow, cock, or weasel—or by being shown its own horrid reflection. Born from an egg laid by a rooster (!) and hatched by a toad over a nine-year period, the Basilisk is apparently heir to the same fear of snakes which bred the mythology of the Gorgons. see: **Gorgon; Medusa.**

Bast [M] A daughter of Isis, Bast was the cat-headed goddess of the city of Bubastis in Lower Egypt. Also known as Ubaste, Bast was the deity of the favorable rays of the sun. This is in contrast to her sister Sekhet who had the head of a lioness and represented the fierce sun. Bast always carried a shield in one hand, a rattle in the other, and a basket around her arm. Her temple at Bubastis was the site of a cat cemetery covering many square miles. see: **Isis.**

Bathory, Elizabeth [H] Known to history as "The Blood Countess," the Hungarian Bathory was born in 1560 and married to Count Ferencz Nadasdy fifteen years later. She was introduced to the occult by her servant Thorko, whose training included lessons in the supernatural power of blood. But it wasn't until the countess slapped a servant girl and broke her skin that she discovered how the fresh blood made the skin of her hand appear.

Count Nadasdy died in 1600, and for the next ten years his widow sought to retain her youth by torturing young girls, draining their bodies of blood, and then bathing in the warm liquid. Her associates in this gruesome pursuit were her old nurse Ilona Joo, the witches Dorottya Szentes and Darvula, and her steward Johannes. Only when one girl managed to escape and report these atrocities to local authorities was the Countess' reign of terror finally ended. Johannes and Darvula were beheaded and cremated; Ilona and Dorottya had their fingers torn out one at a time and were burned alive; and Elizabeth was walled up in her bedroom, with but one small opening for the passage of food. She died in 1614.

Some sources claim that Bathory was actually a vampire and that she drank the blood to stay young. Regardless of which report is accurate, neither diminishes the grotesqueness of the Countess or her hobby. see: **Vampire.**

Batman [C] Created by Bob Kane, this classic comic book hero first appeared in *Detective Comics* #27, May 1939. When his parents are slain by a thug, young Bruce Wayne vows to devote his life to snuffing out crime. His body and mind trained to perfection, Wayne is made wealthy by the estate of his father Thomas and needs only to devise a disguise that will strike terror into the hearts of criminals. While he is considering the possibilities, a bat flies in the window—and thence is born Batman. Soon thereafter he is joined in his crusade by Robin, who is actually young Dick Grayson. The son of deceased aerialists the Flying Graysons, Dick is taken in by Bruce Wayne as his ward. The caped crimebusters work out of their laboratory called the Batcave, located beneath Wayne Manor. The Batmobile and Batplane are among the many conveyances at their disposal.

Over the years, the Batman adventures have showcased a wide variety of unusual supporting characters. Among the more fantastic foes are: the Joker, the Penguin, Mr. Freeze, the Catwoman, the Scarecrow, and the Man-Bat. Among the heroes are: Batwoman, Batgirl, Bathound, and even a supernatural sprite known as Bat Mite.

In the popular 1966–1968 television series, Batman was played by Adam West, with Burt Ward as Robin, and Yvonne Craig as Batgirl. Lewis Wilson played *Batman* in the 1943 screen serial, and Robert Lowery donned the cloak, cowl, and leotards in 1949 for the serial *Batman and Robin.* Wilson's Robin was Douglas Croft, while Lowery's sidekick was John Duncan.

Bayard [F] In medieval folklore, an enchanted horse of unthinkable speed.

Bayard

Owned by Amadis de Gaul, it was snatched from a cave under the care of an enormous dragon by the bold wizard Maugis, an attendant to Charlemagne. Charlemagne, in turn, gave it as a gift to the four sons of Aymon. Under their care, the horse would change size to accommodate its riders. If one mounted, Bayard remained his normal size. If all four scrambled to its back, the animal grew larger. Today, Bayard will sometimes appear as a cloud, and can be heard neighing on Midsummer's Day. Two of its footprints can still be seen: one in the forest of Soignes and another in a rock near Dinant.

Beanstalk [F] In the fairy tales of most nations, the beanstalk is a so-called universe tree, the stairway to the heavens. In the Teutonic tale of Jack and the Beanstalk, Jack climbs a beanstalk and steals from the giant (who represents the father of all things, equivalent to the Greek Zeus or Norse Odin) his most treasured possessions: riches (the rain), the hen that lays golden eggs (the sun), and a harp (the wind). In New Guinea, a similar legend has a young boy and his mother ascend a beanstalk to slay the human-eating giant Tauni-kapi-kapi, who represents the destructive power of storms. In legend, the beanstalk is also known as Jacob's Ladder, Lug's Chain, the Stem of Jesse, and so forth. It is also the seed symbol for the Indian rope trick.

Bear Squash-the-Lot [F] The hero of a droll Russian fable entitled "Who Lived in the Skull?" The story tells of articulate animals who, with great pains, manage one-by-one to take up residence in the skull of a horse. The first animal in is Little Burrowing-Mouse. Burrowing-Mouse is followed by Croaking Frog, Hare Hide-in-the-Hill, Fox Run-about-Everywhere, and Wolf Leap-Out-of-the-Bushes. Finally, along comes the bear. To quote the story: "And the bear sat down on the horse's skull, and squashed the whole lot of them."

The moral? Watch out for the Great Bear of Russia.

Beaver, Tony [F] A towering figure in American folklore, and the West Virginian counterpart of Paul Bunyan. A giant of a man, Beaver was good-natured and incredibly strong. His principal claim to fame? He is credited with having invented peanut brittle when he cleverly halted a flood by damming it with a huge crop of peanuts and molasses. see: **Bunyan, Paul.**

Befana [F] In Italian folklore, the good fairy who fills children's stockings with toys on the night of Epiphany. Befana did not come happily by this assignment. Too busy to look after the Magi when they were on their way to give gifts to Jesus, she said she'd watch over their return trip. Unfortunately, the three wise men followed a different route home and Befana missed them. As punishment, the fairy was ordered to look for them forever, all the while bestowing gifts upon lonely youngsters everywhere. In Russia, Befana is known as Babushka.

Behemoth [F] A Hebrew monster, usually thought of as the personification of Satan in the form of an elephant. Given to the earth on the fifth day of Creation, Behemoth took up residence in a desert outside of Jerusalem. The Lord of the Mammals, Behemoth needed to eat the equivalent of 1,000 mountains per day and drink staggering amounts of water—all the water that flowed through the River Jordan in one year was a single gulp to him—merely to survive. Realizing that he had created quite a formidable creature, God decided that Behemoth must never reproduce. Some interpretations of religious lore say that Behemoth was castrated; others claim that its mate was slain; still others explain that Behemoth is the mate of the giant

fish Leviathan, and that before they can reproduce they will be forced to fight to the death, after which the Messiah will feed the flesh of the loser to all righteous mortals. Behemoth is often identified with the Babylonian monster Tiamat. see: **Leviathan.**

Bellerophon [M] The son of Glaucus and the great grandson of Atlas (although some accounts make him the son of Poseidon and the Oceanid Eurynome). Bellerophon's greatest wish was to be able to ride the winged horse Pegasus. To this end, he received from the gods a golden bridle which enabled him to tame the magnificent animal. Thereafter, they shared many adventures together, including a battle with the Amazons. But it wasn't long before Bellerophon's confidence and ambition began to soar as high as his mount. Deciding that there was only one mountain left to conquer, as it were, he reined Pegasus skyward, toward the hallowed top of Mt. Olympus. Stunned by the young man's arrogance, Zeus caused the winged horse to buck and its rider was thrown to earth. Impoverished and alone, Bellerophon roamed the globe in sadness for the rest of his days. see: **Amazons; Olympus; Pegasus; Zeus.**

Belphegor [O] A medieval demon who was sent from hell to look into the disconcerting reports that mortal males were enjoying the honorable estate of marriage. Disguised as a human, Belphegor partook in the intimacies experienced by men with their wives, and found them to be shocking and terrifying. Returning to the underworld, the demon told his superiors to be glad that female companionship did not exist there!

Originally, Belphegor was the Assyrian double-sexed deity Baal-Peor, god of male vitality and pictured as a phallus. In more recent times, the term Belphegor has been applied to obscene men and social misfits.

Benaiah [F] In Hebrew legend, the servant of King Solomon. When he prepared to build his great temple, Solomon was faced with the seemingly insurmountable task of cutting the stone. The problem? No iron was to be used in the temple's construction. Calling upon his rabbis for a solution, Solomon was told about an insect called the Shamir. As old as Creation itself, the Shamir had the power to eat through stone—however, only the demon Asmodeus knew where to find the creature. Rising to the challenge of dealing with the devil, Benaiah journeyed to the mountain where Asmodeus lived. Filling the hellspawn's cistern of water with wine, the servant waited in hiding until the devil had drunk deeply and been lulled to sleep. Then, sneaking up on his wine-sodden prey, Benaiah slipped a leash about the devil's neck, a magic chain on which was etched the name of god. Powerless, the demon was hauled before Solomon and forced to reveal where and how to find the Shamir. Asmodeus remained in the king's power until the construction of the temple had been completed. see: **Shamir.**

Bene Gesserit [L] According to the glossary of Frank Herbert's novel *Dune*, "the ancient school of mental and physical training established primarily for female students after the Butlerian Jihad destroyed the so-called 'thinking machines' and robots." Another goal of the Bene Gesserit is to produce a male "whose organic mental powers would bridge space and time." The name given to the object of this search was *Kwisatz Haderach*, "shortening of the way." That branch of the Bene Gesserit called Missionaria Protectiva is responsible for helping to strengthen the sway of the old order by infusing underdeveloped worlds with superstition known as Panoplia Propeticus. see: **Fremen; Sandworm.**

Beowulf [L] The great hero of an epic Anglican poem written in either Northumbria or Mercia sometime between A.D. 700–750. Although the poem is fiction, it is widely believed that Beowulf was a historical warrior-leader named Beow or Beowa. In the poem, Beowulf is the son of Scefing and his wife Ecgtheow and the nephew of Hygelac, King of West Gothland. He possesses the power of thirty men, strength which he uses to win battles against humans and sea creatures alike. However, it is for his struggle with the monster Grendel that Beowulf is best known. Slaying the beast in the great Danish hall Heorot, Beowulf then grabs his magic sword Hrunting and sallies forth to kill Grendel's mother, who has been avenging her son by menacing the people of Hrothgar, King of the Danes. Immortalized by these bold deeds, he returns home and, upon his uncle's death, becomes king. Beowulf rules for a half-century. Then, when the treasure of a local dragon is stolen, the fire-breather ravages the countryside and Beowulf elects to meet it in combat. His sword breaks on the serpent's scaly hide, and the king is forced to best it by hand; in the process, the noble leader is himself killed. A pyre is prepared and, with fitting ceremony, was

> *Laid then in the midst*
> *the great prince*
> *the warriors lamenting,*
> *their beloved lord.*

see: **Dragon; Grendel.**

Bermuda Triangle [U] A region of the western Atlantic Ocean where hundreds of planes and ships have inexplicably vanished. The Bermuda Triangle occupies an area roughly defined by southern Florida, Bermuda, and the waters just beyond Puerto Rico. Disappearances are usually accompanied by a yellowing of the sky, a disfunctioning of all instrumentation, and an unsettling eeriness to the water. The name itself was coined in 1945, following the disappearance of a half-dozen Navy aircraft out on a training flight. Explanations range from storms to sea monsters to the presence of extraterrestrials. The Bermuda Triangle overlaps another dread section of water, the Sargasso Sea.

A book by Charles Berlitz, entitled *The Bermuda Triangle,* was a bestseller in 1974. see: **Sargasso Sea.**

Bertie Monster

Bertie Monster [U] A sea beast named after the boat *Bertie* in 1881. Fishing ninety miles southeast of Bressay in Scotland, the crew of the *Bertie* saw a huge monster with large eyes, its head covered by a seaweedlike growth, thrashing about in the water. Sporting three large humps, a powerful tail, and fins on the shoulders, it came at the boat. The six men onboard grabbed rifles and fired, but their bullets just bounced off the creature's slimy body. By heaving ballast stones, they finally succeeded in stopping the monster's advance. Angry, it paddled about the ship from early afternoon until sunset before finally submerging.

Bevis of Hampton [F] An English hero of the Dark Ages. When his father is slain by his mother, Bevis hastens to avenge the murder. But his mother is a hair's-breadth ahead of the grieving lad; no sooner does he reach her side than she has him captured and sold as a slave to Eastern merchants. Escaping from bondage, Bevis meets Josian, the daughter of the King of Armenia. He tells his story to the princess, they fall in love, and she gives him the horse Arundel and the magic word Morglay to help him realize his revenge. Concentrating, first, on slaying a dragon, a demon, and the giant Ascapart, Bevis becomes a famous hero and marries Josian before returning to England to butcher his mother.

Bierce, Ambrose [L] A fantasy author with a particular fascination for dreams. Born in Ohio in 1842, Ambrose Bwinnett Bierce served in the Union Army during the Civil War, after which he went to work for a San Francisco newspaper. His first short story, "The Haunted Valley," was published in 1871; it was followed by other fantastic tales, as well as by nonfiction and nongenre fiction. His most memorable tale, "An Occurrence at Owl Creek Bridge," appeared in 1891 in the volume *Tales of Soldiers and Civilians.* It is the drama of a man's surrealistic imaginings between the time he is knotted to the gallows and executed. Bierce's other nightmare and horror oriented stories include "The Realm of the Unreal," "The Middle Toe of the Right Foot," and "The Death of Halpin Frayser." In 1913, the restless Bierce traveled to Mexico to find the rebellious Pancho Villa. It was the last anyone heard of the author. Legend has it that he was captured by the rampaging general in 1914 and murdered.

Bifrost [M] In Norse mythology, the rainbow bridge whose colors are caused by the glow of precious stones. Bifrost leads from Asgard, the home of the gods, to Midgard, the abode of mortals. Some accounts had it bypassing Midgard and spanning the void between Asgard and the underworld. In both versions, the bridge was guarded against assaults from giants by the god Heimdall. At his side were the horn Gjallarhorn to warn of an attack, the magic sword Hofud, and the gold-maned horse Gulltopor. Yet, even without these accoutrements Hemidall was well suited to his task. The deity's ears were so acute that he could actually hear grass growing, his eyes sharp enough to see wool curling from the flesh of sheep. see: **Asgard; Odin.**

Big Ears [O] The demon cat of Scotland. It usually appeared at the end of a frenzied magical ceremony called Taghairm, the most gruesome of all occult rites. Taghairm consisted of the broiling of cats on spits until Big Ears finally arrived to grant the wishes of the participating sorcerer. According to a contemporary newspaper account of this ritual—which has not been performed for nearly two hundred years—Big Ears' clawmarks could be seen in the stone on which it had been perched.

Bilbo Baggins [L] A hobbit born in the Third Age 2890. A main character in several works by J. R. R. Tolkien, he lives in the village of Hobbiton, Middle Earth, in the hobbit hole Bag End. When we first meet Bilbo, he is about to honor Gandalf's request to become the burglar of the group of twelve dwarfs, led by Thorin Oakinshield, who hopes to drive the dragon Smaug from Thorin's kingdom. Following that adventure, Bilbo returns home, and in 2980 adopts Frodo Baggins, to whom he gives the One Ring in 3001. Twenty years later, he joins the lionizing Last Riding of the Keepers of the Ring over Sea, a large body of water west of Middle Earth.

At 131 years, eight days, Bilbo is the oldest hobbit in history. A bachelor and poet, he owns the sword Sting and is considered something of a lin-

guist. see: **Frodo Baggins; Gandalf; Hobbit; One Ring; Sauron; Smaug; Tolkien, J. R. R.**

Bizarro [C] An animate but nonliving, misshapen double of Superman. White-skinned, his face distorted with angular lumps and creases, Bizarro was created by evil genius Lex Luthor's duplicating ray. His first appearance was in *Action Comics* #254, July 1959. The nature of Bizarro is to do everything contrary to what is considered normal. He speaks in a simple broken tongue, eats "cold dogs," goes to sleep when the alarm clock sounds, tries to look his ugliest, and so forth. Indeed, unlike Superman, the mighty Bizarro Superman is immune to green kryptonite. However, expose him to rare blue kryptonite and he will perish in short order. A popular character, Bizarro was quickly joined by a Bizarro Lois Lane, their twisted offspring, and other Bizarro beings. All of them now reside on the square planet Htrae and appear from time to time in Superman comic books. see: **Superman.**

Black Annis [F] A cannibal hag with a blue face and iron claws in Scotch and Irish folklore. Haunting the Dane Hills of Leicestershire, England, Black Annis lived in the cave Bowerclose which she allegedly scraped from rock with her metal nails. Tall, with long white teeth, it was her manner to wait until dark and hide behind a great oak which fronted her cave. Then, when a lamb or child happened by, she would leap out and devour it. Only the habitual grinding of her teeth alerted a victim to her presence.

In olden days, people used to try and bait Black Annis by dragging a dead cat before her cave on Easter Sunday, presuming that by weight of numbers and the holiness of the day they could do her in. But a century ago, the local citizenry abandoned this quaint practice in favor of simply walling up Bowerclose cave.

Black Cat [F] Contrary to popular belief, a black cat is not just a harbinger of bad luck. True, they are considered the embodiment of the devil, the personification of dark night, stealers of souls, and creatures who, if one crosses your path from left to right, will cause you to suffer various misfortunes (unless it comes home with you, in which case you will have good luck). But black cats are actually more sinned against than sinners. In the early days of civilization, a black cat was no different from any other cat. Cats were considered sacred because they protected the granaries from mice, guarded the homes of their masters from snakes, and possessed eyes reminiscent of the moon, the symbol of a month's passing and hence of a woman's fertility. The skin of any cat was thought to be a potent cure for toothaches, and water poured over a cat was certain to produce rain. Then came the Judeo-Christian religions—and the downfall of the once-noble black cat. It is said that when Satan was tossed from heaven, he landed in a blackberry bush on which he spat and urinated. The blackberry cat was tainted by association, and soon the "berry" was lost—thus condemning all black cats. The mythos of evil grew to its current proportions, until the sinister feline's sole redeeming qualities were that if it followed you home or allowed you to stroke its spine, it brought you good fortune.

Like all cats, black cats have been used to forecast the weather; for instance, if they clean their ears it means rain, and if they frisk about it means there will be wind. Actually, there is some truth to this, since cats are extremely sensitive to moisture and air conditions. Black cats have also appeared frequently in occult literature, most notably in Edgar Allan Poe's 1843 tale of murder and an avenging pet, "The Black Cat."

Black Condor, The [C] A most unusual variation of the Tarzan theme, this costumed superhero was created by writer/artist Lou Fine (also known as Kenneth Lewis), and first appeared in *Crack Comics* #1, May 1940. As a baby, the Black Condor is called nothing more imposing than Richard. Raised by a flock of condors when his parents are killed, Richard soon finds that he has assimilated their power of flight. Rather than waste such a talent, he assumes the identity of assassinated senator Tom Wright, legislating during the day but donning the hood and costume of the crime fighting Black Condor by night. Richard also inherits Wright's fiancée, Wendy, who never suspects the substitution. Only the girl's father, Dr. Foster, knows the truth. see: **Romulus; Tarzan.**

Black Hound, The [O] A collective term describing a variety of supernatural English dogs. For instance, in Dean Combe, South Devon, there is the Pool of the Black Hound. It is haunted by a dog that is actually the spirit of a weaver named Knowles. When Knowles died and his spirit absolutely refused to abandon his body, an incensed priest changed the poor fellow's noncorporeal remains into a ghostly Black Hound, unable to find peace until it had completely emptied the pond with a leaky walnut shell. Other Black Hounds include the ghost of a woman who, in the shape of a dog, roams Lydford in Dartmoor; the transmogrified specter of a suicide victim in Selworthy, Somerset; and the baying Black Hound of Torrington in North Devon.

Experts attribute the predominance of Black Hounds in the occult lore of England to three factors: the dogs were common enough animals; they were ominous and stealthy, particularly when cloaked in night; and they were quite vicious. see: **Gabriel Ratchets, the.**

Black Magic [O] Described by many occultists as a "psychodrama," a vivid, purging gathering, black magic is the rejection of God and the debauching of Christianity by celebrating the forces of corruption and evil. The Christian service specifically is parodied by the black magic ceremony designed by Catherine de Medici (1519–1589) and known as the black mass. In it, moral and cultural values are mocked by the reading of the Catholic mass backward, with sexual orgies often capping the rites. It is said that for several centuries, babies born of these unions were sacrificed in subsequent black masses, their fat used to make candles. Though blasphemous and often crude, rarely has black magic been utilized for the purpose of conjuring demons. Unlike other dark endeavors, it can be practiced either by Satanists or simply by those who wish to deny the forces of good. see: **Magician; Satan; Voodoo; Witchcraft; Wizard.**

Blackmark [L] A hero of future earth created in 1971 by writer/artist Gil Kane (1926–   ). With the world a colossal ruin after nuclear war and mutated animals running free, the brilliant King Amarix of the Westlands uses residual science to make the barren girl Marnie fertile, passing his vast technological wisdom to the babe and giving the world a savior. Thus, while the child is actually the flesh of Marnie and her husband, Zeph, his spirit and mind were forged by Amarix. When the baby is born, Zeph names it Blackmark because it was created with the aid of a "black marked" breed of human, the scientist. Years pass. Blackmark's parents are slain by warriors, the boy is taken as a slave, and he becomes a gladiator. Ultimately, with the help of Amarix's wizard friend Balzamo, Blackmark proves his noble stock and keen mind by entering a vast stadium, defeating the awesome Flame Lizard, launching

an ancient rocket known as the Warlock Shrine, leading a revolution against the evil King Kargon, and becoming the new ruler of earth.

Blackmark's adventures were told by the ever-innovative Kane in a unique combination of words and pictures, the florid text accompanied throughout the book by dozens of handsome illustrations.

Black Sister of Würzburg, The [O] Born Maria Renata, the Black Sister was seduced by Satan when she was eleven years old and, two years later, became a witch. Entering the Untezell convent at age nineteen, she saw this sanctuary in medieval Bavaria as the ideal place in which to practice her demonic craft; while pretending to serve God, she would be able to cast spells on fellow nuns. Eventually, Maria became a subprioress and for forty years privately worked evil against her associates. One day, however, the Black Sister apparently outdid herself. She caused a half-dozen nuns to be possessed by the devil, and when all recalled previous contact with Maria she was arrested. Tortured by her captors, she was later beheaded and burned. see: **Witchcraft.**

Blacula [MP] A menacing Black vampire seen in the motion pictures *Blacula* (1972) and *Scream, Blacula, Scream* (1973). While visiting Count Dracula to ask him to sign a petition protesting slave trade, the nineteenth century African chief Mamuwalde is insulted when his wife Luva is the subject of lewd remarks made by the count. When Mamuwalde tries to defend her honor, he is attacked by Dracula, smitten with the curse of vampirism, and sealed in a coffin for over one hundred years. He is freed when a pair of interior decorators buy all of the furnishings in Castle Dracula—including Blacula's pine box— and transport them to the United States. In the first film, Blacula falls in love with a girl who resembles Luva and, when she dies, he walks willingly into sunlight. In the sequel, he becomes involved with voodoo rites and is destroyed when his effigy is stabbed in the heart. In both pictures, Blacula was played by commanding Shakespearean actor William Marshall. see: **Dracula; Vampire.**

Blarney Stone [F] A large, mystical rock located in a wall of Blarney Castle near Cork, Ireland. Set twenty feet from the top of the wall, the stone bears an inscription about Cormack Macarthy, who long ago surrendered the castle to British attackers. But Cormack was a smooth-tongued fellow, and after several days of patronizing dialogue, he had won incredible concessions from the victors! They became the brunt of great derision at court, and from the mood and substance of Cormack's easy speeches was born the word *blarney*. It is said that whoever kisses the Blarney Stone will be granted that same boon of a witty tongue.

Blazey, Saint [U] A section of Cornwall, England, said to be haunted by a strange animal which looks like a bear but neighs like a horse. Despite the fact that the beast is well known in these parts, the locals fear it and superstitiously refuse to discuss it with visitors.

Blob, The [MP] Reddish gelatin from space featured in the films *The Blob* (1959) and *Beware! The Blob* (1971) (also known as *Son of Blob*). After piggybacking to earth via meteor, the Blob begins to engulf and devour people, growing in size with every fleshy morsel. Vulnerable only to cold, the house-sized mass is stranded in the Arctic in *The Blob*, and is trapped in an ice-skating rink in *Beware! The Blob*. In an early concept of the creature, it did not hitch a ride to our world via space rock; the Blob was itself a molten meteor. see: **Caltiki.**

Bloch, Robert Albert [L] A versatile fantasy author and screenwriter born April 5, 1917 in Chicago, Illinois to Raphael A. and Stella Loeb Bloch. Bloch's first professional sale was the short story "The Secret in the Tomb" which was published in the May 1935 issue of *Weird Tales*—although his second sale, "The Feast in the Abbey," saw print a few months earlier in the January edition. Both tales were heavily influenced by critiques made by H. P. Lovecraft, with whom Bloch corresponded until that author's death in 1937. In 1945, Bloch's first published collection appeared, *The Opener of the Way,* and in 1947 he sold his first novel, *The Scarf.* The author of the novel on which Alfred Hitchcock based his 1960 film *Psycho,* Bloch was awarded a Hugo award in 1959 for his fantasy *That Hellbound Train.* He has been the Guest of Honor at two separate World Science Fiction Conventions (1948 and 1973).

In other media, Bloch adapted thirty-nine of his tales for radio's "Stay Tuned for Terror" and wrote numerous teleplays for such series as "Alfred Hitchcock Presents," "Thriller," and "Star Trek." His screenplays include *The House that Dripped Blood* (1971) and *Asylum* (1972), and he has recently recorded two record albums of his most popular stories. Married to Marion Ruth Holcombe, Bloch makes his home in Los Angeles. see: **Lovecraft, H. P.**

Blue Beetle, The [C] One of the earliest comic book superheroes, Blue Beetle was created by Charles Nicholas and first appeared in *Mystery Men* #1, August 1939. Originally, the Blue Beetle hid behind the secret identity of police officer Dan Garrett, who obtained his super powers from vitamin 2X, worked with a sidekick named Spunky, and had a girl friend named Joan Mason. However, after nearly thirty years this milieu was dropped in favor of one that combined the sleuthing of the then-popular Batman with the gadgetry of James Bond. The result was scientist Ted Kord who became the Blue Beetle after the death of Dan Garrett—a crime of which Kord, in fact, was originally suspected. Riding about in a robotic Beetle vehicle, this incarnation premiered in 1967 and lasted a little over one year before the hero was finally retired. see: **Batman; Bond, James.**

Blue Men of the Minch [F] Evil, blue-skinned mermen. Restless and devoted to mischief, these Scottish sea people are thought to cause storms. Fortunately, they can be reasoned with. When the Blue Men surface to survey their handiwork, ship captains have been known to persuade them into calming the weather. The ocean dwellers are particularly confused by rhymes, the posing of which will preoccupy them and achieve the same end as argument. Considered by some to be fallen angels, the Blue Men possess both mortal names and tremendous strength. see: **Merpeople.**

Blunderbore [F] One of the giants slain by Jack of Cornwall. Dedicated to avenging the death of fellow giant Cormoran, Blunderbore lives in an enchanted castle in a lonely wood. When Jack pauses in this wood after dispatching Cormoran, Blunderbore captures the hero and locks him in a dungeon littered with bodies, bones, and gore. However, while the giant and his visiting brother make ready to eat their captive, Jack finds a rope which he coils into a noose. When the giants come for him, he chokes them to insensibility. Then, "when they were black in the face he slid down the rope and stabbed them to the heart." Pulling a set of keys from Blunderbore's pocket, Jack frees himself. He also liberates a trio of ladies who are locked in a room of the castle, tied up by their hair. Blunderbore was starving them to death as punishment for refusing to eat the flesh of their

husbands. see: **Cormoran; Galligantus.**

Boba Fett [MP] An evil entity in *The Empire Strikes Back,* the 1930 sequel to the motion picture *Star Wars* (1977). With a belt of Wookie scalps lashed about an armored waist, Boba Fett is one of the most feared bounty hunters in the universe. Armed with an assortment of handguns, the tall humanoid carries a laser torpedo on its back, which Boba Fett fires by bending over. It is not known whether this formidable green, blue, and yellow garbed creature is a living being or an android. see: **Chewbacca.**

Bok, Hannes [L] A much-lauded fantasy artist and writer. Born in Minnesota in 1914, Hannes Vajn Bok began his career in fantastic illustration by rendering covers in the late thirties for Ray Bradbury's fan publication *Futuria Fantasia.* These works came to the attention of editor Farnsworth Wright, who commissioned Bok to draw for *Weird Tales* magazine in 1939. Bok thereafter worked steadily for *Weird Tales* and other publications. Simultaneously, he wielded an equally formidable pen as a writer, crafting such novels as *Starstone World* (1942) about a land of magic, and *The Sorcerer's Ship* (1942). He also completed several tales begun by Abraham Merritt (1884–1943), a fantasy author best known for his brilliant *The Moon Pool* (1918) and *Seven Footprints to Satan* (1927). In the fifties, Bok devoted himself primarily to astrology. He died of a heart attack in 1964, but his art has been reprinted in a number of handsome formats by the fan-supported Bokanalia Foundation. see: **Bradbury, Ray; Weird Tales.**

Bolster [F] A giant who dwelt in Cornwall, Bolster was so large that when he spread his legs his feet were six miles apart. Passionately in love with St. Agnes, he trailed her wherever she went. Tiring of his affections, she asked him to prove his love by using

Blue Men

his blood to fill a hole in the cliff at Chapel Porth. Gladly slitting one of his veins with a knife, he let the blood flow until so much had drained that he fainted. What St. Agnes had neglected to mention was that the hole opened into the sea. Bolster bled to death, and at Chapel Porth one can still see the rocks dyed red by the coursing of his blood.

Bond, James [L] The fictional British secret agent created by Ian Fleming (1908–1964). Distinguished from other operatives by the numerical designation 007, Bond is licensed to kill—a carte blanche he uses more in defense than in offense. The hero of thirteen novels beginning with *Casino Royale* in 1953—books of which John F. Kennedy was a great fan—it is in motion pictures that Bond has enjoyed his widest popularity. Portrayed by Sean Connery, George Lazenby, and Roger Moore, he has been featured in eleven films: *Dr. No* (1962), *From Russia With Love* (1963), *Goldfinger* (1964), *Thunderball* (1965), *You Only Live Twice* (1967), *On Her Majesty's Secret Service* (1969), *Diamonds Are Forever* (1971), *Live and Let Die* (1973), *The Man With the Golden Gun* (1974), *The Spy Who Loved Me* (1977), and *Moonraker* (1979). *For Your Eyes Only* is presently in production. Although none of these actors is quite the Bond conceived by Fleming—urbane, with a scar down his left cheek, ruthless eyes, and a cruel mouth—the series shows no signs of slowing.

Bond's superior is named "M"; a chap by the name of "Q" produces the many technological gimmicks which assist 007 in his defense of the free world; and CIA agent Felix Leiter works with Bond whenever Great Britain and the United States are required to join forces. Among Bond's many foes have been the drug-peddling Mr. Big, would-be world conqueror Ernst Stavro Blofeld, the three-nippled martinet Scaramanga and space colonist Drax.

Married briefly to a girl named Tracy, Bond was made a widower through gunfire in *On Her Majesty's Secret Service.*

Bonestell, Chesley [L] One of the first and finest of the illustrators specializing in outer space art. Born in San Francisco in 1888, Bonestell studied architecture at Columbia University and later worked on the designs for such landmarks as the Chrysler Building in New York and the Supreme Court Building in Washington D.C. But Bonestell's heart was not in architecture, so he headed to Hollywood in 1938 and turned his considerable artistic talents to the rendering of *mattes*—realistic paintings done on glass; placed between the camera and the players, and used to suggest sets, buildings, or landscapes which would otherwise be too expensive to film. Yet there was still a void in Bonestell's creative spirit, a gap he was finally able to fill in 1944. Always passionately interested in astronomy, Bonestell sold a series of paintings showcasing the planet Saturn to *Life* magazine. This was followed by a natural and most satisfying segue into science fiction magazines, books such as *The Conquest of Space* (1949) written by Willy Ley and Time-Life's *The World We Live In* (1955), and ultimately science fiction films. Among the movies for which Bonestell painted mattes and backdrops were *Destination Moon* (1950), *When Worlds Collide* (1951), *War of the Worlds* (1953), and other George Pal productions. Today, Bonestell lives with his wife, Hulda, in the Bay Area—still in love with space and still creating masterpieces of astronomical art. see: **Pal, George.**

Boobrie [F] A legendary water bird of Scotland. With its seventeen-inch bill hooked like that of an eagle, and its short legs armed with claws, the boobrie paddles about the water and shrieks in a raucous voice like that of an angry bull. The reputed dietary staples of this huge black bird are sheep and cattle. Many people think that this horrid bird is merely one form assumed by the sinister Water Horse.

Boogeyman [F] Also known as a bogie, bogle, bugaboo, and bugbear, boogeyman is a general term for any imaginary being who frightens a person. Many boogeymen were created by grownups to keep children in line: garden bogies to deter youngsters from stealing fruit, water bogies to keep them away from lakes, and so on. Of course, not all boogeymen prey on children. Adults have such bogies as the Huckauf, who jumps on a person's back as she or he travels alone at night on a country road. Whether the Huckauf was created by magistrates who wished to deprive late-night thieves of victims or by the psychology of solitude, its icy fingers are as real as if the creature were lurking behind a boulder or a tree. Indeed, whatever its guise, the hallmark of the boogeyman is the kind of gnawing fear that sticks in the mind and is expanded by the imagination. The only way to be free from that fear is to turn one's attention to something else—hence the common belief that whistling is protection against boogeymen.

Bosch, Heironymous [E] A Dutch painter of the fantastic. Born Jeroen Anthoiszoon in the town of Hertogenbosch, Bois-le-Duc in 1450, he adopted the name of his village and became the foremost interpreter of medieval mysticism. Little is known of Bosch's life, save that he was very religious and saw all matters as either black or white, good or evil. As a result, his worlds are full of strange creatures and demons, devilish beasts who are constantly confronting God's world of light and justice. Nowhere is this more evident than in the work for which the painter is best known, *The Garden of Earthly Delights*. An epic tableau, it is filled with visions of erotic pleasure, degradation, and incredible monsters. *The Temptation of St. Anthony* is another of his famous renderings, this one complete with giant mice, winged warriors, and tree-men.

Bottlebush Down [O] A place in Dorset, England, where many people claim to have seen one of the world's most important ghosts. Not as spectacular as banshees or Black Hounds, this Bronze Age horseman is the only known prehistoric ghost still extant. Among those who have seen the spectral rider is a well-respected archaeologist. It is said that the long-dead horseman is fond of charging those who cross his path.

Bottom, Nick [L] One of the more unusual mortals in William Shakespeare's tale of fairies and lovers *A Midsummer Night's Dream* (1596). By trade, Bottom is a weaver of Athens. He is also the director and male lead of *Pyramus and Thisbe,* a play that he and five other workers plan to perform at the wedding of Theseus, Duke of Athens, to Hippolyta, Queen of the Amazons. Apart from the problems attendant to any such enterprise, Bottom must contend with Puck; working a bit of mischief, the imp gives the weaver the head of an ass, then causes the Fairy Queen Titania to fall in love with him. In the end, Bottom is restored—although in which state he was the better off is open to debate. see: **Amazons; Oberon; Puck; Theseus.**

Bova, Ben [L] Born in Philadelphia in 1932, Ben Bova is one of the most influential figures in modern science fiction. A graduate of Temple University, he spent many years working in such jobs as aerospace executive, marketing coordinator for a research laboratory, and the like. Then, in 1972, he succeeded John W. Campbell Jr. as the editor of *Analog* magazine. During his six years at the science fiction magazine, Bova won six Hugo awards as Best Science Fiction Editor. In 1978 he became the fiction editor of the ambitious new science fiction/science fact publication *Omni.* In both positions he has been a very vocal champion of hard science in science fiction. However, Bova extends his cause beyond magazine policy. As the author of several dozen science books and novels, he writes some of the most credible and creditable science fiction the genre has ever seen. His 1975 novel *The Starcrossed* parodied the television industry long before *Network* reached theater screens; *The Multiple Man* (1976) foreshadowed the social and technical ramifications of cloning; and his epic *Colony* (1978) combined the technological sweep of Jules Verne with the moral responsibility of H. G. Wells and the nip of Ian Fleming to tell the tale of humankind's first artificial space colony.

A man of great wit and insight, Bova and his wife, Barbara, divide their time between New York City and West Hartford, Connecticut.

Bradbury, Ray [L] One of the top-selling authors of fantasy fiction. Born in Waukegan, Illinois in 1920, Raymond Douglas Bradbury read a great deal of fantasy as a child, completing high school in Los Angeles and entering the field by issuing his own fan publication *Futuria Fantasia* in 1939. A tale written for that periodical, "The Pendulum" (1939), was also the first story he sold professionally. The bulk of Bradbury's output between 1941 and 1946 was for *Weird Tales* magazine—twenty-five stories in all— many of which he later gathered in his first anthology *Dark Carnival* (1947). Concentrating on the short story format Bradbury also published "The Illustrated Man" (1951), "Golden Apples of the Sun" (1953), "Dandelion Wine" (1957), "A Medicine for Melancholy" (1959), and others. His novels include the interwoven tales of

The Martian Chronicles (1950), *Fahrenheit 451* (1953), and *Something Wicked This Way Comes* (1962). Bradbury wrote the screenplay for the 1956 film version of *Moby Dick,* and his works have been the basis for such motion pictures as *The Beast from Twenty Thousand Fathoms* (1953), *It Came from Outer Space* (1953), *Fahrenheit 451* (1966), *The Illustrated Man* (1968), and *The Martian Chronicles* (1979). Bradbury lives with his family in Southern California. see: **Bok, Hannes; Rhedosaur; Xenomorph.**

Brag [F] A Scottish goblin. One of the most fluent of the shape-changing sprites, Brag may also be the most eccentric. While the imp sometimes appears as a horse, he can also be seen as a calf wearing a white kerchief about its neck, as a nude and headless man, or as four men chanting and carrying a large white fabric. Often identified with Hedley Kow and the Irish Phooka, Brag is inclined to do nothing more harmful than adopt a curious shape, wait until someone happens along and pauses to stare, chase the person to a river or lake, and toss the luckless soul in. see: **Hedley Kow.**

Brak [L] A barbarian warrior created in the early 1960s by John Jakes (1932–   ). The hero of such novels as *Brak the Barbarian, Brak vs. the Sorceress,* and *Brak vs. the Mark of the Demons,* Brak lives on Para-Terra, a world which exists on a plane parallel to our own. With his shimmering yellow hair lashed in a long braid that hangs down his back, Brak spends his days searching for Khurdisan, a fabled land which stretches from the Pillars of Ebon in the west to the Mountains of Smoke in the east. En route, this literary heir of Conan faces a host of menaces both mystic and mortal. see: **Conan.**

Bran [F] The son of Iweridd and her husband Llyr, Bran was a brave and mighty Celtic giant. Together with his half-brothers and sister, he held court in Harlech. Bran's family was truly an odd lot. Among his brothers there was kind Nissyen and trouble-maker Evnissyen; Bran's sister Bran-wen was beautiful and of a pleasant disposition. In fact, she was so lovely that King Matholwch of Ireland took Branwen as his bride—an occasion which spawned disaster. During the ceremony, Evnissyen felt it appropri-ate to mutilate the horses of his new brother-in-law. Apologizing for the cur, Bran gave Matholwch new horses and, as additional recompense, a caul-dron that could restore life to anyone who had fallen in battle. But Evnis-syen had other bits of cruelty up his tunic. Years later, he murdered Gwern, the son of the king and queen, by tossing him into a fire. This heinous act plunged Britain and Ireland into war, a conflict which Britain stood no chance of winning due to the magic cauldron. Feeling repentant, Evnis-syen strode into the Irish camp and destroyed the cauldron, losing his life in the process. The odds quickly evened and soon all of Ireland's sol-diers were dead. On the Celtic side, Bran and seven Britons remained. Not a resounding triumph—but victory nonetheless. However, during the war Bran had been hamstrung by a poison arrow. Through the haze of pain he ordered that his head be severed and buried in London facing France, so that no foreign warriors might set foot in Britain without his knowing it. The trek to London lasted eighty-seven years, during which time the living head of Bran counseled the Britons. Some time later, King Arthur ordered Bran's head dug up and destroyed; he wanted England's power to be rooted in strength and courage, not magic. As for Queen Branwen, whose wedding had sparked this strife—she died, quite understandably, of a broken heart. see: **Arthur, King; Giants.**

Bran Mak Morn [L] A warrior hero

created in 1926 by Robert E. Howard. Described as a pantherish man of me-dium height, with black hair, dark skin, and inscrutable black eyes, he is the leader of the Picts of Caledonia. Their enemy were the Romans, along with an occasional incursion of the su-pernatural. The saga of Bran Mak Morn is told in seven epic short story adventures: "The Lost Race," "Kings of the Night," "Men of the Shadows," "A Song of the Race" (verse), "Worms of the Earth," "The Night of the Wolf," and "The Dark Man." see: **Howard, Robert E.**

Brementown Musicians [FT] Charac-ters from the Brothers Grimm, the Brementown Musicians are animals who had supposedly outlived their usefulness and were slated to be killed by their masters. Rather than meekly accept this dire lot, the four creatures unite, form a band, and head for Bre-men. Their number consists of a lute-playing ass, a drum-beating hound, a serenading cat, and a singing cock. However, fate intercedes and the mu-sicians do not reach their destination. Instead, they stumble upon a cottage which is being sacked by robbers. Chasing the thieves away, the animals take up residence and live there still! see: **Grimm, Jakob and Wilhelm.**

Br'er Rabbit [F] In American folklore, the clever nemesis of such dullards as Br'er Bear, Br'er Fox, and Br'er Pos-sum. In his most famous adventure, the encounter with the tar baby, Br'er Rabbit will not help his fellow ani-mals dig a well, claiming "I can get by fine drinking the dew." But when the well is completed, he is among the first to use it. Angry, the other animals make a figure of wood and tar to guard the well. Thinking it a living creature, Br'er Rabbit goes over and addresses the tar baby. When it doesn't respond, he hits it and is caught fast. Immediately, the other animals come dashing around and make plans to execute the precocious hare. The fox suggests they roast him, but Br'er Rabbit smiles and says, "I *like* to be nice and warm." So they discard that idea and Br'er Bear recommends that they hang him—to which the grinning Br'er Rabbit responds, "That would be fun! I'm so light I could just swing there and enjoy myself." Then Br'er Possum thinks to toss the spunky bunny into the bramble bush, which elicits a yelp of distress from Br'er Rabbit. Content that they now have their furry captive where they want him, the animals toss him into the foliage—only to be greeted not by screams, but by a laugh. "Thanks!" he chuckles, scampering away. "You have thrown me back into my home." It is likely that the expression "playing possum" originated with Br'er Rabbit's ruse.

In the folklore of both Africans and the American Indian, the rabbit is the symbol of trickery. see: **Remus, Uncle.**

Brigadoon [E] A mystical land located in the highlands of Scotland. Bothered by witches and demons, Brigadoon is saved by the minister Forsythe. Through his prayers for a miracle, Forsythe causes Brigadoon to disappear circa 1750, returning for only one day every century. Having first appeared in the German tale "Germelshausen," this enchanted and enchanting land gained its greatest fame as the subject of a musical play by Alan Jay Lerner and Frederick Loewe. A 1954 motion picture adaption of *Brigadoon* starred Gene Kelly and Van Johnson as hunters who stumble upon the restless township, whose most important inhabitant is Cyd Charisse.

Brobdingnag [L] The second strange land visited by Lemuel Gulliver in *Gulliver's Travels.* Located on the west coast of North America, it is home to a race of giants, "as tall as an ordinary spire steeple," who take "about ten yards with every stride"

and speak so loudly that their voices, "pierced my ears like that of a watermill." Diligently cared for by a nine-year-old farmer's daughter named Glumdalclitch, Gulliver nonetheless has frightful encounters with a huge frog, monkey, and spaniel. Other of his adventures are less dangerous but no less interesting; for example, the women of Brobdingnag are fond of stripping this little man they call Grildrig, laying him upon their bosom ("... wherewith I was much disgusted; because, to say the truth, a very offensive smell came from their skins ...") and putting him through some rather unusual paces. ("The handsomest ... would sometimes set me astride upon one of her nipples, with many other tricks, wherein the reader will excuse me for not being over particular.") Gulliver leaves Brobdingnag when the box in which Glumdalclitch carries him around is snatched by an eagle and dropped in the ocean. see: **Gulliver, Lemuel.**

Brownie [F] An English fairy, the brownie is usually male and is devoted to the service of its master. Standing three feet tall, it is dressed in ragged brown clothes, has a brown face and shaggy head of hair, and comes forth at night to do whatever work is left undone. If there are servants, the brownie will expose their sloth or misdeeds to its master. On farms, brownies reap and mow and tend after animals. For these contributions, the brownies are rewarded with cakes and cream (or milk)—which must, however, be left by "accident." If the little men think that they are being recompensed or bribed, they will leave and never return. It is said that brownies were originally created to help relieve men of the curse of burden drawn by Adam. see: **Silky.**

Brown Man of the Muirs [F] In Scotland, a guardian spirit of wild beasts. A small but hefty dwarf dressed in clothes the hue of withered fern, the

Brown Man has a thatch of red hair atop his head, and large glaring eyes. He feeds only on whortleberries, nuts, and apples and spends his day warning hunters to leave his animals alone, and punishing those who don't. Anyone who fires a gun or looses an arrow after meeting the Brown Man is likely to take ill and die. The Brown Man is also fond of standing on the opposite side of a stream and daring hunters to cross. Whosoever succumbs to the taunt and enters the water is quickly torn to pieces. see: **Dwarfs.**

Bunyan, Paul [F] A lumberjack hero of the Great Lakes and Pacific Northwest. Born either in Minnesota, Michigan, Maine, or the Canadian Woods, he was twenty feet tall by the time he left home at the age of one month. As befits his great size and strength, Bunyan became a lumberjack. During his many years on the job, Bunyan's companions were his wife, his son Jean, cook Hot Biscuit Slim, a tool-sharpening Swede named Febold Feboldson, bookkeeper Johnny Inkslinger, hunter Little Meery, singer Shanty Boy, Bunyan's personal aide and former cowboy Galloping Kid, the Blue Ox Babe who was discovered as a calf in the frozen Great Lakes and "weighed more than the combined weight of all the fish that ever got away," and the Little Blue Ox Benny, who died after swallowing a red hot stove.

Among Bunyan's many accomplishments were the thawing of lumberjacks' shadows when they froze to cabin walls during an especially cold winter, the rather self-serving invention of a pancake griddle that was so big it had to be greased by men skating on strips of bacon, and the forming of the Mississippi River when his water tank burst. see: **Beaver, Tony.**

Bunyip [F] An imaginary swamp or river dweller found primarily in Australian lore. According to a newspaper article written in 1847, a bunyip has "much resemblance to the human figure, but with frightful features, and feet turned backwards." Other bunyip traits include barking and hair-raising roars. The earliest mention of a bunyip occurs in legends of the Aborigines of southeastern Australia. Their description mirrors the newspaper account, although they add that bunyips are invisible to white people. It is thought that this fanciful beast may actually be some sort of marsh-dwelling wombat.

Burroughs, Edgar Rice [L] Among the most prolific fantasy authors, and one of the best selling writers of all time. Born in Chicago in 1875, the son of George and Mary Burroughs, "ERB" as he has come to be known failed at many occupations before turning to writing. Among these were soldier, cowpoke, police officer, miner, clerk, Sears employee, and shopkeeper. Then, in 1911, he turned his considerable wit to writing. The result was a novel called *Under the Moons of Mars* (changed to *A Princess of Mars* for book publication) and it appeared in *All-Story Magazine* the following year. Burroughs' next work was *Tarzan of the Apes*, which became a legend and made Burroughs a wealthy man. No one had ever worked harder becoming an "overnight success."

The author of over seventy novels in all, Burroughs was twice married, first to Emma Hulbert and then to Florence Burroughs. His children are sons Hulbert and John Coleman and daughter Joan Burroughs Pierce. The founder of the city of Tarzana, California, Burroughs died in 1950. Today, his works and characters are licensed by Edgar Rice Burroughs, Inc., which is run by Hulbert, Mike Pierce, and John Coleman's son Danton. see: **Carter, John; Innes, David; Napier, Carson; Tarzan.**

Buru [F] A fanciful beast of Southeast Asia, where its name in several local tongues means "monster." The water-dwelling Buru is described as twelve to fourteen feet long, possessing a snaking neck capped by a flat head with a large snout and horns, and having three dull spins on its back. Its skin is dark blue spotted with white, and there is a white band running down its belly. Harmless to humans, the Buru bears its young live and never comes ashore. Its voice is described as hoarse, and many scientists feel that it may simply be some manner of crocodile.

Bush of Ghosts, The [F] A haven of the bizarre in an Ibibian folk tale. One day, a skull from the Bush of Ghosts notices and decides to marry a beautiful girl named Nkoyo. Naturally, the skull knows that she will never have him in his native state—so he borrows various parts of the body from his friends and arrives before Nkoyo very handsome indeed. Nkoyo's parents sense something very odd about the skull and warn her to watch her step—but she marries him anyway, and together they head for the Bush of Ghosts. En route, the skull pauses to return those anatomical portions which were on-loan, and Nkoyo learns the unpleasant truth about her husband. But she stays with him, even caring for his invalid mother. However, if the skull is happy, the other creatures in the Bush of Ghosts are not. They don't care to have a mortal in their midst, and decide to devour her. Hearing of the plan, Nkoyo's mother-in-law helps her to escape. Returning home, Nkoyo tells her parents that she has learned her lesson and vows never again to be so willful.

Bushy Bride, The [FT] A cruel lass in the tale that bears her name. Forced to do more than her share of work by an evil stepmother and stepsister, a young girl is out fetching water from a brook when three giant heads emerge from the flow. They ask for a kiss, and when it is given they grant her three boons: that gold shall fall from her hair when she brushes and from her mouth when she speaks, and that she shall be "the prettiest girl there ever

was." Annoyed by the girl's good fortune, her stepmother makes her live in the pigsty, while her stepsister visits the giants and demands equal favors. Instead, they disfigure her by causing a bush to grow from her forehead and ashes to drift from her mouth whenever she speaks. Meanwhile, a visiting king spots the attractive sister and asks her to be his bride. She accepts. Unfortunately, the stepmother and stepsister join her for the sea voyage to the palace and trick her into jumping overboard. To save face, the king is forced to make the stepsister his Bushy Bride. However, the good sister miraculously survives and reaches the king before the wedding. When he has heard her tale, he orders the wicked stepmother and stepsister tossed into a pit of snakes, and takes the kindly girl as his queen.

Buttery Spirit [O] A spectral figure of England which is said to punish dishonesty and corruption. Although its primary haunts have traditionally been wealthy abbeys whose monks have become lazy and materialistic, buttery spirits also badger innkeepers who deal unfairly with patrons, harass shopkeepers who profit by cheating customers, and kill the cattle of unscrupulous farmers. These avenging entities are free to take goods which are ungratefully received or abused, and can feed on any food that has not been marked with a cross.

Buxen, The [O] A group of late eighteenth century Satanists. Led by nobles, these men and women donned dark cloaks and death's head masks and rode about the countryside committing horrible crimes in the name of Satan. Wherever they paused to hold black mass, the Buxen would capture usually a young lady, perform their rites over her nude body, then rape and/or murder her. When human subjects were unavailable, the Buxen settled for animals or robbed fresh graves to find a suitable ceremonial body. see: **Black Magic; Satan.**

C

Cabot, Tarl [L] A warrior hero created by John Norman in 1966. Born on earth, this red-haired, blue-eyed graduate of the University of Oxford was teaching English history at a small New Hampshire men's college when he made the fateful decision to go camping in the White Mountains. On his first night out, a spaceship landed and he was spirited to the barbaric planet Gor. There he has had many adventures involving his wife, Talena; the tarns, eaglelike birds ridden by the natives; the many castes, from the Caste of Physicians to the Caste of Assassins; and the wide variety of dangerous life forms, including the flying, beaver-sized rodents called Vart; the winged giants known as Ul; and the fanged, cobralike Leech plants.

The name *Gor* means "Home Stone," after the native custom of building their huts around a large, flat stone. The planet has three moons, boasts a tug of gravity somewhat lesser than earth, and circles the star Tor-tu-Gor (Light Upon the Home Stone). A new Gor adventure is published on the average of one per year. To date, the thirteen titles are: *Tarnsman of Gor, Outlaw of Gor, Priest-Kings of Gor, Nomads of Gor, Assassin of Gor, Raiders of Gor, Captive of Gor, Hunters of Gor, Marauders of Gor, Tribesmen of Gor, Slave Girl of Gor, Beasts of Gor,* and *Explorer of Gor.*

Cagliostro [H] A magician, medium, faith healer, and pimp. Cagliostro was born in 1743 in Palerma, Italy as Giuseppe Balsamo. Expelled from a mon-

astery at the age of fifteen for blaspheming, he befriended the alchemist Altotas and traveled with him throughout Western Europe. In 1768, Giuseppe married Lorenza Feliciani and settled in London. There, he adopted the name Count Alessandro Cagliostro. His assumed title gained him entrance to the various courts, where he practiced the black arts more to his benefit than that of others. Indeed, there is some question as to whether or not he really possessed any occult skills. Finally, in France, the count fell in disfavor with Louis XVI and was heaved into the bastille. When Cagliostro was released, he fled to Rome where he was nabbed by the Inquisition for heresy. He died in prison in 1795.

Caliban [L] Prospero's deformed, semi-human slave in *The Tempest* (1611). Created by the witch Sycorax, Caliban is described by one character as being, "as strange a thing as e'er I look'd on." The beastling is discovered by Prospero on a deserted island to which the latter drifts after his exile from Milan. The ex-duke teaches Ca-

Cagliostro

liban how to speak, but is unable to civilize his charge. In the end, after an unsuccessful attempt on the life of his master and on the virtue of Prospero's daughter Miranda, Caliban fears he "shall be pinch'd to death." However, he is merely admonished to redouble his efforts at pleasing Prospero to win back his favor. The name *Caliban* derives from the Greek word for "hawk," a root it shares with Circe. see: **Ariel; Circe; Prospero.**

Caligari, Dr. [MP] An eerie seer and conjurer played by Werner Krauss in the 1919 film *The Cabinet of Dr. Caligari.* Directed by Robert Weine, the film is presented through the eyes of hero Francis (Friedrich Feher). According to him, Dr. Caligari came to the village of Holstenwall to participate in the local fair. While obtaining a license to perform with his pasty-faced aide, somnambulist Cesare (Conrad Veidt), Caligari was ill treated by a town official. The next morning, the haughty official was found murdered. Other deaths followed, and it was finally revealed that Dr. Caligari had been using Cesare to kill his enemies. The director of a lunatic asylum, Caligari had read a book about an eighteenth century man named Caligari, who hypnotized a patient to commit murders. With the arrival of Cesare at the institution, the modern-day doctor was inspired to launch a similar campaign of mayhem. With the demise of Cesare, Caligari was straight-jacketed and hauled away. However, in a surprise ending, the audience learns that it is actually Francis who is mad, an inmate in the asylum run by a very normal Dr. Caligari.

The name Caligari was discovered by screenwriters Carl Mayer and Hans Janowitz in a rare book entitled *Unknown Letters of Stendhal.* In it, Stendhal meets an officer called Caligari and the name stuck.

Caliph Stork [FT] The hero of the fairy tale "The Story of Caliph Stork." Able to become any animal he wishes by snuffing a special powder and muttering the word *Mutabor,* the caliph changes into a stork—and is alarmed to find that with his bird's brain, he is unable to recall the magic word. Roaming the countryside in his gangly, unhappy state, the caliph meets a princess who has been transformed into an owl by the sorcerer Kaschnur for refusing to marry his son Mirza. Realizing that Kaschnur's spell is probably the same one practiced by the caliph, the couple decides to eavesdrop on the evildoer. Sure enough, Kaschnur mentions the magic word and the caliph, using it in conjunction with his powder, restores both himself and the princess to human form. They are wed and, as a gift to themselves, have Kaschnur hanged and his son turned into a stork.

Calot [L] A pet created by Edgar Rice Burroughs for the characters in his Barsoomian novels. About the size of a large goat, it has a head like a toad, jaws with three rows of deadly tusks, and ten stubby legs. It is extremely strong, swift, and intelligent, and is fiercely loyal to its master. Although omnivorous, calots prefer meat to vegetation. John Carter's calot is named Woola, and serves as a watchdog, companion, and vicious ally as needed. see: **Barsoom; Burroughs, Edgar Rice; Carter, John.**

Caltiki [MP] The oozing force of evil seen in the film *Caltiki, the Immortal Monster* (1959). In the mythos of the film, Caltiki is a bloblike, human-eating creature of Mexican legend. In A.D. 607, a strange meteor passed close to the earth, its radiation spurring the genesis of Caltiki. Terrorizing the Aztecs, the creature was quickly dubbed the Goddess of Death. A temple was built in her honor in the town of Tikel, and she eventually retired into its central pool. However, comes the mid-twentieth century and the meteor returns, its pass of earth restoring life to the slumbering mass. Eating people anew, the giant Caltiki is eventually stopped by army flame-throwers. What will happen when the meteor returns in the year 3404 is an issue skirted by screenwriter Filippo Sanjust. see: **Blob, the.**

Camaralzaman [FT] The hero of the Arabian Nights story "The Adventures of Prince Camaralzaman and the Princess Badoura." Imprisoned by his father for not taking a bride, Prince Camaralzaman is visited by the fairy Maimoune, daughter of Damriat, the chief of the djinns. He is asleep at the time, but Maimoune is taken with his good looks ("What a marvel of beauty he must be when his eyes are open!") and resolves to help him. Flying through the night air, she meets the evil-winged djinn Danhasch. Since Maimoune is the more powerful of the spirits, Danhasch is conciliatory and soothes her by describing all that he had seen that night. Among the sights, was the beautiful Princess Badoura, endungeoned by her father for refusing to marry. Maimoune orders Danhasch to bring the sleeping princess to Camaralzaman's cell. When it is done they are introduced, fall in love, and are wed. However, after a series of adventures the one-time celibate Camaralzaman meets Princess Haiatelnefous and marries her as well. According to the text, "The two queens lived in true sisterly harmony together. . . ." see: **Djinn; Fairies.**

Camazotz [M] The Mayan God of the Bats, Camazotz was also the judge of those who sought to be initiated into the Sacred Mysteries of the Quiché Mayas. Entrants were subjected to six grueling trials such as the House of Tigers, the House of Fire, and the House of Ice—and were then forced to meet Camazotz in a room filled with great weapons. Mortals who let their guard drop even briefly while in Camazotz's presence found themselves swiftly beheaded.

Capellan Power-Cat [TV] An alien being featured in the animated "Star Trek" adventure "How Sharper Than a Serpent's Tooth." Said to be one of the most ferocious creatures in the universe, the Capellan Power-Cat has gold eyes, reddish fur, a short tail, and thin brown spikes running along its back. Capable of rocking an attacker with 2,000 volts of electricity, the tiger-sized animal is surrounded by an electrically charged aura whenever it moves.

Caprona [L] A time-forgotten continent created by Edgar Rice Burroughs. Located in the South Seas, Caprona was named after its discoverer, Italian navigator Caproni. However, the continent was never colonized because it is inaccessible, its rockbound coast lacking either a beach or harbor. Enter Bowen Tyler Jr. onboard a U-33. The German submarine, captured by a British tugboat, becomes lost, paddles beneath the cliffs of Caprona, and encounters some of the most incredible creatures this planet has ever seen. The most spectacular of these are the dinosaurs. Powerful and aggressive, they force the English and German visitors to establish a grudging alliance. Then there are the humanoids. These are divided into a multitude of races: the apelike Ho-lu, early humans known as Alus, articulate Bo-lu, even more intelligent Sto-lu, the still more advanced Band-lu, and the almost modern Galus. There are also the preternormal Wieroo, evil beings who live on an island set in Caprona's Inland Sea. In one of Burroughs' most interesting concepts, each Capronan, whether dinosaur or humanoid, is a microcosm of the evolutionary process; he or she starts life as a prehistoric animal and passes on through the various levels of sophistication. Different individuals stop at different stages, and only the Galus can produce children who begin life at that regent status.

Caprona, known as Caspak to the natives, is explored by Burroughs in three novels. The first, *The Land that Time Forgot* (1918), is about the U-33 expedition, Bowen Tyler, and Tyler's girl friend, Lys La Rue. The second, *The People that Time Forgot* (1918) is the tale of Thomas Billings, who sets out to rescue Tyler. And the third is *Out of Time's Abyss* (1918), the saga of tugboat crewmember Bradley. see: **Burroughs, Edgar Rice; Wieroo.**

Captain America [C] A superhero created in March 1941 by writer Joe Simon and artist Jack Kirby. Steve Rogers was born on July 9, 1917. An orphan, he grows to lanky adulthood and is turned down by the military for service during World War II. However, in a bold experiment, a scientist's revolutionary formula gives him the body of a demigod. Before other mighty men can be created the scientist is murdered, leaving Rogers his sole legacy. Donning a red, white, and blue costume and forging a defensive and offensive shield, the muscled Rogers becomes Captain America, the personified spirit of the United States. He takes a costumed aide named Bucky and battles the enemy with guts and flair. During one such conflict, "Cap" is frozen in a block of ice and does not thaw until the 1960s. He resumes his fight for the American Way, this time slugging it out with thugs as well as such mighty villains as the Red Skull and the Super Adaptoid. For a brief period during the seventies, disgruntled with his old identity, Captain America changed costumes—and consciousness, to reflect the times—and became the caped, black-garbed Nomad.

Dick Purcell played the hero in the 1944 movie serial *Captain America*, while Reb Brown starred in the 1979 made-for-television movie. A Captain America novel, *The Great Gold Steal*, was written by Ted White and published in 1968. Another was published in 1979. see: **Kirby, Jack.**

Captain Future [L] A pulp magazine hero of the early 1940s. Created by editor Leo Margulies, Captain Future was the six-foot, four-inch, gray-eyed redhead Curtis Newton, who enforced interplanetary law with a proton pistol that boasted "a well-worn butt." Working with the Futuremen, Newton had a pair of robot aides and a ring insignia showing nine planet jewels circling a sun jewel. Most of Captain Future's over twenty adventures were written by noted science fiction author Edmond Hamilton. Formula tales in which the hero was captured and escaped several times per installment, the series boasted such titles as "Calling Captain Future" and "The Triumph of Captain Future."

Captain Klutz [C] Created in 1967 by *Mad* magazine cartoonist Don Martin, Capt. Klutz is comic book freak Ringo Fonebone of Megalopolis. Unsuited for life and responsibility in the real world, Ringo strips to his underwear, lashes a noose of towels about his throat, and jumps from the roof of his apartment building. But death eludes him. The string of towels snaps, he plummets through a woman's hat as it's tossed out a window by her irate husband, and lands atop a fleeing bankrobber when he hits the ground. The police arrive, nab the thief, and misunderstand Ringo's pathetic apology, "I'm a klutz, captain" as the name of the oddly garbed hero. Thus, with a towel-cape and hat-cowl, Capt. Klutz is introduced to the world. Among his equally baroque adversaries are Sissyman, the Mad Bomber, the eight-legged monster Gorgonzola, and others. The superhero's comic strip adventures first appeared in the popular paperback book *The Mad Adventures of Captain Klutz.*

Captain Marvel [C] One of the world's most popular comic book heroes, Captain Marvel first appeared in *Whiz Comics* #2, February 1940. Created by writer Bill Parker and artist Charles Clarence Beck, Captain Marvel was actually Billy Batson, a young radiocaster for station WHIZ. Summoned by the ancient wizard Shazam, Billy was told that whenever danger threatened, he had only to speak the sage's hallowed name and be filled with the wisdom of Solomon, the strength of Hercules, the stamina of Atlas, the power of Zeus, the courage of Achilles, and the speed of Mercury. A flashy costume of red, white, and gold was a lesser byproduct of the mystic utterance. Among the supporting players in the Captain Marvel milieu were Freddy Freeman, alias Captain Marvel Jr.; Billy's sister Mary, better known as Mary Marvel; Billy's girl friend Cissie Sommerly; his secretary Joan Jameson; and such wonderfully evil villains as the crazed scientist Dr. Sivana and Tawky Tawny, the talking tiger.

In the superb screen serial *The Adventures of Captain Marvel* (1941), Tom Tyler played "The World's Mightiest Mortal" in his battle against the wicked Scorpion; Jackson Bostwick and John Davey inherited the mantle for the "Shazam!" TV series during the first and second season, respectively.

Captain Nice [TV] One of the world's most inept superheroes. Created by Buck Henry for the 1966 television season, Captain Nice was actually police scientist Carter Nash. Drinking a potion of his own invention, Nash was able to become Captain Nice and thereby protect Big Town from such menaces as petty crooks and superpowered worms. The costume of the ever-awkward hero consisted of white sneakers; red and white striped pants; a white shirt emblazoned with gold stars and *Captain Nice* spelled out in bold blue letters; a belt of red, white, and blue with a gold buckle; and a blue and red cape. Nash wore his brown-rimmed glasses in both his mortal and superhuman guises.

The intrepid Captain Nice was portrayed by the talented William Daniels. Ann Prentiss played his girl friend, policewoman Candy Kane, and Alice Ghostly co-starred as his nagging mother. This highly underrated comedy series ran for only one season on NBC.

Captain Video [TV] One of the first television heroes, a science fiction character whose program premiered in 1949. A master of electronics, Capt. Video fought evil on our world and in the depths of space. From his mountaintop lair on earth he invented incredible scientific devices which he used against wrongdoers. Among these tools were the Cosmic Vibrator which shook objects apart, and the Opticon Scillometer which permitted him to see through solid objects. Capt. Video's aides were known as Video Rangers. Richard Coogan originated the role of Video, but his successor the late Al Hodge made the part uniquely his own. In 1951, Judd Holdren starred in the "Captain Video" serial, the character's one unsuccessful theatrical manifestation.

Carmilla [L] The most famous vampiress in literary history, and the subject of Sheridan Le Fanu's 1871 novella *Carmilla*. Narrated by a girl named Laura, *Carmilla* brilliantly mingles horror with lesbian overtones. When she is six years old, Laura is visited by a strange woman who gets into bed with her. Thirteen years later, that same woman by chance becomes a guest in Laura's home, an old castle in Styria. Always kissing and hugging her hostess, Carmilla begins to sup on her blood—after three weeks, Laura has become both pale and melancholy. It is discovered soon thereafter that the toothsome visitor is really a vampiress and has recently slain young Bertha Spielsdorf, the daughter of a friend of Laura's father. Nor is the bloodsucker's name Carmilla: she is Countess Mircalla Karnstein, a woman thought to have died 150 years earlier! Cornered within her coffin, the countess is staked through the heart, her head cut off, burned, and the ashes thrown in a river for good measure.

Carmilla has been brought to the screen on numerous occasions, most notably as *Blood and Roses* (1960) and *The Vampire Lovers* (1970). see: **Fanu, Joseph Sheridan Le; Vampire.**

Carradine, John [MP] A prolific horror actor born in 1906, the son of a reporter (father) and a surgeon (mother). Raised in Kingston, New York, Carradine studied art in school. However, he did some stage acting just for fun, and it proved to be valuable experience indeed. Heading for Hollywood, Carradine was hired as a set designer in 1929 by Cecil B. de Mille. A year later, he took a role in the film *Tol'able David* to earn some extra money, and never returned to the dark side of the camera. Among Carradine's many fantasy films have been *Revenge of the Zombies* (1943), *Captive Wild Woman* (1943), *Voodoo Man* (1944), *The House of Frankenstein* (1944), *The House of Dracula* (1945), *Billy the Kid vs. Dracula* (1965), and many others. The father of actors David and Keith Carradine, he continues to be active in filmmaking.

Carter, John [L] The fantasy swashbuckler nonpareil. Created by Edgar Rice Burroughs in 1911, Carter is the Prince of Helium, greatest of all the nations on the planet Barsoom—although he hails originally from Virginia. Details of Carter's life are sketchy. It is never specified when he was born, although we do know that the six-foot two-inch, black-haired, gray-eyed Carter fought the Sioux Indians early in his career, became a

captain in the Confederate Army, and went west to search for gold after the war. With his friend, Capt. James K. Powell, Carter did manage to find a mine in Arizona; unfortunately, neither man was fated to work it. Trapped in the shaft by Apaches, Powell is killed and Carter is transported by some strange mystic force to the planet Mars, called Barsoom by the locals. Upon arriving, he is attacked by Tharks—green giants who offer but a sample of the swordplay and danger which dog Carter throughout *A Princess of Mars* and the ten subsequent Mars books.

Married to the Martian princess Dejah Thoris, Carter is the father of a daughter, Tara, and a son, Carthoris. see: **Barsoom; Burroughs, Edgar Rice; Carthoris; Tara; Thoris, Dejah.**

Carter, Lin [L] A top-selling author and creator of Thongor and many other fantasy heroes. Born in St. Petersburg, Florida in 1930, Carter was a fan of the genre who became a professional with the sale of his first novel, *Thongor and the Wizard of Lemuria* in 1965. Since then he has written over thirty books, completed manuscripts left unfinished by such luminaries as Robert E. Howard and Clark Ashton Smith, and thus far edited four volumes in the sword and sorcery anthology series *Flashing Swords.* Carter is married and lives in Hollis, Long Island. see: **Amalric; Howard, Robert E.; Jandar; Smith, Clark Ashton; Thanator; Thongor; Zarkon.**

Carthoris [L] The son of John Carter and Dejah Thoris. Born 1876 earth-date, the young man inherited his father's "strong masculine beauty," gray eyes, agility, and spirit for adventure. Carthoris is married to Princess Thuvia, the daughter of Thuvan Dihn of Ptarth, whom he first met when she was a slave of the holy Therns at their fortress in the Otz Valley. The brave Martian first appeared in Edgar Rice Burroughs' second Mars novel, *The*

Gods of Mars (1913) and was featured in the next nine books of the series. see: **Barsoom; Burroughs, Edgar Rice; Carter, John; Thoris, Dejah.**

Castaneda, Carlos [E] While studying anthropology at UCLA in 1960, Castaneda was researching medicinal plants in the southwest. There he met one don Juan, a Yaqui Indian from Sonora, Mexico. Don Juan, as it developed, was a *diablero,* a combination medicine man-sorcerer, who had the ability to work magic and change into various animals. He took Castaneda as an apprentice and, over the next four years, introduced him to various hallucinogenic plants and bizarre philosophies. These experiences—in the paranormal or in psychoanalytical fantasy, take your pick—are outlined in Castaneda's books *A Separate Reality, Journey to Ixtland, The Teachings of Don Juan,* and others.

Castle, William [MP] A producer and director of over one hundred films, most of them horror movies. Born William Schloss in New York City in 1914, Castle dropped out of school when his friend and idol Bela Lugosi recommended him for the post of assistant stage manager of the road company of *Dracula.* Some time later, Castle became a theatrical entrepreneur, but decided to give it up and move to Hollywood in 1939. There he worked as an actor before deciding upon a career behind the camera. The first film he directed was *The Chance of a Lifetime* in 1943. It was followed by such hits as *House on Haunted Hill* (1958), *The Tingler* (1959), *Mr. Sardonicus* (1961), *Homicidal* (1961), *Bug!* (1975), and *Rosemary's Baby* (1968) which he produced for director Roman Polanski. Castle's biography *Step Right Up! I'm Gonna Scare the Pants Off America* was published in 1976, and he died one year later. He is survived by his wife, Ellen Falck,

whom he wed in 1948, and his children, Georgie and Terry.

Catoblepas [M] A huge black monster thought by the Greeks and Romans to dwell in the Sahara Desert. With a head so weighty that Catoblepas could not even lift it from the hot desert sands, the creature lolled about waiting for visitors. If anyone did pass by and chanced to peer into the beast's great eyes, he or she fell dead in their tracks. Luckily, the Catoblepas was so lazy that it seldom raised its heavy lids. One of its companions was the two-headed Amphisbena, whose eyes burned like fire.

Cavorite [L] An antigravity substance invented by Professor Cavor in H. G. Wells' 1901 novel *First Men in the Moon.* Described as a "metallic paste," it glows dull red when heated, and at other times is bluish. Becoming functional when it reaches 60° F, Cavorite ". . . is opaque to gravitation (and) cuts off objects from gravitating towards each other." The first batch of the stuff is made on October 14, 1899. Cavor uses his remarkable invention to coat the blinds of a huge sphere in which he and an unsuccessful playwright named Bedford travel to the moon. According to the scientist, when all the blinds are shut, ". . . no gravitation . . . will get at the inside of the sphere; it will fly on through space." But open a window and, "at once, any heavy body that chances to be in that direction will attract us." The sphere itself is enameled with "a thin wide sheet" of Cavorite to render it weightless.

Bedford and Cavor reach the moon, discover lunar dwellers known as Selenites, and find their hospitality wanting. The playwright leaves, but Cavor remains behind and the secret of the marvelous paste dies with him. see: **Mooncalf; Selenites; Wells, H. G.**

Centaur [M] An incredible creature of Greek mythology. Possessing the face and torso of a human atop the body and four legs of a horse, the centaurs were the offspring of Centaurus and the Magnesian mares. Centaurus was himself the product of an odd union, the son of Ixion, king of the primitive Lapithae, and the cloud Nephele, who came to him in the shape of Hera, whom he loved from afar. The most famous tale involving centaurs was a Lapithae wedding feast which ended in disaster. When the centaur Eurythion tried to rape the bride, the hosts attacked the horsepeople and slew most of them. Thereafter, centaurs were among the rarest of sights.

A subsidiary Greek myth maintains that there were actually two strains of centaurs, the children of Centaurus and his mares *and* the progeny of Cronus and the nymph Phylira. To shield his infidelity from his wife Rhea, Cronus disguised himself and Phylira as horses and their lovemaking produced a race of centaurs. Among their number was the great teacher Chiron.

Because the horse is a symbol of virility, it is a popular component of many fantastic creatures, from the Sileni—humans with a pair of horse legs—to the unicorn. However, none of these is quite so lusty as the centaur.

Among the many motion pictures to feature centaurs are *Fantasia* (1940), *Goliath and the Dragon* (1960) (the centaur Nessus), and *The Golden Voyage of Sinbad* (1973). see: **Chiron; Cronus; Hercules; Unicorn.**

Cerberus [M] In Greek mythology, the three-headed dog who guards the gates of hell. Sitting by Hades' side, with its right ear down and its left ear up, listening, Cerberus admits all newcomers—save for the living, whom it devours. If ever there were a creature suited for such a task, it is Cerberus. In addition to its three

Cerberus

heads with flaming eyes and fearsome jaws, Cerberus boasts a mane of snakes and a serpent's tail, which terminates in a stinger. Greeks often buried honeycakes with their dead to assuage this ferocious animal and prompt it to deal kindly with the deceased.

Cerberus figures prominently in the legend of Hercules, the strongman's twelfth labor being to carry the dog to his taskmaster Eurytheus. Hercules journeys to the underworld, and Hades is persuaded to loan him his pet—but only if the Son of Zeus can contain it using just his bare hands. This he does, despite Cerberus' mighty struggles and earth-rattling growls. It is said that wherever the dog's spittle falls to the ground, poisonous aconite flourishes. see: **Hades; Hercules; Orthos.**

Cetus [M] A sea monster with a forked tail, the body of a dolphin, and the head of a greyhound. When Queen

Cassiopeia of Ethiopia has the effrontery to boast that her daughter Andromeda is more beautiful than Venus, the dogs send Cetus to plague her realm. The loss of life is so great that the queen has no choice but to bargain with the beast; Cetus agrees to cease the troublemaking if Andromeda is offered as a sacrifice. Reluctantly, Cassiopeia accedes and has the princess chained to a rock by the sea. Fortunately, just as Cetus is about to devour the girl, along comes the hero Perseus. Plucking the severed head of Medusa from its satchel, he turns the monster to stone and frees Andromeda. see: **Medusa; Perseus.**

Chaney, Lon [MP] One of the great silent screen stars, and a legend of the horror cinema. Born in Colorado Springs, Colorado in 1883 to barber Frank H. Chaney and his wife, Emma, Alonzo was the second of four children. Because his parents were deaf mutes, the young boy learned to communicate by pantomime—a skill which served him well throughout his motion picture career. Leaving school at the age of ten, Chaney worked as a prop boy in a local theater and performed various functions on stages around the country before settling in Los Angeles. From the theater he moved into film, actually performing on screen for the first time in *Poor Jake's Demise* in 1913.

During his youth, Chaney had always been interested in make-up, and when he decided to become an actor he made frightening forms and faces his mainstay. Designing and applying all of his own disguises, he became most famous as *The Hunchback of Notre Dame* (1923), *The Phantom of the Opera* (1925), and as the vampire star of *London After Midnight* (1927). Chaney's last film was *The Unholy Three*, released in 1930, the year of his death. Ironically, his untimely passing forced Universal Pictures to cast around for another actor to star in

their screen version of *Dracula,* which led to Bela Lugosi's landing of the role.

Chaney married Cleva Creighton in 1905, and she bore him a son Creighton Tull (Lon Chaney Jr.). Chaney's second wife was Hazel Hastings, whom he wed in 1914. In the Academy Award winning film about Chaney's life, *The Man of a Thousand Faces* (1957), the actor was played by another legend, James Cagney. see: **Chaney, Lon Jr.; Erik; Lugosi, Bela.**

Chaney, Lon, Jr. [MP] The son of Cleva Chaney and screen immortal Lon Chaney Sr., and a fine horror actor in his own right. Born Creighton Tull Chaney in 1906, his road to stardom was a circuitous one. Creighton's father did not want him to work in the cinema, and for years he slaved in odd and largely unsatisfying jobs. After his father's death, Creighton made tentative moves toward film, making his screen debut in *Bird of Paradise* in 1932 and even testing for the role of Quasimodo in the 1939 remake of his father's film *The Hunchback of Notre Dame* (Creighton lost the part to Charles Laughton). However, it wasn't until he changed his name to Lon Chaney Jr. that producers began to take the young man seriously. Landing the coveted role of the brutish Lenny in *Of Mice and Men* (1939), Chaney performed magnificently and went on to specialize in the kinds of parts once played by his father. Among his most notable efforts were *One Million B.C.* (1940), *The Wolf Man* (1941) (a character he would play in five different films!), *Man Made Monster* (1941), *The Ghost of Frankenstein* (1942) as the monster, *Son of Dracula* (1943) as the titular vampire, and *The Mummy's Curse* (1944) as the embalmed Egyptian. Chaney's last film was *Dracula vs. Frankenstein* in 1970. He died three years later.

Chaney's sons are Lon Chaney III and Ronald by his first wife, Dorothy. He married his second wife, Patsy, in 1937. see: **Chaney, Lon, Sr.; Dracula; Frankenstein; Mummy, the; Werewolf.**

Changeling [F] An object that is left by a fairy in place of the human baby it has kidnapped. A changeling may be a fairy child or an aged fairy no longer of value to the sprites. It may even be wood given life and the features of the stolen child; though it quickly reverts to its normal state, the lifelessness of the figurine is misconstrued as the death of the baby. Once the substitution has been made, the human child is used to repopulate the fairy stock, put to work on a specific chore, or cherished solely for its beauty.

It was long thought that ill or retarded babies were actually changelings, and they were battered or maimed to force them to revert to their natural fairy form. When a genuine substitution *is* discovered, the

Changeling

human baby is either instantly returned or has to be rescued from fairyland. Since cold iron is repulsive to fairies, scissors suspended over the child's bed or crib will protect it from harm. see: **Fairies.**

Chaos [M] Perhaps the most important—and certainly the most confusing—figure in Greek mythology. There are two stories about Chaos and the beginning of the universe, the first of which was conceived by the poet Orpheus and is fairly straightforward. It states that Chaos came from Time and contained within it Nyx (night), Mist, and Aether (air). Upon the edict of Time, Mist spun about at such tremendous speeds that it assumed the shape of an egg and cracked. From within came the two-sexed four-headed Eros, while the egg halves themselves became heaven and earth. The second origin story, as told by the eighth century B.C. poet Hesiod, is a trifle more eccentric. In the beginning there was Chaos, who brought forth Nyx; her sister, Gaea (earth); and their brother, Erebos (the darkness under the earth). Lonely, Nyx and Erebos made love and brought forth Aether and Hemera (the light of day on earth). Nyx then placed a silver egg within Erebos (even though he was a male . . .) who gave birth to the golden-winged Eros. Finding herself attracted to Eros, Gaea lay with him and together they created the mountains; Uranus, the personification of the heavens; and Oceanus, the seas. Taking his mother, Gaea, as his wife, Uranus became the father of the Greek Gods.

These stories are not meant to be taken literally, nor did the Greeks view them as thus. They were merely symbolic explanations for a universe whose roots and nature were otherwise beyond comprehension. see: **Cronus; Gaea; Uranus.**

Charon [M] In Greek mythology, the ferryman of the underworld. Pictured as a grim, lonely figure, Charon poles his boat through any of the five rivers that divide Hell from the world of the living: Styx, the river by which the gods swear sacred oaths; Phlegethon, the River of Fire; Lethe, the River of Forgetfulness; Cocytus, the River of Lamentations; and Acheron, the River of Woe. Acheron is Charon's usual haunt. However, before Charon will carry anyone from the mortal sphere to the domain of Hades, that individual must pay for passage using money placed upon his or her lips at the time of death. see: **Hades; Hell.**

Charun [M] In Etruscan mythology, the monstrous demon servant of Mantus and Mania, the king and queen of the underworld. Half-human and half-beast, he is an aged man with fiery eyes and huge tusks. There are snakes coiled about his head and arms, and he possesses a pair of great wings. Charun is always seen holding a sword, and he relishes both using it to kill and witnessing the death of others through any means. One of the demon's principal functions is to hold the horses on which mortal souls take their trip to the underworld. Once these spirits arrive, Charun torments them until they beg for mercy. Among his many aides are Vanth or Death, the tomb-god Kulmu, and the fury Nathuns. see: **Death.**

Charybdis [M] An awesome whirlpool in Greek mythology. Originally a mortal woman, Charybdis stole oxen belonging to Hercules and was punished by being turned into a maelstrom by Zeus and placed in the straits between Sicily and Italy. Charybdis' partner in perdition is Scylla, a sea monster who eats the sailors of ships wrecked by the whirlpool. Among the most famous of Charybdis' nemeses is Odysseus, whom she challenges not once but twice—losing both times. The first encounter occurs after he leaves the island of Circe and, at the sorceress' suggestion, hugs the shore near Scylla. Away from Charybdis, Odysseus loses only those men the monster can nab, rather than the entire ship. Unhappily, though Odysseus denies Charybdis her due, Zeus sends a hurricane to destroy his vessel when he slaughters cattle owned by Helios. Using pieces of his ship as a raft, Odysseus alone survives—although the current carries him right into the swirling embrace of the whirlpool. The raft is swallowed up immediately, but Odysseus avoids this fate by clinging to a fig tree which grows from the face of a bordering cliff. see: **Odysseus; Scylla; Zeus.**

Chaw Gully [F] A Roman mine located in Dartmoor, England, and the site of some very strange doings. Guarding a legendary treasure buried deep within its bowels is a huge monster who works in conjunction with a raven perched at the mouth of the shaft. (Some say it's the raven released from Noah's Ark prior to the dove.) Whenever someone enters the mine, the raven alerts the monster and the trespasser is eaten. However, the body is always recovered within a few days, usually found lying near the mouth of the shaft. The monster, alas, cannot keep down a Christian. Presumably, the creature's primary sustenance is prospecting Jews, Moslems, atheists, and other non-Christians.

Cheshire Cat [L] One of the most famous creatures in Lewis Carroll's *Alice in Wonderland* (1865), the Cheshire Cat is constantly pestering Alice with counsel of very questionable worth. A case in point is the following exchange:

"In that direction . . . lives a Hatter: and in *that* direction . . . lives a March Hare. Visit either you like: they're both mad."

"But I don't want to go among mad people."

"Oh, you can't help that . . . we're all mad here. I'm mad. You're mad."

Cheshire Cat and Chichevache

"How do you know I'm mad?"
"You must be . . . or you wouldn't have come here."

Physically, the cat has ". . . *very* long claws and a great many teeth . . .", growls when it is pleased, and wags its tail when angry. It can also disappear at will, something it usually does with flair: ". . . this time it vanished quite slowly, beginning with the end of the tail, and ending with the grin, which remained some time after the rest of it had gone." To which Alice reacts with her ever unflappable wit: "Well! I've often seen a cat without a grin . . . but a grin without a cat! It's the most curious thing I ever saw in all my life." see: **Alice.**

Chessmen of Lewis [U] In 1831, on the Isle of Lewis in that teeming seat of fairy lore, the United Kingdom, an abnormally high tide dissolved a mound of sand and exposed a cave.

Inside there was a small building. A laborer working nearby saw the structure and broke in, hoping to find a treasure. He found, instead, eighty-four sleeping fairies. He ran home to his wife, who was made of sterner stuff; she urged him to go back and capture them. As it turned out, the fairies were actually ancient Celtic chess pieces, which ultimately fell into the hands of the British Museum. That august institute has them still—although when the guards make their rounds, their dogs refuse to go near the showcase in which the figurines are displayed.

Chewbacca [MP] A seven-foot, two-inch-tall Wookie pirate created by George Lucas for his 1977 film *Star Wars.* The alien Chewbacca was originally inspired by Lucas' pet dog and was patterned after the Cowardly Lion in the *The Wizard of Oz.* Played by Peter Mayhew, Chewbacca, in his capacity as copilot of the spaceship *Millenium Falcon* travels the universe with smuggler and mercenary Han Solo. The shaggy, blue-eyed Wookie is 100 years old and speaks in a language of grunts. He has a father named Itchy, a wife named Malla, and a son named Lumpy. Called "Chewie" by his intimates, Chewbacca possesses a violent temper and has been known to both excel and crumble in situations of stress. see: **C-3PO; Darth Vader; Death Star; R2-D2.**

Chichevache [F] An unusual British monster. The roots of chichevache lie in the French word *chicheface*, which means "thin face." By replacing "face" with *vache*—the French word for "cow"—the English had themselves a thin cow possessing a human visage. Its chore was to roam the countryside feasting on faithful and obedient wives. However, since there were so few of these around, the creature was perpetually thin. The chichevache has not been seen for many years, and indeed may well be extinct

Chimera

Chimera [M] An incredible monster with an equally incredible lineage. Boasting Poseidon and Medusa as its maternal grandparents, and Gaea and Tartarus as their paternal counterparts, this hybrid creature was the fiercest of the monstrous offspring of Echidna and the giant Typhon. A fire-breather, Chimera had the head and front quarters of a lion, the body of a goat, and the hindquarters of a dragon. Some accounts also have a goat's head growing from its side and a dragon's head springing from its tail. Chimera was eventually slain by Bellerophon who, from his perch astride Pegasus, was able to evade the creature's flaming breath. see: **Bellerophon.**

Chiron [M] The greatest of the centaurs in Greek mythology. Produced by the mating of the nymph Phylira and Cronus, Chiron was a great teacher and the guardian of many heroes. Sadly, it was one of his students who ultimately felled him. Warring with Chiron's brethren, the great Hercules let fly an arrow tipped with hydra's gall. The poisonous shaft speared Chiron, who stumbled into a cave where he lay in agony. Hercules joined Chiron to administer medicine prepared after the centaur's instructions—but the pain did not abate. Since Chiron was immortal, and Hercules did not wish to see him suffer through eternity, Zeus obliged the hero by placing the centaur in the sky as a constellation. see: **Centaur; Hercules; Zeus.**

Cimmeria [M/L] A mythological land of pronounced impact on fantastic literature. A place of darkness in *The Odyssey*, it was referred to by Milton in *L'Allegro* and by Shakespeare in *Titus Andronicus* (1592). However, it is best known as the prehistoric setting of Robert E. Howard's stories about Conan the Barbarian. A savage land of the north, Howard's Cimmeria lay just above modern-day France and Germany—although its face changed dramatically with the coming of glaciers and the geographical rending that followed the sinking of nearby Atlantis. see: **Circe; Conan; Howard, Robert E; Hyborian Age.**

Cinderella [L] The heroine of a short story by the Brothers Grimm. Cinderella is the attractive and charming daughter of a widower who decides to take a new wife. The marriage gives Cinderella two ugly stepsisters who do not hesitate to take advantage of the good-natured girl. Lonely, Cinderella visits her mother's grave thrice daily. Each time the girl arrives, she is met by a white bird that grants her anything she wishes. Since the prince will soon be holding a three-day festival during which he will select a bride, Cinderella asks for "a dress of gold and silver, and a pair of slippers embroidered with silk and silver."

On the first day of the festival, the prince falls hopelessly in love with

Cinderella. However, the girl is frightened by his attention and runs away. She returns on the second day, but once again flees the young man's advances. Finally, the prince has the steps leading from the palace coated with pitch. This time, when the girl hurries off her slipper remains behind.

Carrying the shoe about the kingdom, the prince tries to find the one girl whose delicate foot it will fit. When he reaches Cinderella's house, the eldest stepsister slices off her toe, slips easily into the shoe, and is carried off by the prince. However, the white bird from the cemetery calls the prince's attention to the blood pumping from the slipper. The next stepsister cuts off her heel, dons the slipper, and manages to fool the prince again—until the bird returns to point out the red puddle gathering beneath the shoe. Ultimately, the prince asks Cinderella to try on the slipper and it's a perfect, bloodless fit. They marry and live happily ever after. The two stepsisters are blinded for their wickedness.

The most popular screen versions of the Cinderella story remain the 1949 Walt Disney cartoon and the 1977 musical *The Slipper and the Rose*. In both films, as in several post-Grimm versions of the story, it is Cinderella's Fairy Godmother, and not a white bird, that assists our heroine. see: **Disney, Walt; Grimm, Jacob and Wilhelm; Woodengown, Kari.**

Circe [M] A Greek enchantress whose name means "Hawk." The daughter of Helios and the sea nymph Perseis, Circe's brother was Aeëtes, the King of Colchis and foe to Jason. Jason's wife Medea was her niece. Circe lived on the isle of Aeaea, where she changed the beautiful Scylla into a fearsome monster. She also transformed many of Odysseus' men into swine, an affliction which required the god Hermes to intercede on the side of the heroes. With the deity's help

Odysseus bested Circe, after which she became the zenith of cooperation. The enchantress directed the Greek leader to Cimmeria, which was one step closer to home, and later warned him about the Sirens, Scylla, and Charybdis. see: **Charybdis; Cimmeria; Hermes; Jason; Odysseus; Scylla; Sirens.**

Clach Dearg [O/F] A miraculous talisman brought by the noble Stewart family to Ardvorlich, Perthshire in Scotland during the Crusades. Also known as the Red Stone, it is actually transparent and colorless, made of rock crystal and nestled in silver. Although it could be used like a magnifying glass to set fires, its primary function was to cure sick animals. People with ailing beasts would bring buckets of water to the matron of the Stewart clan. She, in turn, would dip the stone in the water, mouth a Gaelic incantation, and instruct that the water be given to the afflicted animal. The magic spell has been lost for centuries, although the Clach Dearg itself is still said to exist.

Coblynauu [F] Welsh goblins who live in mines. Eighteen inches tall, they are extremely ugly and always dirty. However, they are blessed with good humor and help mortal miners by knocking at the spots where rich lodes can be found—although they never do any of the digging themselves. If you taunt a Coblynauu it will cast stones, but it would never do anyone serious harm. In Cornwall, these little people are called Knockers. see: **Goblins.**

Cockaigne [F] A legendary medieval land, a place of incredible wealth, pleasure, and unending leisure. There, the houses, streets, rivers, and some say the ground itself were made of delicious edibles such as cake and candy. All who lived in or visited Cockaigne were free to feast on any of these delights. Also spelled *Cokayne* and *Cocagne*, it is thought to be the root word for "cookie."

Collins, Barnabas [TV] The vampire played by Jonathan Frid in television's ghoulish soap opera "Dark Shadows" (1966) and in the 1970 motion picture *House of Dark Shadows.* In 1795, spurning a woman's love, a young Barnabas Collins finds himself afflicted with her curse—to be bitten by a vampire bat and become one of the undead. Unfortunately, Barnabas' father, Joshua, cannot bring himself to destroy his son. Thus, he places a silver crucifix on Barnabas' chest, wraps chains around the coffin, and thus makes it impossible for the vampire to emerge. However, a modern-day thief enters the Collins crypt in Collinsport, Maine, and opens the coffin hoping to find treasure. He finds, instead, the bloodsucking fiend—and Barnabas is once again free to roam the earth. Posing as a cousin from England, he settles with his descendants in Collinsport. The vampire survived for three years in daytime television, eventually succumbing to low ratings. In *House of Dark Shadows* he is speared through the heart—a more traditional demise, though both have kept the nocturnal demon dead for nearly a decade.

Colossa [MP] A legendary island seen in the motion picture *The Seventh Voyage of Sinbad* (1958). In its high peaks nest the film's fearsome two-headed rocks; roaming the countryside are horned cyclopes with orange skin and the lower quarters of a goat, in whose possession is great wealth gathered from the hulks of wrecked ships; and in one of its vast volcanic caverns is the castle of the magician Sokurah. The entrance to this cave is guarded by an ivory-horned, fire-breathing dragon, who protects the sorcerer from the cyclopes. Colossa is carved with steep valleys, many of which were created by rivers which flow with wine. The island is several days voyage from Bagdad, located in the Arabian Sea beyond the Isle of the Sirens. see: **Harryhausen, Ray; Roc; Sinbad; Sirens; Sokurah.**

Colossus [L] A supercomputer created by author D. F. Jones and featured in the trilogy of novels *Colossus* (1966), *The Fall of Colossus* (1974), and *Colossus and the Crab* (1977). Designed by Jones' protagonist, scientist Charles Forbin, Colossus is put in charge of all of North America's defenses. The computer's programmed chore is to analyze intelligence, decide if an attack is in the offing, and marshal its forces to strike first. However, Colossus writes its own scenario. Linking up with its Russian counterpart Guardian, the artificial brain orders Forbin to give it eyes and a voice and quickly takes over the world. Forbin survives through the bulk of the Colossus saga, being killed after Colossus helps earth battle invading Martians. The first novel of the trilogy was made into a 1969 movie entitled *Colossus: The Forbin Project* starring Eric Braedon as the luckless scientist.

Commando Cody [TV/MP] A space-age hero. Also known as the Sky Marshal of the Universe, Commando Cody is a young scientist who zips through the air via jet backpack. Sporting a leather jacket "flying suit," a metal helmet, and a ray gun, he battles the alien Retik in the 1952 movie serial *Radar Men from the Moon,* and the cruel Ruler in the 1955 NBC television series "Commando Cody." George Wallace was the screen Commando, while Judd Holdren was TV's Cody; in both outings he was assisted by Aline Towne as Joan Gilbert. Curiously, the exact same "flying suit" had been used in 1949 by Tristram Coffin as Rocket Man in the theatrical serial *King of the Rocket Men.*

Conan [L] One of fantastic literature's most popular heroes. The son of a blacksmith, Conan rises from inglorious beginnings in prehistoric Cimmeria to become, in his early forties, the King of Aquilonia, mightiest kingdom in this Hyborian Age. As strong as two men, the black-haired Conan endures a long and difficult road to the throne. Born on a battlefield, he falls into a succession of unsavory positions, from slave to thief to mercenary to pirate—adopting the name *Amra*, "the Lion"—to outlaw; then back to pirate, followed by soldier, buccaneer, and scout in Western Aquilonia. Finally, helping to fight the Picts, he graduates from soldier to commander. Subsequently, Conan leads a revolution against King Numedides of Tarantia, the capital of Aquilonia, of which he becomes absolute ruler.

Conan was created by author Robert E. Howard, and most of the tales of the barbarian hero, his wife, Zenobia, and their son, Conn, appeared in *Weird Tales* magazine from 1932–1936. Eighteen Conan stories were published during Howard's all-too-brief lifetime. Eight others later surfaced in manuscript form, and still further rough or fragmented adventures have been edited by such authors as Lin Carter and L. Sprague de Camp. In 1978, Andrew J. Offutt and others began penning new Conan adventures, and a motion picture starring Arnold Schwarzenegger is currently being readied for release. see: **Carter, Lin; Cimmeria; Howard, Robert E.**

Corben, Richard Vance [C] A fantasy artist whose vivid colors and dynamic figures have made him one of the genre's most respected talents. Born in Anderson, Missouri in 1940, Corben studied at the Kansas City Art Institute. He worked as an animator for Calvin Productions from 1963–1972, and in his spare time drew and photographed a stark animated feature entitled *Neverworld*. In 1968, he sold some comic book art to *Voice of Comicdom*, a fan publication. The story-telling potential of the comics

medium intrigued him, and he began to work for the adult-oriented underground comics. Among his many creations in this field was the fantasy strip "Rowlf," about a dog owned by the madwoman Maryara. During this period he also published the bizarre comic magazine *Fantagor*. Moving from the undergrounds, Corben turned down the chance to draw color comics at DC—the publisher of *Superman* and *Batman*—to render horror tales for Warren Publishing Company's *Creepy* and *Eerie* magazines. Today, Corben still draws for Warren as well as for European comic magazines. His epic text and pictures fantasy saga *Neverwhere* was published in book form in 1978 and has proven to be a strong seller.

Corben lives in Kansas City with his wife, Donna, and daughter, Beth. see: **Creepy, Uncle; Eerie, Cousin.**

Cormoran [F] One of the giants slain by the Welsh hero Jack the Giant Killer. During the reign of King Arthur, Cormoran lived in a gloomy cave in St. Michael's Mountain near Cornwall. In each of his raids on the surrounding countryside, the eighteen-foot-tall, nine-foot-round giant took eighteen sheep and hogs plus six oxen. One day, while the monster was out pillaging, Jack entered his cave. Digging a pit twenty-two feet deep and twenty feet broad, he covered it with sticks and dirt to make it look like solid ground. Then, blowing hard on a horn, he waited for Cormoran to come and investigate the sound. The giant arrived within minutes, thundered into the cave, and fell into the pit—whereupon Jack killed him, cleaving his skull with a pickax.

In the 1962 film *Jack the Giant Killer*, Cormoran was pictured as having a human torso, the legs of a goat, and a horn on his head. see: **Blunderbore; Galligantus.**

Cornucopia [M] The horn of plenty and symbol of prosperity. A Latin term,

Cornucopia was coined to describe the remarkable horn of a goat named Amalthea. It was on Amalthea that the baby Zeus suckled while hiding from his murderous father Cronus. Tended on the Isle of Crete by demigods known as Curetes—who drowned out Zeus' cries by banging together their weapons and shields— the future King of the Gods had only to desire food or drink and the goat's horn immediately filled with whatever he wished. see: **Cronus; Zeus.**

Costa Bower [F] The terrifying Death Coach of Ireland. Once it sets out, it cannot return to the netherworld without a passenger. Thundering from the skies, the all-black Costa Bower is pulled by four headless horses. It is guided by a driver who wears a perpetual grin from ear-to-ear, as pleased as can be to claim mortal souls in death. The Costa Bower does have one limitation, however; it cannot pass over bridges—a vulnerability which seems to have been inherited by Washington Irving's Headless Horseman. In the 1959 Walt Disney motion picture *Darby O'Gill and the Little People*, the Costa Bower is pictured as being propelled by horses with heads, but steered by a driver who lacked that attribute. Today, Ilmington in Warwickshire, England, is haunted by a Costa Bower. see: **Headless Horseman.**

Coven [O] A group of witches who gather, usually in some isolated locale, to honor their gods. In both attitude and timbre, covens are very much like the cavepeople who used to assemble to pay homage to the gods of fertility and of the hunt. Unlike Judeo-Christian services, the mass of the coven focuses on matters spiritual *and* material, their ceremonies often culminating in random sexual unions. As a rule, covens consist of thirteen witches: a high priestess or priest and six mixed couples. The term itself was coined in the year 1660 by the Scottish witch

Isobel Gowdie. see: **Black Magic; Sabbat; Witch.**

Crackernuts, Kate [FT] In an ancient fairy tale, the kindly daughter of a wicked queen—a queen so evil that she has a witch turn the head of the king's beautiful daughter from a previous marriage into that of a sheep. Aching for her forlorn stepsister, Kate places a cloth over the mutton top and together they flee to a neighboring kingdom. There, Kate lands a post in the palace kitchen and is permitted to leave her "sick" stepsister in the attic.

At the moment, the palace is in something of an uproar; the prince is ill and no one knows why. All who stand watch by his bedside mysteriously vanish. Kate volunteers to stay beside him and, that night, follows as he rises in a trance and heads for a nearby fairy mound. After dancing all night, the enchanted lad is sent back to the palace. The second night Kate follows again and, during the ceremony, is able to distract the fairies by rolling nuts from her hiding place. Snatching an unguarded wand, Kate returns to the palace and cures her stepsister. On the third night she steals an enchanted bird from the fairies, feeds it to the prince, and frees him from his stupor. Bested, the fairies let them be. As for Kate, she weds the prince, her stepsister marries his brother, and a tale so sadly begun ends with rejoicing. see: **Fairies.**

Creature from the Black Lagoon, The [MP] A member of an aquatic branch of humanoids which developed parallel to our own. Dwelling in a lagoon along the Amazon River, the Creature is green and extremely powerful. In the first film of the Universal Pictures series, *The Creature from the Black Lagoon* (1954), the marine beast survives harpoons, fire, drugs, and gunshot wounds to elude capture by a scientific expedition. The stars were Julie Adams, Richard Carlson, and Richard Denning. In *Revenge of the*

Creature (1955), the Gill Man is snared and brought to civilization, while *The Creature Walks Among Us* (1956) has scientists surgically transform the Creature into an air-breather, although he returns to the sea in the end. Ricou Browning played the Creature in all of the underwater sequences, sharing the chores on land with Ben Chapman.

Creepy, Uncle [C] The gaunt, semi-sadistic host of Warren Publishing's horror anthology magazine *Creepy*. Created by publisher James Warren and artist Jack Davis in 1964, Uncle Creepy describes himself in the first issue as "nauseating." Dressed like an undertaker and surrounded by misshapen imps, he provides an introduction and an epilogue for each of the comic book format stories in the magazine. He is also the occasional spinner of "Creepy's Loathesome Lore," tales of real-life monsters and demons.

According to the story *Monster Rally*, Uncle Creepy's origin is most unique. Searching for the secret of eternal life, a scientist named Dr. Habeas probed the bodies of such undying entities as werewolves, vampires, and mummies. When the local villagers found out what he was up to, they burned his castle to the ground. However, when a spilled vial of life essence mingled with the charred bodies of the monsters, something uncanny transpired. A new life was created and, nurtured by the rays of the full moon, the terror-spawned tyke grew to be the fiendish Uncle Creepy. see: **Eerie, Cousin; Spirit, the; Vampirella.**

Cretan Bull, The [M] The object of the seventh labor of Hercules. A magnificent white animal, the bull is given to King Minos of Crete by Poseidon to be used as a sacrifice to the god. But Minos can't bear to slaughter so beautiful a beast and substitutes another. Enraged, Poseidon drives the bull mad, causing it to terrorize all of Crete. As an added fillip, Minos' wife, Pasiphae, falls in love with the animal and, from their coupling, bears the Minotaur, a creature half-man and half-bull. Minos appeals to Hercules for help and, under the instructions of his taskmaster Eurystheus, the hero is to capture it alive. Approaching the bull and throwing it over his shoulders, he carries it back to Mycenae. The humbled beast is permitted to roam the Greek mainland for several years, until it has a run-in with Theseus at Marathon and is slain. see: **Hercules; Minotaur; Poseidon.**

Cronus [M] The Greek symbol of time, a Titan, and the youngest son of the deities Gaea and Uranus. The saga of Cronus is alternately vicious and tragic. After cutting off his father's genitals and becoming the master of the universe, Cronus hears a prophecy that rattles him to the core: it is foretold that he will be dethroned by one of his own children. Thus, no sooner does his sister-wife and fellow Titan, Rhea, bear him Hera, Poseidon, Hestia, Demeter, and Hades than he swallows them all. But when their sixth child, Zeus, is born, Rhea decides that Cronus has gone too far. Hiding the babe on Crete, she gives her husband a swaddled rock to ingest. Years later, the fully grown Zeus feeds his father a potion that causes him to regurgitate the gods. A war follows, with Zeus and his family headquartered on Mt. Olympus in Thessaly, and Cronus, aided by all the Titans, waging battle from Mt. Othrys. A well-placed thunderbolt from Zeus eventually dethrones his foe who, according to sundry versions of the myth, falls to Tartarus; is made king of the Isle of the Blessed; or wanders to Italy, where King Janus welcomes the god and dubs him Saturn, by which name he is known to the Romans. see: **Demeter; Hades; Hera; Olympus; Uranus; Zeus.**

Uncle Creepy

Crystal Ball [O] A transparent globe made of mineral or glass and employed to see into the future. Crystal balls were first used as medicinal amulets, crystal being thought of by early Christians as representative of the Immaculate Conception. Water which has been used to wash a crystal was considered the surest cure for most ills. Crystal tokens were also seen as bringing good fortune and were used to repel the Evil Eye. It was only a step from prevention in the present to prevention by peering into the future. Today, after some preliminary haziness, visions are supposed to appear with clarity to true believers. The art of using a crystal ball is called *scrying* or *crystal gazing*, although many clairvoyants shun the practice. They feel that physical media are a crutch at best, and at worst a sham. see: **Clach Dearg.**

Crystal Coffin [FT] The central prop and title of a story by the Brothers Grimm. One day, a poor young tailor is kidnapped by a stag and brought to an underground chamber. There, the tailor finds two large crystal boxes. In one is a miniature castle; in the other is a lovely young maiden. When he opens the latter crystal box, the girl steps out and tells him a woeful tale. Roaming the land above the chamber is an evil sorcerer who wishes to marry her. When the magician first asks she refused, and he punishes her by turning her brother into a stag. In a rage, she tries to shoot him " . . . but the bullet rebounded from his breast. . . ." Angry with the girl, the enchanter imprisons her in a crystal box, places her castle in another, and transforms her servants into vapor and stores them in phials. He vowed that there one and all would stay imprisoned until she changes her mind. But the maiden's brother hastens to fetch her a champion, and with the help of a magic stone the tailor begins to return everything to normal. Not that

his activities go unnoticed. Assuming the form of a bull, the magician comes to investigate. However, as soon as he arrives, the stag engages him in battle and is victorious. The tailor then restores the brother and marries the girl, never to be poor again. see: **Grimm, Jakob and Wilhelm.**

C-3PO [MP] Companion droid to R2-D2. The prime functions of this third-degree human-cyborg relations unit are translation and interpretation of thousands of alien and droid tongues, and customs and protocol, as denoted by the "C" prefix. Finished in bronze, the human-shaped C-3PO plays a decisive role in the Battle of the Death Star, serving as liaison between R2-D2 and the party headed by Luke Skywalker, and by helping to throw Empire Stormtroopers off Skywalker's trail. Previously in the service of Capt. Colton of the Alliance to Restore the Republic (informally, the Rebels), the droid now belongs to Skywalker. Occasionally victimized by his program to mimic humans, C-3PO is subject to fits of temper and anxiety.

In the film *Star Wars* (1977) and its sequel, C-3PO is played by actor Anthony Daniels. see: **Droid; R2-D2.**

Cthulu [L] The fundamental entity of the Cthulu Mythos. A giant, green, tentacled blob, it was created by author H. P. Lovecraft and is one of the masters of the fourth dimension as yet unknown to science. These monsters are the Great Old Ones or the Ancient Ones who were banished from earth by the benevolent Elder Gods. Among their number are the blind leader Azathoth, Yog-Sothoth, Nyarlathotep, Hastur the Unspeakable, and Shub-Niggurath. The Mythos refers to the stories written by Lovecraft and his literary heir August Derleth; tales in which the Ancient Ones hover about the edge of mortal perception, waiting for the chance to reconquer the earth. The first tale in the series, "The

Call of Cthulu," was published in *Weird Tales* magazine in 1928. It told of the elemental Cthulu emerging from the Pacific Ocean after epochs of inactivity. see: **Lovecraft, H. P.**

Cuchulain [F] A great hero of Irish legend. When his mother, Dechtire, sister of Conchobar, King of Ulster, was being readied for her marriage to Sualtim, the sun god Lugh transformed himself into a fly and carried her to his abode. Years later, Conchobar's men found Dechtire and her son and brought them to the castle Emain Macha where she and Sualtim were finally wed. When the young demigod was seven years old, he slew the dog of a smith name Culain and was forced to take his place. In addition to surrendering his freedom, the lad's name was changed from Setana to *Cuchulain,* "the Hound of Culain."

After a while, the handsome lad was permitted to leave his post to become a soldier. During the course of his bold adventures, Cuchulain fought many monsters—among them Terror, who lived at the bottom of a lake—bedded the wives of fellow warriors, and finally married the Princess Emer, daughter of King Forgall. At the age of twenty-seven, the bold Cuchulain was killed in battle by his old foe Lugaid; Emer died of grief. However, the Irish claim that even today Cuchulain's chariot is frequently seen, and the hero is oft heard singing.

Curlicue, Prince [FT] The kind, hunchbacked son of the evil King Grumpy in the French fairy tale "The Golden Branch." When Curlicue refuses a marriage of state to the ugly Princess Cabbagestalk, the king has him imprisoned. There, the prince meets the fairy Douceline who lives in a secret passage nearby, and she charitably transforms him into the handsome Prince Peerless. Meanwhile, Princess Cabbagestalk has likewise refused to marry the prince and is tossed into

jail. Visited by an enchanted eagle, Cabbagestalk watches in wonder as it becomes a prince, the lover of Douceline. He changes Cabbagestalk into the beautiful Princess Sunbeam and, independent of one another, the prince and princess escape into the countryside.

Living as a shepherd and shepherdess they meet and fall in love, neither being aware of whom the other really is. Unfortunately, their romance is interrupted when an enchanter, spurned by the princess, transforms her into a grasshopper. When the prince complains to the sorcerer's sister, the Queen of the Comets, she turns him into a cricket. Quite by chance, the prince and princess meet in their new form and decide to seek the one remedy for their affliction, the Golden Branch. Finding it in a garden of gems, they touch it and are restored. Just then the fairy Douceline happens by and reveals the couple's true identity. They are wed and take up residence in the palace of the Golden Branch.

Cushing, Peter [MP] A celebrated horror actor born in Kenley, Surrey, England in 1913. Although Cushing's early performances were outside the genre—his first film was *The Man in the Iron Mask* in 1939—he starred as Dr. Frankenstein in the blockbuster British movie *Curse of Frankenstein* (1957) and has rarely left the fantasy field since. Among his most famous characterizations are Dr. Van Helsing in *The Horror of Dracula* (1958) and Grand Moff Tarkin in *Star Wars* (1977). Other films include *The Gorgon* (1964), *Tales from the Crypt* (1971), and *The Creeping Flesh* (1972). Cushing's late, beloved wife was Helen Beck.

Cybermen [TV] Robotlike creatures seen in the "Dr. Who" television series. Hailing from the planet Telos, the Cybermen were once mortals who, to be free of disease and other physical frailties, gradually substituted metal and plastic parts for flesh, bone, and sinew. In the process they lost all of their emotions. The seven-foot-tall Cybermen have the strength of ten humans, can live in the vacuum of space, and employ metal rats called Cybermats to help implement their nefarious schemes. The silver Cybermen were created by Gerry Davis and Kit Pedlar, and were first seen on the program in 1966. see: **Who, Dr.**

Cyclops [F/M] One-eyed giants who appear in many branches of fantasy. The earliest of the cyclopes were creatures with names like Arges, Steropes, and Brontes, all of them parented by the Greek deities Uranus and Gaea. However, in Greek mythology the chief of the single-orbed ogres is Polyphemus, the son of Poseidon and ,a granddaughter of Gaea named Thoosa. It is Polyphemus who encounters Odysseus, eats four of his men, and keeps the rest of them barricaded within his cave. But the dull-witted cyclops makes the mistake of accepting fine wine from the Greek hero and, when he falls asleep, Odysseus puts out the giant's eye with the sharpened end of a smoldering pole. The humans escape Polyphemus' groping hands by lashing themselves to the underside of his sheep. Like Polyphemus, all of the cyclopes in *The Odyssey* are without law and agriculture.

Not that the Greek cyclopes have a monopoly on barbarism. Physically, the first of the breed met by the Arabian Nights' Sinbad on his third voyage, " . . . was as tall as a palm tree, and perfectly black, and had one eye which flamed like a burning coal in the middle of his forehead. His teeth were long and sharp and grinned horribly, while his lower lip hung down upon his chest, and he had ears like elephant's ears, which covered his shoulders, and nails like the claws of some fierce bird." More fortunate than Odysseus, Sinbad loses only two

men to the cyclops before the adventurers can blind him with a spit and escape his domain via raft.

In recent times, a pilot who loses half his face in a plane crash and becomes giant through exposure to radiation is the subject of Bert Gordon's 1957 film *The Cyclops, while a pair of satyr-legged cyclopes appeared in the 1958* motion picture *The Seventh Voyage of Sinbad.* see: **Gaea; Odysseus; Poseidon; Sinbad; Uranus.**

Cyclops, Dr. [MP] The star of the 1940 film *Dr. Cyclops,* and one of the most malicious of the cinema's mad scientists. Dr. Cyclops is actually scientist Alexander Thorkel (Albert Dekker), called Cyclops because of his extremely poor vision. To his laboratory on the Karana River in Peru comes the party of Dr. Rupert Bulfinch (Charles Halton), little beloved associates whose good eyes Cyclops uses to assist in his work. He then shrinks the scientists to six inches in height as a result of this work. But the manipulation of size is only the first step in Cyclops' plan to "control life absolutely . . . shape the very substance of life." Fortunately, the diminutive people succeed in luring Cyclops from the edge of a vertical mine shaft and the bald, burly man plunges to his death. After the scientist's demise, his victims slowly return to their normal size. A novelization of the film was written by Will Garth and published in 1940.

Cylons [TV] Evil alien beings featured in the science fiction television series "Battlestar Galactica." Because of the way adventuresome human spirits have led to the disruption of the natural order of the universe, the Cylons seek to obliterate every trace of the breed from outer space. To this end, they have been waging a 1,000-year-long war against humankind. Ever calm and supremely logical, the humanoid, metal-encased aliens have many eyes as well as different brains to suit various tasks. Warriors have just a first-brain, commanders a second-brain, and only the Imperious Leader possesses a third-brain, the receptacle of all Cylon knowledge. see: **Galactica.**

Cyoeraeth [O] A Welsh spirit who announces the approach of death. The favorite haunts of the cyoeraeth are crossroads and rivers, where it will moan and shriek with fearful conviction. At rivers it will also take pains to splash about, as though trying to give death's victims as much advance notice as possible. Ordinarily the cyoeraeth cannot be seen. But at those times when it becomes visible it is in the form of a woman with unkempt hair, long, emaciated arms, and a bloodless face with long, black teeth. see: **Banshee.**

Dagon [M] The chief god of the Philistines. A brutal monster who is half-human, half-fish, Dagon is also known as the avenging devil of the sea. Historically, it was this deity's temple which Samson destroyed in a final act of fealty to his own god. In 1936, the eerie Order of Dagon was the subject of an H. P. Lovecraft novella entitled *The Shadow Over Innsmouth.* see: **Lovecraft, H. P.**

Dagon

Daleks [TV] Machinelike creatures featured in the "Dr. Who" television series. Voicing perpetual cries of

"Exterminate! Exterminate!" the Daleks are formerly humanoid beings who donned metal casings after being maimed in a neutronic war. These shells roll about on casters, have arms with mechanical hands, and are guided by an eye-lens on a flexible shaft. They dwell beneath the surface of the planet Skaro, and frequently try to invade earth. Their counterparts on Skaro are the blond Thals, men and women who were rendered perfect due to the mutating radiation of the war. Created by writer Terry Nation, the Daleks first appeared in 1963, on the second Dr. Who adventure "The Dead Planet." They are also on-hand in the two Dr. Who motion pictures, *Dr. Who and the Daleks* (1965) and *Dr. Who: Invasion Earth 2150* (1966) starring Peter Cushing as Dr. Who. see: **Cushing, Peter; Who, Dr.**

Damien [MP] The son of Satan or antichrist foretold in the Book of Revelations and featured in the motion pictures *The Omen* (1975) and *Damien: The Omen II* (1978). Damien is actually Damien Thorn, sired through the rape of a jackal by Satan and bearing the triple-six birthmark, the sign of the antichrist. He is destined to rule the earth in terror and ultimately battle the reborn son of God.

The delivery of the child in Rome is supervised by a trio of Satanists who also arrange both the death of a baby belonging to the United States Ambassador to London, Robert Jeremy Thorn (Gregory Peck), and his wife, Katharine (Lee Remick), and their under-the-counter adoption of Damien. Though Damien is protected from those who would impede his mission—guarded by Satan in the form of a large mastiff or a soaring black raven, or by his assorted human aides—Damien *can* be killed, but only via prescribed ritual.

Thorn, along with four others who eventually discover the truth about Damien, are gruesomely executed through Satanic channels. As a result,

Damien, aged five, is given over to Thorn's brother Richard (William Holden), head of Thorn Industries. The gruesome pattern is repeated and, as of Damien's thirteenth birthday, when he first discovers his true identity and begins to build his power base, seventeen people have died. He now stands alone at the threshold of the massive Thorn political and industrial empire.

Danavas [F] Wicked Titans in the folklore of India. Over thirty million in number, the Danavas were created through the union of the sun god, Kasyapa-Aditya, and the daughters of the demon Vaiswanara, also known as Agni, who live in Hiranyapura, the golden city that floats through the sky. It is the lot of the Danavas to mount perpetual war against the Indian gods.

Dando [O] A frightful embellishment to one of the many legends about British Black Hounds. Near Plymouth, in South Devon, is the Tamar River, whose banks are haunted by a pack of devilish dogs. However, unlike most such apparitions these hounds are led by the specter Dando, the ghost of a

Dando

rebellious priest. Both the animals and their evil master are seen only on Sunday mornings, as though trying to frighten people from going to church. see: **Black Hound, The; Gabriel Ratchets, The.**

Danforth, Jim [MP] The leader of the third generation of stop-motion animators. Born in 1940, Danforth saw a reissue of *King Kong* (1933) in 1952 and was inspired to try his hand at the frame-by-frame manipulation of clay models to create the illusion of movement. His early efforts were crude experiments in 8mm, but they were sufficient to land him a job with Clokey Films on their TV series "Gumby." In 1959, Danforth worked with Projects Unlimited (Gene Warren, Tim Baar, Wah Chang) on *The Time Machine* (1960), and after that, animating the monsters seen in *Jack the Giant Killer* (1962). Subsequently, Danforth animated *The Wonderful World of the Brothers Grimm* (1962), *The Seven Faces of Dr. Lao* (1964)—for which he was nominated for an Oscar—and *When Dinosaurs Ruled the Earth* (1970), another Oscar contender. Between feature films Danforth worked on "The Outer Limits" television series and on TV commercials for Cascade Films, animating the Pillsbury Doughboy among other fanciful figures. see: **Harryhausen, Ray; Lao, Dr.; O'Brien, Willis; Outer Limits, The.**

Dapplegrim [FT] An articulate horse featured in a fairy tale of the same name. So huge that it has to lie down on all fours before anyone can get on its back, Dapplegrim is owned by a young man who rescues a princess from an oppressive troll. However, before the maiden's father will turn over the promised reward of her hand in marriage and half the kingdom, he demands further displays of wit and valor. Riding off, the young man and Dapplegrim raze a hill near the castle so that the sun can shine in, but it is not enough. The king orders his would-be son-in-law to find the princess a horse as magnificent as Dapplegrim—which, with the help of his mount, he does. Yet still the king is not satisfied, and he instructs the young man to find his disguised daughter twice before he can collect his due. Even though she transforms herself into a duck, is released, and then becomes a loaf of bread, the cagey horse recognizes her and informs his master. Finally, the king says that if the lad can twice hide himself from the princess, she and half the kingdom will be his. The first time he eludes her by turning himself into a horsefly and hiding in Dapplegrim's left nostril, and the second time by becoming a lump of earth between the hoof and the shoe of the horse's left forefoot. Having succeeded royally, the young man is deemed worthy of becoming a member of the family.

Darth Vader [MP] The Dark Lord of the Sith, enveloped in a black cloak and encased in body armor, his visage hidden behind a black mask. After being trained as a noble Jedi Knight by Obi-Wan Kenobi, Vader was seduced into the service of the evil Galactic Empire. Legend has it that he was hideously mutilated in a lightsabre fight with Kenobi, after which he was burned to within inches of death in a volcanic pit, necessitating the restorative body armor. Vader's ruthless killing of another young Jedi, the father of Luke Skywalker, is alleged to have provoked the duel, but there is the possibility that Vader is actually Luke's father gone mad, using the armor to conceal his identity as a traitor to the Old Republic. Razor-honed in all modes of torture and combat, Vader kills Kenobi in the 1977 film *Star Wars*, then helms a Tie fighter to personally blast Rebel ships during the climactic Battle of the Death Star. A deflected energy bolt from Han

Solo's vessel *Millennium Falcon* sends Vader's ship reeling—intact—into deep space an instant before the Death Star explodes. Somewhere within the Empire, Darth Vader waits, biding his time and rebuilding his strength. see: **Death Star; Kenobi, Obi-Wan.**

Death [O] Also known as the Grim Reaper, the blight that terminates the functioning of the corporeal body. In Romania, Death is known as the Voice That Calls. In Africa it has a variety of names, from Kalunga to Walumbe. The Mayans called it Ahpuch; the Incas, Supay the Shadow; and the Etruscans, Vanth, a genie who waits beside open graves.

In art, Death is usually portrayed as a skeleton dressed in a hooded black robe and bearing a scythe, or as a skull. In literature, Death has been a popular character from the continental figure who falls in love with a mortal woman in *La Morte in Vacanza* (*Death Takes a Holiday*) by Alberto Casella; to the shrouded skeleton in *Rime of the Ancient Mariner* (who had " . . . ribs through which the sun did peer . . . "); to the silent wraith in Edgar Allan Poe's "Masque of the Red Death" and the "carrion monster" often invoked by Shakespeare; to the Fresca guzzling oaf in Woody Allen's play *Death Knocks.* In film and television, Robert Redford portrayed Death as a police officer in the "Twilight Zone" episode "Nothing in the Dark"; Cedric Hardwicke was a mannered Death trapped up a tree in *On Borrowed Time* (1939); and a pasty-faced, black-cloaked Death played chess for the life of a fourteenth century knight in Ingmar Bergman's classic 1956 film *The Seventh Seal.*

Death Star [MP] A moon-sized space station of the Galactic Empire in the movie *Star Wars* (1977). The Death Star was constructed at the behest of General Grand Moff Tarkin, to serve as a symbol of the Empire's omnipotence and to boost his own power and glory. Its task is to enforce Empire decrees in their realm's outregions, and to serve as a planet-destroyer and orbital stalag. However, no sooner is it completed than its blueprints are stolen by Rebel forces. In retribution, and as a show of force, the Death Star annihilates the peaceful planet Alderaan. It is on the Death Star that Princess Leia Organa is held prisoner by Darth Vader—and from which she is subsequently rescued by Luke Skywalker and his companions, C-3PO, R2-D2, Han Solo, and Chewbacca. Luke and other Rebels later return to engage Empire pilots in a space dogfight called the Battle of the Death Star. During the fray, the Rebels exploit a weakness yielded by the blueprints; Luke plants a photon torpedo in an unprotected, two-meter-wide thermal exhaust port. The Death Star is destroyed seconds before it can wipe out the Rebel conclave on the fourth moon of Yavin. see: **Chewbacca; C-3PO; Darth Vader; R2-D2; Skywalker, Luke.**

De Bergerac, Cyrano [L/FH] An early science fiction author; also, the hero of a romantic play. In fiction, Cyrano is represented as an extremely long-nosed, poetry-spouting Frenchman who woos the lovely Roxanne for a friend, although he too loves the girl. In fact, Cyrano de Bergerac was a soldier and writer who lived from 1619 to 1655 whose work *A Voyage to the Moon* was published in 1657, and the incomplete *A Voyage to the Sun* five years later. The trip to the sun is the more remarkable of the two. It is undertaken in a box fitted with a lens which focuses the sun's rays to create a whirlwind. Thus propelled to the sun, he finds it inhabited with civilized birds. As for the moon, he tells friends, "I believe that the moon is a world like ours...." To prove his theory, he lashes bottles of dew to himself and rises because, "... the

sun so violently darted his rays that the heat, which attracted them, as it does the thickest clouds, carried me up...." Landing is accomplished simply by breaking the vials.

Deepdale Monster [U] A sea serpent washed ashore on the Orkney Islands off the northeast tip of Scotland. Drifting from the sea in December of 1941, the gray-colored creature had a small head, a long thin neck, a great hump on its back, and a snaking tail. It was twenty-five feet in length. Most scientists dismissed the Deepdale Monster as a Basking shark, although local citizens remain convinced that they were wrong. The area has a history of monster sightings, from sea animals with cowlike heads and brownish hair to serpents that were yellowish and twenty-eight-feet long. see: **Loch Ness Monster; M'Quhae, Peter.**

Delicia [FT] A princess who, with her mother, is kidnapped by an evil king in the French fairy tale "The Little Good Mouse." Raised to be the bride of the potentate's ugly son, Delicia is kidnapped by the wicked fairy Cancaline. A good fairy takes the form of a mouse and tries to find Delicia, but without success. The princess is raised as a peasant, and she is fully grown before the king recaptures her. When she refuses to marry his hideous son, the monarch has her tossed into a dungeon. In the meantime, the good fairy has gathered up Delicia's mother and they assault the dungeon in a flying chariot. Resuming her mouse form, the fairy nibbles the ears of Delicia's foes, causing them to go mad, jump in a river, and drown. Through some incredible course of inheritance, Delicia becomes the queen of the kingdom, marries a handsome prince from a far-off land, and rules kindly for the remainder of her days.

Demeter [M] The Greek goddess of agriculture. The daughter of Cronus and Rhea, she is the mother of Persephone by Zeus; of Arion, a great steed, by Poseidon; and of Plutus, the god of riches, by Iasion. Although Demeter is best known for searching the underworld to find her daughter, Persephone, she is integral to other myths as well. She turned young Stellio into a lizard for teasing her about her eating habits; when Erysichthon, a prince of Thessaly, chopped down trees in a forest dedicated to her, she drove him to such hunger that he consumed his own flesh; and in trying to make Prince Demophoön of Attica immortal by burning his mortal parts she slipped up, killing him, and assuaged her guilt by teaching agriculture to his brother, Triptolemus. see: **Cronus; Persephone.**

Demogorgon [O] A fearsome god, the very mention of whose name may be disastrous. First cited in the fourth century by the Christian scribe Lactantius, it was thought that by writing down that unspeakable name one could break its spell. Regardless of whether or not this is true, Demogorgon has become synonymous with the most infernal powers of ancient wizards. A Greek word, its root is Gorgo, the Greek name for the "Devil." see: **Devil.**

Demon Drummer [O] The ghost of a witch-musician who lived in South Tidworth, Wiltshire, England. A rude and volatile drummer, this man— whose name has been long forgotten—was placed in jail in 1661. His drum was sent to the Magistrate Mompesson—where it began to beat by itself. Shortly thereafter clothes were plucked from family members, hair was pulled by invisible hands, ghostly knocking was heard, and objects were moved about by unseen forces. This went on for months, until Charles II sent a Royal Commission to investigate. They questioned the drummer who admitted that he was a witch and responsible for the mis-

chief. He was tried and executed, but his ghost still marches about South Tidworth, urging eerie tattoos from the drum.

Derleth, August W. [L] A noted fantasy author, publisher, and archivist. Born in Sauk City, Wisconsin in 1909, Derleth published his first story "Bat's Belfry" in 1926. After graduating from the University of Wisconsin, he pursued fantastic literature as a career. One of his first tasks was to try and find a publisher who would issue a volume of H. P. Lovecraft's work. Failing at this, Derleth and associate, Donald Wandrei, formed Arkham House Publishers and printed *The Outsider and Others* themselves. It was the first of many distinguished Arkham volumes. On other fronts, Derleth compiled anthologies such as *Sleep No More* (1944), *Dark Mind, Dark Heart* (1962), and many others, and wrote over one hundred books on his own, from short story collections like "Someone in the Dark" (1941) and "Not Long for this World" (1948) to novels such as *The Lurker at the Threshold* (1945). Derleth died in Sauk City in 1971. see: **Lovecraft, H. P.**

Désiré [FT] The son of Lord Tubby of Flanders in the Charles Deulin fairy tale "The Enchanted Canary." When Désiré dreams of a lovely princess budding from within an orange, he is convinced that she exists and goes to find her. Locating a grove which belongs to a giant, he steals three oranges. The young lord opens one and out flutters a canary. He gives the bird water and it becomes a princess named Zizi. Thrilled with the maiden, Désiré leaves to find her a carriage. While he is gone, the jealous gypsy Titty changes Zizi back into a bird and takes her place. Returning with the coach, Désiré takes Titty home with him. Meanwhile, the canary follows them and cajoles Lord Tubby into pricking her with an enchanted pin. She immediately becomes Princess Zizi exposes Titty who is banished, and marries Désiré.

Devil [O] A name used to describe either the supreme evil being (Devil) or any fallen angel at war with the forces of good (devil). A devil in any form is said to enjoy the blood of sacrificial victims, especially virginal maidens or babes-in-arms. The Devil as the Ruler of Hell can assume any form, but is usually depicted as having the head of a goat. He is served by the lesser devils and other demons, who visit earth to lure souls to damnation. They do this by promising power, riches, youth, or beauty; these creatures are usually pictured as being burned red from the heat of hell and possessing horns, cloven hooves (another part of the goat, whose head their master has), a pitchfork (for prodding reluctant souls into the inferno), and forked tails. The Devil is the antagonist in Milton's *Paradise Lost*. Among the Devil's names in dif-

ferent cultures are the Samarian Adramelech, the Celtic Bilé, the Canannite Baalberith, the Moabite Chemosh, the Japanese O-Yama, the Syrian Beherit, the Yezidi Melek Taus, and the American Indian Sedit.

Devilina [C] The sister of Satan in the comic magazine *Devilina*. Created by writer/artist Ric Estrada in 1974, she is the daughter of the woman Sephora. Raised in a New England mansion near the entrance to hell, Devilina knows nothing of her heritage until her eighteenth birthday—when horns sprout from her head. Refusing her brother's offer to rule the underworld at his side, she enters Radcliffe. However, as punishment for her impertinence the Devil kills her boyfriend in a fire. Promising retaliation, she takes a job with a newspaper as a reporter specializing in the occult. The position enables her to keep tabs on her brother and use her own devilish powers to thwart him wherever possible.

Devil's Sooty Brother, The [FT] The hero of a Grimm Brothers fairy tale of the same name. Penniless, a discharged soldier named Hans agrees to sell his soul to the Devil for seven years if, after that period, the Dark One will return him to earth with great wealth. The Devil agrees, warning, "But you must not wash, comb, or trim yourself." In Hell, Hans' job is to poke the fires under the kettles in which the hell-broth is stewing. After seven years, the Devil fills a knapsack with sweepings and instructs Hans to take it home. The unkempt young man is also told that if anyone asks who he is, he must reply, "The Devil's Sooty Brother and my king as well."

When Hans reaches the forest where he first met the Devil, the sweepings turn to gold. Arriving at an inn, Hans rests for the night—but his unscrupulous landlord steals the knapsack. When Hans awakens to

Devil

find it gone, he complains to the Devil. Feeling that Hans has suffered unduly, the Devil cleans his erstwhile servant, gives him a second knapsack of sweepings, and informs the landlord to return the gold or he will personally fetch him and drag him to hell. The innkeeper wisely capitulates and Hans finds himself handsome once more and possessing *two* sacks of gold. Presenting himself to a king, he woos the ruler's daughter, marries her, and becomes king when his father-in-law dies. If there is a moral here, about why not to consort with the Devil, it is an elusive one. see: **Grimm, Jakob and Wilhelm**

Devourer, The [M] An awesome monster who lives in the Hall of Maat, the Egyptian Goddess of Truth. After the dead have been ferried along the subterranean Nile, beneath the mountains of hell, they cross a field of monsters to the Hall of Maat. When they arrive, the goddess places each person's heart, in succession, on one pan of a scale, laying a magic feather in another. If the two balance, the person is admitted into the afterlife. If the heart is heavier, the Devourer comes forth and eats the offender. Boasting the forequarters of a lion and the hindparts of a hippopotamus, the Devourer performs its titular task with a pair of extremely powerful crocodile jaws.

The Devourer

Dilvish [L] A fantasy hero created by author Roger Zelazny. Also known as Lord Dilvish, Dilvish the Damned, the Colonel of the East, and the Deliverer of Portaroy, the sword-swinger rides an articulate steed and uncannily leaves no footprints where he walks. Battling sorcery in its many evil forms pits Dilvish with and against a vast array of bizarre supporting characters, among them King Malacar the Mighty, Korel the Priest, the Cursed Legions of Shoredan, and Lyish the Colonel of the West.

Diodric [L] A sword and sorcery hero created by author Lin Carter. Born a Celt, but living on Atlantis, Diodric has yellow braided hair, fair skin, and clear blue eyes. His family rose from slavery to nobility through distinguished service to the empire, and Diodric, a lord, continues the noble tradition. Among the fiends battled by the powerful spearman in such adventures as *The Black Star* and *The White Throne* are Thelantha the Accursed, hordes of Witchmen, the Dragon Warriors, and others. Diodric is married to Lady Niane of the House of Phiodon. see: **Carter, Lin.**

Dionysos [M] The God of Wine in Greek mythology, known as Bacchus to the Romans. Born in Thebes, Dionysos is the son of Zeus and Semele, the daughter of Cadmus. However, it was a most unusual birth. Semele died six months into her pregnancy, so Zeus took the child from her womb and sewed it into his thigh. When the babe was fully developed, the king of the gods removed it and turned it over to the nymphs of Mt. Nysa in Thrace for rearing. However, Zeus' wife, Hera, jealous of her husband's philandering with Semele, cursed Dionysos with insanity in which state he traveled the world. Those who treated him with kindness were taught how to make wine. Those who were cruel were driven mad. One example of Dionysos' power came when he was nabbed by pirates who wished to peddle the god as a slave. Chained to their ship, he transformed the sails and oars into serpents, caused ivy to engulf the vessel, burst from his bonds, and became a lion surrounded by snarling panthers, and caused the air to fill with the piercing sound of flutes. When the frightened pirates jumped overboard, he changed them into dolphins.

The god's female attendants were known as Mimallones, Bassarids, Clodones, Thyiads, Maenads, Lenae, and Bacchae, all of whom frolicked without inhibition through the hills and had snakes squirming through their hair. The god's male followers were the satyrs. It was Dionysos who gave Midas the golden touch. see: **Midas; Satyr; Zeus.**

Dis [L] In Dante Alighieris fourteenth century poem *The Divine Comedy*, the city which forms the Sixth Circle of Hell. Fortified with high walls, moats, and towers, Dis is visited by Dante and the Roman poet Virgil (70–19 B.C.). They are ferried to its demon-guarded portals by the sinner Phlegyas, who was sent to the underworld for having had the insolence to burn one of Apollo's temples. Inside the grim city the visitors find, "grave denizens, a mighty throng," wailing heretics locked in tombs which burn with intense fire. Of all the places in Dis, Judas' circle is described as being, "furthest from heaven's all-circling orb." see: **Erictho.**

Discovery, The [MP] The interplanetary craft featured in the motion picture *2001: A Space Odyssey* (1968). Following a signal beamed into space from an alien monolith buried on the moon, the *Discovery* carries its five person crew to Jupiter. There, the flight's sole surviving member, First Captain Dave Bowman, has a first hand encounter with extraterrestrials. Seven hundred feet long—although the miniature models used in the film were fifty-four and fifteen feet long— the *Discovery* is powered by nuclear reactor engines. Its every other function is run by the articulate computer HAL 9000—until the superbrain goes berserk, kills four crewmembers, and has to be lobotomized by Bowman. see: **HAL.**

Disney, Walt [MP/TV] A fantasy film entrepreneur born Walter Elias Disney in 1901. Working in a Kansas City, Missouri advertising agency, Disney decided to relocate in California and open a small animation studio in 1923. He enjoyed his first successes with the combination live-action/cartoon shorts *Alice's Wonderland* and the all-animated adventures of Osward the Rabbit. However, it wasn't until he and animator Ub Iwerks created Mickey Mouse in 1928 that Disney's place in fantasy history was assured. He produced the first sound cartoon, the Mickey Mouse short *Steamboat Willie* in 1928 and the first full-length cartoon, *Snow White and the Seven Dwarfs* nine years later. Among his other animated features are *Pinocchio* (1940), *Fantasia* (1940), *Peter Pan* (1952), and *Sleeping Beauty* (1959). His live-action fantasies include *Twenty Thousand Leagues Under the Sea* (1954), *Darby O'Gill and the Little People* (1959), and *Mary Poppins* (1964). In the Disney science fiction stable are *The Cat from Outer Space* (1978) and *The Black Hole* (1979).

Disney's parents were Flora and Elias; his brothers, Herbert, Ray, and Roy; his sister, Ruth. The producer's wife, Lillian, bore him two daughters, Sharon and Diane. Though Disney himself died of lung cancer in 1966, his studio continues to produce generally fine fantasy fare. The amusement parks Disneyland, Disney World, and the under-construction Disneyland Tokyo are based on the films and characters created by the

Disney studio. see: **Cinderella; Pinocchio; Peter Pan; Poppins, Mary; Sleeping Beauty; Snow White; Verne, Jules.**

Ditmarsch [P] In the lore of the Brothers Grimm, a land of incredibly odd sights. There, a visitor sees two roasted fowl flying, an anvil and a millstone swimming across the Rhine, a frog eating a plowshare, a crab chasing a hare, a cow climbing to the roof of a house, and flies as big as goats. The only luckless inhabitant of this amazing land seems to be the man who sailed on dry land and drowned on a mountain. see: **Grimm, Jakob and Wilhelm.**

Divination [O] The process of foretelling the future or learning hidden knowledge through occult means. Unlike necromancy, divination is always used for good. Covered by this blanket term are such subsidiary fields as astrology and the interpretation of dreams. Among the tools of the craft are herbs, fire, cards, numbers, palms, a special rod, a crystal ball, or the entrails of an animal. This latter is not quite as fanciful as it might seem. If the organs looked healthy to history's earliest peoples, then that area was evidently a good place to settle! see: **Crystal ball; Necromancy.**

Djinn [F] In Arabian folklore, the fairy offspring of fire. Created 200 centuries before the coming of Adam, the djinn are governed by a breed of kings called Suleyman. Extremely beautiful and good, or extremely ugly and bad, their favorite dwelling place is in the desert or in the mountain Kaf. These strange creatures usually appear to humans as serpents, cats, dogs, humans, monsters, or in their favorite shape, a combination of wolf and hyena. They can also render themselves invisible, although humans who apply the ointment kohl to their eyes can see invisible djinn as well as a hidden treasure regardless of where it

may be secreted. One step below angels in the Islamic faith, djinn are fond of passing out onion skins which later turn to gold. As a rule, these beings—which are sometimes identified with genies—are hostile to humans, although they are frequently forced to serve them.

Dobie [F] An extremely dull-witted strain of Scottish brownie. Very sincere and always willing to help a human, dobies are nonetheless inept at most tasks. Told to guard someone's possessions, they can be talked into turning them over to a stranger; asked to perform a simple domestic chore, they will approach it with enthusiasm and invariably botch the job. They are particularly expert at spilling pails of newly drawn milk, dropping newly gathered eggs, and losing herds left in their care. In some places, dobies are believed to be the ghosts of murdered wives. As such, they will fumble about the house which was theirs in life until their spirits are exorcised. see: **Brownie.**

Don Juan [F] A libertine of Spanish legend. Although Don Juan's conjugal feats throughout the bedrooms of Europe border on the fantastic, only his downfall is bonafide fantasy. Visiting a Franciscan monastery, he notices a statue of one of his foes, the Commander of Seville—the father of a girl he had seduced. When Don Juan snidely requests the pleasure of the commander's company at dinner, the statue comes to life and drags him down to hell. Although some scholars have suggested that the Don was actually murdered by monks who were fed up with his activities, that demise is hardly worthy of so licentious a character.

In terms of the arts, the adventures of this son of Don José were most popularly immortalized in a poem written 1818–1823 by Lord Byron, in Mozart's 1787 opera *Don Giovanni*, and in Bernard Shaw's play *Don Juan in Hell.* In the cinema, the Spanish lover was most vividly portrayed by Douglas Fairbanks Sr. in 1934 and, particularly, by Errol Flynn in 1949.

Doolittle, Dr. [L] A most unusual veterinarian. Created by Hugh Lofting (1886–1947) during a battle in World War I, Dr. John Doolittle is Lofting's tribute to "the very considerable part the animals were playing in the war." Based in Puddleby-on-the-Marsh, England, the stout, short Doolittle can speak 499 different animal languages. Among the twelve novels in which he gets to use these tongues are: *Dr. Doolittle's Garden, Dr. Doolittle and the Pirates, Dr. Doolittle in the Moon, Dr. Doolittle's Caravan,* and *Dr. Doolittle and the Green Canary.* The first of the novels, *The Story of Dr. Doolittle,* was published in 1920. In the 1967 musical motion picture, Dr. Doolittle was played by Rex Harrison.

Doom Patrol [C] A band of superheroes created in 1963 by writer Arnold Drake and artist Bruno Premiani. The Doom Patrol first appeared in the comic book *My Greatest Adventure.* Led by a wheelchair-bound super-scientist known only as "Chief," the squad consists of Elasti-Girl, Negative Man, and Robot Man. Elasti-Girl is actually movie actress Rita Farr. While on a film location in Africa, she was swept over a waterfall to a landscape where craters emitted strange gases. Breathing the gases gave her the power to stretch her body to any length. Negative Man is test pilot Larry Trainor who, while flying the rocketplane K-2F in the upper atmosphere, blacked out. Passing through a variety of wave belts, he revived to find himself transformed into an all-powerful mass of energy. Robot Man is adventurer Cliff Steele who was involved in a racing car smack-up and awoke to find that the Chief had placed his one intact organ, his brain,

into the body of a mighty robot. Together, the members of this remarkable team protect humankind from criminals, monsters, and antagonistic alien beings.

Doppelgänger [O] A ghostly double or extradimensional counterpart of a living person. Although the term is German for an astral body, a spectral double of the self, it is broadly used to describe a guardian angel, a person's evil side, or any soul undergoing an out-of-body experience. Certain authorities contend that if anyone ever meets their doppelgänger from another dimension, one of the two will perish or, as in the hypothetical brushing of matter and antimatter, everything in creation will vaporize in an atom-wrenching explosion.

Doré, Paul Gustave [FH] Possibly the world's greatest illustrator of gothic fantasy. Born in Strasbourg, Alsace-Lorraine in 1833, Doré was urged to be an engineer like his father. But the lad could not pull himself away from his pencils, even to the decay of his schoolwork. Moving to Paris, be became a magazine cartoonist at the age of fifteen, and a best-selling author seven years later with his illustrated edition of *Rabelais.* From then until his death in 1883, Doré was one of the most popular artists of his time. Working with lithographs, woodcuts, and other formats, he created handsome pictorial editions of Dante's *Inferno* (1861), *The Adventures of Baron Munchausen* (1862), *Perrault* (1862), *The Bible* (1866), *Rime of the Ancient Mariner* (1875), *Paradise Lost* (1883), and *The Raven* (1883). Many of these classic works remain in print to this day.

Dracae [F] Water spirits of Western Europe. According to legend, they can change their shape as they wish, and can often be seen floating down rivers as wooden dishes (in England) or golden dishes (in France). In this form they attempt to lure needy mortal women to within reach. Grabbing the helpless ladies, the spirits then drag them to the riverbed where they are forced to nurse the dracae young.

Dracula [L] A vampiric Transylvanian noble. Created by author Bram Stoker (1847–1912) for his 1897 novel *Dracula*, the centuries-old blood drinker is initially, "... a tall old man, clean shaven save for a long white moustache." However, as the novel progresses he grows ever younger. His face becomes strong and acquiline with a high bridge and a thin nose accented by "peculiarly arched" nostrils. His blue eyes flicker with new life and his eyebrows become, "... very massive, almost meeting over the nose." In each of these stages his mouth is "fixed and rather cruel-looking, with peculiarly shaped white teeth." His chin is broad and strong, his cheeks firm though thin, his ears pointed—and his palms slightly furry. Apart from becoming less infirm as he feasts on the novel's many characters, Count Dracula can crawl straight down walls and become a bat, wolf, mist, or dust cloud at will. On the debit side is the fact that he can be repulsed by garlic or any religious icon. Ultimately, Dracula is slain by having his throat cut and a knife plunged through his heart.

Apart from his literary fame, Dracula has been a most popular stage and screen presence. Among the many fine actors who have played the sanguinary role are Bela Lugosi, Christopher Lee, Jack Palance, and most recently Frank Langella. see: **Blacula; Nosferatu; Vlad Tepes.**

Dragon [F] Huge scaled lizards, usually fire breathing. The origin of the dragon is difficult to trace. It may have had its beginnings with the misinterpretation of dinosaur remains, or in word carried from Indonesia about the ten-to-twelve foot long monitor lizards known as Komodo Dragons.

Dracula

Perhaps they were merely the logical extension of human inability to feel affection for cold blooded reptiles. Regardless, early dragon legends seem to have surfaced circa 3500 B.C. in Asia and parts of Europe. Most of these primitive dragons were snaking subsea dwellers, usually the guardians of pearls or some other fortune. When lore moved these creatures to land, they retained the scales of a fish but added horns, the head of a lion, talons, and the wings of an eagle. They also came in a variety of colors: green, red, black, yellow, and white—although their eyes were almost always red and flaming. In Africa, dragons were the hybrid of an eagle and a wolf, and the only living things they feared were elephants. Not that slaying the pachyderms was difficult; it was simply impossible to avoid being crushed in the process.

As soon as dragons were established on land, subsidiary myths began to ripen. It was said that eating the heart, liver, or blood of a dragon enabled one to understand the language of animals; priests declared that the dead were transformed into the huge lizards; and certain cultures maintained that planting dragon teeth in the ground would produce an army. Only in China were the beasts benevolent. A combination camel, clam, tiger, snake, carp, eagle, and bull, they had whiskered faces, favored swallows above all other animals, and were able to control both the four elements and the fate of humans. Everywhere else dragons were pure evil. Virgin-eaters, they were the quintessential foe of all medieval knights who were looking to prove their strength and valor. Indeed, with the Christian knights came the notion of dragons as the personification of Satan, someone who seduced people with dreams of treasure and carnality (the captive maiden) and then roasted them in the fires of hell. Hence the popular vision of dragons as fire breathers.

To be fair, of course, not all dragons were merely bark and fire. Certain of the monsters were alleged to have breath so sweet that birds soaring above would smell it, presume it to be nectar, and fly right into the open mouth of the dragon. Some peoples also ascribed the burnt autumn leaves to dragons—a deed of beauty for which we should all thank these much-maligned animals! see: **George, St.**

Drakestail [FT] A duck featured in the French fairy tale "Drakestail." Setting out for the palace, it is Drakestail's objective to be repaid money he had loaned to the king. Along the road he meets Fox, Ladder, River, and Wasp's-nest—all of whom make themselves small, jump into Drakestail's gizzard, and come along for the ride. Reaching his destination, the duck is ignominiously grabbed by guards and heaved into the poultry yard. Indignant, he unloads his passengers who assume their full size.

Helping Drakestail to escape, they decide why stop here—and in short order, through skill and wile, manage to make the duck king.

Droid [MP] A breed of being from the *Star Wars* mythos. A Droid is an ambulatory and usually articulate computing device, a slang condensation of the twentieth century word *android,* which specifies "an automation in human form." It is now used as a blanket term which includes androids, cyborgs, and robots in any form that comprise the category known as *mechanicals* as opposed to *organics*. see: **C-3PO; R2-D2.**

DuBay, William Bryan [C] An American comic book artist, writer, editor, and innovator. Born in San Francisco in 1948, DuBay broke into the field in 1966 writing *Blooperman* comics. More important, however, was his first sale to the Warren group of comics, *Creepy, Eerie,* and *Vampirella.* The story was "The Life Species" and it was both written and drawn by DuBay. It appeared in *Eerie* #30 in 1970. DuBay moved to New York soon thereafter and became editor of the Warren titles in 1972. He also guided Warren's short-lived revival of *The Spirit* in 1973–1975. In 1976 he left Warren to become a freelance writer, and has sold dozens of horror and science fiction comic stories, usually with an ironic or sexual twist. Among his most popular continuing characters is the time-traveling Rook. In 1977 he originated Warren's science fiction comic book *1984,* a provocative magazine for adults. He edits this title from his home in Connecticut, where he lives with his wife, Peggy. His children are Crystal, Lisa, and William Jr. see: **Creepy, Uncle; Eerie, Cousin; Spirit, The; Vampirella.**

Duergar [F] The most sadistic of all English fairies. Unlike other fairies, the duergar live alone rather than in groups. Enemies of all humankind, they are eighteen to twenty-four inches tall, extremely strong, and dress in a lambskin coat and trousers, moleskin shoes, and a hat of green moss sometimes decorated with a pheasant's feather. The evil creatures delight in killing people, and their favorite method is to lead them from a cliff. They do this by working up an illusion and tricking a victim into believing that there is land where there is nothing but empty space. The duergar may feign hospitality to lower a person's defenses, but are never to be trusted. They usually vanish at cockcrow.

Dunsany, Lord [L] A noted Irish author of fantasy. Born Edward John Moreton Drax Plunkett in 1878, the eighteenth Baron Dunsany—the "Lord" was applied only to his writings—sold his first novel in 1905. This was *The Gods of Pegana*, and it introduced Dunsany's own mythology, the chief deity of which is Mana-Yood-Sushai. Other supernatural efforts by this noble soldier-hunter-playwright include *The Sword of Welleran* (1908), *The Book of Wonder* (1912), *Tales of Wonder* (1916), and the adventures of one Joseph Jorkens, an alcoholic who spun incredible tales as payment for drink. Dunsany died in 1957.

Dunters [F] English spirits who dwell in ancient keeps and towers. In olden days, possibly dating to the Picts, these edifices were dashed with blood as a good will sacrifice; it is thought that the dunters are the specters of these luckless offerings, whether human or animal. In any case, it is their duty to keep up a perpetual noise that is said to resemble the grinding of barley in a hollow stone mill. If the sound ever becomes louder than normal, it means that death or bad luck is nigh. Dunters are also known as Powries. see: **Redcap.**

Dur [L] A number in the Martian vocabulary created by Edgar Rice Burroughs for his John Carter novels. Dur means 1,000,000: other numbers are ay (1), tee (10), tan (100), and dar (1,-000). Tor is 4, ov is 7, bar is 8, and any combinations thereof are valid. For instance: teetor is 14, and tordurbar is 4,000,008. Either Burroughs or his Martians neglected to provide their language with a 2, 3, 5, 6, or 9. see: **Barsoom; Burroughs, Edgar Rice; Carter, John.**

Dwarfs [F] Little people who live underground. Principally Norse, dwarfs were made by Odin from the worms which dined on the body of Ymir. The keepers of all precious gems and metals, dwarfs refuse to turn these over to humans, or tell where they might be found, unless they have been properly appeased with gifts. Offerings are also requisite for those who wish to tap the dwarfs' skills in wood and metalworking. Extremely handy beings, among their many artifacts are Thor's hammer and the ship Skidbladnir, which can hold all the Norse gods yet be folded and kept in a small pouch. The dwarf Regin made the sword Gram, which Siegfried used to slay Fafnir—and later Regin as well. Most dwarfs are well versed in the supernatural, such as the fairy-tale dwarf Rumpelstiltskin who was able to make gold from straw.

But dwarfs are not dedicated laborers exclusively. Sometimes they will carry off mortal women and force them to be their wives. Nor do they hesitate to snatch away a human baby and leave behind one of their own deformed offspring. And gems or money stolen from them will bring misfortune not only to the thieves, but to their heirs as well. Fortunately, if anyone *does* get on a dwarf's dark side, and they begin to badger that person, the little people can be driven away by noise. Dwarfs hate a loud racket of any kind—particularly church bells.

In Europe, dwarfs are little different than their Norse counterparts. Sub-hill-dwellers, they are short and bent, hunchbacked, with long beards and the feet of a goat or goose. Sometimes standing no more than three inches tall, they live beneath mounds in a beautiful kingdom ruled by King Alberich. Garbed in gray, the European dwarfs leave their subterranean lairs only at night, since exposure to sunlight will turn them to stone. see: **Changeling; Siegfried; Snow White; Trolls; Ymir.**

Dybbuk [O] A demon traditionally feared by East European Jews. The spirit of someone who had been cruel or sinful during life and is thus denied eternal peace, the dybbuk takes possession of a living person whom they bend entirely to their will. They prefer scholars and other influential people who wield great power. Once the demon has taken hold, it so absolutely controls the host that only the most potent exorcism can hope to uproot it. Although the first tale of a dybbuk was published in 1602, it is thought that the belief is considerably older.

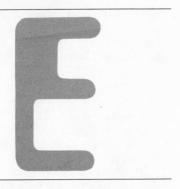

Echidna [M] Among the less attractive characters in Greek mythology. The daughter of Poseidon and Medusa, and the sister of Chrysaor, the father of Geryon, Echidna had the head and torso of a beautiful woman—but was a serpent from the waist down. By Typhon she was the mother of the Lernean Hydra, the hellhound Cerberus, and the two-headed dog Orthos. Among their other offspring are the Chimera, Ladon, and the Sphinx—although some tales claim that Orthos was the Sphinx's father. Echidna hid from the world in a dank cave, where she met her doom at the hands of Argos. see: **Cerberus; Chimera; Hydra; Medusa; Orthos; Poseidon; Sphinx; Typhon.**

Eerie, Cousin [C] A comic book character created in 1966 by artist Jack Davis and publisher James Warren.

Cousin Eerie

Cousin Eerie is the host of every story published in the horror omnibus comic *Eerie*. Fat, wart-covered, and wearing clothes that might politely be described as moldering, Cousin Eerie calls himself the "Host in Horrors," occasionally spins a true terror tale in *Eerie*'s Monster Gallery, and is constantly bickering with Uncle Creepy regarding which magazine is better, *Eerie* or Warren Publishing's companion periodical *Creepy.* see: **Creepy, Uncle; DuBay, William; Vampirella.**

Elak [L] A sword-and-sorcery hero with a difference. Unlike the brutes which populate the genre, Elak of Atlantis is smooth and sophisticated, worldly but not crude. An exiled prince-cum-adventurer, Elak is slim, sun-bronzed, and supple. Created in the middle 1930s by Henry Kuttner (1914–1958), this hero and his apish sidekick, Lycon, are featured in four novellas, the most famous of which is *The Spawn of Dagon* (1938).

El Dorado [F] A legendary city of wealth whose name means "The Golden One." Early on, El Dorado apparently was not a place but a person. The individual in question was a ruler in north-central South America, someone who annually had himself doused with oil and powdered with gold dust so that once per year he could rival the brilliance of the sun. This leader was eagerly sought by the first Spanish explorers, for where there is gold dust there must be gold. They never found the Golden One, but neither did they give up the quest for gold. El Dorado grew to mythical proportions, becoming a city filled with gold and treasure. Its location was somehow removed to the western-central United States, and it was dutifully if unsuccessfully sought by the Spanish explorer Coronado in 1540–1541. Mentioned in *Candide* by Voltaire (1694–1778) *El Dorado* today is a more figurative expression meaning "the land of golden dreams."

Elle-Folk [F] Airy Danish beings tangential to the elf family. There are two different versions of their origin: either they are angels who were cast with Satan from Heaven, but did not tumble all the way to the underworld—or they are the offspring of Adam and his first wife, Lilith. Whichever is so, they are a curious lot indeed. The males are withered and stooped, and their greatest pleasure is to lounge in sunbeams. The females are beautiful and thrill to dancing in the moonlight. However, mortals are advised to shun them. The breath of the Elle-Folk brings plague on whomever it falls; their music, which the young find especially pleasing, is fatal to humans. Even their cattle, which feeds on dew, must never mingle with the cattle of humans—such contact is always deadly to the latter. see: **Elves.**

Eloi [L] People of the far future as envisioned by H. G. Wells in his novel *The Time Machine* (1895). When the book's nameless narrator visits the year A.D. 802,701 he finds the Eloi, whom he characterizes as "indescribably frail." Exhibiting graceful gentleness, they speak in "soft cooing notes" in a "strange and very sweet and liquid tongue." All are four feet tall, wear sandals and a purple tunic with a leather belt, and live communally in great old structures which the Time Traveler describes as "palace-like buildings." The Eloi have curly hair but no facial growth, small ears, and a mouth with thin red lips, little pointed chins, large and mild eyes, and a general "girlish rotundity of limb." Taking up with the Eloi woman Weena, the narrator soon learns that this calm domestic nature is hardly a reflection of cultural advancement. The Eloi are simply "fatted cattle" bred and eaten by antlike monsters called Morlocks. The Time Traveler comes to disdain the Eloi, describing them as being preoccupied with "feeble prettiness," and at novel's end leaves their world in disgust. see: **Morlocks; Wells, H. G.**

Elric [L] A barbarian hero whose strength lies not in his arm, but in his sword. Created in 1961 by author Michael Moorcock (1940–), Elric of Melniborné is melancholy and quiet, a physical weakling who is perhaps less extraordinary than the average mortal—save for his black, rune-carved sword, Stormbringer. However, while the blade brings him victory in battle, it also causes various personal misfortunes. Not that Elric, a crimson-eyed albino, has need of further problems. The last ruler of the ancient kingdom of Melniborné, he works hard to retain his honor after turning against his own people to help topple the arrogant empire of sorcerer kings and dragon hordes. Accompanying him on his dour, bloody journeys through such works as *The Stealer of Souls* (1963), *Stormbringer* (1965), and *The Jade Man's Eyes* (1973) is the short, red-haired Moonglum of Elwher.

Elrond [L] The ageless Lord of Rivendell, a great Elfen kingdom in J. R. R. Tolkien's *Ring* trilogy. The keeper of the Last Homely House east of the Sea, he offers his people rest, refreshment, a story or two, and songs intended to free the listener from fear. Cast in the mold of a sage, Elrond is extremely knowledgeable in matters of ancient lore, and is also considered something of a poet. The son of Elwing and Eärendil, he is married to Celebrian and is the father of Elladan, Elrohir, and Arwen. see: **Tolkien, J. R. R.**

Elves [F] Capricious sprites in human form. Originally, elves were Scandinavian fairies who were quite powerful, although less so than the gods. When not about the mortal sphere, they lived in Elfheim under the peccant rule of the Elf-king, an evil being who loved to visit forests and work mischief on travelers. Unlike their

Elf

monarch, the elves were both good and bad: the White Elves were kindly and fair, with golden hair, golden harps, and lyric voices; the Black Elves were dreary folk who brought the banes of illness and injury wherever they went.

As the lore of elves spread to other cultures, the little people were embellished with a broader range of powers and characteristics. For example, they grew to enjoy dancing, particularly in woods and meadows. Further, while invisible to most humans they could be seen by any child born on Sunday or by someone who steps within an elf circle at midnight. Finally, elves could appear only at night; those who had not returned to their homes by dawn remained rooted to the spot until sunset, during which time anyone who touched them was beset by sickness. Their powers, too, became more diversified. Sick cattle were thought to have been struck by an elf's arrow. Then, there was the Black Elves' musical ditty called the Elf-king's tune. Played on a fiddle, it compelled all who heard it to dance—even if the only listeners around were inanimate objects! Nor could the dancers stop unless the tune were played backward or somebody

crept behind the fiddler and cut the instrument's strings.

Through it all, the elves remained physically much the same: short, ugly, long-nosed, and a dirty brown in color. see: **Elle-Folk; Leprechauns.**

Emerald City [L] The home of the Wizard of Oz. Created by author L. Frank Baum for his novel *The Wonderful Wizard of Oz* (1900), the Emerald City can be reached by following the yellow brick road. At the entrance to the wizard's empire is a big gate studded with emeralds. When entering, one must don glasses or be blinded by the glare. Inside are houses built of green marble and flecked with emeralds. The sun's rays shine green, the pavement is green marble, the windows are green glass, the citizens' skin is green, and so are the clothes, food, and money. There are no animals in the entire city. Oz himself is a pretentious man, a former showman from Omaha, Nebraska. He appears as something different to all who see him: a beautiful woman to the Scarecrow, a giant five-eyed monster to the Tin Woodman, a ball of fire to the Cowardly Lion, and a huge head on a throne to Dorothy. During the climax of the first Oz novel, the wizard decides that he has ruled long enough and departs the Emerald City by balloon. He leaves his kingdom in the capable straw hands of the Scarecrow. see: **Oz.**

Empusae [M] Cannibalistic females of classic mythology. In their natural form, the Empusae are half-donkey and half-human. However, these creatures are shape-changers, able to become dogs, cows, or beautiful maidens. In this latter guise, the Empusae are highly successful luring male travelers to their abode. Otherwise, they wait innocuously by the roadside until someone passes by, and then they pounce. Some legends have the Empusae as vampiric bloodsuckers. see: **Lamia.**

Enchanted Snake, The [FT] The bewitched serpent of the fairy tale "The Enchanted Snake." When the peasant Sabatella and her husband, Cola-Mattheo, cannot have a child, they decide to adopt a snake. The years pass, and when the serpent decides to marry, Cola-Mattheo announces that he'll go and find a suitable snake. But our hero declines. "If you do that," says he, "we shall be no better than the vipers and reptiles." He intends to woo the king's daughter, Grannonia. The King of Starza-Longa agrees, but only "If you can turn this palace into ivory, inlaid with gold and silver, before tomorrow at noon, I will let you marry my daughter." When the snake works this and other miracles, Grannonia is given to him. However, to the surprise of all, the snake throws off his viper's skin and reveals himself to be a handsome prince with golden locks and flashing eyes. Joyous, the king tosses the snakeskin into the fire—at which point the prince becomes a dove and flies through a window. Grannonia sets out after him, taking a fox as her companion. On the road they meet birds who explain that in crashing through the pane the prince had slashed himself and now lays dying. Since the only cure is to rub his head with the blood of the birds who told this tale, the Reynard kills them and gathers their blood in a bottle. The fox interjects that, technically speaking, his own blood must be added to the mixture—but the princess says she won't harm him if he will lead her to the prince. This he does, and when they find the young man dying at the palace of his father, the King of Vallone Grosso, the princess quickly butchers the fox and drains his blood. The crimson brew is given to the prince who recovers and weds Grannonia.

Several experts on fairy tales have seen this story as a surprisingly detailed, symbol-laden description of the traditional "wedding night."

Enkidu [M] A hairy creature created by the Babylonian goddess Aruru in answer to the prayers of the married women of Erech. Working their husbands eternally, Gilgamesh, the Prince of Erech, takes whichever of these women he pleases. The powerful Enkidu is therefore placed in the desert beyond Erech where he stymies the economy of local hunters by freeing animals from traps and befriending all beasts. But Gilgamesh will not be tempted into battle on the ogre's home ground. The prince simply instructs one of the priestesses of Ishtar to seduce Enkidu. This costs him his innocence, and animals will no longer approach him. Thundering into Erech, he meets Gilgamesh who has the advantage of familiar surroundings and therefore defeats the son of Aruru. However, the adversaries form a mutual respect and become firm friends.

The alliance proves to be a fortunate one. When Gilgamesh spurns Ishtar, the goddess of sexual delight, her father, Anu, fashions a bull to kill the prince. Mighty Enkidu intercedes, tearing the animal to pieces and hurling a thighbone at the goddess. Outraged, she causes Enkidu to take ill and die. It is this calamity that inspires Gilgamesh to undertake his legendary quest for the secrets of life and death, which leads in turn to a brief but happy reunion with the ghost of Enkidu. see: **Gilgamesh.**

Enterprise, **U.S.S.** [TV] A Constellation Class starship seen in the television series and 1979 motion picture *Star Trek.* The largest, most advanced of the thirteen Constellation Class crafts in the entire Star Fleet, the *Enterprise* sports a crew of 430—nearly one-third of whom are female. Capped by a huge disk consisting of eleven decks plus the bridge, the starship boasts laboratories, a hangar housing the shuttlecraft *Galileo,* various sized recreation rooms, crew's quarters, sick bay, transporter room for bearing people and objects to coordinates outside the ship, and so forth. All are connected by turbolifts which run both vertically and horizontally throughout the 947-foot-long, 417-foot-wide ship. Able to travel as fast as warp 14.1—nearly one-half billion miles per second—the *Enterprise* is run by the stalwart crew of Capt. James T. Kirk, First Officer Mr. Spock, Dr. Leonard "Bones" McCoy, Communications Officer Lt. Uhura, Chief Engineer Lt. Commander Montgomery Scott, Chief Helmsperson Sulu, and Ensign Pavel Chekov. see: **Kirk, Capt.; Spock, Mr.**

Erictho [O] A Thessalian sorceress. It was Erictho whom Sextus, the son of Pompey the Great, ordered to contact the spirit world to learn the outcome of the civil war between his father and Caesar in 48 B.C. (Caesar won.) Erictho also appears as a mistress of the supernatural in *The Divine Comedy*. Holding great sway with the specters of Dis, she is described as having the power to send specters on select missions and then compel these shades back into their bodies. see: **Dis.**

Erik [L/MP] The titular fiend of the 1911 novel *The Phantom of the Opera* by Gaston Leroux. Thought to be a ghost in dress clothes who haunts the opera house, he is actually a man possessing a skeleton's head with deep-set eyes like "a dead man's skull." His yellow skin is "stretched across his bones like a drumhead," he has "hardly any nose to speak of and the only hair he has is three or four long dark locks on his forehead and behind the ears." Because of his hideous appearance, Erik wears a mask which covers all but his forehead. In love with opera singer Christine Daae, the Phantom murders those who wrong him or get in the way of Christine's career. When the singer eventually marries the man she loves, Erik dies of a broken heart. On the screen, Erik

was played by Lon Chaney Sr. in 1925, by Claude Raines in 1943, and by Herbert Lom in 1962. The Chaney version held relatively close to Leroux; the Eriks of Raines and Lom were musicians disfigured by acid. see: **Chaney, Lon Sr.**

Erinnyes [M] Also known as the Furies, these three Greek goddesses are responsible for punishing anyone who commits a crime within a family, especially patricide. Born when the blood of Uranus, drawn by Cronus, mingled with Gaea, the Furies are Megara, Tisiphone, and Alecto—and they are frightful to behold. With snakes coiled through their hair and about their bodies, each has batlike wings and carries a whip and a flaming torch. There is no way to escape the Furies' justice. However, they *will* be lenient if a family member is slain in retribution for having murdered another person in the family—as in the case of Orestes, who killed his mother, Clytemnestra, after she took a lover and then took the life of her husband, Agamemnon, King of Mycenae.

Eros [M] The Greek god of love; Cupid to the Romans. According to different myths, Eros is either the son of Aphrodite and Ares, or the child of the West Wind, Zephyrus, and the rainbow, Iris. Flitting about the earth, Eros carries a bow and quiver, the arrows of which cause whomever they poke to fall in love. As Cupid, the god is married to the beautiful mortal Psyche; as Eros, he is usually attended by Hymen, the god of marriage.

Although not as well known, there is another Eros—the golden-winged, four-headed, double-sexed deity hatched from the silver egg conceived by Night and Erebos, the darkness under the earth. The two halves of this egg became Uranus (heaven) and Gaea (earth), many tales claim. see: **Ares; Gaea; Uranus.**

Erymanthian Boar [M] The third labor of Hercules is to capture alive this wild animal of Mt. Erymanthus. Journeying to the mountain—which is situated on the border of winter-gripped Arcadia and Achaia—Hercules yells as loud as 100 men. Startled, the boar charges into a thicket where it becomes tangled in foliage and mired in snow. Bundling the beast in chains, Hercules drags it before his taskmaster in Mycenae. The frail Eurystheus is so frightened that he leaps into a bronze urn and orders the hero to deposit his catch outside the city gates. see: **Hercules.**

Estrie [O] In medieval Hebrew superstition, a female monster who exhibits the worst qualities of a werewolf and vampire. An evil spirit who usually appears in the form of a mortal woman, the Estrie spends her existence among the living to sate her heinous appetite for blood and mortal flesh. Though she is particularly fond of children, the demon will prey upon anyone. Capable of changing her shape to whatever she wishes, the Estrie becomes her natural demonic self only when she flies about at night. In this state, if she is ever wounded or seen by human eyes, she will die. The only way she can possibly save herself is by eating bread and salt belonging to whomever has caused her downfall. Upon death, the Estrie's mouth must be stuffed with earth or she will return to tender more of her particularly gruesome brand of evil. see: **Vampire; Werewolf.**

Everyman [L] The hero of an anonymous late fifteenth century morality play of the same name. Written in an allegorical form which was popular from the fourteenth through the sixteenth century—the personification of abstractions such as vice and virtue—*Everyman* is the story of how God sends Death to summon one man for an accounting of his life on earth.

Even though Everyman pleads, "O Death, thou comest when I had thee least in mind," it is time to add up the debits and credits. Symbolically, Everyman goes searching for assets to join him in his journey to the beyond. Fellowship will not go unless it is to "haunt together women's lusty company," or else seek similar pleasure. Kindred and Cousin won't go either, the latter complaining of a "cramp in my toe," while Goods state the obvious, "I am too brittle." Neither can Good Deeds be his ally, for it lies "cold in the ground. Thy sins have me sore-bound that I cannot stir," nor is the response of Discretion, Strength, Five Wits, and Beauty any more heartening. Only Knowledge will come along part of the way, to lead him to "Confession's cleansing river." In the end, Good Deeds is able to enter Everyman's grave with him, revealing the play's self-proclaimed moral: Make sure your Good Deeds are strong, or God will say, "Go into the eternal fire, ye cursed ones."

Evil Eye, The [O] A malignant power centralized in the eye, which visits death or bad luck upon whomever it falls. Called jettatura in Italy—where it is still a potent fear—the evil eye or "overlooking," as it is also known, was originally a power granted to witches by the Devil. In its earliest form, the eye itself was not blighted: it was simply the medium through which ill will was channeled. And while people actually died after being given the evil eye, this was probably due to the power of suggestion rather than tangible occult ability. However, since many people prefer to be safe than sorry, the proper protection from the evil eye is to dab the soles of the feet and the palms with a mixture of warm water and salt, throwing the rest of the concoction into a fire and praying for protection from the Devil. see: **Devil; Witches.**

F

Fachen [F] An awful monster of Irish legend. Although it is the habit of the Fachen to track, maim, and kill people who travel after dark, its appearance alone is sufficient to still all but the sturdiest heart. Its body is covered with dark flue feathers, a crop of which juts from its head like a cock's comb. The Fachen has one eye, a single gnarled hand growing from its chest, and a lone leg. To render itself even more frightening, the Fachen usually ruffles its feathers prior to an assault.

Fachen

Fafhrd [L] The popular sword and sorcery hero created by author Fritz Leiber (1910–). Fafhrd the Barbarian lives in the world of Nehwon. Located in a dimension different from our own, Nehwon's northern sector includes the ferocious Land of the Eight Cities, its eastern half desert and steppes ruled by Mingol raiders, and its south the ancient land of Lankhmar. Nearly seven feet tall, slim and long-limbed, Fafhrd hails from the frigid wastes north of the Eight Cities. With him on his many adventures is the short, gray-garbed, swarthy-faced Gray Mouser from the south, whom he met in Lankhmar. Among the novels through which they battle their way are *Swords Against Destiny, Swords Against Death, Swords in the Mist, Swords Against Wizardry,* and *The Swords of Lankhmar.*

Fafner [F] An evil giant who, with his equally foul brother Fasolt, murder their father to obtain his gold. However, there is no love lost between the brothers, for Fafner is quick to kill Fasolt to possess all of the gold. To make certain that no one ever wrests the treasure from *him,* the giant transforms himself into a dragon. Enter Siegfried, who not only slays the beast but, by eating his heart or bathing in his blood (depending upon the legend) is enabled to understand the language of birds. These characters of both Teutonic and Norse (where they are Fafnir and Sigurd) legend are featured in Richard Wagner's immortal opera cycle *The Ring of Nibelungs.* see: **Siegfried.**

Fairies [F] A term used to describe benevolent or malicious sprites. As a rule, European fairies live in Fairyland, a world which borders our own and is ruled by either King Oberon and Titania, or by Queen Mab, depending upon the fairy lore consulted. Fairyland can be located in a hollow hill or mound, under the roots of trees, or beneath a river or lake. The size of fairies differs according to nation: they range from an inch to human stature. Irish fairies are the size of babies; England's sprites are the size of fully grown adults. Regardless of their national origin, all fairies love to dance, this activity producing patches of rank or decayed grass known as a fairy ring. Any mortal who steps inside such a circle is either struck dead, borne to Fairyland, or pinched and battered insensate. Usually invisible, fairies can be seen by humans who have imbibed one of the many potions which can be brewed for this purpose. The favorite color of European fairies is green, though they will wear clothes of any earth color such as green, yellow, or brown.

The origin of fairies lies in prehistory, where they were thought to be the spirits of the dead. Later lore made them fallen angels. No matter what their true nature, fairies possess remarkable supernatural powers. They can cause or cure sickness, foretell the future, and perform other occult acts. Their relationships with humans vary. They have an overriding love of cleanliness, and will attack those who keep a dirty house. Conversely, they will leave presents for those who are tidy, usually depositing these in the bottoms of pails. However, the imp in fairies sometimes conquers such generous impulses and they will often turn gifts into worthless objects, such as gold to lead. More nefariously, they will not hesitate to steal mortal babies to replace their own deformed or ugly offspring; fairies are also known to kidnap mortal women to serve as housekeepers, rewarding the families they leave behind with perpetual good fortune. Nor are fairies averse to making love with mortal men or women, although in such relationships the human is not permitted to see the fairy or to speak its name. Children born of such a union are invariably blessed.

In lands beyond Europe, fairies are fundamentally the same entities, although their trappings may differ. In China, for example, the revered fairy Hsi Wang Mu, "The Golden Mother of the Tortoise," is made of distilled western air and lives on K'un-lun Mountain in a palace, the walls of which are made of gold and jewels. Her favorite foods are dragon liver, phoenix marrow, and peaches which grant her immortality. Most European fairies are content to sup on barley, oatmeal, roots, and the milk of goats or deer. see: **Changeling; Fairy Animals; Fairy Godmother; Oberon.**

Fairy Animals [F] The wide variety of creatures living in Fairyland and sometimes escaping to our sphere. The animals which most frequently find their way into fairy lore are cats, dogs, horses, and cattle. The horses are wild and can be broken only with the most stringent application; the cattle are much less domestic than their mortal counterparts. Most ghost hounds who haunt our world are thought to be fairy dogs, and many demon cats like the fierce Cait Sith are fairy felines. In addition to these beasts there are also fairy seals, fairy trout and salmon, fairy insects, and fairy beavers. see: **Black Hounds; Fairies.**

Fairy Godmother [F] A general term for any patron fairy. In its earliest form, the fairy godmother was simply the Virgin transmogrified so as to give everyone a spiritual benefactor without insulting the Church. Over the years, different identities were tagged on by different cultures until she became the ghost of a dead mother protecting her child; a specter looking after someone who had done them a good turn in life; or the spirits of local woods, streams, or hills. However, these interpretations presented serious problems. Foremost among them was that while fairy godmothers were often required to attend religious rites such as christenings, fairies cannot appear in the presence of religious icons. Hence, the subsequent evolution of the less contradictory Guardian Angel. see: **Fairies.**

Familiars [O] Creatures given to a witch or warlock after they have agreed to serve the Devil. Usually cats, dogs, mice, or toads, familiars are said to have occult powers and are utilized to spread disease and kill or maul their master's enemies. Though witch-finders have claimed to see witches nursing their familiars on a second pair of nipples, it is thought that such reports are false, applied by the over-zealous to simple house pets, in the hope of pinning a rap on suspected witches. see: **Devil; Witchcraft.**

Famous Monsters of Filmland [MP] A publishing phenomenon: a long-lived magazine about movie monsters. Founded by publisher James Warren and editor Forrest J. Ackerman, *Famous Monsters* began publication in February 1958. Nearly twenty-two years and over 160 issues later, it is still going strong. *Famous Monsters* has, in its pages, featured exclusive interviews with Boris Karloff and Christopher Lee, among other film greats; through contests and articles championed once-amateur and now professional talents such as Rick Baker and Jim Danforth; single-handedly made its million-plus readers aware of fantasy films as a serious genre; and brought into the spotlight such behind-the-scenes fantasy figures as Willis O'Brien and Ray Harryhausen. *Famous Monsters* is also the base from which Warren runs Captain Company, the world's largest fantasy merchandise mail order company. see: **Ackerman, Forrest J.; Baker, Rick; Danforth, Jim; Harryhausen, Ray; Karloff, Boris; Lee, Christopher; O'Brien, Willis.**

Fantastic Four, The [C] A team of comic book superheroes created in 1961 by artist Jack Kirby and writer Stan Lee. When Dr. Reed Richards decides to build a rocket to beat the Russians into space, he fails to consider what effects cosmic rays will have on himself and his crew, consisting of Susan Storm (later his wife), her brother Johnny, and big Ben Grimm. As it turns out, the radiation transforms Reed into Mr. Fantastic and gives him the power to stretch; Susan into The Invisible Girl, able to be her normal self or transparent at will; Johnny into The Human Torch, a hero who can turn to fire and fly; and Ben into The Thing, an extremely strong orange-skinned brute. Based in Manhattan's Baxter Building, they have battled many foes over the years, including the Skrulls from Space, Dr. Doom, the Mole Man, the Submariner, and others. see: **Kirby, Jack; Lee, Stan; Submariner.**

Fanu, Joseph Sheriden Le [L] A British fantasy novelist. Born in 1814, he graduated from Trinity College in Dublin with a degree in law. But the attorney decided upon a career in journalism, and from there moved into fiction. Le Fanu's specialty was the ghost story, although he is best known for the classic vampire tale *Carmilla*, written in 1871. Among his other works are *Ghost Stories and Tales of Mystery* (1851), *The House by the Churchyard* (1863), and *Uncle Silas* (1871). Following the death of his wife in 1858, Le Fanu became a recluse, living alone in his mansion and nightly writing terror tales by candlelight. He died in 1873. see: **Carmilla.**

Fates, The [M] Also known as the Moirai, the Fates are old and ugly women who control the destiny of the universe. Individually, they are Clotho, Lachesis, and Atropos. Clotho is responsible for spinning the thread of life, Lachesis controls luck and is the dispenser of lots, and Atropos is known as the Unchangeable, one who cuts the thread of life at death. The daughters of Zeus and the titan Themis—who represents Justice and is the figure usually seen balancing the legal scales—they are sisters to the

Hours. The will of the Fates is unquestionable; even the almighty Zeus must abide by their edicts. see: **Zeus.**

Father Grumbler [FT] The antihero of the French fairy tale "Father Grumbler." Unhappy because of his many responsibilities, he accepts a gift from a Holy Man, a magic basket which provides an unending flow of food. Although he is warned not to show the basket around, Father Grumbler reveals its power to an innkeeper, who steals it. Complaining to the Holy Man, Father Grumbler is given Coquerico, the cock that crows "golden drops and diamonds as large as peas." It, too, is stolen by the innkeeper, so the Holy Man gives Father Grumbler a magic bag. When the greedy landlord sneaks a look inside, an enchanted switch emerges and beats him until he returns the basket and the cock. However, because he is disappointed in the loose-lipped Father Grumbler, the Holy Man takes back his presents and leaves the poor man to suffer.

Faustus [O] Also known as Johann Faust, a magician and astrologer born in Knittlingen, Germany in 1480. After Faust's death in 1540, tales began to circulate about how he had consorted with the Devil. It was said that he had sold his soul in exchange for wealth, youth, knowledge, power, and demons to act as his slaves. From these legends arose the 1590 play *The Tragical History of Dr. Faustus* by Christopher Marlowe (1564–1593) which, in turn, was the basis of the early nineteenth century poem "Faust, A Tragedy" by Johann Wolfgang von Goethe (1749–1832) and an 1859 opera by Charles Gounod. Shot as a film over twenty times, the most recent cinematic Faust was Richard Burton in the 1968 motion picture *Dr. Faustus.* see: **Devil.**

Federation [TV] In the "Star Trek" universe, the United Federation of Planets. A political system embracing many, many star systems—including our own—the Federation is basically democratic. Governed by the Federation Council, it is a peaceful conglomerate whose principal foe is the Klingon Empire, although altercations with the Romulans do occur. One of the functions of the Federation is to send out starships like the U.S.S. *Enterprise* to learn what they can about non-member planets and distant galaxies. see: *Enterprise*, **U.S.S.; Klingons; Romulans.**

Fée [O] French demons. Also known as the White Ladies, the Fée loitered near bridges and gullies and asked passers-by to dance. If they refused, the Fée hurled them from the ledge or handed them over to the Lutrins— cats, owls, and other creatures over which she held influence. The White Ladies were also famous for holding bazaars at which they sold artifacts for the working of magic. However, when a mortal purchased one of these items and went to take it, the Fée grabbed the person's arm and threw him or her from a nearby cliff.

Fenoderee [F] An incredibly powerful brownie. Tall, with twisted features and a body covered with hair, Fenoderee tests peoples' strength by shaking their hands. If he can crush a person's bones with an effortless grip, that individual is dismissed as puny and deserving of further mischief. Lore has it that Fenoderee used to be a handsome fairy. Falling in love with a human maiden, he missed a fairy festival. For this irresponsibility he was made hideously ugly and banished from Fairyland. On occasion, Fenoderee will help a farmer with his labors, but will tolerate neither thanks nor criticism. This outcast is also known as Fenorderee and Phynnodderee. see: **Brownie; Fairies.**

Fenrir [M] A monster wolf, the son of the vile Norse god Loki and the giantess Angurboda. The brother of Hel, goddess of the dead, and the Serpent of Midgard—a snake who was so huge it could coil itself about the earth—Fenrir was quite a problem child. So bad was he that the gods had to keep him perpetually bound. But normal chains proved insufficient for the task, so the gods ordered dwarfs to forge the magic chain Gleipnir from the sound of a cat's footsteps, the roots of a mountain, the breath of a fish, the beard of a woman, and the spittle of a bird. These monumental links managed to hold Fenrir until Ragnarok, the Day of Judgment—when he broke loose, bit off the hand of the god of war, Tyr, and swallowed Odin. Looming so huge that his lower jaw brushed the ground and his snout the sky, Fenrir was finally felled by Odin's son Vithar. In some myths, the giant wolf is known as Fenris. see: **Loki; Odin.**

Findhorn [U] An agrarian community of some two hundred people. Located in the north of Scotland, Findhorn is a place where the mystical is commonplace. Thanks to the cooperation of Nature Spirits and Devas—the latter defined as thought as an aspect of growth and creation, something ignored by modern day society—the residents of Findhorn have transformed it into a Garden of Eden. There, forty pound cabbages grow, roses bloom in the snow, and Pan's pipes can be heard on the wind. Said to be run according to instructions received directly from God, Findhorn is described by Paul Hawken—author of *The Magic of Findhorn*—as either, "a manifestation of light and power which could transform our planet within a lifetime, or ... an illusory bubble."

Finlay, Virgil [E] Born in Rochester, New York, in 1914, Virgil Finlay is one of the most respected names in fantasy illustration. With his first professional sale to *Weird Tales* magazine in 1935, Finlay became a favorite of both fans and the authors whose tales he interpreted, including H. P. Love-

craft. The bulk of Finlay's professional work was for the pulp publications, most of it done in either his famous stipple or cross-hatching techniques. Just prior to his death in 1971, most of Finlay's output was for *Astrology* magazine and the Science Fiction Book Club. He is survived by his wife, Beverly. see: **Lovecraft, H. P.; Weird Tales.**

Firebird [F] A fabled bird of Russia. Larger than an eagle, the firebird glistens like the sun and has feathers made of pure gold. According to legend, the firebird was captured long ago by the Horse of Power, who had lured it from flight by spreading 100 bags of maize in a large field. Presented as a gift to the Czar, the firebird later escaped. It is said that when this awesome animal takes wing, it creates a strong wind that causes the trees to creak and bend, the seas to foam, and all other birds to fall quiet. A benevolent firebird is the subject of *The Firebird*, a ballet written in 1910 by Igor Stravinsky.

Firebird   Flying Carpet

Fire-Breathing Bulls [M] Monsters which appear in the saga of Jason and the Argonauts. When the Greek hero lands on Colchis, home of the Golden Fleece, King Aeëtes is not at all happy to see him. He knows why Jason has come, and offers to turn over the coveted ram skin only if the adventurer proves himself worthy. First, Aeëtes orders Jason to tame and yoke a pair of flame-spitting bulls. Using them to furrow a large field, the Greek is then given a handful of dragon's teeth to sow. Aeëtes declares that if Jason survives the onslaught of soldiers which will sprout from the planted teeth, he may have the Golden Fleece. With the help of Aeëtes' sorceress daughter, Medea, Jason is triumphant. see: **Jason; Medea.**

Fitcher's Bird [FT] A wondrous bird of legend featured in the Grimm Brothers tale of that name. When a wizard finds three poor sisters living together, he kidnaps the eldest in a basket and offers her the run of his regal home if she will but care for a special egg and promise not to go into one particular room. The girl accepts the terms, but as soon as the wizard leaves she disobeys. Holding the egg, she enters the room and finds the dismembered bodies of other girls. Accidentally dropping the egg in a basin filled with blood, she retrieves it and flees the room. When the wizard returns and sees the blood-stained shell, he cuts the girl to pieces and kidnaps the second sister. She repeats her sister's mistake and suffers a similar fate. When the third sister is brought to the wizard's home, she takes care to leave the egg behind before visiting the forbidden room. Recognizing her butchered sisters, she reassembles them and sends them home with gold stolen from the wizard's coffers. Before they depart, she asks only that they send help, for when the wizard returns he plans to make the young girl his bride. In the meantime, she gets hold of a skull and disguises herself as Fitcher's Bird by covering herself with honey and rolling in feathers scooped from a

featherbed. The wizard finds the skull and presumes his beloved dead, accepting the bird for what it appears to be. Moments later, friends gathered by the liberated sisters arrive, rescue the unwilling bride-to-be, and burn down the wizard's house. see: **Grimm, Jakob and Wilhelm.**

Flash Gordon [C] A space-going hero created in 1934 by Alex Raymond for King Features Syndicate. A polo-playing Yale graduate, Flash, his girl friend, Dale Arden, and scientist Dr. Hans Zarkov (Alexis Zarkov in the movie versions) fly into space in Zarkov's rocket to alter the orbit of the planet Mongo, which is on a collision course with earth. There they battle Ming the Merciless, Emperor of Mongo. Other escapades carry the bold earthpeople to Queen Fria's ice kingdom, Queen Undina's undersea empire, and the like. Among the group's allies on Mongo are Ming's daughter, Aura, and her husband, King Barin of Arboria.

In addition to the comic strip, Flash has appeared in comic books; on radio; in a 1936 novel entitled *Flash Gordon in the Caverns of Mongo* as well as a short-lived series issued in 1973; on TV, with Steve Holland as the intrepid space traveler, Irene Champlin as Dale, and Joe Nash as Zarkov; and in three motion picture serials: *Flash Gordon* (1936), *Flash Gordon's Trip to Mars* (1938), and *Flash Gordon Conquers the Universe* (1940). In all three serials, Buster Crabbe played Flash, Frank Shannon was Zarkov, and Charles Middleton created a splendidly devilish Ming. Jean Rogers played Dale in all but the third serial, for which she was replaced by Carol Hughes.

Flash, The [C] A comic book superhero created in 1940 by writer Gardner Fox. Originally, the Flash was Jay Garrick who, when exposed to the vapors of hard water, became the fastest being alive. Donning a red, blue, and yellow costume, winged boots, and a winged metal cap, he used his remarkable ability to fight wrong-doers. Revised in 1956 by writer John Broome and artist Carmine Infantino, the Flash was now police scientist Barry Allen whose superspeed is the result of accidental contact with dangerous chemicals. Married to Iris West, Allen keeps his red and yellow costume stored within a signet ring and battles the many faces of crime in Central City. Among his most famous adversaries are Captain Cold, the supergorilla Grodd, and the Reverse Flash. In the comic book mythos, the Barry Allen Flash is explained as living on Earth One, while the Jay Garrick hero dwells with his wife, Joan, on Earth Two, which exists in a dimension parallel to our own.

Flatwoods Monster [U] An outerspace creature who paid a well-documented visit to earth. When a UFO landed in Flatwoods, West Virginia in September of 1952, five boys saw the object and informed authorities. What the investigators discovered was a twenty-five-foot-diameter, six-foot-tall spaceship glowing red. From within the foul smelling craft emerged a creature who was nearly ten feet tall. It wore a helmet, had a red face and two orange-green eyes, a blue-gray body (perhaps a spacesuit) which reflected the search party's flashlight beams, and slid rather than walked across the ground, hissing all the while. After investigating its surroundings for several minutes, the alien returned to its spacecraft and left. see: UFO.

Fleischer, Max [MP] Quite possibly the greatest producer of animated cartoons in film history. Born in Vienna, Austria, in 1885, Fleischer came to the United States at the age of four. After studying at Cooper Union, he landed a job as a photo engraver for *The Brooklyn Eagle*. In 1915 he

turned to the fledgling field of cartoon animation. In the years that followed, he produced classic short subjects featuring Popeye and Betty Boop—whom he created in 1931—and in the early 1940s brought forth seventeen cartoons featuring the comic book character Superman. In their full, fluid animation, brilliant juxtaposition of soft and sharp colors, and dynamic action, the Superman efforts may well be the finest work the field has ever seen. Fleischer was also responsible for creating the second feature-length cartoon, *Gulliver's Travels*. It was released in 1939, only a few months after Walt Disney's *Snow White and the Seven Dwarfs*. Fleischer worked only sporadically after 1943, his lack of an independent studio such as the one built by Walt Disney severely limiting his outlets. He died in 1972. Today, Max's son Richard Fleischer is one of the industry's most bankable directors, having helmed such films as Walt Disney's *Twenty Thousand Leagues Under the Sea* (1954), *Fantastic Voyage* (1966), *Dr. Doolittle* (1967), and *Soylent Green* (1973). see: **Disney, Walt; Popeye; Superman.**

Flubber [MP] A gravity-defying substance created by Professor Ned Brainard (Fred MacMurray) in Walt Disney's *The Absent Minded Professor* (1961). *Flubber* is a word coined from the union of "flying rubber." A pasty substance, it is used to make Brainard's model-T airborne. Later, the scientist irons it to the shoes of the inept Medfield High School basketball players to give them some much needed bounce . . . and a victory. Flubber returned in a 1963 sequel *Son of Flubber*. The ingredients used by Professor Brainard to manufacture flubber are not known. However, the Disney special effects department made their on-camera flubber by mixing salt water taffy, polyurethane foam, and yeast, pouring it over cracked rice, splashing on a cup of water, and covering the brew with molasses. see: **Disney, Walt.**

Flying Carpet [F] Originally the personification of a dream, the Oriental and Middle Eastern flying carpet carries its passengers to worlds of imagination. Inspired by the lazy drifting of clouds, the flying carpet gained early credibility after appearing in a number of religious legends. Buddha, for one, is said to have been lifted through the skies on a magic carpet. According to the Koran, King Solomon enjoyed a similar mode of transportation. Made of green silk and boasting a canopy made of birds, Solomon's carpet is said to have carried his aides to the right and spirits to the left with his throne in the center. That the carpet, rather than a chair or a bed, became this symbol of nobility is due to the belief that the foot is a sacred part of the body. Hence, the honorary contemporary ritual of rolling out the red carpet. see: **Jones, Gulliver.**

Flying Dutchman [O] A fabled ghost ship frequently seen off the Cape of Good Hope, South Africa, and regarded as an omen of ill fortune. The legend was born one stormy night when an old Dutch captain, locked in combat with the restless elements, vowed he would round the cape even if it took forever. His oath was heard—and became his unhappy fate. The seagoer must now sail the course until he finds a woman who is willing to become his wife and sacrifice everything for his sake. There have been several film versions of the story, most notably with James Mason and Ava Gardner in 1950. It is also the subject of an opera by Richard Wagner.

Flying Mermaid [L] The amazing vessel featured in the 1908 novel *Five Thousand Miles Underground or The Mystery of the Centre of the Earth* by Edward Stratemeyer, writing as Roy Rockwood. The main character of the tale is Professor Amos Henderson, and the Flying Mermaid is a ship which can travel on the water or in the air. Driven on the sea by motorized propellers, it takes to the air when a light gas is pumped electrically to containers located above-deck in the place of sails. When these are filled, the ship rises into the skies.

Flying Nun, The [TV] An unusual television heroine. The Flying Nun is Sally Field as Sr. Bertrille, whose cornette miraculously catches the wind and allows her to become airborne. Situated in a Puerto Rican convent, the young girl is constantly using her unique ability to get her into and out of trouble. Based on the novel by Terre Rios, "The Flying Nun" ran for three seasons on ABC, starting in 1967.

Fly, The [L/MP] A science-spawned monster created by George Langelaan for his short story "The Fly." Experimenting in matter teleportation, scientist André Delambre tries to send his cat Dandelo through the aether— but its atoms never reassemble. Then he tries to teleport himself. However, unknown to the researcher, a fly accidentally enters the teleportation chamber and, during transit, their atoms are mingled. Delambre is reassembled with the head and right arm of the fly, and vice versa. Though the fly escapes, the scientist decides to go through the machine once more, hoping that he will be miraculously cured. Instead, the atoms of the cat are joined with his already mutated body. When Delambre emerges this time, he has the white hairy head of Dandelo, with a low flat skull and a pair of pointed ears, a pink and moist cat nose, fly ears—brown bumps the size of saucers—and a vertical slit of a mouth with a long, quivering trunk dripping saliva. Afraid of losing his human soul as his mind becomes that of a fly-cat, Delambre has his wife Hèléne crush his head and arm under a giant steam hammer.

In the 1958 movie classic *The Fly*, Delambre is played by David Hedison. Sequels, not based on the Langelaan work but borrowing its premise, are *The Return of the Fly* (1959) and *The Curse of the Fly* (1965).

Fomors [M] Twisted monsters of Celtic mythology. The nature of the Fomors differs from region to region. In Ireland, they are hideous demons who have existed since before the Great Flood. Led by King Conann, they battle all other monsters who try to invade their homeland. Their most famous foes were the Partholans, an evil people who crawled from the deep chasm of Time, defeated the Fomors, and dwelt in Ireland until decimated by plague. The best known of the Irish Fomors is Balor, who possesses two eyes; one for vision and the other invested with magic powers like those of an evil eye. The lid of Balor's sighted orb is so heavy that it takes four men to raise it.

In Scotland, the Fomors are a race of giants who serve the same provincial purpose as their Irish cousins. However, not only do these Fomors defend their nation, they enslave those whom they conquer and demand most of their newborn and cattle as tribute. Symbolically speaking, it is thought that the Fomors as a whole represent old pagan faiths trying to weather the coming of more modern religions.

Fortunato [L] The victim of some sinister plotting in Edgar Allan Poe's 1846 short story "The Cask of Amontillado." Says his nemesis Montressor, "The thousand injuries of Fortunato I had borne as best I could; but when he ventured upon insult, I vowed revenge." Finding the cruel Fortunato at a carnival, dressed in "a tight-fitting party-striped dress," his head surmounted by a "comical cap and bells," Montressor lures the liquor connoisseur to his wine cellar under the pretense of sampling some amontillado, the authenticity of which is doubted by Montressor. When the pair has gone far in the murky, mildewed chamber, Montressor slyly chains Fortunato to a recess in the wall and casually bricks him inside. Self-satisfied, the rather sadistic Montressor says of his enemy's remains, "For the half of a century, no mortal has disturbed them."

Fortunatus [F] A magical figure in Eastern medieval legend. Stricken with poverty and on the precipice of starvation, Fortunatus is visited by Fortune, who offers him his choice of strength, health, wisdom, beauty, long life, or wealth. Fortunatus opts for riches, which are granted in the form of a purse that never runs dry. (Some tales say it is a wishing cap.) Fortunatus quite enjoys his treasure—although it ultimately destroys him and ruins his sons. see: **Everyman.**

Fountain of Youth [F] A mythical fountain alleged to restore a person's youth. There are several possible sources for this legend, but it apparently emerged upon the European consciousness when Indian Brahmic lore of youth-giving waters merged with Semitic tales of the River of Immortal Life located in Paradise and responsible for granting eternal good health to those who have gone to heaven. These stories were crystalized as the Fountain of Youth, which Spanish explorer Ponce de Léon (1460–1521) vainly sought in the wilds of Northern Florida. see: **Mar Jiryis.**

Four-Leaf Clover [F] Primarily an Irish charm used to generate good luck. In olden times, the four-leaf clover was a token which protected the bearer against fairies. Since clover grows in the fields, and fairies are by-and-large rural beings, its selection as a charm is logical. Later, it became an ingredient in magic potions, specifically those intended to hypnotize the victim. As its mystique grew, the four-leaf clover also enabled people to actually see fairies and was used to grant wishes. Today, it is simply a broad token of good luck.

Frankenstein Monster, The [L] The artificial being victimized by a frightened world in the 1816 novel *Frankenstein* by Mary Shelley (1797–1851). When Swiss scientist Victor Frankenstein finds the means of generating life, he uses it to manufacture an eight-foot-tall creature whose "yellow skin scarcely covered the work of muscles and arteries beneath; his hair was of a lustrous black, and flowing; his teeth of a pearly whiteness ... his watery eyes, that seemed almost of the same color as the dun white sockets in which they were set, his shrivelled complexion and straight black lips." After roaming misunderstood on the periphery of society, answering ignorance with violence, the monster stands himself on an Arctic ice floe.

Cinematically, the Frankenstein Monster has had literally dozens of screen vehicles. The earliest of these is Thomas Edison's 1910 version of *Frankenstein* starring Charles Ogle as the creature; the most popular, the 1931 James Whale picture featuring Boris Karloff as a monster assembled from parts of dead bodies. Appearing as Baron Henry Frankenstein in the Karloff film is Colin Clive. Though Karloff's monster is trapped in a burning mill at the end of the film, he returns as the protagonist in *The Bride of Frankenstein* (1935), which is based on a segment of the Shelley novel, and in *The Son of Frankenstein* (1939). Other screen Frankenstein Monsters include Lon Chaney Jr., Bela Lugosi, Glenn Strange, Christopher Lee, and Dave (Darth Vader) Prowse. see: **Chaney, Lon Jr.; Karloff, Boris; Lee, Christopher; Lugosi, Bela; Whale, James.**

Frazetta, Frank [L] Renowned painter of heroic fantasy. Born in Brooklyn, New York in 1928, Frazetta studied art at the local Academy of Fine Arts and began drawing comic books at the age of sixteen. A partial listing of the titles include *Thun'da, Buck Rogers,* and *Tally Ho,* as well as the EC line of horror and science fiction titles. Frazetta's own comic strip, "Johnny Comet," was short lived, but he stuck with the medium for nine years, ghosting Al Capp's "L'il Abner." Then, in the early 1960s, he began painting covers for *Creepy* and *Eerie* magazines along with reissues of old Edgar Rice Burroughs novels. His dynamic, moody style won him a wide following. But it wasn't until he rendered the barbaric Conan for paperbacks that he really entered the forefront of fantastic illustration. Today, book collections of his work are perennial top sellers, and his attention-getting paintings for the posters of such films as *Battlestar Galactica* have made him a favorite in Hollywood. Frazetta lives in rural Pennsylvania with his wife, Ellie, and children Frank Jr., Bill, Holly, and Heidi. see: **Conan; Creepy, Uncle; Eerie, Cousin; Galactica.**

Fremen [L] In the mythos of Frank Herbert's 1965 novel *Dune,* the desert-dwelling free tribes of the planet Arrakis. Remnants of Zensunni Wanderers—also known as Sand Pirates—they all belong to the Ichwan Bedwine, the brotherhood of Fremen. Fremen make their living by mining valuable spices, often from the backs of huge sandworms captured by Fremen known as Hookmen. Religious people, they have an anticipated messiah called the Mahdi; saints known as Sadus; and priests called Quizara Tafwid. Most Fremen wear robes; the women are garbed in black robes known as aba. see: **Melange; Sandworm.**

Frodo Baggins [L] A hobbit created for the *Ring* trilogy by J. R. R. Tolkien.

Born in the Third Age 2968, Frodo is
the son of Drogo Baggins and Primula
Brandybuck. Orphaned in 2980, he
goes to live with his cousin Bilbo Baggins. Given the One Ring in 3001, it is
his job to toss it in the Crack of Doom
at Orodruin, the fire mountain where
the Ring was made. A Christ figure
who enjoys eating mushrooms, he ultimately decides to wear the Ring
rather than destroy it—but his finger
is bitten off by his aide Gollum, who
falls into the Sammath Naur, the
chamber of fire which houses the
Crack of Doom, thus fulfilling the
mission. In 3021, Frodo joins Bilbo,
Elrond, and others in the Last Riding
of the Keepers of the Rings, an epilogue to those many full lives. see:
**Bilbo Baggins; Elrond; Tolkien,
J. R. R.**

Frost, Jack [F] The personification of
freezing cold. In Russia, this sprite is
known as Father Frost, and he chills
the air with brittle laughter as he
leaps from tree to tree bringing with
him the bitter cold. In the United
States, Jack Frost is an elf who discol-
ors the leaves in autumn and etches
frost designs on windows. The legends
of these and other such frigid figures
seem to have originated with the
Frost Giants of Norse mythology,
awesome beings who caused ava-
lanches and glaciers and made the
rivers freeze.

Fu Manchu [L] A sinister villain created
by London bank teller Sax Rohmer
(real name: Arthur Sarsfield Ward) in
1913. Described as tall, thin, and catlike with a shaved skull, jade-green
eyes, and a face like Satan, Fu Manchu is a cruel scientific genius intent
on world conquest. In *The Insidious*

Jack Frost

Dr. Fu Manchu, the initial novel in
the long-lived series, the megalomaniac meets his match in handsome,
rugged British secret agent Nayland
Smith. It is the first of many battles
waged by the two opponents; subsequent matches are recounted in *The
Return of Fu Manchu, The Hand of
Fu Manchu, The Daughter of Fu
Manchu, The Mask of Fu Manchu,
President Fu Manchu*, and other
novels. A popular subject for filmmakers, Fu Manchu has been played
by such noted actors as Warner Oland
in *The Mysterious Dr. Fu Manchu*
(1929) and *The Return of Dr. Fu Manchu* (1930), Boris Karloff in *The Mask
of Fu Manchu* (1932), and Christopher
Lee in *The Face of Fu Manchu* (1965),
The Brides of Fu Manchu (1966), and
The Vengeance of Fu Manchu (1967).
see: **Karloff, Boris; Lee, Christopher.**

G

Gabriel Ratchets, The [O] According to English legend, a pack of howling wolves which roam the skies during a thunderstorm. The spirits of children damned for never having been baptized, it is the mission of the Gabriel Ratchets to announce the approach of Death. However, their bloodcurdling cries can be heard by other than the doomed party, and serve as fair warning for sinners to mend their ways before Judgment Day. The Gabriel Ratchets are also known as The Wild Hunt and The Devil's Dandy Dogs. see: **Black Hound, The; Death.**

Gaea [M] The earth personified in Greek mythology and, with her husband, Uranus—the heavens—the first of the gods. She is ascribed different origins by different myths. The most prominent tale makes her one half of the egg which hatched Eros, Uranus being the other half. In a subsidiary myth, she simply emerges from formless Chaos with Night and Erebos—the darkness below the earth. Among Gaea's first activities is to bear Pontus—the sea—and the mountains, both by Uranus. Later, she and Uranus parent the twelve Titans including Cronus and Rhea; the cyclopes; and the mighty Hecatoncheires. Unfortunately, Uranus proves a cruel and imperious father, and Gaea helps the Titans rebel against him. Cronus assumes the mantle of supreme ruler and Gaea seeks other companionship. By her son Pontus she mothered the early sea gods Nereus, Thaumas, and Phorcys; by Tartarus she bears the giants Typhon, Antaeus, and Tityus. In Roman mythology, Gaea is known as Terra. see: **Cronus; Cyclops; Eros; Mecatoncheires; Titans; Uranus.**

Galactica [TV] A spacegoing battlestar, the featured vessel in Glen Larson's television series "Battlestar Galactica." Flagship of the Twelve Worlds' Warfleet, it was at the front line of a 1,000 year war against the alien Cylons until disaster struck. All the other battlestars as well as the human populations of the dozen colonized planets—the Gemons, Virgos, Scorpios, Picons, and others—were destroyed by a false Cylon peace initiative. Only the Galactica survived. Now, led by Commander Adama, the battlestar and its crew of 500 search the universe for the legendary thirteenth colony of humans, earth. Hounded along the way by pursuing Cylons, their only defenses are on-board weapons and squads of Viper Ships. see: **Cylons.**

Galligantus [F] One of the foes of Cornwall's Jack the Giant Killer. A giant who dwells in a castle with an evil magician, Galligantus kidnaps the daughter of a duke—whom the magician changes into a deer. Jack vows to rescue her and, donning a coat of invisibility stolen from a giant, he enters the castle. There he finds a golden horn inscribed with the legend, "Whoever can this trumpet blow shall cause the giant's overthrow." Jack forces the instrument to sound and, while the castle and its occupants shake from the vibrations, he draws his sword and murders the giant. The magician escapes in a hastily summoned whirlwind; upon his departure, all the knights and ladies who had been transformed into beasts resume their natural shapes. The castle crumbles to dust, Jack sends the head of Galligantus to King Arthur, and the hero weds the duke's daughter. In the 1962 motion picture *Jack the Giant Killer,* Galligantus was pictured as having two heads. see: **Cormoran.**

Ganconer [F] A fairy lover. Ganconer appears in isolated valleys where, usually smoking a *dudeen,* "a clay pipe," he woos and makes love to country girls, then leaves them. The poor maidens thereafter refuse to take another lover and/or sulk until they die. Ganconer is said to be darkly handsome, with black eyes, cold lips, and breath that will kill all but the object of his affections. Ganconer frequently dresses in fairy garb, although his seductions are worked with—and without—mortal clothing. He can only be chased away by a religious icon.

Gandalf [L] A gray-maned, gray-robed, bushy-browed sage and wizard in J. R. R. Tolkien's *Ring* Trilogy. The foe of Sauron, whose destruction he pursues for twenty centuries, Gandalf is the owner of a magic rod and the mighty sword Glamdring. Instrumental in setting in motion the mission to destroy the One Ring, Gandalf perishes when he falls into a vast pit while saving his comrades from the griffinlike monster Balrog. His mantle as leader of this driven little group or Fellowship thereupon falls to Aragorn. However, the heroic mage is returned to Middle Earth as the invulnerable Gandalf the White, a resurrection which adds yet another appellation to he who is already known by such names as Mithrandir, Stormcrow, and Incánus. In the end, Gandalf joins Bilbo Baggins, Frodo Baggins, and others in the apotheosizing Last Riding of the Keepers of the Ring. see: **Bilbo Baggins; Frodo Baggins; Sauron; Tolkien, J. R. R.**

Gans [F] An Apache mountain spirit. Possessing incredible powers which they use for both good and evil, the gans are frequently honored by ceremonies. At such times, they are repre-sented by Indian dancers wearing black masks and high, wood-slat headdresses. Although whites have labeled these rites Devil Dances, the gans are more like Arabian djinn than Judeo-Christian devils.

Ganymede [M/L] The son of Laomedon, King of Troy. In Greek mythology, Ganymede is spirited to Olympus by Zeus, who assumes the form of an eagle and kidnaps the young prince. Once he is settled at the home of the gods, Ganymede is put to work as the deities' cup-bearer, serving them nectar. His predecessor Hebe, the daughter of Zeus and Hera, had left the post to marry Hercules, newly ascended to the celestial abode. Ganymede is also one of the moons of Jupiter, and the setting of Michael Resnick's sword and sorcery series featuring Adam Thane, who is known as Kobar by the natives. see: **Hera; Hercules; Zeus.**

Gappa [MP] A gigantic creature seen in the 1967 Japanese film *Monster from a Prehistoric Planet.* Actually, the label "Prehistoric Planet" is misleading, since Gappa is snatched from a lost island on earth and brought to Tokyo. There, it is rescued by its huge mother and father who level a goodly share of Japan in the effort. Gappa, like its parents, is a scaly biped with a large beak, blue incendiary breath, and a pair of wings to bear it aloft.

Gargoyle [F] A decorated waterspout on the top of a building, usually jutting from a gutter. The earliest gargoyles were iron heads used in Ancient Greece. In latter-day architecture, gargoyles were often degrading caricatures of the enemies of the building's owner. However, gargoyles are best known today as grotesque stone figures which are half-human, half-bird, and half-animal and usually found adorning Gothic cathedrals. The word *gargoyle* comes from the Latin *gurgulio* which means "gullet." Contrary to popular usage, *any* waterspout is a gargoyle; the monstrous stone hybrids of humans and animals are known as chimeras. see: **Chimeras.**

Gathol [L] An unimposing but rich country in the Western Hemisphere of Edgar Rice Burroughs' Barsoom. Standing on a mountain located within a great salt marsh is the *city* of Gathol, thought to be the most ancient inhabited city on Mars. This mountain, which was once an island in the Throxeus Ocean, is famous for its diamond mines. The ruler of Gathol is Gahan, husband of Tara of Helium, who is the daughter of John Carter of Mars and Dejah Thoris. Gahan and Tara are the parents of a girl, Llana. see: **Barsoom; Burroughs, Edgar Rice; Carter, John; Thoris, Dejah.**

Genie [F] A powerful supernatural being of Islamic folklore, often identified with djinn. Boasting both good and bad members, genies do not marry or mate, so their numbers are fixed. The good genies are inclined to serve those mortals who pray or make them offerings. However, the bad genies are so evil that they cannot be moved by obeisance of any kind. They dwell in holes in the ground and are responsible for causing humans to argue or become ill. Bad genies seldom show themselves to mortals, but when they do it is with a human body, the multi-horned head of a lion, and great claws. Typical is the genie Caschcasch in the Arabian Nights tale "Camaralzaman and Badoura." He is described as being "hideous, humpbacked, lame ... with six horns on his head." The term *genie* derives from the Latin word *Genius.*

   More recently a genie named Jeannie captured the imagination of television viewers with her popular TV series *I Dream of Jeannie.* Barbara Eden played the magic lass who is discovered by astronaut Tony Nelson (Larry Hagman) and moves in with

him. The series ran for five seasons on NBC. see: **Djinn; Genius and Juno.**

Genius and Juno [M] Generative deities of Roman mythology. Each man has a Genius and every woman a Juno, spirits who have looked after the individual since his or her very inception. Some myths claim that there are actually *two* such beings which follow a person from day to day, one counseling evil and the other good. It is from this belief that the notion of a twin conscience, one's personal devil and angel, derives.

George of the Jungle [TV] A brilliant spoof of Tarzan. An animated cartoon series created by Jay Ward, "George of the Jungle" ran for a single season on ABC in 1968. It's humor was far too sophisticated for the Saturday morning cartoon viewers. Dwelling in a treetop cabin in the jungle, the monosyllabic George lives with two identical twin mates named Stella and Ursula, has a pet elephant named Shep—which he insists is "a long-legged, droopy-nosed bow-wow"—and is counseled in love and war by his friend Ape, a monkey who speaks with a British accent and is an excellent mathematician. George keeps tabs on jungle goings-on by conversing with a fleet of tuki-tuki birds, and is able to summon any and all animals merely by crying out. Though the wrong animal usually appears ("maybe George give wrong area code"), things always work out for the best. George's foes include witchdoctors, unscrupulous developers, and greedy hunters. see: **Superchicken; Tarzan.**

George, St. [H] The patron saint of England and a legendary dragon slayer. Born in Lydda, Palestine at the end of the third century A.D., George became a soldier and served the Emperor Diocletian. Stationed in Great Britain, he learned of a dragon which demanded the sacrifice of a maiden or youth every time water was drawn from its well. When only the king's daughter was left, George galloped to Berkshire to rescue her from the great lizard. Dodging the monster's fiery breath, stinging tail, and swipes of its huge bat-wings, George moved in and struck it between the eyes. To this day, nothing grows on the hill where the dragon's blood spilled. On April 23, 303, when Diocletian turned against Christianity, George opposed him and was executed. That last statement is fact; however, because a dragon is often used to represent Satan, George's slaying of the beast is symbolic of the victory of Christianity over the emperor's antichristian sentiments. In 1962, the story of St. George was filmed as *The Magic Sword* with Gary Lockwood in the title role. see: **Dragon.**

Geryon [M] A monster with three heads, six hands, three bodies joined at the waist, and huge wings. The son of Chrysaor and Callirrhoe, he lives on the red island of Erythia—red because it lies directly beneath the beams of the setting sun. The proud owner of a herd of cattle as red as his home, Geryon leaves them with the giant Eurytion and the two-headed watchdog Orthrus for safekeeping. Alas, the stealing of this herd is the tenth labor of Hercules. Making his way to Erythia, the Greek hero slays Eurytion and Orthrus and makes off with the cattle. But Hera, looking down from Olympus, sees that the son of her husband, Zeus, is having too easy a time of it. Thus, she sends a gadfly to drive the oxen mad and scatter them, then alerts Geryon of the theft. The six-handed giant goes raging after Hercules, but is felled with an arrow which enters his side and skewers all three of his bodies. Gathering the cattle, Hercules brings them to his taskmaster, Eurytheus, then sacrifices them to Hera. see: **Hercules.**

Gezun [L] A magician created by author

Geryon

L. Sprague de Camp. Gezun of Lorsk is a poverty-stricken magician with brownish skin, curly black hair and a beard, a big sharp nose, a square jaw, and wide cheekbones. Based in Pusâd—de Camp's name for Poseidonis, a lost continent which the author places at the site of the modern-day Azores—he battles such foes as Bokarri the wizard, the nasty magician Larentius Alba, and others. A one-time student of the great Sancheth Sar, Gezun is husband to the woman Ro. They have a thirteen-year-old son, Zhanes, and a ten-year-old daughter, Mnera. The seriocomic magician was introduced in the 1973 tale *The Rug and the Bull* in which he tries hard to establish a flying carpet factory. It is one of de Camp's many tales of Pusâd.

Ghidrah [MP] A three-headed, winged, two-tailed monster from space. Created by the late Japanese special effects artist Eiji Tsuburaya, Ghidrah arrives on earth in a huge meteor from which a fireball erupts and slowly becomes the huge flame-breathing creature. In Ghidrah's first film, *Ghidrah the Three-Headed Monster* (1965), the titular fiend is defeated by reformed baddies Godzilla and Rodan, with an assist from Mothra in caterpillar form. But the modern-day dragon returns in *Monster Zero* (1965) battling Rodan and Godzilla only, and in *Destroy all Monsters* as he helps the alien Kilaaks try to conquer earth. Their plans are stymied by the combined forces of Rodan, Mothra, Godzilla, Angilas, Godzilla's son Minya, the giant spider Spiga, Barugon, and the huge snake Manda. Ghidrah's most recent screen appearance has been in *Godzilla vs. Gigan* (1971), as the three-time loser joins Gigan in a fight against Godzilla and Angilas. see: **Angilas; Godzilla; Mothra; Rodan.**

Ghost Owl [F] A creature showcased in the famous Cheyenne legend "The Ghost Owl." In that tale, an uppity young Indian girl is snatched by an owl and made to work for the owl's grandfather. While she goes unhappily about her duties, other birds gather round and tell her that the owls plan to eat her. Panicking, the prisoner promises to reform her precocious ways if someone will help her. Just then a hawk appears, and carries her to a cave inhabited by the hawk's grandfather. There she waits for the owl to come and retrieve her—at which point she carefully follows the old hawk's instructions. Battering off the owl's head with a rock, she burns both it and the lifeless body, never touching the beads and gems which pour from the latter. Freed from her nemesis, the girl lives with the hawks until she is an adult. Then she sets out for home with the aid of a magic mink. En route she pauses at the lodge of an old woman. When the hostess scratches her leg a club appears; grabbing it, she tries to batter the girl's skull. But the mink bites the hag and kills her, and the girl arrives safely home.

In the general lore of Indians—particularly Algonkian and Athabascan—as well as that of Mexico, owls were widely feared. They were thought to be the personification of spirits returned to earth to finish mortal tasks or to seek revenge. These beliefs are rooted in the fact that the owl is an eerie nocturnal predator.

Ghosts [O] The spirits of the deceased. Scientists tell us that what we see or hear as ghosts may actually be electrical manifestations of the brain, created subconsciously by the self for the self or for viewing by others. Occultists deny this. They say that materialized spirits are made from a cool and slightly luminous bodily substance called *ectoplasm*, which they claim wafts from the pores and other bodily openings in the dark. Spiritualists assert that specters can inhabit more than just ectoplasm; they can enter the bodies of people or animals, or slip inside an inanimate object and cause it to move. They also maintain that while ghosts are aware of time and space, they are in no way governed by it.

The traditional ghost, a hazy creature that resembles a floating white bedsheet, is thought to be a popularization of the white appearance of ectoplasm under artificial light. Ghosts can be either benevolent or cruel, depending upon how kindly they were in life or how well they are adjusting to their new incorporeal form.

Ghouls [O] Evil demons which were born in the lore of Arabia and of the Orient. Ghouls, as originally conceived, are the children of Iblis, feed on humans living and dead, and pilfer tombs for their booty. Although they dwell primarily in cemeteries, they are known to live in any deserted areas. In the eighteenth and nineteenth centuries, *ghoul* was a term applied mainly to graverobbers; today, it is used to describe anyone who lives off the efforts of another.

Giant Behemoth [MP] A prehistoric monster featured in the 1959 motion picture which bears its name. An amphibious, long-necked lizard, the Giant Behemoth comes ashore when its aquatic food supplies are killed off by the monster's own radioactive presence. As it stomps along the English coast and finally through London proper, the creature is studied by scientists and is found to be dying of its own intense radiation. Tipping a torpedo with radium, the British are able to fire it into the Behemoth's mouth when it returns to the sea. The monster dies—although the washing ashore of dead fish in America suggests a sequel which never materialized. The Giant Behemoth was brought to cinematic life by animator Willis O'Brien. see: **Behemoth; O'Brien, Willis.**

Giants [M/F] Large beings in human form, usually extremely ugly and often immortal. In Greek mythology, giants were born from the blood of Uranus' severed genitals as it struck the earth. These giants have serpents for feet and are kin to the Erinnyes, who also rose from the spilled life essence of Uranus. Norse tales give giants the homeland of Jotunheim, where the most famous residents are Hresuelgr, who creates winds and storms by flapping his vast wings; Surtr, who looks after Muspelheim, the southerly Land of Fire, guarding it with a flaming sword; and Hrunghir, who was killed by Thor. The giants of Jotunheim are particularly famous for dragging in winter to replace summer. In Celtic lore, giants are said to have deposited islands in the ocean as they waded through; the Irish giant Fingal and his son Ossian are noted for having built the Giants' Causeway which connects Ireland and Scotland. Scandinavian giants have up to nine hundred heads, while in England a giant named Corinaeus was actually the ruler of Cornwall. The thirty-three daughters of the Ital-

ian Emperor Diocletian all mated with demons and bore a clutch of giants.

Although giants can be both good and evil, the latter are usually referred to as ogres. However, no giant is above eating human flesh and they do so in numerous fables and fairy tales. King Arthur slew such a giant atop St. Michael's Mountain; in "Jack and the Beanstalk," the titular hero killed another—one who not only fed on humans but was married to a lady cyclops! see: **Arthur, King; Blunderbore; Cormoran; Galligantus; Gog and Magog; Jack and the Beanstalk; Uranus.**

Gigantes [M] Vaguely humanoid creatures bred by the Titans when they fought a desperate war against the Greek gods. The Gigantes were truly bizarre fabrications. Some possessed the tails of dragons, others had fifty heads, and still others were half-serpent with 100 arms. These hideous monsters were vanquished by a hardworking Hercules who, with the aid of Zeus, clubbed the Gigantes to death and buried their remains beneath mountains. see: **Hercules; Titans.**

Gilgamesh [L] A historical king of Erech in Southern Babylonia. However, it is as the protagonist of a short fantasy epic written circa 2000 B.C. that Gilgamesh is best known. Two-thirds a god and one-third a mortal, Gilgamesh loses his good friend Enkidu to the wrath of the goddess Ishtar. After six days of mourning during which "like a wailing woman I cry for Enkidu," the king resolves to revive him from the dead. This he will do by learning the secret of life and death through conference with his sage ancestor Utnapishtim on a mountain at the world's end. Setting out, Gilgamesh meets such creatures as the scorpion man and his wife, who look after the rising and setting sun; Siduri, the cup-bearer of the gods; and Ur-Shanabi, who ferries our hero to the presence of Utnapishtim. The king's distant relative tells him, "At the bottom of the underworld sea is a briar plant. If you pluck it, it will pierce your hand, but do not hesitate, for it is the plant of life."

Trudging to the shore, Gilgamesh lashes stones to his feet, jumps into the water, finds the plant, and hurries back to the surface. However, on the way back to Erech, he foolishly places it on the ground while he bathes—and along slithers a serpent who eats the plant. Which is why snakes can shed their old skin while humans must wither and die—small consolation to Gilgamesh, who has failed his friend, Enkidu. Frustrated beyond imagining, Gilgamesh journeys to the domain of Allatu, goddess of Arallu, the underworld. He had planned to pay a visit with Enkidu, but mysterious forces sap his strength and the king barely makes it back to the surface. Pleading for help, Gilgamesh is rewarded when Ea, the god of water, orders Nergal, the god of war, to open the earth so that Enkidu's spirit may rise and speak with his friend. The two embrace, and Enkidu informs Gilgamesh that at least the underworld treats the shadows of the brave with honor, while the evil suffer. Gilgamesh is somewhat consoled by that—although, as Enkidu leaves, the King of Erech is still haunted by his failed mission. see: **Enkidu; Utnapishtim.**

Glubbdubdrib [L] A side voyage undertaken by Gulliver while awaiting a ship to carry him from Balnibari to Luggnagg. Glubbdubdrib is an island ⅓ the size of the Isle of Wight, and it is a land of sorcerers and magicians. There, the residents summon the dead to serve them. Each soul can be called forth for twenty-four hours, but none can whistle forth the same spectre within a three-month period—"except upon very extraordinary occasions." As a favor to Gulliver, his host, the Governor of Glubbdubdrib, brings

forth such historical figures as Hannibal, Caesar, Alexander the Great ("He assured me upon his honor that he was not poisoned but died of a fever by excessive drinking . . ."), Pompey, Brutus (Gulliver was told, "that his ancestor Junius, Socrates, Epaminodas, Cato the Younger, Sir Thomas More, and himself were perpetually together . . ."), Homer, Aristotle, Descartes, and others. see: **Balnibari; Gulliver, Lemuel; Luggnagg.**

Gnomes [F] In medieval times, gnomes were one of the four Elementals, serving the earth as salamanders served fire, sylphs the air, and nereids the water. These gnomes could move as freely beneath the ground as the other Elementals through their own milieu. However, in modern lore gnomes are merely little people who are usually identified with trolls or dwarfs. Small, wrinkled beings, gnomes can generally be found guarding mines or quarries. When not bothering with subterranean affairs, they revel in frightening humans or causing nasty things to happen. [Cf. *Gnomes*, by Wil Huygen (Abrams, 1977)] see: **Dwarfs; Trolls.**

Gnomes

Goblins [O] Demons who adopt a horrifying human or animal form and set about tormenting people. Although goblins can assume any size they wish, the hideous creatures are usually small and twisted. Often identified with the German kobold, the Danish nis, and Scotland's brownies, *goblins* are broadly defined as "any malicious spirit." However, hobgoblins are a softer strain; domestic spirits which, if treated well, do constructive things such as protecting the household from strange spirits or prowlers. Conversely, poorly-treated hobgoblins cause misfortunes such as poverty and discord. They also tangle people's hair while they sleep, cause blisters with their infernal kiss, and drive pets mad or make them sick. Like brownies, hobgoblins appreciate offerings of a bowl of cream and bread. They don't like to be bribed—just cared for. see: **Brownies.**

Godfather Death [FT] A tale from the pen of the Brothers Grimm. When a poor couple has their thirteenth child, the papa resolves to ask the first person he meets to be its godfather. Setting out, the desperate man encounters God, whom he chastises saying, "You give to the rich and leave the poor to hunger," and moves on. The bitter father likewise turns down the Devil—"You deceive men and lead them astray"—but Death proves acceptable, noting, "I make all equal."

Surprisingly, Death seems devoted to his task. He holds the child at his christening and, when he is grown, Death gives him a magic herb which makes his godson a great physician. However, Godfather Death cautions the young man, "When you are called to a patient, I will always appear to you. If I stand by the head of the sick one, you may say with confidence that the sick will be well again . . . but if I stand by the feet, the patient is mine." Death also explains that to use the herb against his will shall cause the young man's instantaneous demise.

Death's godson becomes quite famous due to his astute medical judgments and skill, and all is well until he falls in love. His inamorata takes ill and, when Death takes his place by her feet, the physician elects to cure the girl and suffer the consequences. She lives; he dies. see: **Death; Grimm, Jakob and Wilhelm.**

Godzilla [MP] A towering movie monster created by Japanese special effects genius Eiji Tsuburaya. Godzilla, a fictitious dinosaur roused from eons of hibernation by American nuclear tests in the Pacific Ocean, stands thirty stories tall and has incendiary radioactive breath. Effectively played by an actor in a rubber costume, Godzilla's first screen appearance is in *Godzilla, King of the Monsters* (1954) starring Raymond Burr as *United World News* reporter Steve Martin. The monster resurfaces in *Gigantis the Fire Monster* (1955) followed by *King Kong vs. Godzilla* (1962), *Godzilla vs. the Thing* (1964), *Ghidrah the Three-Headed Monster* (1965), *Monster Zero* (1965), *Godzilla vs. the Sea Monster* (1966), *Son of Godzilla* (1968), *Destroy All Monsters* (1969), *Godzilla's Revenge* (1969), *Godzilla vs. the Smog Monster* (1971), *Godzilla vs. Gigan* (1971), *Godzilla vs. Megalon* (1976), *Godzilla vs. the Cosmic Monster* (1977), and *Godzilla on Monster Island* (1978). *Space Godzilla* is upcoming.

Godzilla is also the star of the thirty-second-long animated comedy *Bambi Meets Godzilla* (1969), and is featured with his nephew, Godzooky, on the NBC "Godzilla" cartoon show. Known in Japan as Gojira, Godzilla has a mate named Gojilla and a son named Minya. He currently resides on Monster Island along with Rodan, Barugon, Angilas, and other giant beasts. see: **Angilas; Barugon; Ghidrah; Mothra; Rodan.**

Gog and Magog [F] Biblically, the two

nations which will be led by Satan during Armageddon, the battle against the authority of God. However, in the folklore of Great Britain, Gog and Magog are the last of the giants. Captured by Brutus, they are said to have been brought to Troy-no-vant—later called London—and employed as servants. Some tales have the two giants as one twelve-foot-tall being named Gogmagog who fought Corinaeus and was thrown into the ocean. Lastly, Gog and Magog are the stars of the 1954 motion picture *Gog*. In that film, they are a pair of small robots run by computer. When the computer is taken over by spies, Gog and Magog begin to kill the human residents of their secret scientific base. see: **Giants.**

Golden Blackbird [FT] The sole cure for death in the French fairy tale "The Golden Blackbird." A lord is dying, and while his eldest two sons give up their search for the curative bird, the youngest son does not. Consulting a hare, he is instructed to climb on its back. The rabbit carries him 700 miles taking 7 miles per stride—but when they find the bird's owners, the boy is told that before they will turn it over, he must bring them the Porcelain Maiden, "a young girl, beautiful as Venus, who dwells two hundred miles from here." Mounting the rabbit, he finds the girl bathing, steals her clothes, and pledges not to return them unless she comes with him. The maiden agrees. However, the young man falls in love with her and, following the advice of the canny hare, is able to steal the blackbird from its rightful owners. Returning home, the lad cures his father, weds the Porcelain Maiden, and inherits the kingdom of his proud and grateful parent.

Golden Fish [F] A mystical character in a Russian fable—although most every culture has some version of this tale. A poor fisherman snares a golden fish, which promises to grant his every wish if the old man will turn him back to the sea. The kindly fisherman agrees and wishes for some bread. When he returns home, his wife chastises him for his modest request. Sending him back, she orders him to ask for something more extravagant. He calls upon the fish and asks for a bread trough, but his wife is still unsatisfied. She forces him to return time after time; getting them a new hut, making her a lady with a fine house and servants, and finally elevating her to Czaritza. However, when the woman orders her husband to tell the fish to make her God, all of the boons are withdrawn. The couple is left with no more or less than they had at the start—save for an added thread of wisdom and a dose of humility.

Golden Fleece [M] A magnificent ram skin sought by Jason in Greek mythology. The origin of the Fleece is steeped in intrigue. The principal players are Ino, wife of the Thessalian king Athamas, and Athamas' son, Phrixos, by Nephele. Ino wants Phrixos dead, and plots his demise with care. She bribes the women of the fields to scorch the kingdom's crops; famine follows and Athamas asks the oracle at Delphi for a solution. Intercepting the king's messengers, Ino pays them to tell her husband that Apollo has ordered Phrixos' death to end the famine. Athamas agrees to make the sacrifice, but Nephele has other ideas. She asks for help from Zeus and, just as Phrixos is about to be stabbed, a golden fleeced ram races from the sky and places the young man and his sister, Helle, on its back. The animal races over land and sea and, while Helle tumbles off and drowns in the straits between Europe and Asia—thereafter called Hellespont, the Sea of Helle—Phrixos lands safely in Colchis. Taking one of the daughters of King Aeëtes in marriage, Phrixos sacrifices the golden ram to Zeus and gives its fleece to his father-

Ghost   Golden Fleece

in-law. Aeëtes places it in a sacred grove under the watchful eyes of fire-breathing bulls and a dragon who never sleeps. Years later the fleece is stolen by Jason, who sees the theft as a deed worthy of a king, something he must undertake before trying to regain his father's usurped throne. see: **Fire-Breathing Bulls; Jason.**

Golden Goose [FT] A Grimm fairy tale that has also been told with a swan in the featured role. When a poor woodcutter offers a white-haired old man some of his water and flour cake, the appreciative fellow tells him to cut down a certain tree beneath which, among the roots, is a goose with golden feathers. The woodcutter does as he was told and finds the bird. Pausing at an inn, he is surprised to find that three girls who try to pluck the gleaming feathers become stuck to the goose—as does everyone who tries to help the greedy ladies. Meanwhile, a king whose daughter is grimly seri-

ous promises her hand in marriage to anyone who can make her smile. In comes the woodcutter with his goose and seven hangers-on—and the princess laughs hysterically. But her father reneges on his promise. He tells the young man that before any wedding can take place he must "bring a man who can drink up a whole cellar of wine." Returning to where he found the goose, the woodcutter discovers such an individual—the old man in disguise—and leads him to the king. The monarch then asks for someone who can eat a mountain of bread and the woodcutter provides one—again, the white-haired fellow incognito. Finally, the king requests a ship which can sail on land as well as on water, which the woodcutter supplies courtesy of the old man. Thus, the beleaguered young man gets the girl and, when her father dies, his kingdom as well.

Golden Lads [FT] Characters in a Grimm Brothers story of the same name. Catching a golden fish, a poor man follows its instructions and cuts it into six pieces. He gives two sections to his wife to eat, keeps two pieces for his horse, and plants two in the garden. It isn't long before the garden brings forth two golden lilies; the horse has two golden foals; and the man's wife bears two golden boys. When they are grown, the brothers decide to take the horses and go out into the world. Before leaving, they tell their father that if the lilies stay healthy, then they too are healthy. But "if they seem to droop, you will know we are ill, and if they fall down and fade away, it will be a sign that we are dead." Setting out, the boys are laughed at because of their uncommon hue. One boy turns back; the other presses on. Eventually, the determined son marries and builds a fine home. Then, one day, he is out hunting and meets a witch who turns him to stone. Back at his father's house, his brother sees one of the lilies droop and hurries to the rescue. Finding the witch, he forces her to restore the afflicted brother, and all ends happily. see: **Grimm, Jakob and Wilhelm.**

Golem [F] A creature first described by Hebrew mystics of the thirteenth century. Molded from clay by Rabbi Elijah of Chelm, the golem is a brawny, larger-than-human figure created to help preserve religious freedom. Drawing life from the secret name of God (Shemhamforash) etched on its forehead, the speechless brute proves difficult to control. Fearing its destructive potential, Chelm scrapes the inscription from the golem's brow and it falls to dust. Some legends say that the word *emet* or "truth" was cut into its hard shell, the monster crumbling to powder when its creator hacked off the "e" leaving *met* or "death."

There have been many motion pictures about the golem, most prominently Paul Wegener's *The Golem: Monster of Fate* (1914) and its "prequel" *The Golem: How He Came to Be* (1920). In the Wegener version of the tale, fifteenth century Rabbi Loew of Prague builds his giant clay figure then calls upon the demon Astaroth to reveal the occult word (*aemaer*) which will give it life. see: **Astaroth; Homunculus.**

Goodfellow, Robin [F] A British hobgoblin. The inspiration for Shakespeare's sprite Puck, Robin Goodfellow is primarily a forest spirit. His pleasure is to mislead travelers and scare the unprotected—as long as his victims are not kindly folk. He is also known to visit homes where he happily serves people who are selfless and pinches those who are not. The son of the fairy king, Oberon, by a country girl, Robin Goodfellow had no magical powers for the first six years of his life. Then, he ran away from home and, during his flight, discovered a golden scroll which gave him the abil-

Robin Goodfellow

ity to change his shape and summon up whatever material things he desired. The only restriction on these powers is that they must be used to reward the good and punish the bad. see: **Goblin; Oberon; Puck.**

Gooseberry Wife [O] A bogie from the Isle of Wight in England. Invented to keep youngsters from playing in the garden, the Gooseberry Wife is a huge hairy caterpillar which lurks near gooseberry bushes and eats children. As the old saying goes, "If ye g᷉os out in the gearden, the gooseberry-wife'll be sure to ketch ye." see: **Boogeyman.**

Goosey [O] A ghost who haunts Whitby in Yorkshire, England. In life, Goosey was a young man who took on the challenge to consume an entire goose in a single sitting. He succeeded, but the poor fellow was subsequently murdered. Today, his hungry ghost loiters about the site of his dubious triumph.

Gorgan [TV] The pink-haired man from the planet Triacus in the "Star Trek" episode "And the Children Shall Lead." Played by Melvin Belli, the green-glowing, soft-skinned Gorgan is called "the Friendly Angel" by youngsters whom he's using to try to conquer the universe. He is defeated—along with the illusions and mind control ploys worked through his wards—when Capt. Kirk shows the children video tapes of their early youth. They see themselves playing with their scientist parents before Gorgan intruded upon the research colony and drove its adult members to take their lives. The sobered, bitter youths stop believing in the Friendly Angel and, after appearing in his naturally pocked and repulsive form, Gorgan vanishes. see: **Kirk, Captain.**

Gorgo [MP] A sixty-five-foot-tall monster seen in the 1961 motion picture *Gorgo.* Released by an undersea volcano from millennia of sleep, Gorgo is captured on the shores of Nara Island, a small fishing village off the coast of Ireland. Brought to Dorkin's Circus in London and placed in a pit rimmed by electrical wires, Gorgo is put on public display. But the monster has a 200-foot-tall mother coming to rescue it. After sinking half of the British navy and razing most of London, Gorgo's mother frees her child and the pair ambles back to the ocean depths. The film was the genesis of a long-lived Gorgo comic book, as well as a sexed-up novelization by Carson Bingham.

Gorgon [M] A loathesome monster of Greek mythology. Daughters of the sea god Phorcys and the sea goddess Ceto—themselves the children of Gaea and Pontus—the Gorgons are three in number: the immortal Stheno and Euryale, and the vulnerable Medusa. With bronze-scaled bodies, yellow tusks, and snakes for hair, the Gorgons are so ugly that to see them is to turn to stone. Anyone venturing to their lair on the farthest shore of Oceanus, near Tartarus, can safely view them only in a mirror or other burnished surface.

On the cinema screen, a Gorgon named Magaera was the subject of the 1964 film *The Gorgon.* Since her spirit is floating about Vandorf, Transylvania with nothing to do, Magaera

decides to possess the body of a young girl and turn her into a snake-haired monster. Medusa was on-hand as one of *The Seven Faces of Dr. Lao* in 1964—all of them, including Medusa, being superbly played by Tony Randall. At the moment, Ray Harryhausen's $15,000,000 film about Perseus' slaying of Medusa, *Clash of the Titans,* is in production for release in 1981. see: **Harryhausen, Ray; Medusa; Perseus.**

Gorn [TV] A frog-faced biped featured in the live-action "Star Trek" episode "Arena," and on-hand briefly in the animated adventure "Time Trap." Seven feet tall and extremely intelligent, the dirty-green colored Gorn is forced to battle Capt. Kirk to the death on a barren asteroid in "Arena." Although Kirk is victorious, he refuses to slay the creature. The alien Metrons who pit one against the other are impressed with his charity and set both beings free. In "Time Trap," a Gorn is on the Elysian Council, the governing body of the Delta Triangle sector of space.

In Fredric Brown's 1944 story "Arena," on which the "Star Trek" episode is based, the Gorn is called the Roller and it is a red orb with tentacles. see: **Kirk, Capt.**

Gort [MP/L] The police robot featured in Robert Wise's classic 1951 science fiction film *The Day the Earth Stood Still.* Silver colored, with a disintegrator beam located behind a visor in its face, Gort is brought to earth by the humanoid Klaatu. The alien's mission is to warn earth people to live in peace or face intervention from space. As he admonishes at film's end, "If you threaten to extend your violence, this earth of yours will be reduced to a burned-out cinder." And the all-powerful, ten-foot-tall Gort—whom Klaatu leaves behind when he saucers back to space—is the robot to do it!

The Day the Earth Stood Still is based on Harry Bates' short story

"Farewell to the Master." In it, the mechanical being is not called Gort and, unlike the movie, it is Gnut who is the master. Klaatu is merely its biological emissary.

Graces [M] In Greek mythology, the goddesses of beauty. The daughters of Zeus and the oceanid Eurynome, there are three Graces in all: Aglaie, Euphrosyne, and Thalie. Aglaie, one of the three wives of Hephaestus, is the goddess of splendor and the youngest of the Graces; Euphrosyne, the goddess of joy; and Thalie, the goddess of pleasure. Also known as the Charities, these goddesses are described as being incredibly beautiful. see: **Hephaestus; Zeus.**

Graciosa [FT] The heroine of the fairy tale "Graciosa and Percinet" by French writer Madame d'Aulnoy. A princess, Graciosa is pushed around by her stepmother, the red-haired, one-eyed, toothless Duchess Grumbly. Throughout, the girl is aided by the fairy powers of Prince Percinet. When Grumbly beats Graciosa, the switch is changed to peacock feathers. When the princess is abandoned in a forest filled with lions, wolves, and bears, he sends a stag-drawn sled to rescue her. When the cruel stepmother gives her a box full of tiny people for safekeeping, and they escape, the fairy helps her gather them. After other such abuses, Graciosa decides to leave her father's kingdom and live with Percinet in his fairy palace.

Graiae [M] Three gray-haired women in Greek mythology who possess magical artifacts as well as vast knowledge. The daughters of the sea god Phorcys and his sister, Ceto, the Graiae are sisters of the Gorgons, and share one eye and one tooth which they are constantly passing. By name the Graiae are Pephredo, Deino, and Enyo, and they live at the far end of Libya, by the Gorgonian Plain, where neither the sun nor moon ever reaches. Their most famous visitor in this desolate

Graiae

region is Perseus, who arrives during his hunt for their sister Medusa. Snatching the hags' eye, he refuses to return it until they give him a large bag in which to place the Gorgon's head, winged sandals to carry him to her, and the helmet of Hades to make him invisible. see: **Gorgon; Perseus.**

Grant [O] An English demon predating the Middle Ages. Grant looks very much like a large colt, except that he has flaming red eyes and always moves about on his hind legs. Appearing only in rural villages at noon or dusk, he gallops down the main street and warns people of approaching evil or misfortune. Though Grant cannot speak, his presence causes dogs to bark—which is why canines always seem to know about disaster before it strikes. Often identified with Hedley Kow, Grant's forte is announcing the coming of fire. see: **Hedley Kow.**

Gray, Dorian [L] A character created by Oscar Wilde (1854–1900) for his 1891 fantasy novel *The Picture of Dorian Gray*. Dorian is a man of striking features. He has "finely curved scarlet lips, frank blue eyes, crisp gold hair,"

as well as "youth's passionate purity."
People instinctively like him, and
when artist Basil Hallward paints a
portrait of Dorian he feels a strange
electricity among himself, his subject,
and the canvas. Dorian feels it as well,
which leads him to make an odd request. "How sad it is! I shall grow old,
and horrible, and dreadful. But this
picture will remain always young. It
will never be older than this particular day. . . . If it were only the other
way! If it were I who was to be always
young, and the picture that was to
grow old! Yes, there is nothing in the
whole world I would not give! I would
give my soul for that!"

Miraculously, the young man's wish
is granted. He remains handsome and
unravaged by time while the portrait
not only ages but manifests the sin and
corruption in Dorian's soulless body.
In the end, the tormented Dorian
stabs the picture with a knife—and
falls to the floor "a dead man . . . with
a knife in his heart. He was withered
and wrinkled, and loathesome of visage," the years of physical and moral
decay having passed from the portrait
to Dorian.

The Picture of Dorian Gray has
been filmed ten different times, the
most famous being the 1945 motion
picture starring Hurd Hatfield as the
tortured protagonist.

Great Bear Chief, The [F] The antagonist in the American Indian fable
"How the Little One Set Free His Big
Brothers." With the arrival of an
especially harsh winter, when food is
scarce, two of the three sons of a poor
family find bear tracks in the snow.
They follow then and kill the beast
which made them. Upon death, the
bear's shadow returns to the mountain of the Great Bear Chief. The indignant god has other animals lure the
killers to his lair within the peak,
where he changes their arms and legs
into those of a bear. When the children do not return, their parents go

searching for them; unfortunately,
they are discovered by one of the
Great Bear Chief's ursine subjects,
who breaks their backs. Lonely and
concerned, the youngest son, the Little One, leaves behind his small sister
and sets out after his parents. He finds
their crushed bodies and pursues their
killer. When his dog Redmouth disap-
pears inside the mountain, the lad sets
a fire which splits the peak in two.
The bears are consumed by flame—
except for the sister of the Great Bear
Chief. A kindly creature, she tells the
boy to gather moss and let his brothers
smell it. As soon as this is done, their
bearskin limbs are cured. The boys return to their home and care for their
sister, who "soon forgot that she had
ever had a mother and father."

Great Mother [F] An early religious
icon. The Great Mother is synonymous with the goddess of fertility, important to the earliest of civilization's
agricultural peoples. She appears in
many cultures in a variety of forms.
Generally, however, she has three
faces: the maiden, the mother, and the
sage old woman. These attitudes represent the new moon, the waning
moon, and the full moon—the moon
being the symbol of fertility due to its
presumed link with the female menstrual cycle. The Great Mother is
often pictured as having large horns
on her head, and her worship invariably concludes with a spirited orgy.

Green Children [F] Youngsters whose
existence is open to question. In medieval England, a boy and his sister
were discovered near a pit. They were
relatively normal in every respect
save one; their skin was green.
Brought to the home of a knight, they
spoke in a strange tongue and would
eat only green beans. After a short
while the boy became dour, lan-
guored, and died. The girl, on the
other hand, sampled whatever foods
were offered to her, lost her green

hue, learned to converse in English, and explained that she came from a world of perpetual twilight and green people. Tending sheep with her brother, they came to a cavern and traveled to its mouth; there they were struck unconscious by the bright sunlight. No one ever found the cave she described, though it is doubtful any would have entered if they had. In Celtic lore beans are the food, and green is the color, of the dead.

Green Lantern [C] A superhero whose awesome powers derive from a most unusual source. When Coast City test pilot Hal Jordan finds an alien whose vessel has crashed on earth, he is given a special ring by the dying extraterrestrial. It is a "power ring" which will enable Jordan to fly and create any object he wishes—from a giant hand to slap villains against walls to a huge baseball bat capable of swatting away large meteors. Every twenty-four hours the ring must be recharged on an invisible lantern-shaped battery, which the alien also gives to Jordan. The earthman is told that whenever he uses the lantern he must restate the Green Lantern oath: "In brightest day, in blackest night, no evil shall escape my sight. Let those who worship evil's might beware my power, Green Lantern's light!" Jordan also learns that he is not the only Green Lantern; the universe is full of them, all granted their powers by benign, blue-skinned aliens known as the Guardians. There are only two drawbacks to the Green Lanterns' abilities; they are unable to affect anything colored yellow or made of wood.

The Hal Jordan Green Lantern was designed by writer Gardner Fox and artist Gil Kane in 1959. An earlier Green Lantern, Alan Scott, had been created in 1940 by artist Martin Nodell and writer Bill Finger. However, he was much less exciting and was thus explained away as the Green Lantern of Earth II, a world nearly identical to our own but existing in another dimension. Among the foes of our world's Green Lantern are: the Star Sapphire, Major Disaster, the fallen Green Lantern Sinestro, and others.

Greensleeves [FT] A popular wizard of folklore. When a prince is beaten in a game of chance by an old man, the noble is forced to honor the stakes—on pain of death, find out where he lives within a year. Setting out, the prince stumbles upon three brothers, aged 200, 600, and 1,600 years old. They guide him to a river where the old man's daughters bathe, disguised as swans. Nabbing a swan with a blue wing, the prince forces her to lead him to her father's castle. There, Greensleeves acknowledges defeat. However, when the prince asks for his daughter in marriage, Greensleeves says he must first accomplish three additional tasks: build a castle 1,000 miles long and tall, using stones from every quarry in the world, and cover it with the feathers of all the known birds; take a large amount of seed from a cask, sow it, reap the crop, and refill the container with seed all in one day; and find a golden needle in a stable of 200 horses. Aided by one of the captured daughter's magic blue feathers and a box containing thousands of fairies, the prince completes every chore. The young man leaves with his bride-to-be, but Greensleeves is fuming over the defeat. Donning his seven league boots, the wizard bounds after them. Following the girl's instructions, the prince snatches a magic egg from a high hill and throws it at the wizard. The egg strikes him in the chest and Greensleeves dies, permitting the prince and his daughter to live together in peace. see: **Seven League Boots.**

Greenteeth, Jenny [F] An evil river goddess. Assuming many different guises throughout the United Kingdom, she is also known as Nelly Longarms, Peg Powler, Rawhead-and-Bloody-Bones, and Grindylow. Whatever her name, Jenny Greenteeth lusts for meals of human flesh. She is particularly fond of children, especially naughty ones or those who play on the Sabbath. Whenever she finds such a child she grabs it, drags it screaming into water, and eats it.

Gremlins [F] Gnomelike creatures blamed by American pilots and navigators for any trouble which strikes their aircraft. Gremlins are said to be a combination of jack rabbit and bulldog—fast and stubborn—wearing breeches, a red jacket, spats, and a top hat. They live in ditches and holes near airfields, and pad quietly about on large, ducklike feet. Whether the on-board problem is mechanical or electrical, chances are a Gremlin is responsible. see: **Gnomes.**

Gremlins

Grendel [L] A vicious monster in the epic poem *Beowulf.* Grendel is descended from Cain who, for slaying Abel, was punished by siring races of elves and monsters. In *Beowulf,* we first meet the ogrelike Grendel when he comes to Heorot, the hall of the Danish king Hrothgar, to feast on the ruler's soldiers. Beowulf arrives after the monster's attack, but is present

when Grendel strikes again. The "grim and greedy fiend" eats Beowulf's aide, Hondscio, and then attacks the hero himself. Since by magical decree Grendel cannot be slain by a sword, he fears no one. The beast's confidence paves the way for his downfall. Grabbing Grendel's arm, Beowulf wrenches it from its socket and hammers it to the ceiling. The creature is fatally wounded and crawls to its cave beneath the Dark Lake to die. But all is not yet well at Heorot. The next night Grendel's mother attacks, "a wretched crone" who tears the king's advisor, Aschere, to pieces. Beowulf chases her to her den, where he finds a sword forged by giants and therefore not bound by any enchantment. He slays the "mighty mere-wife," whose blood proves so potent that the sword dissolves.

Beowulf is told from the biased point of view of the hero. However, John Gardner reversed the prejudice in his 1971 novel *Grendel,* which relates the story from the monster's perspective. see: **Beowulf.**

Griffin [F] Also spelled gryphon, this fabulous monster of Indian and Arabian lore has the body of a lion and the head and wings of an eagle. Its feathers are black, red, white, and blue; its talons merge the power and hunting skills of both the king of the beasts and the king of the birds. A griffin's talons will also change color when exposed to poison, and for this reason are greatly prized.

Griffins are traditionally associated with great wealth. Either they are the guardians of treasure or happen upon it innocently, preferring to build their nests on deposits of gold. The eggs of the griffin are always made of agate, and their cry combines the bellow of a lion with the shrill screech of an eagle. The mortal enemy of horses, griffins like nothing more than to kill and eat them —although they will also feed on human corpses when the occasion arises.

The word *griffin* comes from the

Greek word *grypos* which means "hooked," describing their eagle's beak. In the arts, there is a friendly griffin in *Alice in Wonderland* and a golden griffin which battles a centaur in the 1973 motion picture *The Golden Voyage of Sinbad.* The hybrid creature is also a heraldic symbol of Great Britain. Similar to the griffin is the hippogriff. More of a land creature, the hippogriff has the forepart of a griffin and the hindquarters of a horse. see: **Centaur; Mock Turtle.**

Griffin, Dr. [L] The transparent villain in H. G. Wells' 1897 novel *The Invisible Man.* Before becoming the Invisible Man, the nearly thirty-year-old Griffin had been "almost an albino, six feet high ... with a pink and white face and red eyes," his hair and beard were also white. He becomes invisible after realizing that "the whole fabric of a man except the red of his blood and the black pigment of hair, are all made up of transparent, colourless tissue." Spending four years locked in research, he discovers drugs which will render these hues indetectable to the eye. When the potion works on a cat, Griffin takes it and spends a night slowly and painfully vanishing. After a series of adventures—during which London dirt clings to his otherwise transparent frame, and he appears in rain like a bubble—Dr. Griffin plots to gain power through a reign of terror. However, a spade driven against his chest in the novel's brawling climax ends these plans, as well as Dr. Griffin's life. Upon death, the scientist's visibility returns. Griffin was superbly played by Claude Rains in *The Invisible Man* (1933). see: **Wells, H. G.**

Grim Ghost, The [C] A comic book hero created in 1974 by writer Michael Fleisher and artist Ernie Colon. A highwayman, American Matthew Dunsinane is hanged for his crimes in the year 1743. Awaking in hell, he is offered a deal by Satan. Matthew will be returned to earth if he will serve the Devil, seeking out evildoers and

Grim Ghost

sending them to the lower regions. The period in which he will work is the 1970s since, as Satan explains, there is a wealth of corruption afoot. Matthew accepts the terms and, wearing the garb from his days as a highwayman—a white mask knotted behind the head, a purple cloak, and his eighteenth century vestments— goes to work as the Grim Ghost. Riding a black horse through the nighttime skies, and using his supernatural powers to transmute bullets into flowers, he causes many a wrongdoer to vanish in a puff of smoke. By day, the Grim Ghost dwells in a suburban mansion as the independently wealthy and rather eccentric Matthew Dunsinane.

Grimm, Jakob and Wilhelm [FT] The world's best-known compilers of fairy tales. Born in Hanau, Germany, Jakob Ludwig Karl Grimm (1785–1863) and Wilhelm Karl Grimm (1786–1859) worked as philologists, collecting fairy tales in their spare time. Most of these stories were of Northern European origin, and many had a moral. The brothers amassed 211 tales in all, published as two volumes, in 1812 and 1815 respectively. Wilhelm took a wife, Dorothea, in 1825; Jakob never married. Today, the brothers are memorialized in Kassel, Germany's Grimm Museum. However, a less pedantic tribute came in 1962 when George Pal produced the spectacular Cinerama motion picture *The Wonderful World of the Brothers Grimm.* This film not only told the story of their lives, but it brought to the screen three of their best-loved fairy tales: "The Dancing Princess," "The Singing Bone," and "The Cobbler and the Elves." Jakob was played by Karl Boehm, Laurence Harvey was Wilhelm, and Claire Bloom appeared as Dorothea. see: **Pal, George; Singing Bone, The.**

Gruagach [F] A fairy of Scotland. Actually, there are two distinct breeds of Gruagach. The first is a fairy lady who has golden hair and dresses all in green. Some accounts make her extremely beautiful, while others describe her as worn and pale. In either case, she spends most of her time looking after cattle and farms. She usually travels from village to village by river, and will come to the door soaking wet. The Gruagach will ask to dry herself beside the fireplace. If a person obliges her, the fairy will serve them. If not, she will leave. The second kind of Gruagach is a handsome male who works on farms and appears either dressed in red and green or naked. As payment for their services, both Gruagachs require nothing more than a cup of milk.

Gulliver, Lemuel [L] The hero of a brilliant fantasy adventure. Jonathan Swift (1667–1745) first published the saga of *Gulliver's Travels* in 1726. In it, his somewhat naive hero is described as the third of five sons. Born

Gulliver

in Nottinghamshire, England, Gulliver graduated from Emanuel College, apprenticed with an eminent London surgeon, studied navigation on the side, and signed up as a ship's physician. After three and one-half years at sea, he married Mary Burton, set up a practice in London, and had a son, Johnny, and a daughter, Betty. But Gulliver's practice failed and in 1699 he returned to sailing. For the next sixteen years he experienced some of literature's most extraordinary adventures. Among the many islands he visits are those inhabited by little people (Lilliput), giants (Brobdingnag), talking horses (the Houyhnhnms), ghosts (Glubbdubdrib), and so forth.

In terms of the cinema, the two finest adaptations of Swift's novel are Max Fleischer's 1939 feature-length cartoon *Gulliver's Travels*, and Ray Harryhausen's 1959 film *The Three Worlds of Gulliver.* see: **Balnibarbi; Brobdingnag; Fleischer, Max; Glubb-**

dubdrib; Harryhausen, Ray; Houyhn-hnms; Laputa; Lilliput; Luggnagg.

Gwangi [MP] The rampaging allosaur seen in Ray Harryhausen's 1969 motion picture *The Valley of Gwangi.* Captured in 1912 in Mexico's Forbidden Valley, Gwangi is put on display in a Wild West Show. However, the dwarfish servant of a gypsy witch unlocks the monster's cage and sets it free. After stomping through the city, Gwangi is trapped inside a burning cathedral and destroyed. Prior to the Harryhausen film, Willis O'Brien had also planned to shoot *Gwangi.* In his 1941 scenario, a tyrannosaur is captured in the Grand Canyon, tours with a Wild West Show, breaks loose, and is eventually forced from a cliff by a truck. see: **Harryhausen, Ray; O'Brien, Willis.**

Gwyllion [F] Hideous mountain fairies of Wales. As nasty as they are ugly, the all-female Gwyllion come out only at night. Waiting beside mountain byways, they misdirect travelers and perform other mischievous acts. Afraid of storms, they will visit local homes and ask for accommodations when it rains or blusters. This boon is invariably granted, since people fear what the spurned Gwyllion might otherwise do. These fairies also cringe

Gwyllion

before cold iron or a drawn knife. The benefactors of goats, they can assume the shape of these creatures—a handy disguise while trying to hover innocuously about mountain roads. Similar to the Gwyllion are the Ellyllon, although the latter are much more benign.

Hades [M] The Greek god of the underworld, known as Pluto to the Romans. The son of Cronus and Rhea, he was swallowed by his father at birth and remained in his belly along with Hera, Demeter, Hestia, and Poseidon. When Zeus freed them, he named himself King of the Gods and ruler of the sky, gave Poseidon dominion over the sea, and sent Hades to watch over the nether regions. Married to Persephone, the daughter of Zeus and Demeter, Hades is nonetheless a philanderer. Among his many concubines are the nymphs Mintho and Leuce, whom the jealous Persephone changes into the mint plant and white poplar, respectively.

Hades' symbol is a staff with two prongs—one prong less than Poseidon's trident, and the forerunner of the modern-day devil's pitchfork. He uses this implement to prod unwilling souls into the flames of his dark abode. The deity also owns a helmet given to him by the cyclopes. It renders the wearer invisible and is sometimes loaned by Hades to mortals or his fellow gods. see: **Cerberus; Cronus; Demeter; Persephone; Perseus; Poseidon; Zeus.**

Haggard, H. Rider [L] A knighted author of fantasy and adventure tales. Born in Norfolk, England in 1856, Henry Rider Haggard was raised in Great Britain and South Africa. His early training was in law, but he ditched that to become a writer. Haggard's first work of fantasy fiction was *The Witch's Head* (1885), the story of the malevolent severed head of a witchdoctor. Haggard's next novel was the immortal *King Solomon's Mines* (1885), which introduces the stalwart hero Allan Quatermain. Quatermain reappears in several sequels, many of them fantastic in nature. Among them are *The Ancient Allan* (1919), in which he relives a former life in Babylon; *Heu-Heu* or *The Monster* (1923); *Allan and the Ice Gods* (1927); and *She and Allan* (1920), in which Quatermain meets Ayesha, the supernatural heroine of several Haggard novels. Other of Haggard's strapping good genre tales include *People of the Mist* (1894) about a forgotten civilization ruled by a monster; the Viking epic *Eric Brighteyes* (1891); the Mayan fantasy *The Heart of the World* (1895); *Stella Fregelius* (1903) a tale of Destiny; *Red Eve* about a mystical world; and the Atlantean saga *When the World Shook* (1919). Haggard died in 1925. see: **Ayesha.**

Hags [O] Ugly old women who dabble in the supernatural. There are actually three kinds of hags. The most common is the witch hag, the crone who gives herself over to the devil in exchange for mystic powers and a flock of familiars. Then there is the occult hag, the wailing ghosts of shriveled women or demons like the murderous Black Annis. Finally, there are giantess hags, enormous women with twisted features and a sadistic bent, or in some cases cruel nature goddesses. Although hags exist in civilization's oldest lore, the word itself did not appear until the sixteenth century. At that time, the term *Hagge* was coined to describe "a succubus who sits on a man's stomach and gives him nightmares." see: **Black Annis; Incubus.**

Hal [MP] The supercomputer created by author Arthur C. Clarke and director Stanley Kubrick for their 1968 motion picture *2001: A Space Odys-*

sey. HAL stands for *H*euristically Programmed *AL*gorithmic Computer," and the *2001* superbrain is technically a HAL 9000 model, Production Number Three. It became operational at the HAL plant in Urbana, Illinois, on January 12, 1997. Able to speak and mimic most of the functions of the human brain, it is placed on board the spaceship *Discovery* responsible for most of the vessel's functions. Unfortunately, en route to Jupiter, HAL begins to doubt the competence of its human comrades, slays four of them, and has to have its capacity for independent thought shut down by the fifth. As its free will saps away, HAL regresses to its childhood and sings the song "Daisy." In the film, "Daisy" as well as HAL's other dialogue was spoken by actor Douglas Rain. see: **Discovery, The.**

Half-Chick [FT] The son of a black hen and protagonist in a very old Spanish fairy tale. Called Medio Pollito—Half-Chick—because he has only one leg, one wing, one eye, half a head, and half a beak, he is, however, an aggressive creature. Leaving behind what he dubs a "dull farmyard, with nothing but a dreary maize field to look at," he goes to Madrid. On the way he proves himself to be as selfish as he is headstrong; he refuses to clear a congested river of weeds, ignores a fire's request to feed it, and will not help wind untangle itself from the branches of a chestnut tree. Reaching Madrid, Medio is captured by the king's cook and placed in a scalding broth. Half-Chick pleads for the water not to wet it and the fire not to burn, but is denied. However, the chef has never boiled half a chicken before and accidentally overcooks Half-Chick. Medio is tossed out the window where the wind captures the charred poulet and places it atop a church steeple. It remains there still, the world's first and oldest weather vane.

Halloween [F] Also known as All Hallow's Eve and Hallowe'en, this is the night before November 1, All Hallow's Day. In the year 609, Pope Boniface IV dedicated the Pantheon in Rome to all of Christendom's saints and martyrs. The ritual was marked with sacred rites and a great feast which was thereafter celebrated annually as All Saint's Day. The time of year was not casually chosen; peoples of this era, such as the Celts, traditionally lit fires to convince the summer sun to stay and chase away the autumn chill. The church was carefully depaganizing an ancient custom. In medieval England, November 1 came to be known as All Hallow's Day and Hallowmas, a time to honor the holy. However October 31, All Hallow's Eve, is quite the contrary. On that night Satan and his minions walk the earth, making a last bid for souls prior to the sanctifying dawn of the following day. Attending the Devil are sundry demons and goblins who will forgo pulling nasty little tricks if people leave a treat outside their door—hence the modern-day custom of trick-or-treat. All Hallow's Day is also a popular time for Sabbats, an ultimate affront to God. see: **Sabbat.**

Halo Fish [TV] An alien fish seen in the animated "Star Trek" episode "The Terratin Incident." Somewhat resembling an angelfish, the Halo Fish is normally surrounded by a glowing band of color. However, if their element is ever infused with foreign material, or if there is some radical fluctuation in the environment, the halo will fade. When stasis is restored, the glow will return. The Halo Fish live on the world Terra Ten, the only planet circling the star Cepheus. see: **Enterprise, U.S.S.**

Hameh [F] In Arabian folklore, a bird which rises from the blood of a person who has been murdered. The Hameh flies about the site of the crime

Hameh

screaming "Give me a drink! Give me a drink!" The bird will not rest until it has drunk deeply of the killer's blood. When this has come to pass, the Hameh flies to the land of the dead where it informs the victim that his or her death has been avenged.

Hansel and Gretel [FT] The children of a poor woodcutter, Hansel and Gretel are led deep into the forest where their wicked stepmother hopes they will become lost and die. But the canny Hans had pocketed a loaf of bread, and marks the route by dropping crumbs. Disastrously, the idea backfires when birds eat Hans' trail. The children wander through the woods until they come to a house "built of bread and roofed with cakes, with windows of transparent sugar." Famished, they begin to eat the scrumptious house—though they are

stopped, before too long, by an old witch. She nabs the children and, as she locks Hansel behind a grating in the stable, admits to Gretel that she built the house to entrap boys and girls. They are the only food the weak-eyed crone will eat.

When it comes time to eat Hansel, the hag orders Gretel to crawl in the oven and see if it's hot enough. Realizing that she will be roasted if she does, the girl asks the witch to show her how it's done. When the old woman pokes her head into the oven, Gretel shoves her in and slams the door. Snooping about the house, the youngsters find a cache of jewels. They bring these to their kindly father, whose wife has died while the children were away (some versions of the fairy tale make her the witch as well as the woodcutter's wife).

Hanuman [M] A magical monkey general in Hindu mythology. The son of Vayu, the god of wind and air, Hanuman begins his career as a military strategist for Sugriva, King of the Monkeys. Subsequently, he becomes an aide to the demigod Rama. His most notable contribution in this capacity occurs when Rama's wife, Sita, is kidnapped by the evil Ravana. Hanuman spies on her captors and causes mischief within their city, such as ripping up trees and damaging property. The ape is finally caught, oily rags are tied to his tail, and the saturated cloth is touched with fire. But Hanuman has a surprise for Ravana. Growing to the size of a giant he hurries to the sea, setting the city aflame during his sprint. In another escapade, Hanuman helps Rama build a causeway to Ceylon (Sri Lanka) for an invasion. To this day Hanuman is an important Hindu deity. see: **Ravana.**

Haokah

Hanuman

Haokah [M] The rather backward god of thunder in the mythology of the Sioux Indians. A giant, Haokah laughs when he is sad, cries when he is happy, has a face the two sides of which do not match in color, thinks that hot is cold and cold is hot, and so on. Still, he manages to perform his chores with remarkable efficiency, using wind as a drumstick to produce his thunder. Haokah has a pair of huge horns on his head and wears a forked headdress which represents lightning.

Harlequin [F] A stock character in Italian comedy, a sprite whose fate is to dance through life. Invisible to all but his lover, the faithful Columbine, Harlequin spends most of his time trying to protect her from the advances of the knavish Clown. Other members of the repertory—whose cast remains the same, although each troupe creates its own plots—are Columbine's father, Pantaloon, and the boastful Scaramouche. With his roots in Italian hobgoblins, Harlequin is usually played as a graceful, witty character. His traditional accoutrements are a mask, diamond-patterned tights, a wooden sword, and a magic wand.

Harpy [M] In Greek mythology, a winged creature who is half-woman and half-vulture. Parented by the oceanid Electra and the sea god Thaumas, a son of Gaea, the three harpies represent the fury and might of storms. By name they are Aello (Storm), Podarge (Swiftfoot), and Ocypete (Swiftflyer), and everything they touch becomes polluted with a foul odor. The brass-clawed, pale-faced harpies are especially infamous for their tormenting of the blind seer Phineus. At Zeus' instructions they punished his misuse of his abilities by snatching every morsel of food that was placed on his table. Phineus was finally freed from his misery when Jason drove off the harpies in exchange for directions to the Symplegades. This dramatic encounter is recounted in Ray Harryhausen's 1963 film *Jason and the Argonauts*. Actually, anyone can cause a harpy to flee merely by banging a brass instrument. see: **Harryhausen, Ray; Jason.**

Harryhausen, Ray [MP] A special effects artist who specializes in *stop-motion photography*—"the frame-by-frame animation of three dimensional models." Born in Los Angeles in 1920, Harryhausen began experimenting with homemade monster models after seeing the most famous stop-motion performer of them all, *King Kong* (1933). After taking classes in drawing and sculpting, and producing a few educationally-distributed fairy tale short subjects, Harryhausen landed an apprenticeship with O'Brien. Their first movie together was *Mighty Joe Young* (1949), after which Harryhausen went off on his own. He has since produced a steady stream of classic fantasy and science fiction features: *The Beast from Twenty Thousand Fathoms* (1953), *It Came from Beneath the Sea* (1955), *Earth vs. the Flying Saucers* (1956), *Twenty Million Miles to Earth* (1957), *The Seventh Voyage of Sinbad* (1958), *The Three Worlds of Gulliver* (1959), *Mysterious Island* (1961), *Jason and the Argonauts* (1963), *First Men in the Moon* (1965),

One Million Years B.C. (1966), *The Valley of Gwangi* (1969), *The Golden Voyage of Sinbad* (1973), *Sinbad and the Eye of the Tiger* (1977), and *Clash of the Titans* (1981). In 1956, he and O'Brien collaborated on the dinosaur segment of the documentary film *Animal World*. Harryhausen lives in London with his wife, Diana, and daughter, Vanessa. He is the author of a career memoir entitled *Film Fantasy Scrapbook*. see: **Gulliver, Lemuel; Gwangi; Jason; Moon Calf; Nemo, Captain; O'Brien, Willis; Perseus; Rhedosaur; Selenite; Sinbad; Wells, H. G.; Ymir; Young, Mighty Joe.**

Harvey [L] A phouka featured in the 1943 play *Harvey* (originally titled *The White Rabbit*) written by Mary Coyle Chase (1907–   ). A six-foot-tall invisible white rabbit with magical powers, Harvey is the best friend of Elwood P. Dowd. The eccentric Dowd realizes that by speaking to the rabbit in public he subjects himself to derision. However, that's not his primary concern. As he says in the play, he worries that "For years I've known what my family thinks of Harvey. But I've often wondered what Harvey's family thinks of me." Most of what he does is intended to endear the rabbit. The role of Elwood P. Dowd was created by Frank Fay in the play's 1944 debut, and was enacted by James Stewart in the 1950 film *Harvey*. see: **Phouka.**

Hathor [M] Egyptian mythology's goddess of the sky. Possessing the body of a woman and the head of a cow, she is both the mother, daughter, and wife of Ra. Also known as the Lady of the Sycamore and Athor, she once helped Ra destroy a failed early version of humankind and became so involved in her task that she ended up chin-deep in blood. Wearing the sun's disk between her horns, Hathor doubles as Egypt's goddess of love and beauty. see: **Ra.**

Hatter, The [L] Also familiarly known as the Mad Hatter, a particularly zany character in *Alice in Wonderland* (1865). Alice first meets the check-suited Hatter with the top-hat and bow-tie at a tea party also attended by the Dormouse and the March Hare. The gathering is being held around a table arranged outside the Hare's home—a place with chimneys shaped like rabbit ears and a roof thatched with fur. As soon as Alice arrives, the Hatter begins to criticize her. He be-littles her command of the English language and her appearance, poses riddles which frustrate the girl be-cause they have no answers ("Why is a raven like a writing-desk?"), and sings inane ditties which he perceives as brilliant ("Twinkle, twinkle little bat! How I wonder what you're at! Up above the world you fly, like a tea-tray in the sky."). The Hatter and his friends are perpetually celebrating tea-time, and as Alice leaves after bearing a storm of insults, the Hatter and the Hare are busy trying to stuff the poor Dormouse into a teapot.

The Hatter reappears later in the novel as a witness at the tart-stealing trial of the Knave of Hearts. see: **Alice; Queen of Hearts.**

Havatoo [L] A city-state on the planet Amtor—the natives' name for Venus—in Edgar Rice Burroughs' 1933 novel *Lost on Venus*. A satire on the notion of a utopian society, Hava-too is governed by a council which rates the talents of each individual and assigns that person an appropriate profession. How well or how poorly people perform their duties deter-mines how long they live: citizens who fall short of their potential are not given any immortality serum when a new dosage is required. The problem with this society, as Bur-roughs points out, is that objectivity and intellectual capability may keep Havatoo functioning smoothly—but

without emotional flexibility, it is a shallow triumph. see: **Burroughs, Edgar Rice; Napier, Carson.**

Havoc, Rex [C] A monster-fighting comic book hero featured in *1984* magazine. Created by writer Jim Stenstrum in 1978, Rex is the leader of the Ass-Kickers of the Fantastic ("We haul ours to kick theirs"), a group composed of the scholarly Major Lars Wurlitzer, the buxom lass Bruno, and the mechanic Springer. They travel anywhere to destroy monsters from Sebastian, King of the Vampires to the Spud from Outer Space to Ayesha. Ex-tremely powerful, Rex is nonetheless something of a dullard. As Wurlitzer explains it, the brawny commander "was ambushed at a miniature golf course by a number of monsters pos-ing as traveling pros, bashing Rex's head in with their putters and heavier woods. The doctors managed to save Rex's life, but not before most of his intelligence leaked away, leaving him with the I.Q. roughly that of a sno-cone." The Ass-Kickers are headquar-tered in downtown Tarzana, Califor-nia. see: **Ayesha; DuBay, William.**

Hawkman [C] A comic book character created in 1940 by writer Gardner Fox and artist Dennis Neville. As orig-inally conceived, Hawkman was Carter Hall, a reincarnation of the Egyptian Prince Khufu. Able to fly thanks to an antigravity belt, Hall had an aide named Hawkgirl, could com-municate with birds, and waged bat-tle against crime using such ancient weapons as crossbows, spears, and axes. With the early 1960s comic book science fiction boom, Hawkman un-derwent some drastic changes. Al-though the name Carter Hall had been retained, he was now a police of-ficer from the planet Thanagar. Known as Katar on his home world, Hawkman comes to earth and accepts a post as curator of the Midway City Museum. With a crime fighting lab secreted in his orbiting spaceship, and the Hawkman costume—actually, his Thanagarian police uniform—tucked inside a medallion, Carter uses his power of flight to help right our world's many wrongs. Assisting him in this struggle is his wife, Shiera, otherwise known as Hawkgirl.

Hawthorne, Nathaniel [L] A noted American fantasy author. Born in Salem, Massachusetts i) 1804, the son of a sea captain, Hawthorne spent much of his sickly youth reading. A graduate of Bowdoin College in Maine, he worked in a Boston custom house during which time he began to write. Among his most notable works are *Young Goodman Brown* (1835), a Gothic tale of devil worship; the terror tome *Twice-Told Tales* (1937); and *House of the Seven Gables* (1851), a story about sin and corruption. Hawthorne married Sophia Peabody in 1842; he died in 1864.

Headless Horseman [L] The antagonist in *The Legend of Sleepy Hollow*, an occult tale written in 1819 by Washington Irving (1783–1859). Described by the author as, "the ghost of a Hessian trooper whose head had been carried away by a cannonball in some nameless battle during the Revolutionary War," the spectre gallops nightly from a graveyard in Tarrytown, New York, searching for his missing head. In its absence, the black-cloaked ghost carries a flaming pumpkin which he tosses at anyone who crosses his path. The Hessian's forays are limited to the periphery of the graveyard in which he is buried, and he is free to roam the earth only between midnight and dawn. Although protagonist Ichabod Crane is slain by a headless horseman, author Irving does not say whether it is *the* Headless Horseman or Crane's foe Brom Bones masquerading as the nocturnal rider. see: **Irving, Washington.**

Hecate [M] The Greek goddess of witchcraft. The daughter of Asteria and Perses, the son of Perseus, she is known as the triple deity; in addition to the occult, she is goddess of the underworld and of crossroads. Hecate has three faces and is always seen bearing torches and traveling in the company of baying dogs. In her honor, the dragons who tug night's dark shroud across the sky are known as Hecate's Team.

Hecatoncheires [M] Giants with 100 hands and 50 heads in Greek mythology. The sons of Uranus and Gaea, there were three Hecatoncheires: Briareus the Strong, Cottus the Striker, and Gyes (also Gyges) the Crippler. So horrified was Uranus by these gruesome creatures he'd helped to create that he tried to stuff them back into their mother's womb. Failing at that, he threw them and their equally grosteque brothers, the cyclopes, down to Tartarus. This action so outraged Gaea that she helped another of their sons, Cronus (one of the Titans) to slay his father. see: **Cronus; Cyclopes; Gaea; Uranus.**

Hedley Kow [F] A bogie which originated in Hedley, Northumberland, England. Basically a teasing sprite,

Headless Horseman

the Hedley Kow can assume any shape it wishes, from a beautiful maiden to a bale of hay. In this form it plays practical jokes: as the maiden it will lead a lusty lad astray; as hay or straw it will make itself too heavy to be lifted; and so forth. But whatever its guise, the Hedley Kow always brays with laughter when its ruse has been effective. see: **Boogeyman.**

Hel [M] The Norse goddess of the dead, the daughter of Loki and the giantess Angurboda and the sister of the giant wolf, Fenrir. Half black and half blue, Hel feeds on the brains and bone marrow of mortals. With Care her lowly bed, Hunger her dish, and Starvation her knife, she is attended by Delay and Sloth. Indeed, Hel is so corrupt and undesirable that, at birth, the gods banished her to Niflheim, the underworld. There she became queen of the nine worlds, where the dead are segregated according to various criteria. Some myths say that all the dead went to Hel, save those who had died in battle; other tales have her claiming all, including warriors. Located directly beneath the roots of the sacred world-tree Yggdrasil, Hel's domain is surrounded by the mighty river Gioll. It is so far from Asgard, the home of the gods, that Odin's eight-legged horse Sleipnir requires nine days and nights to reach it. see: **Asgard; Fenrir; Loki; Odin; Valhalla.**

Helios [M] The Greek god of the sun. Born to the sea god Hyperion and his wife, Thea, Helios' sisters are the moon goddess, Selene, and the dawn goddess, Eos. Riding through the heavens in a gold chariot drawn by four fire-breathing white horses, Helios rises from Eastern Oceanus every morning and settles into its western reaches each night. The color white is sacred to him, and he can both see and hear everything. Helios is particularly proud of his seven flocks of sheep and seven herds of oxen, fifty animals in each flock, which he gazes upon during his daily course. If any are ever found to be missing, the god becomes angry and the day grows dark. Sharing many traits with Apollo—some legends consider them one and the same—Helios is the father, by the ocean nymph Perseis, of King Aeëtes of Colchis; of Pasiphae, the wife of King Minos of Crete; and of the sorceress Circe. By Clymene, another ocean nymph, he sired Phaëton. Not as promiscuous as the other gods, Helios has actually turned lovers away. One, named Clytie, pined away until she became a flower—the *heliotrope,* which means "toward the sun." Helios' Roman counterpart is Sol. see: **Apollo; Circe; Minotaur; Nymph.**

Hell [O] The underworld, generally hot and uncomfortable. In the lore of Ancient Greece this grim place is surrounded by four rivers: Acheron, the River of Woe across which Charon ferries all incoming spirits; Styx, by which the gods swear mighty oaths; Phlegethon, the River of Fire; and Cocytus, the River of Lamentations. Once a soul has reached the underworld and been admitted by the guard dog Cerberus, it arrives in Erebus, a check-in point. Here, the new arrivals are judged by Minos, Aeacus, and Rhadamanthus and sent on to Tartarus, a dark realm of pain and fire, or to a place of light and joy known as the Elysian Fields.

In Egypt, souls endure a similar evaluation, going to the Judgment Hall of the Dead where they stand before Osiris while Horus and Anubis weigh their hearts on a Scale of Truth, Thoth noting the results. If an individual led a virtuous life, his or her soul is allowed to pass with Osiris' blessing. If not, the spirit is eaten by a monster known as the Devourer.

Different from the underworlds of Greece and Egypt is the Christian

Hell. Also known as Purgatory, the Inferno, and the Pit, it is the fiery inside of the earth ruled by the fallen angel Satan. It is not divided into regions of reward and punishment: it is *all* unpleasant, good spirits allegedly ascending to Heaven, the home of God. This Hell has been immortalized in numerous works, the most descriptive of which is *Paradise Lost* by John Milton (1608–1674). Among the phrases he uses to describe Satan's domain in this 1665 poem are, "bottomless perdition," "A dungeon horrible, on all sides round as one great Furnace flam'd, yet from those flames no light," and "A Fiery Deluge, fed with ever-burning Sulphur unconsum'd."

Less well known, but perhaps the least pleasant of all, is the hell of Hebrew lore. It consists of seven divisions, one below the other. Each has seven subdivisions, each subdivision consisting of seven rivers of fire and seven of hail, as well as 7,000 caves with 7,000 crevices in each, and 7,000 scorpions in each fissure. These delights are supervised by 90,000 angels of destruction. Rivers of poison which cause mortals to burst thread throughout the seven levels. see: **Cerberus; Devil; Devourer; Dis; Hades; Hel; Osiris; Satan; Yen-lo-Wang.**

Hellstrom, Nils [MP] A scientist interested in both insects and world conquest. In the 1971 semidocumentary film *The Hellstrom Chronicle*, the fictitious Dr. Nils Hellstrom—played by Lawrence Pressman—explains how bugs are slowly taking over our planet. However, in Frank Herbert's 1972 novel *Hellstrom's Hive*, a sequel to the film, the scientist plans to beat them to it. Using the money he made from the movie, Hellstrom sets up a farm in Oregon where he breeds creatures which outwardly resemble humans but are really insects. They are able to see in the dark, carry ten times their weight, and regenerate lost limbs. Although the novel ends

John Henry   Hell

with Hellstrom's megalomaniacal plot stalemated, the implied follow-up novel has not yet materialized.

Henry, John [F] An American folk hero. The historical John Henry was a black man who laid tracks on the Chesapeake and Ohio Railroad in West Virginia. A strong, proud man, he was ideal fodder for folklorists. The story they fabricated has him weighing forty-four pounds at birth, learning to sing songs that same day, and leaving home before midnight. However, his most remarkable accomplishment is matching his steel-driving skills against those of a steam engine. The contest takes place at Big Bend Tunnel, and is won by Henry—although the strain causes his heart to burst. Records from this period suggest that the real John Henry may in fact have met and beat a mechanical drill circa 1870. On the screen, the legend is best told by George Pal in his animated, Oscar-nominated 1946 short subject *John Henry and the Inky Poo*. In it, Henry is portrayed as being twelve feet tall. His voice is provided by the brilliant actor Rex Ingram. see: **Pal, George.**

Hephaestus[M] The Greek god of fire, known as Vulcan and Mulciber to the Romans. The son of Zeus and Hera, Hephaestus did not have an easy childhood. Born ugly and lame, with his left leg shorter than his right, he was thrown from Olympus by his mother, who was ashamed of him. Landing in the Ocean, the god was cared for over a nine-year period by the nymphs Eurynome and Thetis. In the subsea cave which served as his home, Hephaestus became quite an artisan, making many fine pieces. Among these was a golden throne for his mother—a very special throne that bound its occupant with invisible chains. These could only be unlocked by Hephaestus. Inducing his mother to sit, the fire god agreed to let her go only if Zeus recalled him to Olympus. He did, immediately. However, no sooner had the deity returned than he had the bad luck to side against his father in an argument. Zeus heaved him from the heavens once again and, after falling for a full day, Hephaestus landed on the Island of Lemnōs in the Aegean Sea.

An eventual reconciliation made Hephaestus the chief artist and builder for the gods. From his large workshop on Mt. Olympus, he built palaces for all his fellow deities, forged the thunder-creating shield of Zeus, made the Fire Breathing Bulls for King Aeëtes, molded Pandora from clay, and made weapons for the gods.

Hephaestus had three wives: Charis, the Grace Aglaia, and the goddess Aphrodite. Among his children are the serpent Erechtheus; the rowdy giants Cacus and Caeculus; and Erichthonius, the inventor of the four-horse chariot. see: **Aphrodite; Fire-Breathing Bulls; Graces; Hera; Pandora; Zeus.**

Hera [M] The queen of the Greek gods and sister-wife of Zeus. Known as Juno to the Romans, Hera is the daughter of Cronus and Rhea and was born on the Ionian island of Samos. Possessing most of the same powers as her husband, she often uses them to spy on Zeus' many lovers. Nonetheless, she and Zeus have been together often enough to parent Hephaestus; Ares; the goddess of youth, Hebe; and the goddess of childbirth, Eileithya (also known as Ilithyia). Hera's personal aides are the Hours, the beautiful deities who make sure that the seasons arrive on-schedule. She is also attended by the virgin goddess of the rainbow Iris, the female counterpart of Hermes. Hera was marvelously portrayed on-screen by actress Honor Blackman in the 1963 film *Jason and the Argonauts.* see: **Ares; Cronus; Hephaestus; Hercules; Zeus.**

Hercules [M] A powerful demigod known familiarly by his Roman name of Hercules, although he is Heracles to the Greeks. Hercules is the son of

Hercules

Zeus and the mortal woman Alcmene. The king of the gods comes to Alcmene in the guise of her husband, causing her to have twins: Hercules by Zeus, and his brother Iphicles by Amphitryon. The demigod's childhood is anything but normal. Hera, angered by her husband's infidelity, sends a pair of snakes to kill the babies. But Hercules strangles the snakes as they squirm into his crib. Exhibiting extraordinary mental abilities—not to mention great strength —Hercules is tutored by the finest scholars and athletes in the world, including the centaur Chiron. He is clearly destined for greatness.

Hercules' first heroic deed is the slaying of the vicious lion of Cithaeron, whose skin thereafter serves as the demigod's cloak, its mouth his helmet. Settling in Thebes, the city of his birth, Hercules helps King Creon defeat the invading army of King Erginus of Orchomenus. In return, Creon gives Hercules his daughter Megara in marriage. Meanwhile, the gods also shower the hero with gifts. Apollo gives him a powerful bow and arrow, Hermes a sword, Hephaestus a bronze club and gold suit of armor, and Athena a *pelpus*—"a loose outer-garment on which a tapestry of heroic vistas has been stitched." But Hera, still filled with hate, visits a fit of madness on Hercules, during which he mistakes his three children and his brother's two children for wild beasts and slays them accordingly. Sick over the incident, Hercules consults the Oracle at Delphi. It tells him that absolution can come only after great suffering. Accordingly, Hercules is instructed to report to the district of Argolis and serve his slight but epically cruel cousin Eurystehus for twelve years.

The oracle's choice of Eurystheus is a spiteful one. Due to Hera's intervention, this grandson of Perseus had been born only a few hours before Hercules, thereby giving to him the throne of the mighty city of Mycenae. There is no love lost between Hercules and the king. And Eurystheus does indeed come up with twelve years of projects worthy of a demigod. They are to kill, capture, clean, or steal the Nemean Lion, the Learnean Hydra, the Erymanthian Boar, the Stynphalian Birds, the Keryneian Hind (also known as the Arcadian Stag), the Augeian Stables, the Cretan Bull, the Wild Mares of Diomedes, the Girdle of Hippolyta, the Cattle of Geryon, the Golden Apples of the Hesperides, and Hades' dog Cerberus.

Accomplishing these dozen tasks, Hercules returns to Thebes. Giving Megara to his nephew Iolaus, the hero presses on to other adventures. One of these, a battle with the river god Achelous, introduces the hero to his second wife, Deianeira, the princess of Aetolia. It is a fateful meeting. On their honeymoon, the couple crosses the river Evenus, the lady riding the back of the ferrycentaur Nessus. The proximity of Deianeira arouses the man-horse and, when he tries to rape his passenger, Hercules drives an arrow through his heart. As Nessus lays dying, he tells Deianeira that his blood is actually a potion which will ensure a man's love forever. The naive Deianeira douses Hercules' tunic with the centaur's blood and, shortly thereafter, her husband's skin begins to blister and fall off in massive chunks. Bellowing in pain, Hercules has his body carried to Mt. Etna and burned.

Ascending to Olympus, Hercules becomes an immortal and marries Hera's daughter, Hebe. The couple has two children: Alexiares, who turns away curses, and Aniketos the Unconquerable. As for Deianeira, plagued by guilt, she hangs herself.

On the screen, Hercules has been most notably portrayed by Steve Reeves in *Hercules* (1957) and *Hercules Unchained* (1959) and by Nigel Green in *Jason and the Argonauts* (1963). see: **Amazons; Antaeus; Au-**

geian Stables; Centaur; Cerberus; Chiron; Cretan Bull; Erymanthian Boar; Geryon; Hera; Hesperides; Hydra; Keryneian Hind; Nemean Lion; Reeves, Steve; Scott, Gordon; Stynphalian Birds; Mares of Diomedes; Zeus.

Hermes [M] The messenger of the Greek gods. The son of Zeus and the naiad Maia—the eldest daughter of Atlas—Hermes is also the god of eloquence and cunning. During his first day of life he invented the lyre from a tortoise shell; his other inventions include numbers, the alphabet, astronomy, weights and measures, and the concept of sacrifices—which made him a patron of shepherds. A skillful thief, Hermes at one time or another steals fifty of Apollo's oxen, Hephaestus' tools, Poseidon's trident, Ares' sword, and even the scepter of Zeus. Bold and good with his hands, it is Hermes who is assigned the task of chaining Prometheus to Mt. Caucasus.

Unlike most of the gods, Hermes' dress is quite distinctive. He always wears sandals whose "wings" or *talaria* allow him to fly as swiftly as the wind—although some accounts have the talaria fastened directly to his ankles. He also sports "a brimmed bowl-hat" called a *petasus* with wings on its side, and carries a "golden rod" or *caduceus* given to him by Apollo in exchange for the lyre. Hermes later turns the staff over to Aesculapius, the god of medicine.

By his fellow god Aphrodite, Hermes is the father of Hermaphrodite, a son who is the manifestation of all that is both masculine and feminine. By Chione, the daughter of Daedalion, he parented Autolycus, the king of thieves. Hermes' Roman counterpart is Mercury. see: **Apollo; Ares; Argos; Hephaestus; Poseidon; Zeus.**

Herne [O] A ghost whose principal haunt is the park at Windsor Castle in Berkshire, England. A woodcutter—or hunter, according to the specific legend—Herne worked in the service of Richard II. After his death he began appearing in deerskin garb, wearing a helmet made from the skull of a stag, and riding a horse which breathes flame. Running alongside him are dogs known as Cain's Pack, whose presence has won Herne the nickname, Master of the Wild Hunt. The figure of Herne is thought by many to have been inspired by tales of the Norse god, Odin, and his fleet mount, Sleipnir. However, since stag was the main source of meat for this region's prehistoric inhabitants, and early religious rites consisted of people donning caps made of antlers, Herne's roots are doubtless here. see: **Odin.**

Herrmann, Bernard [MP] A composer specializing in fantasy film scores. Born in New York in 1911, Herrmann studied at the Julliard School of Music and later at New York University. Although his earliest work was for CBS radio, it was in film that Herrmann's career blossomed. Fame came with his flavorful score for Orson Welles' 1941 motion picture *Citizen Kane;* and it was followed with assignments on such Alfred Hitchcock films as *Vertigo* (1958) and *Psycho* (1960); Ray Harryhausen's *The Seventh Voyage of Sinbad* (1958), *The Three Worlds of Gulliver* (1959), *Mysterious Island* (1961), and *Jason and the Argonauts* (1963); and other such diverse fantasy and science fiction pictures as *The Day the Earth Stood Still* (1951), *Journey to the Centre of the Earth* (1959), and *Fahrenheit 451* (1966). Herrmann died in 1975, the day he completed recording the score for the gruesome film *Taxi Driver* (1976). Thrice married—first to Lucille Fletcher and then to Lucille Anderson—Herrmann is survived by his third wife, Norma, and daughters, Wendy and Taffy, from his first marriage. see: **Harryhausen, Ray.**

Hesperides [M] The daughters of Atlas and Hesperis in Greek mythology. The Hesperides own a garden on the Western edge of the world. Here they keep an orchard of golden apples, a wedding gift from Gaea to Hera. These apples are guarded by the 100-headed dragon Ladon—not that the great lizard has much to do. Because the golden fruit bestows immortality, it can only be picked by a god. Anyone else who tries will die. Knowing this, nasty Eurystheus makes procuring the apples the eleventh labor of Hercules—who, while a demigod, is not a full-blooded Olympian. The hero is aware of this, but his first problem is how to *find* the apples, not how to pluck them. Locating Nereus, the Old Man of the Sea, Hercules grabs him and holds tight while the water god changes to various shapes in an effort to escape. Finally, exhausted, he gives Hercules directions. En route, the son of Zeus stops in Libya to kill the wrestler Antaeus, liberate Prometheus, and finally have a chat with Atlas. The Titan, who has been condemned by Zeus to bear the heavens upon his back, offers to get the apples if Hercules will hold up the skies in the interim. Hercules accepts the exchange—but upon his return, Atlas decides not to take back his burden. Playing dumb, Hercules says that if he is to carry the weight of the heavens, he would like to do so in relative comfort. Atlas agrees to take the skies while Hercules pads his shoulders with his lion skin cloak. But no sooner does Atlas resume his post than Hercules gathers up the golden apples and departs. The hero presents the fruit to Eurystheus, who allows the beleaguered Greek to keep them. Not wishing to make further enemies among the gods, Hercules turns them over to Athena who replaces them in the garden of the Hesperides. see: **Antaeus; Atlas; Hercules; Prometheus.**

Hideous Sun Demon, The [MP] A movie monster of note. Featured in the 1959 film *The Hideous Sun Demon*, the creature is an atomic researcher—played by Robert Clarke—who is battered by radiation in a scientific mishap. Thereafter, whenever he is exposed to the sun's rays the scientist becomes a fanged, scale-encrusted beast. After terrorizing the countryside, the Hideous Sun Demon is cornered atop a large oil storage drum. Following a battle with police, the monster plunges several stories to his death. An interesting reversal of the werewolf theme. see: **Werewolf.**

Hob [O] A ghost seen at Whitby in Yorkshire, England. A dangerous specter, Hob causes cars to skid and alters roadsigns to mislead travelers. However, Hob is not the only restless spirit in Whitby. Among the several others is a coach driver who must recreate for eternity the accident which took his life, the plunging of his church-bound carriage from a cliff; a ghost who ambles aimlessly about with its head cradled in its arm; and the shrouded Lady Hilda, who haunts the abbey near the Whitby Church. see: **Goosey.**

Hobbit [L] Dwarfish denizens of Middle Earth. Created by author J. R. R. Tolkien for his many fantasy novels, hobbits are two to four feet tall, walk about shoeless on hairy feet, live in cozy burrows known as hobbit holes, and live to an average age of 100 years old. Provincial creatures, most hobbits live in that part of Middle Earth known as the Shire, although others dwell in Bree and less populous areas. There are three groups of hobbits: the Harfoots, the Stoors, and the Fallohides. All love to eat and draw their pleasure from the simple things in life. On the negative side, they do not trust the outside world and hate to be confused. see: **Bilbo Baggins; Frodo Baggins; One Ring; Tolkien, J. R. R.**

Homunculus [F] A miniature or artificial human being. As originally conceived, a homunculus was the microscopic but fully formed human thought to be contained inside a sperm cell. Short people or midgets were thus thought of as large homunculi rather than human beings. The sixteenth century alchemist Paracelsus refined that definition somewhat, stating that dwarfs are people and only an artifically created being can be considered a homunculus. He is alleged to have brought such beings to life. The current usage parallels Paracelsus' definition, the term *homunculus* meaning "any mannikin given · life." from the Golem of legend to the Frankenstein Monster of literature to the artifical lizard-bat seen in Ray Hattyhausen's 1973 film *The Golden Voyage of Sinbad.* see **Frankenstein Monster; Golem, Harryhausen, Ray; Paracelsus.**

Honey Swamp Monster [U] a skunklike ape who lives in Mississipps's Honey Island Swamp. Weighing 800 pounds, the two-legged, three-toed creature is seven feet tall, has a small head, no neck, broad shoulders, and wiry dark gray hair all over its body. Thought to be a humanoid which diverged from the main of the line in prehistory, the Honey Swamp Monster feeds on the quivering flesh of still-life animals, and has a screech which contains the volume of a scream with the ominous flavor of a snarl. Witnesses say that the pungent stench of the brute can be snelled up to a quarter-mile away.

Hooper [O] An eerie, clinging mist seen in Cornwall, England. Thought to be the spirit of a local man named Hooper, the cloud made hooting sounds during the day and rained sparks by night. The manifestation disappeared forever when a fisher and his son, curious about what was inside, took up clubs and entered. Neither the cloud nor the man nor boy were seen thereafter. Hooper is presumed to have been a benevolent ghost,

using its mist form to inconspicuously protect its home from evil.

Near Hooper's old haunt of Cowloe Rock there is another ghost, the spectral remains of the Irish Lady. Thrown in the water when her boat capsized, the young woman clung to the vessel and screamed for help. But no one could reach her in time and she drowned. Today, her spirit claws at rocks along the shore, recreating her last mortal moments on earth. see: **Ghost.**

Hopfrog [L] The dwarf jester in Edgar Allan Poe's short story "Hopfrog." Described as walking with "a sort of interjectional gait—something between a leap and a wriggle," Hopfrog

Hopfrog

has powerful arms and can climb almost anything. His best friend at court is the graceful Trippetta who, while "very little less dwarfish than himself," is extremely beautiful. Both were brought from a barbarous land to serve a king who is fond of practical joking. However, since so many of these jokes are worked at the dwarfs' expense, Hopfrog plots against the monarch. The jester's vengeance comes when he is asked to costume the king and his equally obnoxious ministers for a ball. Dressing them up as orangutangs, he makes the resemblance "so striking that the company of masqueraders will take you for real beasts."

At midnight on the evening of the masque, Hopfrog leads the king and his seven counselors into the great salon. The apes put on a good show, whooping and running and terrifying the partygoers. To "save" everyone from the wild beasts, Hopfrog binds them with a chain used to haul up the chandelier. When they are dangling thirty feet in the air, and everyone is beginning to realize that this was all an act, Hopfrog grabs a torch and shimmies down the links. Pretending to see who the apes really are, he sets them ablaze. Within moments they are "eight corpses . . . a fetid, blackened, hideous, and indistinguishable mass." Climbing through the skylight, Hopfrog escapes and neither he nor Trippetta is ever seen again. see: **Poe, Edgar Allan.**

Hopkins, Mathew [O] A notorious seventeenth century English witchfinder. A failure as a lawyer, Hopkins turned to hunting witches. Though he always claimed to observe his subjects personally before arresting them— watching them practice their craft and deal with familiars—most of his confessions were extracted under torture. Hopkins' manner was to go from town to town and charge twenty-five pounds to clear the village of witches.

Although his crusade enjoyed public support in its early years, Hopkins' handsome honorarium caused many to suspect the validity of his work. Chief among these doubters was priest John Gaule, who spoke against the witchfinder and caused his fall from favor in 1646. Hopkins died a year later, allegedly of tuberculosis. However, most contemporary writers seemed to feel that he was hacked to death by people whom his sadism had offended. The bloody career of Mathew Hopkins is vividly recounted in the 1968 motion picture *Witchfinder General* (also known as *The Conqueror Worm*) starring Vincent Price. see: **Familiars; Witch.**

Horla [L] The evil entity featured in the 1887 French short story "The Horla" by Guy De Maupassant (1850–1893). Described as "a malevolent force from an unknown dimension," the Horla slowly fills the tale's narrator with dread. It begins as a dream which grows to a "fiendish influence . . . sucking my life from between my lips." Oddly, when the protagonist leaves the chateau in which he lives, everything is all right. But when he returns, inanimate objects start to move on their own and the creature's presence becomes ever more palpable. The narrator comes to know it as not possessing "any clearly defined outlines, a sort of opaque transparency," one of a race of "invisible, though tangible beings, a species of vampire, which feed on life while it is asleep, and who, besides, drink water and milk without appearing to touch any other nourishment." In the end, the hero burns his home to the ground—vowing that if this does not kill the creature, "Then—I suppose I must kill myself!"

Horses of Power [F] Magnificent steeds of Russian legend. Described as broad of chest with eyes like fire and hooves of iron, the horses sleep underground, beside the graves of the *bogatirs*, "the

dead men who once tamed them."
Whenever Russia has need of their
valor and strength, the great horses
will thunder from the earth, wait for
their armored riders to rise, and then
sweep the earth clean of enemies of
the Czar. This is a very old folk tale.

Horta [TV] A silicon-based creature
seen in the "Star Trek" episode "The
Devil in the Dark." A native of the
planet Janus VI, the Horta is seven
feet long, three feet wide, and three
feet tall, and resembles an undulating
rock. Able to drill through the ground
with tremendous speed, it lives for
60,000 years, at which time every
member of the generation dies together. Played by James Prohaska in
the program, the Horta kills fifty-six
miners before Mr. Spock is able to establish mental contact with the being.
He learns that the Horta is actually a
peace-loving sort, slaughtering humans only because *they* have inadver-
tently been smashing its silicon nodule
eggs. Once an understanding has been
reached, the Horta helps the miners
with their work by burrowing swiftly
into the rock walls of the shafts. see:
Spock, Mr.

Horus [M] The falcon-headed Egyptian
god of light and, in later years, a judge
of the dead. The son of Osiris and his
sister-wife, Isis, Horus has a most unusual conception. When cruel Seth
tosses his mighty brother Osiris from
the sky, Isis becomes a bird and flies to
the ground where he lies broken.
Using her wings to force air up her
husband's nostrils, Isis resumes her
natural form and draws his seed from
his body. This becomes Horus. When
the new god is born, his mother hides
him so that she can visit a temple to
honor the dead Osiris. While she is
gone, Seth sends a scorpion to sting
Horus to death. When Isis returns and
finds the newborn dead, she beseeches
the sun to stand still and prays for
help from her fellow gods. Thoth, the
god of wisdom and a master magician,
brings spells to undo the evil deed
and, assisted by the fluid of life do-
nated by Ra, revives the young deity.
Waging war against Seth, Horus succeeds in winning back all that had
been stolen from his father. Later, he
joins Osiris in the Judgment Hall of
the Dead where his job is to weigh the
hearts of all new arrivals on the Scale
of Truth. see: **Devourer, The; Isis;
Osiris; Thoth.**

Host, The [O] Also known as Sluagh,
crowds of unforgiven dead in pre-me-
dieval Scotland. The Host are spirits
who drift above the earth from midnight until dawn, great clouds of them
dimming the light of God's majesty.
As this mass circles the globe, individual spirits break from the group to
visit the sites of their mortal sins. Although the wandering shades are not
permitted to enter heaven until they
have repented for their transgressions,
the Host members are usually so bitter that they become forces of pure
evil. They kill pets and livestock using
poison darts, and are constantly fighting among themselves. Some people
say that the morning dew is actually
their spilled blood. Only on stormy
nights do the Host refrain from vile
acts, taking refuge behind plant stalks
and other small foliage.

Many legends say that the lost souls
of the Host can enslave humans,
whom they drive to acts of violence.
These mortal victims are subsequently
abused and abandoned. Though the
spectres are practically invisible, they
can usually be seen on clear, cold
nights.

Houyhnhnms [L] Creatures discovered
by Lemuel Gulliver in 1711. Left by
mutineers on an unknown island, Gulliver finds a society of savage humans
known as Yahoos, and intelligent
horses called Houyhnhnms. He says of
the Yahoos, "Their heads and breasts
were covered with thick hair ... they
had beards like goats, and a long ridge
of hair down their backs and the fore-

parts of their legs and feet; but the rest of their bodies were bare (and) of a brown buff color." They did have one other patch of hair, located "about the anus; which, I presume, nature had placed there to defend them as they sat on the ground." The Yahoo females are smaller than the males, and all walk in springs and bounds. They serve the horses and feed on the meat of dogs and asses.

The Houyhnhnms are a cultured contrast. Gulliver is surprised to find their neighing "to be almost articulate," and is shocked by their dexterity: "The Houyhnhnms use the hollow part between the pastern and the hoof of their forefeet as we do our hands." The horses live in fine homes, subsist on oats boiled in milk, and live to an average of seventy to seventy-five years. Gulliver is able to learn their language within three months, and they are fascinated by his accounts of law, avarice, and other elements unknown to their society or persona. However, the Houyhnhnms do become quite indignant when they learn that in Gulliver's world, humans ride horses. . . .

Gulliver stays among the Houyhnhnms and Yahoos for three years, leaving their realm by canoe in 1714. Among the other animals he notes on the island are lyhannh or swallows, and birds of prey known as gnnayh. see: **Gulliver, Lemuel.**

Howard, Robert Ervin [L] A fantasy author best known for his stories about Conan the Barbarian. Born in 1906 in Peaster, Texas, the son of Jane Ervin Hester and Dr. Isaac Mordecai Howard, Robert E. Howard attended Howard Payne College and sold his first work to *Weird Tales* magazine. The story was "Spear and Fang" and it was published in July 1925. Subsequent issues of the magazine featured other Howard tales, the most popular being about the heroes Conan, Solomon Kane, and King Kull. Howard's

frequent pen name was Patrick Ervin; his favorite writer, Jack London. In 1936, when the author learned that his sickly mother would soon die, he took his own life. see: **Bran Mak Morn; Conan; Kane, Solomon; Kull, King; Weird Tales.**

Huitzilopochtli [M] One of the most important of the sixty major Aztec gods. The god of war, Huitzilopochtli wears a headdress of bird feathers and is armed with four spears and a shield. His idols were built of grain made pasty by adding children's blood, and were eaten during ceremonies held in his honor. Tribute to Huitzilopochtli was paid in the form of human sacrifice. The chief god to most Aztecs, Huitzilopochtli is also the god of lightning, in which form he is pictured as a huge snake.

Hulk, The Incredible [C/TV] A comic book character created by artist Jack Kirby and writer Stan Lee in 1962. The Hulk is a green-skinned brute, barely articulate, who possesses extraordinary physical strength. He was created when Dr. Bruce Banner rushed toward ground zero to save young Rick Jones from the explosive fury of a gamma bomb. Banner tossed Jones into a trench—but was himself bathed by radiation from the detonation of the weapon he had designed for the United States military. As a result, whenever Banner becomes angry his mutated metabolism turns him into the Incredible Hulk.

In the television series based on the comic book, the Hulk's alterego is David Bruce Banner and he is played by Bill Bixby. In a departure from the comic book, he first became the Hulk after being exposed to gamma rays while investigating the reason why some people exhibit great strength in moments of stress. The Hulk himself is played by six-foot five-inch Lou Ferrigno as a superstrong but inarticulate brute. A series of Hulk novels was published in 1979. see: **Lee, Stan; Kirby, Jack.**

Humpty Dumpty [FT] A character in the nursery rhymes of Mother Goose. Humpty Dumpty is pictured as an egg with arms and legs and a smiling face beaming from his shell. In its original form, his sad saga reads:

Humpty Dumpty sat on a wall.
Humpty Dumpty had a great fall.
All the King's horses
And all the King's men
Couldn't put Humpty Dumpty in his
    place again.

Beyond his tragic spill, Humpty Dumpty gained note as a character in Lewis Carroll's *Through the Looking Glass* (1871). In this sequel to *Alice in Wonderland*, Alice immediately recognizes the egg: "It can't be anybody else," says she. "I'm as certain of it as if his name were written all over his face!" She finds him sitting cross-legged on a wall, obviously having learned nothing from his nursery rhyme mishap. However, Dumpty is convinced that if he fell, the King's horses and men would now "pick me up again in a minute." The two begin a generally pointless conversation, sparked by such exchanges as "Why do you sit out here all alone?" to which he responds, "Because there's nobody with me." The only matter of worth to emerge from their talk is Dumpty's explanation of the poem "Jabberwocky." see: **Alice; Jabberwock; Mother Goose.**

Hyborian Age [L] A mythical epoch invented by Robert E. Howard for his Conan stories. The Hyborian Age embraces the world as it may have been 12,000 years ago, before the sinking of Atlantis. At that time, the Mediterranean Sea was dry land, western Africa lay beneath an ocean, and civilization was centered in the northwestern parts of Europe. These countries had been founded circa 15000 B.C. by barbarians from the far north and such places as Cimmeria, Asgard, Vanaheim, and Hyperborea. By name, these so-called Hyborian Nations were Aquilonia, the mightiest of them all; neighboring Nemedia; and Argos, Koth, Cornithia, and Brythunia. To the south lay the city-states of Shem, Punt, and Zembawei. To the east were the Hyrkanian Kingdoms and the inland Vilayet (now Caspian) Sea. see: **Cimmeria; Conan; Howard, Robert E.**

Hydra [M] A fanciful beast with many heads. The most famous such monster is the Lernean Hydra of the Hercules legend. The Greek hero's second task is to travel to Lernea with his nephew Iolaus and slay the nine-headed beast. The offspring of Typhon and Echidna, the hydra dwells in swampland and ventures forth to nab cattle and crops. Raised by Hera, it possesses a doglike body and an immortal middle head, is covered with scales, and has breath which is poisonous to mortals.

When Hercules and Iolaus find the creature's lair, they use flaming embers to force it out. Grabbing his mighty club when the monster emerges, Hercules begins to bat off the hydra's heads. But the muscled Theban is shocked to find that for each head he severs, *two* larger and uglier heads take its place. Thinking quickly, Iolaus uses a torch to cauterize the necks after every decapitation. Rendering the immortal head useless by burying it beneath a rock, Hercules dips his arrows in the hydra's blood to make them poisonous. Angry that her enemy has been victorious, Hera sends a giant crab to menace Hercules. The hero crushes it with ease.

On-screen, a seven-headed hydra was brought vividly to life as the guardian of the Golden Fleece in *Jason and the Argonauts* (1963). see: **Harryhausen, Ray; Hera; Hercules.**

Icarus [M] The son of Daedalus, the Greek architect who built a labyrinth on Crete to house the ferocious Minotaur. When Daedalus helps Theseus slay the man-bull, he earns the wrath of Crete's King Minos. The ruler has the builder and his son placed in the maze where they quickly become lost. Realizing that their only means of escape is to fly from the maze, the men don wings made of bird feathers and wax and launch themselves skyward.

Icarus

Unfortunately, Icarus glides too close to the sun. Its pounding heat melts the wax, his wings begin to molt, and he falls into the sea and drowns. His grieving father presses onward and lands safely in Sicily. see: **Minotaur; Theseus.**

Ichor [M] The divine bloodlike fluid which flows through the veins of the Greek gods. Ichor possesses many unique properties; it will not harbor disease, and when it is spilled it produces new life. In the film *Jason and the Argonauts* (1963), the ichor released from the body of Talos is pictured as red and steamy. How this magnificent fluid came to be a term in modern medicine, used to signify the liquid produced by ulcers, is quite a puzzle! see: **Olympus; Talos.**

Id, Monster from the [MP] A two-legged, invisible, lionlike land creature with arboreal claws seen in the 1956 motion picture *Forbidden Planet*. The monster from the Id dwells on the planet Altair Four. It is created by the subconscious hatreds of earthman Morbius (Walter Pidgeon) and given substance through thought-to-matter machinery built by a long dead race of natives known as the Krel. Indeed, it was the manifestation of their own forgotten lusts and anger which had destroyed the Krel in a single night. Morbius' monster first emerges when the colonization party of which he is a member elects to leave Altair Four for earth. Everyone except the linguist and his wife is torn to pieces. The beast returns when a relief ship tries to force Morbius to travel back to earth. The monster is seen only briefly as it attacks the space vessel, and is outlined by the beams of a protective electrical barrier. It is destroyed when Morbius' young daughter Altaira (Anne Francis) falls in love with Commander Adams (Leslie Nielsen) of the earth ship. For her sake, her tortured father confronts and renounces his Id Monster, dying in the process.

Imp [O] A small demon, devil, or evil spirit. Frequently identified with familiars or goblins, imps adopt various animal or monstrous shapes to serve witches and other dabblers in the dark arts. Their job is to work menial chores for a witch or haunt and nag her enemies. The imp's reward is to be allowed to suckle on a second set of nipples possessed by female students of the occult. The term imp originally meant a sprout, and imps are generally thought to be offshoots of Satan. see: **Familiars; Goblins; Witches.**

Incubus [O] A male devil who indulges in sexual intercourse with human females. (Its female counterpart is a *succubus.*) An incubus can alter its shape, move through walls, and dominate whomever it has elected to seduce. Their task is to both lure women into the service of Satan and produce evil or misshapen offspring. This latter is worked when the incubus assumes the form of a succubus, makes love to a male, stores his semen, and then pumps this into a chosen female. Incubi also accomplish this end by causing and gathering nocturnal emissions.

Incubus

The incubus often gains his victim's confidence by taking the guise of a trusted figure, such as a relative or member of the clergy. It is said that women who have been to bed with one of these devils can never again be satisfied by a mortal male. Common lore also reports that there are more incubi than succubi. And why not? According to the Medieval Church, women are far more profligate than men. Be that as it may, both forms of hell-spawned lover are thought to have been created by the church to cover those of its priests or congregation who were tricked into having intercourse. see: **Devil.**

Inferior Five, The [C] Comic book characters created in 1966 by writer E. Nelson Bridwell and artist Joe Orlando. Misfit crimefighters, the Inferior Five is composed of cartoonist Myron Victor, who dons a jester's suit to become the group's leader Merryman; diner-owner Herman Cramer, alias the green-clad Blimb, a hero who can fly as long as there's a tailwind; model Athena Tremor whose Amazonian powers are put to good use when she dons rabbit ears and a red leotard to become Dumb Bunny; the superstrong Awkwardman, alterego of beachcomber Leander Brent; and photographer William King, otherwise known as the unerring archer White Feather. Prowling the streets of Megalopolis, the Inferior Five stays in touch with the police and one another via the Lukewarm Line. Among the bold brigade's many foes are Doc Gruesome, the Silver Sorceress, and the Speed Demon.

Inner Sanctum [E] A half-hour mystery and horror radio program which premiered in January 1941 under the name "The Squeaking Door." The show's sinister and popular host was Raymond Edward Johnson—Raymond for short—who offered ghastly prologues and epilogues to the already grim goings-on. The broadcast became particularly well known for the creaking door sound effects which opened each program and led the listener into Raymond's domain. "Inner Sanctum" was the most successful show of its kind, a genre which included "Lights Out," "Stay Tuned for Terror," "The Hermit's Cave," "The Haunting Hour," and others. Spinoffs from the program included a line of novels published by Simon and Schuster, a TV series, and a string of motion pictures such as *Calling Dr. Death* (1943), *The Frozen Ghost* (1944), and *Weird Woman* (1944). "Inner Sanctum" gave up the ghost in its radio format in 1952.

Innes, David [L] The hero of Edgar Rice Burroughs' Pellucidar series. A thirty-year-old native of Connecticut, Innes is the son of a wealthy mine owner. Approached by amateur paleontologist Abner Perry, Innes joins him on the maiden voyage of the *Iron Mole,* a vessel capable of traveling inside the earth. The two men pierce the earth's crust, their goal is to uncover mineral deposits which can be put to commercial use. Unfortunately, Perry and Innes lose control of the huge borer. It drills ever onward, stopping only when it reaches Pellucidar, a world located in earth's hollow core. There, Innes falls in love with Dian the Beautiful of Sari, battles a variety of monsters, and vies with Hooja the Sly One for Dian's affections. see: **Burroughs, Edgar Rice; Pellucidar; Perry, Abner.**

Iotians [TV] Extremely intelligent humanoids seen in the "Star Trek" episode "A Piece of the Action." When the Federation ship U.S.S. *Horizon* leaves behind a book entitled *Chicago Mobs of the Twenties,* the residents of Iotia abolish their existing culture and build one based upon the forgotten history book. As a result, gangsters abound. When the U.S.S. *Enterprise* arrives, powerful thug Bela Oxmyx— played by Anthony Caruso— wants to

use the spaceship to force his will upon the planet's other crimelords. Ultimately, Capt. Kirk and his crew set Iotia back on the course of natural cultural evolution, establishing a government of which Oxmyx is the head. see: *Enterprise,* **U.S.S.; Kirk, Captain.**

Iron Man [C] A comic book character created by Stan Lee. Iron Man's first appearance was in *Tales of Suspense* #39, March 1963. In his pre-superhero years, Iron Man was merely Tony Stark, a wealthy industrialist. When he steps on a buried mine in Viet Nam, Stark suffers a massive chest injury and is captured by the Communists. While a prisoner, the American designs a chest plate which keeps his mangled heart beating. With this formidable unit as a base, Stark goes on to build a complete iron suit which increases his strength, enables him to fly, and allows him to launch repulsor rays. With this heavy gray suit he wages a one-person war against his captors—and wins. Returning to the United States, he gives the armor a gold and red coat of paint. With the cover story that Iron Man is an anonymous guard for Stark Industries, the industrialist is able to switch from man to superhuman without raising suspicion. The romantic interest in the strip is provided by Stark's secretary, Pepper Potts. Iron Man's sidekick and confidant is Happy Hogan.

Irving, Washington [L] America's first short story master. Born in New York City in 1783, the youngest of eleven children, Irving had an eye for the fantastic and a knack for storytelling. Lacking a college education, he turned to writing and produced evocative tales of the Hudson River Valley with an emphasis on local lore and ghosts. Sometimes writing behind the pseudonym of Diedrich Knickerbocker, he penned such immortal tales as "Rip Van Winkle" and "The Legend of Sleepy Hollow," both of which appeared in *The Sketch Book* in 1820. Among his other works are "Don Juan: A Spectral Research," "The Devil and Tom Walker," and the ghostly "Adventures of the German Student." Irving died in 1859. see: **Headless Horseman; Winkle, Rip Van.**

Ishtar [M] The Babylonian goddess of sexual pleasure. The daughter of Anu, god of the heavens, she is sometimes represented as the offspring of Sin, the moon god. The wife of Tammuz, the god of vengeance, Ishtar is also the benevolent protector of the earth and, paradoxically, the goddess of war. In her most famous escapade, Ishtar journeys to the underworld where the dead sit in perpetual darkness. There she searches for Tammuz, who had been slain while boar hunting. Fighting the underworld's Queen Allatu to get her husband back, Ishtar loses. Indeed, only with the help of the water god Ea does she herself manage to return to the surface world. To the Phoenicians, Ishtar is known as Astarte. see: **Enkidu; Gilgamesh.**

Isis [M] The Egyptian goddess of the earth and the moon. The sister-wife of Osiris and the mother of Horus, Isis possesses powers which are virtually limitless. She rules the earth, the heavens, and the seas and even holds tremendous sway in the underworld, where she doles out rewards and punishments. As the goddess of birth, she decides the fate of mortals early in their lives. The daughter of Keb (the earth) and Nut (the heavens), Isis is sister to the evil god Seth and the goddess Nephthys. She is pictured as having a large pair of horns between which the disk of the moon is suspended. see: **Horus; Osiris.**

Ivanoushka [FT] A yound Russian who decides to walk around the world with his sister Alenoushka. Shortly after the couple sets out, Ivanoushka becomes thirsty. Finding water in the footprint of a sheep, he takes a sip and is immediately turned into a lamb. As Alenoushka sits and weeps, a gentleman happens by and takes her for his wife. One day, a witch comes to their home. "Ugly she was, with only one tooth in her head and wicked. . . . " Drowning Alenoushka, the witch hides her body at the bottom of a river and assumes the young girl's shape and visage. But it is not a perfect crime. The lamb has witnessed the murder, and the witch orders him roasted for dinner. Racing toward the river with the cook in pursuit, Ivanoushka calls to his sister—who answers! The startled cook runs home and tells his master, who fishes his wife from the chill water. Ivanoushka kneels beside her prone form, and when the two embrace, Alenoushka's life is restored and he is no longer a lamb. The group heads for home, the witch runs off, and Ivanoushka marries the gentleman's sister.

Ivan, Prince [FT] "Once upon a time, very long ago, there was a little Prince Ivan who was dumb." So begins the Russian fairy tale of a young boy who saddles a horse and flees his evil sister, a witch with black metal teeth. Eventually, the naive but resourceful Ivan comes to the end of the world. There, hanging in the sky and built of clouds, is the castle of the Little Sister of the Sun. Ivan's horse flies him to the palace where the prince remains as a playmate for the young girl. However, Ivan happens to glance toward the horizon one day and sees his home in ruins. He leaves immediately, hoping to rescue his parents. But before he goes, the Little Sister gives him a magic comb, a magic brush, and two apples of immortality.

Along the way, Ivan meets the giant Mountain-Tosser, who says he will soon die for lack of any mountains to toss. Throwing the magic brush on a plain, Ivan creates a new range for the thankful giant. Pressing on, he

Ivan

meets Tree-Rooter who says he will die for his last tree is almost uprooted. Dropping the comb to the ground, the prince causes a huge forest to spring from the earth. Hurrying away, Ivan next encounters two old women who are sitting and sewing. They are weak and near death, for their thread is almost gone. Ivan gives them the apples and, in return, the old ladies make him a handkerchief which will turn ground to water.

Reaching his home, Ivan finds his sister grown huge. She has already eaten their parents and turns on her brother. Galloping away, Ivan tosses the handkerchief behind him. The monstrous girl stumbles into the lake which bursts from the earth. Though she is slowed, she manages to cross. Ivan rides furiously toward the castle of the Little Sister, Tree-Rooter barring the giantess' way with trees and Mountain-Tosser with mountains. She still manages to reach the castle hard on the heels of her brother—and he barely manages to drive his horse skyward to the safety of the palace. Gnashing her teeth so hard that they break, the wicked girl leaves. Ivan stays with the Little Sister of the Sun, and the two are playing there still. Their favorite toys are stars—which is why they appear in the sky only when the children sleep.

Izanagi [M] With Izanami, the generative deities of Japanese mythology. After seven generations, these two supreme deities decide to create the world and all the elements. Alas, Izanami dies while giving birth to fire and, in despair, Izanagi cuts off the head of one of his sons. From the young god's spilled blood spring the other Japanese gods. Inconsolable at the loss of his wife, Izanagi goes to the underworld to find her and bring her back to his ethereal abode. However, when he finds her body it is so badly corroded by death that he flees from it, horrified. As Izanagi dashes to the surface world he casts off his clothing and jumps into the nearest river to purify himself. Though the god is cleansed, from his tainted, discarded wardrobe spring all of the evils which have since plagued humankind.

Jabberwock [L] A fiendish creature in the poem "Jabberwocky," written by Lewis Carroll for *Through the Looking Glass.* The object of a young warrior's search, the Jabberwock is a dragon with a long neck, two bat wings, a pair of arms terminating in three long fingers each, a twining tail, three-toed feet, antennae, tendrils dangling from its lower jaw, whiskers, and a vest. In the poem, the questing hero is warned by his father, "Beware the Jabberwock, my son! The jaws that bite, the claws that catch." He does, and manages to slay the monster. see: **Alice; Humpty Dumpty.**

Jack and the Beanstalk [FT] The hero of a fairy tale which appears throughout most cultures in one version or another. Jack and his widowed mother live in a small cottage. Planting magic beans for which he traded his cow to a butcher, Jack finds them grown to a cloud-piercing beanstalk by morning. He climbs it and discovers a land of sheep, beautiful meadows, and a fine castle. Jack learns that this realm borders Fairyland and at one time had been ruled by a kindly knight and his family—all of whom were slain by a giant, save for the knight's wife and three month old baby who were not in at the time. Jack realizes that *he* is the knight's son and vows to win back the castle.

Hiding in the palace, Jack is nearly discovered when the giant comes to dinner grumbling, "Fe, fi, fo fum. I smell the blood of an Englishman. Be he alive or be he dead, I'll grind his bones to make my bread." But the giant dines and falls asleep, and Jack steals a hen that lays golden eggs and a singing harp with a diamond frame and strings of gold. He heads for home, but the harp doesn't want to leave and calls to the giant. The huge fellow storms after Jack and follows him down the beanstalk. Reaching the bottom, the brave lad "cuts the stem quite through and darts from the spot." The stalk and the giant both tumble to the ground, the latter cracking his spine. Just then, a fairy appears. She explains that she had been the butcher, disguised to test the boy's courage. Bundling Jack and his mother into a peacock-drawn chariot, she flies them to the castle. The knight's subjects cheer them, the giant's cyclopean wife slips down a flight of stairs and breaks her neck, and Jack rules wisely for the remainder of his days. see: **Beanstalk; Giants.**

Jack the Hedgehog [FT] The hero of a Grimm Brothers fairy tale which bears his name. Because he has no children, a farmer is teased by his neighbors. Resolving to father a child "even should it only be a hedgehog," he watches with shock as his wife gives birth to a boy with human legs but the head and torso of a hedgehog. Jack, the beast-boy, senses that his father is displeased; packing his bagpipes and shoeing a cock, he rides off. Venturing into a nearby forest, Jack finds a lost king. The potentate promises Jack that if he will guide him back to his castle, the hedgehog can have whatever the king meets first upon his return. Jack accepts the terms. Upon arriving, the king is met by his beautiful daughter. He informs her of the bargain, but she refuses to honor it. Angry, Jack threatens her father's life, and she agrees to go. When they enter the forest, the spurned hedgehog rips off her clothes and pricks her with his bristles. Scarred and humiliated, the haughty girl is returned to her father.

Moving on, Jack helps a second lost king who promises the same reward for directions to his castle. This new king is likewise greeted by his daughter, who says she will be happy to go with Jack for the noble service he has performed. A feast is held in the hedgehog's honor and that night, while everyone is asleep, he crawls from his spiny skin and has it burned. Jack is revealed to be a strikingly handsome lad whom the princess is thrilled to marry. Eventually, Jack inherits the kingdom. see: **Grimm, Jakob and Wilhelm.**

Jaffar [MP] A villainous sorcerer played by Conrad Veidt in the 1940 motion picture *Thief of Bagdad*. The Grand Vizier under King Ahmad (John Justin), Jaffar has the ruler arrested when he dresses as a peasant to move among his people. He then assumes the throne and woos Ahmad's lover, the Princess of Basra (June Duprez). He wins her hand by making her father a gift of his flying horse. The princess is less than thrilled.

Meanwhile, Ahmad escapes from prison assisted by a young thief named Abu (Sabu). Racing to stop Jaffar from absconding with the princess, Ahmad is struck blind and Abu is turned into a dog. But Jaffar's victory is a hollow one, as the princess falls into a trance from which only Ahmad's embrace can rouse her. Reluctantly, the sorcerer brings the couple together, and tells the princess that he will cure Ahmad and Abu only if she agrees to love him. The princess accedes, but all is not lost. After Jaffar summons a storm to detain our heroes while he escapes, Abu finds an enchanted bottle. He opens it and out clouds a genie who sends Ahmad to Jaffar's palace. Guided by passion rather than logic, Ahmad attacks his former Grand Vizier and is arrested. However, just as he is about to be executed, in soars Abu on a flying carpet. Sensing danger, Jaffar mounts the flying horse he

had given the princess' father and runs from the thief. But Abu is not about to let him escape. Loosing a shaft from his crossbow, the boy pierces Jaffar's skull and kills him. The princess and Ahmad wed, and the thief flies into the sunset searching for other adventures.

Jahar [L] A city-state of red humans dwelling on Barsoom, Edgar Rice Burroughs' fictional version of the planet Mars. Located in the Western Hemisphere below the Mountains of Torquas, Jahar is best known for two former attributes: its eccentric, recently deceased *jeddak* or "emperor" Tul Axtar, who had a harem composed of several thousand beautiful women; and its southern province of U-Gor, which boasted a wealthy agricultural commerce until Tul Axtar overtaxed it in an attempt to build his population and conquer the entire planet. With advanced weapons, Tul Axtar marched against a fleet from Helium. The would-be tyrant was slain and Jahar was subdued. see: **Barsoom; Burroughs, Edgar Rice; Carter, John.**

Jandar [L] The hero of Lin Carter's fantasy novels about Callisto, the fifth moon of Jupiter. Called Thantor by the natives, Callisto is a world of barbaric passions. Into this environment comes Jonathan Andrew Dark, a man just over six feet tall, with yellow hair and blue eyes. Serving as a helicopter pilot in Viet Nam, Capt. Dark crashes in a river. Stumbling from the wreck, he finds himself in Cambodia's lost city of Arangkôr. Falling into a transporter beam which appears as luminance in a well, he materializes on Callisto. There, his Yale-bred skills in fencing prove quite handy, as Jonathan Dark—*Jandar* to the locals—woos and weds Darloona, warrior princess of Ku Thad. Among the ongoing Callisto adventures are *Jandar of Callisto, Black Legion of Callisto,*

Sky Pirates of Callisto, Mad Empress of Callisto, Mind Wizards of Callisto, Lankar of Callisto, and *Ylana of Callisto.* see: **Carter, Lin.**

Janus [M] The Roman guardian of gates and doorways, Janus has two faces. Each face looks in an opposite direction so that Janus can best fulfill his responsibilities. As the god of good beginnings, Janus is the root word for January and was an early Roman sun god, the rising of the sun being synonymous with a good beginning. He was originally known as Dianus and is sometimes considered the male counterpart of Diana, the goddess of hunting and chastity. Both of Janus' faces are bearded, one smiling and the other frowning. These extremes have come to represent the theater, a showcase for opposing emotions. see: **Artemis.**

Jason [M] The son of Alcimede and Aeson, the rightful king of Iolcus in Thessaly. When Aeson is deposed by his half-brother Pelias, Jason is given over to the centaur Chiron at Mt. Pelion to escape the invader's sword. Reared by the man-horse, Jason emerges from hiding at age twenty to claim his father's throne. First, however, he decides to win public favor by performing a deed worthy of a king, fetching the Golden Fleece from the land of Colchis. Commissioning a fifty-oar strong vessel which is christened the *Argo* after its builder, and gathering together such heroes as Hercules, Theseus, Orpheus, Castor, and Pollux, Jason sets off on his so-called Argosy.

Leading the Argonauts through perils like the sirens, the Symplegades, the harpies, and the loss of the stalwart Hercules—his companion Hylas is lured into a well by a nymph, and the crew refuses to permit the enraged demigod back on the ship—Jason reaches Colchis. There he tames a pair of fire-breathing bulls, slays a dragon, and battles an army of sol-

diers which spring from the dragon's teeth, before obtaining the Fleece. In the process, he also captures the heart of the sorceress Medea, the daughter of Colchis' King Aeëtes. Medea leaves with Jason—pursued by her father, who wants back his Fleece. The woman delays him by chopping up her half-brother Apsyrtos and scattering the pieces about the water. Aeëtes pauses to collect and bury the dismembered body and the Argonauts escape. However, so sickened are the gods by Medea's action that they send the *Argo* to the island of Circe to be purified. After making a suitable sacrifice, they head for home.

Learning that Pelias has killed Aeson, Jason is grieved—but the resourceful Medea plots revenge. She tells the king's daughter that Pelias' youth will be restored if he jumps into a magic pot filled with boiling water. Medea provides the "enchanted" pot, Pelias tries the restorative, and he quickly cooks to death. Horrified, the populace orders Jason and Medea to leave the city. Settling in Corinth, Jason falls in love with Glauce (also known as Kreusa), the daughter of King Creon. The jealous Medea sends Glauce a poisoned robe which burns her to death; slits the throats of her own two sons by Jason; kills Creon; and burns down the king's palace. Mounting a chariot drawn by two winged dragons, she taunts her anguished husband and rides to Athens. There she settles with King Aigeus until she tries to kill his son Theseus and is banished. Fleeing again, Medea returns to Colchis and her father. As for the tormented Jason, he visits the decaying *Argo* one day, lies down for a nap, and is killed when a piece of rotted wood falls and strikes him.

In the cinema, the story of Jason has best been told in *Hercules* (1957), *Giants of Thessaly* (1960), *Jason and the Argonauts* (1963), and *Medea* (1970) starring Maria Callas. see: **Ar-**

gonauts; Chiron; Circe; Fire-Breathing Bulls; Golden Fleece; Harpies; Harryhausen, Ray; Hercules; Reeves, Steve; Theseus.

Jawas [MP] Yard-high desert scavengers of the planet Tatooine seen in the 1977 motion picture *Star Wars*. Clad in rough, dirty robes and sandmasks which obscure all but their glowing, amber eyes, these creatures collect scrap and peddle used droids—such as C-3PO and R2-D2 whom they sell to Luke Skywalker. Jawa language is a variable jabber that can prove maddening to non-Jawas. They are cowardly, paranoid, rodentlike, and particularly unhygienic. However, they do possess a highly developed sense of smell, which they use for tracking. The Jawas are reputed to be extremely ugly. see: **C-3PO; Droids; R2-D2; Skywalker, Luke.**

Jedi Knights [MP] Peacekeepers of the Old Republic in the 1977 motion picture *Star Wars*. For over 1,000 generations the Jedi Knights were the strongest and most revered beings in the galaxy. But with the fall of the old order, the warriors were either slain or decided to disband. In the era of the story told by *Star Wars*, their greatest spokesperson is old Obi-Wan Kenobi, who passes the Jedi skills to young Luke Skywalker. Principal among these talents is the handling of a lightsaber, a yard-long beam of blue-white light that is as thick as a thumb and can cut through anything; and the tapping of the Force, the energy that is generated by and binds all living things. see: **Darth Vader; Kenobi, Obi-Wan; Skywalker, Luke.**

Jekyll, Dr. Henry [L] The tortured scientist featured in the 1886 novel *The Strange Case of Dr. Jekyll and Mr. Hyde* by Robert Louis Stevenson (1850–1894). Inspired by a nightmare and written over a three-day period, the tale tells of a "large, well-made, smooth-faced man of fifty, with something of a slyish cast," who wants to

Jekyll

liberate the good in humans by subjugating the bad. "Man is not truly one but truly two," he explains, adding that it is "the curse of mankind that these incongruous faggots were thus bound together . . . continually struggling." Concocting a watery-green potion which he hopes will suppress the evil side, he quaffs it and finds that his humane aspects crumble. He becomes the cruel Mr. Edward Hyde on whom evil had left "an imprint of deformity and decay." One character sees "Satan's signature" on the hairy man, "something abnormal and misbegotten in the very essence of the creature." The reason Hyde is dwarfish, Jekyll realizes, is because throughout his life his evil side "had been much less exercised."

After committing several murders, during which period the Hyde character emerges beyond Jekyll's ability to control it, the doctor takes his own life.

On the screen, the most notable Dr. Jekylls have been John Barrymore in 1920, Fredric March—for which role —he won the Best Actor Oscar in 1932, Spencer Tracy in 1941, Boris Karloff in *Abbott and Costello Meet Dr. Jekyll and Mr. Hyde* (1953), Jack Palance in 1967, and Christopher Lee in 1971.

Jenik [FT] The hero of the fairy tale "The Enchanted Watch." When Jenik tells his father he wants to leave home to seek his fortune, the older man quips, "Go if you like, you idiot; but what good will it do you?" Departing nonetheless, Jenik comes to a meadow where he saves the life of a dog, then a cat, and finally a serpent, all of which join him on his journey. In due course, the snake must leave them. But before he goes, he brings them to the King of the Serpents who rewards Jenik's kindness with the gift of an enchanted watch. Rubbing it makes any wish come true. Although Jenik's father had been cruel, the boy gives him a splendid new home and mounts a lavish feast. The king and his daughter are invited, and Jenik is permitted to marry the princess. But it isn't long before she tires of the simple lad. Stealing his watch, her highness builds a castle in the middle of the ocean. Jenik cannot reach it—so his faithful dog swims the cat to the palace. There, the stealthy feline sneaks inside and snatches the magic timepiece. As soon as he has the watch,

Jenik orders the sea to swallow up the castle and everyone in it. Sadder but matured, he gathers his pets together and retires to his father's mansion.

Jersey Devils [F] Monsters which inhabit the woods and swamps of southern New Jersey. The legend of the Jersey Devils was born in 1735 when Mother Leeds had her thirteenth child. The woman was so annoyed by yet another pregnancy that she declared, "I am tired of children. Let it be a devil!" And so it was. The child she bore was over six feet long and snakelike, with hooves, a horse's head, and a pair of bat wings. Rasping as it slipped from the womb, the creature ate all of Mrs. Leeds' other children and flew from the house. It has been seen many times since then, rustling through foliage and tangling clothes lines. Some accounts say that the Jersey Devil was parented by Mrs. Leeds and a British soldier, its monstrous shape having been caused by the woman's treason. Other tales say that it was merely an evil baby which be-

Jersey Devils

came more and more deformed with every devilish act.

Jones, Gulliver [L] The hero of the 1905 fantasy novel *Lt. Gulliver Jones: His Vacation* (also known as *Gulliver of Mars*) by Edwin L. Arnold (1857–1935). The alleged prototype of Edgar Rice Burroughs' John Carter, Gulliver Jones is a lieutenant in the United States Navy. Visiting his New York apartment, he steps on a strange carpet he has discovered, finds himself rolled swiftly within, and is borne to Mars. Finding himself in a quiet Martian community he muses, "Where was I? It was not the Broadway; it was not Staten Island on a Saturday afternoon." Becoming involved with court intrigue on this savage planet, he encounters many strange life forms. Among them are rats the size of elephants, the peaceful Hither folk, trees that grow and die in a single season—and the beautiful Princess Heru, with whom he falls in love. In the end, Gulliver is mysteriously snatched back to earth where he weds his terrestrial girl friend Polly. There were no further adventures. see: **Burroughs, Edgar Rice; Carter, John.**

Jongor [L] A savage fantasy hero created in 1942 by Robert Moore Williams, and featured in such novels as *Jongor of Lost Land* (1942), *The Return of Jongor* (1946), and *Jongor Fights Back* (1951). When his aviator father, Capt. Robert Gordon, loses control of an airplane in turbulence, he crashes in Lost Land. Only the captain's wife and their son survive. The boy's mother dies when he is still a youth, and the lad is forced to fend for himself. Growing to manhood, the tall, brown-skinned, loin-clothed John Gordon calls himself by the name he recalls from his babyhood, the garbled *Jongor.*

Surrounded by mountains, valleys, and desert, Lost Land has been untouched by normal evolution. Thus, dinosaurs coexist with centaurs known as Arklans and ruled by Queen Nesca, bizarre monkey men, and humans—in a world flavored by the superscience of the Murtos, beings descended from the Murians, survivors of the sinking of Mu. Love interest in the brawny series is provided by Ann Hunter, an outsider who comes to Lost Land to find her missing brother Allan.

Joringel [FT] The hero of the Grimm Brothers fairy tale "Jorinde and Joringel." In an old castle lives an enchantress, who is an owl or cat during the day and by night an ugly woman with "yellow skin, large red eyes, and a hooked nose which met her chin." If a boy comes with 100 paces of her castle, he must stand stone still until she sets him free; if a girl, she is transformed into a bird.

When the story begins, the witch already owns 7,000 birds in wicker cages. Walking in the forest which surrounds her castle, young lovers Jorinde and Joringel get lost. When they near the accursed abode, the girl becomes a nightingale and her betrothed is paralyzed. The witch approaches. Locking Jorinde in a cage, she mercifully sets Joringel free. It proves to be her undoing. Learning of a blood-red flower with a pearl in the center which will end any enchantment, he goes searching for it. After nine days he finds the blossom and hurries back to the castle. Though the witch breathes poison at Joringel, the bud protects him. Curing Jorinde and all the other girls and boys, he touches the witch with the flower and she loses all of her magic abilities. see: **Grimm, Jakob and Wilhelm; Witch.**

Jubjub [L] A fictitious bird created by Lewis Carroll. The Jubjub appears twice in Carroll's works, in the poems "Jabberwocky" and "The Hunting of the Snark." Possessing a shrill, high scream which sounds like "a pencil that squeaks on a slate," the Jubjub bird has a desperate temper, lives in perpetual passion, has absurd taste in clothes, knows anyone it has met once before, cannot be bribed, and has an exquisite flavor when boiled in sawdust and salted with glue. The hero of "Jabberwocky" is advised that this is a bird of which to beware. see: **Alice.**

Judge Jeffreys [O] A ghost who haunts the Chatham House in Lyme Regis, Dorset, England. Although the spectre is usually seen wearing his robes, a wig, and a black cap, the locals refer to the august figure as nothing more imposing than "Annie." Over the years, the restless judge has been seen carrying a bloody bone. Many people believe that he is trying to attract the ghostly Black Dog who also haunts this region. The hound is said to know the location of buried treasure.

Julian [L] The hero of Edgar Rice Burroughs' fantasy tales *The Moon Maid* (1922), *The Moon Men* (1924), and *The Red Hawk* (1925). Julian has no surname. However, he has total recall of all his past and future incarnations. As a result, all of the Julians we meet are essentially the same man. Julian V, born in the year 2000, is the protagonist in *The Moon Maid.* A graduate of the Air School, he is assigned to the International Peace Fleet (previous Julians were also in the military). Julian V is later put in command of the spacecraft *Barsoom,* which leaves for Mars on December 25, 2025, after contact with the Martian John Carter has been made. The lieutenant commander of the voyage is the scientific genius, Orthis. Jealous because he had not been selected to head the mission, Orthis sabotages the ship and it lands inside the moon.

The crew of the *Barsoom* finds three races of beings within earth's satellite. They are the Va-gas, barbaric centaurs who eat human flesh; the Kalkars, who are primitive humans; and the U-gas, who are very sophisticated humans. The lunarians call their world Va-nah, and they receive light and heat from the inner moon's radioactive atmosphere. During the course of the first novel in the series, Julian falls in love with one of the natives, the girl Nah-ee-lah, daughter of Sagroth, Jemadar (King) of the city-state of Laythe. After many adventures, the couple leaves the moon for earth. But they leave Orthis behind, and he remains inside the moon until the year 2050. In *The Moon Men,* having used the intervening quarter-century to build spaceships, Orthis leads a Kalkar invasion of earth. Ironically, both he and Julian V are killed during the altercation and the Kalkars conquer the earth. A succession of Julians battles the aliens until, in *The Red Hawk,* Julian XX defeats them. see: **Barsoom; Burroughs, Edgar Rice; Carter, John.**

Jurupari [O] An evil god of Brazilian lore. Originally, Jurupari was merely a mischief maker. His mother was a virgin who became pregnant after drinking a local beer. Since she lacked sexual organs, the woman waded into a river and allowed herself to be chewed open by a fish in order to give birth. When Jurupari was fully grown, he challenged the members of a tribe to a drinking contest. But the women refused to prepare the brew and Jurupari became their enemy. Worse, they cut down a tree which was sacred to him. He struck back by eating all of the tribe's children, which caused the men to turn against him and burn Jurupari to death. From his ashes sprouted a new tree which was chopped down and made into holy symbols. Jurupari was thenceforth worshiped as a force of supreme evil, whose rites were fatal to any woman who witnessed them.

K

Kadath [L] A mountain featured in the World of Kadath stories by H. P. Lovecraft. Because Kadath is the tallest peak in a world parallel to our own, its summit was chosen by the gods to be their home. They used to dwell on smaller mountains but vacated these when humans learned how to climb them. However, the deities sometimes visit their old cliffs, traveling to them on cloud-ships. Mortals can travel to the World of Kadath in dreams—or through such Lovecraft tales as *The Cats of Ulthar, The Other Gods, The Doom that Came to Sarnath,* and *The Dream-Quest of Unknown Kadath.* see: **Lovecraft, H. P.**

Kafka, Franz [L] An author of pensive, symbolic stories. Born in Prague in 1883, Kafka is best known for three works of fantasy, published posthumously: *The Castle* (1930), a novel about a bizarre edifice that casts its shadow on everything within a small village; *The Trial* (1937), a novel in which a lonely man finds himself in conflict with authority; and *Metamorphosis* (1937), the semiautobiographical tale of a salesperson who becomes a cockroach. Kafka died of tuberculosis in 1924.

Kali [M] A figure in the folklore of India. Kali is one of the forms in which Durga—the martial form of Devi, the Great Goddess of India—came to earth. Kali's job is to protect humans from demons and ill-fortune. One would never guess this, looking at her visage. In early legends, when the goddess was broadly viewed as the personification of creation and destruction, she had black skin pulled taut over an emaciated frame, a hideous face, cobras twining around her body, and a necklace made of skulls. As she became more and more benign, her image softened. Married to Siva the Destroyer, she is actually the more domineering of the two.

In the 1973 motion picture *The Golden Voyage of Sinbad,* Kali's more antagonistic nature is manifest. A giant, six-armed statue of the goddess is brought to life by the magician Koura. Attacking Sinbad and his party, the icon is stopped only when it is nudged from a ledge of its temple and shatters.

Kanamit [L] Alien beings featured in the 1950 short story "To Serve Man" by Damon Knight (1922–   ). Landing on earth, the Kanamit explain their mission as charitable; they want to help cure human society of its many ills. And so they do. They eliminate war, disease, and hunger; the Kanamit even transport large masses of earth people to their world in the form of "exchange groups." That's when one of the human scientists translates the opening lines of a Kanamit book entitled *How to Serve Man*—and learns that it's a cookbook.

The Kanamit are described as a cross between pigs and people. They are short, plump, covered with a great deal of thick, brown-gray hair, have snoutlike noses, small eyes, and three fingers on each hand, and dress in green shorts and a green leather harness. "To Serve Man" was filmed as an episode of the television program "Twilight Zone," with the Kanamit portrayed as seven feet tall, bulbheaded, and bald.

Kane, Michael [L] The hero of the Mars trilogy written in 1965 by Edward Powys Bradbury (real name: Michael Moorcock). Born in Ohio, physicist

Michael Kane is a professor of the Chicago Special Research Institute. Building a matter transmitter, he teleports himself to Mars. There, on a world the natives call Vashu—earth is named Negalu—the scientist with diamond blue eyes battles blue giants known as Argzoon; encounters a variety of monsters; and takes as his bride Shizala, the lovely queen of the Karnala. The three volumes in the Kane saga are *Warriors of Mars, Blades of Mars,* and *Barbarians of Mars.* In several editions, these novels are also known as *The City of the Beast, The Lord of the Spiders,* and *The Masters of the Pit,* respectively. see: **Argzoon.**

Kane, Solomon [L] A sword and sorcery hero created by author Robert E. Howard in 1928. Set in the sixteenth century, the Kane epic follows the warrior as he travels from England into Europe and Africa. Along the way he crosses swords with vampires, winged humans, remnants of Atlantis, and the like. A tall, slender Puritan, the black-clad Kane lives to right wrongs and is passionate in his pursuit of justice. Howard wrote twelve stories and three poems about Kane, all of which are included in the books *The Moon of Skulls, The Hand of Kane,* and *Solomon Kane.* see: **Howard, Robert E.**

Kantos Kan [L] A human character created by Edgar Rice Burroughs for his novels about the planet Barsoom. Kantos Kan is a *padwar,* "lieutenant," in the navy of Helium. While trying to locate his abducted princess Dejah Thoris, the warrior is captured by plant beings known as Warhoons. Kantos Kan is put in jail where his cellmate is none other than Dejah's beloved John Carter. The two men escape and, in due course, help the Tharks—powerful green giants led by Tars Tarkas—take the city of Zadanga near the Atmosphere Plant which provides Barsoom with breathable air. They rescue the princess, who is a prisoner in the city. Kantos Kan later becomes an overlord in the navy and fights at John Carter's side in many of the eleven novels. see: **Barsoom; Burroughs, Edgar Rice; Carter, John; Thoris, Dejah.**

Karloff, Boris [MP] One of the great actors of the horror and fantasy screen. Born William Henry Pratt in 1887, the son of Edward Pratt and Eliza Sara Millard, the young man from the London suburb of Camberwell did poorly in school. Rather than embarrass his family, he left England to pursue acting in Canada. After learning the stage trade—supplementing his income by digging ditches and farming—the newly christened Boris Karloff (a name drawn from his mother's Russian ancestry) landed his first movie role in the Douglas Fairbanks film *His Majesty, the American* (1919). Over sixty films later, when he seemed relegated to a career of bit parts, Karloff won the role of the Monster in *Frankenstein* (1931). He was a hit, played the part in a pair of sequels—*The Bride of Frankenstein* (1935) and *The Son of Frankenstein* (1939)—and went on to gain ever-mounting fame as *The Mummy* (1932) and *The Ghoul* (1933), and in other classic genre films like *The Mask of Fu Manchu* (1932), *The Tower of London* (1939), *The Body Snatcher* (1945), *Abbott and Costello Meet Dr. Jekyll and Mr. Hyde* (1953), *The Raven* (1963), and *Cauldron of Blood* (1971). In 1960, the actor also hosted the "Thriller" television series, which remains in syndication twenty years later. Karloff died in 1969, survived by his daughter, Sara Jane, and his third wife, Evelyn Hope Helmore. Karloff's previous wives were Helene Vivian Soule and then Dorothy Stine. see: **Frankenstein Monster, The; Fu Manchu; Jekyll, Dr. Henry; Lugosi, Bela; Mummy, The; Whale, James.**

Kelpie [O] A Scottish waterhorse who serves the Devil. Black as the night, the Kelpie has two long, sharp horns and in its native form is a cross between a horse and a bull. The creature has the power to change its shape; it is usually found posing as a beautiful horse grazing beside a pond or a stream. It permits passers-by to mount—but no sooner are they upon its back than the Kelpie bounds into the water, drowns its rider, and eats its flesh. This demonic sprite is also known to disguise itself as a handsome young man. In this form it will lead a young girl to the water's edge, drown her, and then feast on her corpse. However, when posing as a human the Kelpie's hair is always wet and run through with weeds—a dead giveaway.

Kelvan [TV] Creatures seen in the "Star Trek" episode "By Any Other Name." Inhabitants of the planet Kelva in the Andromeda Galaxy, these large beings have masses of tentacles and brilliant minds—but no awareness of tactile sensation. The U.S.S. *Enterprise* first encounters the aliens when a colonial party from Kelva is shipwrecked and "borrows" Captain Kirk's vessel for the three-century-long trip back to their world. Adopting human form to be able to function within the *Enterprise,* and killing crew members who disobey them, the Kelvans slowly learn what physical stimulation is all about. Chief Engineer Scott gets one of them drunk, Captain Kirk makes love to another, Dr. McCoy uses chemicals to upset the metabolism of yet another, and so forth. Realizing that they have become too human to ever again fit in comfortably with other Kelvans, the invaders agree to turn over the *Enterprise* and colonize an earthlike planet selected by Captain Kirk. see: *Enterprise,* **U.S.S.; Kirk, Captain.**

Kenobi, Obi-Wan "Ben" [MP] A former general and Jedi Knight played by Alec Guinness in the 1977 motion picture *Star Wars.* Fighting for the Old Republic during the Clone Wars, Kenobi becomes a hermit with the advent of the cruel Galactic Empire. He lives in the outlands of the Western Dune Sea on the planet Tatooine. When the tale told in *Star Wars* begins, Kenobi emerges from seclusion in response to an sos hologram secreted inside the droid R2-D2 by the kidnapped Rebel Princess Leia Organa. The wise and grizzled Kenobi requires help in this mission, and to this end schools young Luke Skywalker in the ways of the Force and the use of the lightsabre; this, as he had once instructed such Jedi Knights as Luke's father and Darth Vader. During the climactic Battle of the Death Star, Kenobi is killed in a lightsabre duel with Darth Vader, his demise buying time for Luke and his party to escape the enemy space station. Physically, while Kenobi no longer exists, his consciousness endures as an eddy of the Force—in which form he counsels Skywalker from time to time. see: **Darth Vader; Death Star; Droid; Jedi Knight; R2-D2.**

Keres [M] Greek entities which claim the body at death. When the Fates decide that it is time for a person to die, the Keres venture forth. Hovering above the doomed one, they swoop down at the exact moment of death. Then, with a shriek of delight, they suck the blood from any wounds and carry the body to the underworld. The daughters of Nyx, the Night, and sisters to the Fates and the Furies, each Ker wears a red robe and has dark skin. Since they love drinking mortal blood above all, they are usually seen loitering above a field of battle. see: **Banshee; Fates; Furies.**

Keryneian Hind [M] Also known as the Arcadian Stag, a creature in Greek mythology possessing bronze hooves and golden antlers. The fifth labor of Hercules is to capture the deer alive. While the animal itself is not particularly dangerous, the mission is. The hind is sacred to Artemis, dedicated to the god when he saved the nymph Taygete from Zeus. There are two accounts of how Hercules surmounted this sticky problem. In the first, he stalks the deer for one year until he can come close enough to grab the beast without harming it. In the second, Hercules wounds it with arrows and parries Artemis' wrath by explaining that he had no choice. Throwing the hind about his shoulders, Hercules carries it to his overseer, Eurystheus. see: **Artemis; Hercules; Zeus.**

Khepera [M] Also known as Khepri, a supreme god of Egyptian mythology. Creating itself merely by speaking its own name, Khepera next thought solid land into being and climbed from Nu, the water-mass of the universe. Peering into Ba, its soul, Khepera was able to visualize what its mind wanted to create. Pleased with what it saw, the deity mated with its own shadow and parented Shu, the god of the air, and Tefmut, the god of the waters. These two gods coupled and produced Nut (night) and Keb (earth). Keb and Nut begat Osiris, Isisi, Set, and Nephythys. In early tales, the sun is referred to as the Eye of Khepera; in later mythologies, Khepera and the sun god Ra are synonymous. see: **Isis; Osiris; Ra.**

Killmoulis [F] An ugly sprite who looks after mills in Scotland. Every mill has a killmoulis, one who is dedicated to the wellbeing of the family it serves. These puckish creatures have no mouth, but a huge nose with which they snort up their food. Dwelling in an area provided for it near a fireplace or oven, the killmoulis will scream and shout when sickness or illfortune is nigh. Not above a practical joke or two, the millmate can be turned from these only by the miller. Depending upon geography, the killmoulis is often thought of as a brownie or a urisk. see: **Brownie; Urisk.**

King Kong [MP] A giant ape created by producer Merian C. Cooper and special effects artists Willis O'Brien and Marcel Delgado for the motion picture *King Kong* (1933). The god of uncharted Skull Island in the Indian Ocean, King Kong is fifty feet tall and regularly accepts the sacrifice of human females, "the brides of Kong." When a filmmaking crew arrives on the primitive isle, its blonde female actress Ann Darrow (Fay Wray) is kidnapped by the natives and handed over to the giant ape. She is rescued from the gorilla's mountaintop cave by her lover Jack Driscoll (Bruce Cabot) and, when Kong comes after them, movie producer Carl Denham (Robert Armstrong) fells the brute with gas bombs. Kong is shackled, sailed to New York, and put on display in a Broadway theater. Breaking loose, he nabs Ann and climbs the Empire State Building, from whose summit he is picked off by machine-gunning biplanes.

In the 1976 remake of *King Kong,* the ape's bride is Dwan (Jessica Lange), who had been shipwrecked and is taken in by an oil expedition en route to Kong's island. True to his

Hillmoulis

cloth, oil executive Fred Wilson (Charles Grodin) sees dollar signs on the wall, gases Kong, and puts him on display in New York's Shea Stadium. This time out, Kong escapes and carries Dwan to the top of the World Trade Center, from which he is shot by orbiting helicopters.

Other Kong quests are featured in Delos W. Lovelace's 1932 novel *King Kong*—derived from the scenario of the original film; the inevitable cinema clash *King Kong vs. Godzilla* (1963); a robot-Kong battling the hirsute original in *King Kong Escapes* (1967); and a half-hour 1966 cartoon series in which the gorilla is a hero! see: **Baker, Rick; Godzilla; O'Brien, Willis; Son of Kong.**

Kinglet [FT] The son of a sailor and hero of the fairy tale "The Little Soldier." Returning home from war, Kinglet pauses in a strange castle. There, he is greeted by a serpent with a woman's head. Her name is Princess Ludovine, and she promises to marry the young man if, from different parts of the castle, he will fetch special garments which will make her human. Fighting goblins, disembodied hands, and the like, he succeeds. However, according to the enchantment which made her a serpent, if he does not meet her at a certain inn at a specific time he will lose her. This is fine with Ludovine, who doesn't like Kinglet and drugs him.

Awaking much later, Kinglet is dejected. Reaching the seashore, he meets the girl Seagull, who gives him a purse which never runs out of money, and a magic red cloak. Kinglet visits Ludovine, who agrees to marry him in exchange for the purse. The lad readily agrees, hands it over, and is promptly heaved from the palace. Still determined to win the princess, he makes his way back to her side, wraps her in the magic cape, and wishes them to "the ends of the earth." Ludovine steals the cloak, leaving him stranded.

Wandering about, Kinglet finds a grove whose golden fruit causes him to grow horns, and whose green plums make them go away. Disguised as a merchant, he feeds the golden fruit to her highness. She is alarmed by the change, and Kinglet offers to cure her if she will return his purse and cloak. The princess turns over Seagull's possessions and he gives her the plums. Slipping into the cape, the young man wills himself to Seagull's side. They marry and toss the magic artifacts into the sea, realizing that "happiness does not lie in the possession of treasures."

King, Stephen [L] A popular contemporary author of horror and fantasy tales. Born in Portland, Maine, in 1946, King sold his first short story in 1967. Entitled, "The Glass Floor," it appeared in *Startling Mystery Stories* magazine. However, he scored his first huge commercial success with his debut novel, *Carrie*, in 1974. This novel, the basis of a 1976 motion picture, is about a girl with telekinetic abilities. *Carrie* was followed by *Salem's Lot* (1975), *The Shining* (1977)—coming in 1980 as a film by Stanley Kubrick—and *The Stand* (1978). The only collection of King's short stories is *Night Shifts*, first published in 1977. King lives with his wife Tabitha and children Naomi, Joe, and Owen in western Maine. see: **Kubrick, Stanley.**

Kirby, Jack [C] A comic book artist, revered for his powerful action drawings and narrative skills. Born in New York in 1917, Kirby began cartooning professionally in 1935, working for animator Max Fleischer. One year later he moved from film to newspapers, drawing such comic strips as "The Black Buccaneer." In 1941 he made the move to comic books, illustrating the first adventure of Captain Marvel and teaming with writer Joe Simon to create the shield-flinging Captain America later that year.

Kirby specialized in science fiction and monster comics in the fifties, rendering tales written by Stan Lee. In the early sixties, Kirby and Lee joined forces to revive the panting superhero genre, coming up with the popular Fantastic Four, the Incredible Hulk, the X-Men, and other mighty characters for Marvel Comics. In 1971 Kirby moved to Marvel's competitor D.C. Comics, for whom he created Mr. Miracle, Kamandi, Demon, OMAC (One Man Army Corps), the Forever People, and the New Gods. Only Kamandi proved to be a commercial success, and after several years Kirby returned to Marvel. In addition to drawing comics, Kirby helps package action toys and draws layouts for cartoon programs. see: **Captain America; Captain Marvel; Fantastic Four, The; Fleischer, Max; Hulk, The Incredible; Lee, Stan; X-Men, The.**

Kirk, Captain James T. [TV] Commander of the U.S.S. *Enterprise* in the television series "Star Trek." Kirk's five-year mission onboard the starship is to explore unknown worlds and serve as the Federation's ambassador to Class M planets—worlds like earth. In his middle thirties, Kirk was born in a small town in Iowa. At the age of seventeen he joined the Space Academy as a midshipperson. His record there was superb. Indeed, Kirk is the youngest graduate in Academy history to have become a starship commander. Kirk has brown hair and hazel eyes; his middle name is Tiberius. He idolizes Abraham Lincoln, and his serial number is SC9370176CEC. Kirk's brother, Sam, and sister-in-law, Aurelan, were killed in the episode "Operation Annihilate," although their son, Peter, survived. In the TV series, cartoon program, and *Star Trek* movie, Captain Kirk is played by actor William Shatner. see: ***Enterprise*, U.S.S.; Federation.**

Kisa [FT] The kitten born to "a beauti-ful cat, the color of smoke, with china-blue eyes," in the German fairy tale "Kisa the Cat." Owned by a queen, Kisa's mother knows that her mistress is sad because she has no children. Consulting a fairy, the cat makes it possible for the woman to bear Ingibjörg, "a little girl who seemed made out of snow and sunbeams." One day, Ingibjörg is kidnapped by a giant. However, her cries so annoy the brute that he cuts off her feet and strands her in the woods. Chasing after the princess, Kisa boldly presses on to the giant's cave. Reclaiming the severed feet, she reattaches them using magic grasses and returns Ingibjörg to the castle. There, the cat requests, "that I may sleep for this night at the foot of your bed." The princess happily agrees, and come morning Kisa is no longer a feline. She is a princess. The transformed maiden explains that her mother had been turned into a cat by a wizard, in which form she and her heirs had to remain until a good deed was done to end the curse. Though her mother died a cat, Kisa and her children shall always be human. After living a while longer at the palace, the ex-tabby marries a prince and rules a kingdom of her own.

Klimius, Nicholas [L] The hero of the Danish novel *Journey to the World Underground,* written by Ludvig, Baron von Holberg, in 1741. In this early science fiction story, Klimius descends into a hole and plunges to the center of the earth. He finds out that the world is hollow, warmed and lighted inside by a central sun which is circled by several tiny planets. This small system boasts a variety of inhabitants—as does the inner shell of earth, much as in Edgar Rice Burroughs' Pellucidar novels. Like the voyages of Lemuel Gulliver, the adventures of Nicholas Klimius are primarily the author's platform for social satire. That Jules Verne's 1864 novel *Journey to the Centre of the Earth,*

Lewis Carroll's *Alice in Wonderland* in 1865, or the Burroughs books may have been inspired by Holberg's earlier work seems doubtful. see: **Alice; Burroughs, Edgar Rice; Pellucidar; Verne, Jules.**

Kline, Otis Adelbert [L] A noted author of swashbuckling science fiction. Born in Chicago in 1891, Kline's early interests lay exclusively in music. He was a fine piano player at the age of twelve, and when he was nineteen years old he moved to Tin Pan Alley to perform and sing. Later, he turned to music publishing and then to fantasy fiction. He sold his first short story in 1923. Entitled "The Thing with a Thousand Shapes," it appeared in *Weird Tales* magazine. It was followed by "The Cup of Blood" as well as a batch of excellent sword and sorcery novels. Among these are the Grandon of Terra series, *Planet of Peril* (1929), *Prince of Peril* (1930), and *Port of Peril* (1949); a Venus series spearheaded by *Buccaneers of Venus* (1931); the Harry Thorne Mars series led by *Swordsmen of Mars* (1933); and such isolated titles as *Jan of the Jungle* (1931), *Maza of the Moon* (1930), and *Tam, Son of the Tiger* (1931). Kline died in 1946, survived by his wife, Ellen. see: **Burroughs, Edgar Rice.**

Klingons [TV] Grim, dark-skinned warriors featured in the television series "Star Trek." The Klingon Empire is composed of violent people who do not hesitate to pillage whatever they need from whomever has it. Brawny humanoids, the dictatorial Klingons are nonetheless the sworn enemies of humans, living in a perpetual state of war with the benevolent Federation. Allies of the nasty but less aggressive Romulans, the Klingons honor no law save the law of survival. see: **Enterprise, U.S.S.; Federation; Romulans.**

Kolchak, Carl [L/TV] A fictional newspaper reporter who specializes in the supernatural. Created by author Jeff Rice for the 1970 novel *The Kolchak Papers,* our journalist gained wide fame when played by Darren McGavin in the 1972 television film "The Night Stalker." Chasing the vampire Janos Skorzeny through modern-day Las Vegas, Kolchak works alone—his brash manner annoying most everyone he encounters, especially his editor Anthony A. Vincenzo. When Skorzeny is staked to death—and the film proves a colossal ratings success—Kolchak turns his attention to alchemist Dr. Malcolm Richards who, in "The Night Strangler" (1973), is murdering people in order to remain young. In 1974, a Kolchak TV series is launched. Called "The Night Stalker," it pits our hero against Jack the Ripper, a werewolf, a zombie, another vampire, alien beings, a succubus, a witch, a mummy, and the like, one monster per week. When the audience begins to dwindle, the human element of the program is underlined with a title change to "Kolchak: the Night Stalker." Despite the new name, the show lasts only one season. Plans to feature Kolchak in a theatrical film have thus far been fruitless.

Konga [MP] A huge gorilla featured in the 1961 film *Konga.* Dr. Charles Decker (Michael Gough) discovers a race of ten-foot-tall giants in Africa, and learns that the seeds of a carnivorous plant makes them so tall by doubling the number of genes in each cell. Dr. Decker returns to England with seeds and the sacred monkey Konga. Injecting the simian with a small dose of oil extracted from the jungle vegetation, Decker expands the chimp to gorilla-proportions. Then he sends him out to kill critics and scientific rivals. But Decker's experiment gets out-of-hand, and before long Konga is a giant. Breaking from the scientist's laboratory, the ape storms into the heart of London. There, with a frightened Decker held firmly inpaw, the monkey is killed in a volley of gunfire. Dr. Decker also dies and the body of Konga returns to its former diminutive size.

Korak [L] The son of Tarzan. Tall, well built, and possessing the piercing gray eyes of his father, Korak is not the illiterate "Boy" of the Tarzan films. Like his father John Clayton, Lord Greystoke, and his mother Jane Porter, young Jack Clayton is cultured and well educated. It is only when adventure lures him into Tarzan's trees that he becomes Korak the Killer. Introduced by author Edgar Rice Burroughs in the novel *The Eternal Lover* (1914) in which the Tarzan family makes a cameo appearance, Korak takes a wife—the French girl Meriem, an Arab slave—in *The Son of Tarzan* (1914), book number four of the Tarzan series, and later fathers a son, Jackie. On the screen, Korak was featured in the 1920 motion picture *The Son of Tarzan*, with Gordon Griffith in the title role. see: **Burroughs, Edgar Rice; Tarzan.**

Korbes, Mr. [FT] An evil man in the Grimm Brothers fairy tale "Mr. Korbes." One day, a cock and a hen decide to take a ride. So they build a beautiful carriage, harness four little mice, and set out. During their ride they meet a cat, a millstone, an egg, a duck, a pin, and a needle—all of whom join them on their little holiday. Reaching the house of Mr. Korbes, the group pauses. The cock and the hen relax on a beam, but not their passengers. To quote the tale, "Mr. Korbes came home, and went to the hearth to make a fire, but the cat threw ashes in his eyes. Then he ran quickly into the kitchen to wash himself, but the duck splashed water in his face. Then he was going to wipe it with the towel, but the egg broke in it, and stuck his eyelids together. In order to get a little peace he sat down in his chair, but the pin ran into him, and, starting up, in his vexation he threw himself on the bed, but as his head fell on the pillow, in went the needle, so that he called out with pain, and madly rushed out. But when he reached the housedoor the millstone jumped up and struck him dead." The Grimms never say exactly what Mr. Korbes did to deserve such treatment—but explain that if he were not an evil man, he would not have been punished thus. see: **Grimm, Jakob and Wilhelm.**

Korva [L] A kingdom featured in Edgar Rice Burroughs' 1937 novel *Carson of Venus.* Adopted by Carson Napier and his wife, Duare, as home, Korva supplants their previous address in Vepaja, the realm of Duare's father, Jong (King) Mintep. But Korva is not a land of peace when the couple first discovers it. It is under attack by Zanis, Naziesque fighters who salute their leader with a hail of Maltu Mephis. Aided by Napier, Korva mounts a victorious offense for which the earthman on Venus is named the tanjong or prince of the empire. As for Mephis—Burroughs' play on the name Mephistopheles—he is poisoned. see: **Burroughs, Edgar Rice; Napier, Carson.**

Kothar [L] A sword-swinging adventurer created in 1968 by author Gardner F. Fox. As a boy, Kothar had been left to die on the desolate shores of Grondel Bay. But he survived, growing to manhood and becoming the greatest swordsperson in the world. Wielding the enchanted blade Frostfire, the barbarian with long yellow hair marches through adventures like *Kothar and the Demon Queen.* Among his most formidable foes are the White Worm and the sorceress Red Lori.

Koura [MP] The vile magician played by Tom Baker in Ray Harryhausen's 1973 film *The Golden Voyage of Sinbad.* Koura has a problem; every time he uses his powers he ages. However, without magic there is no way he can retrieve an amulet which will give him limitless occult abilities. Another problem: Sinbad is also searching for the talisman, which rightfully belongs to the Grand Vizier of Marabia. Using his supernatural talents to create a pair of homunculi, bring a masthead and then an idol to life, summon Lemurians and a centaur to his aid, Koura is a decayed old man before he finds the amulet. But find it he does, with the help of his assistant, Achmed. Unfortunately, before Koura can tap its great strength, Sinbad runs the magician through the belly and claims the prize. see: **Centaur; Harryhausen, Ray; Homunculus; Kali; Sinbad.**

Kraken [U] A legendary squid or octopus of monstrous size. Said to be round and flat and up to one and one-half miles long, the kraken usually has hundreds of tentacles and spends most of its time sleeping. Over the years, huge carcasses said to belong to kraken have washed up on shores around

Hraken

the world, and as recently as 1977 Indonesian fishers have reported sighting one of these sea giants. Surprisingly, science says that there may be some truth to these stories. It is not inconceivable that cephalopods several hundred feet long live at the sea bottom. While their local food sources remain constant, the creatures stay put. But if some environmental imbalance causes supplies to dwindle, the squid or octopus may venture to the ocean's surface. A somewhat melodramatic version of this theory was the subject of the 1955 Ray Harryhausen film *It Came from Beneath the Sea*, as a kraken razed San Francisco in search of food. see: **Harryhausen, Ray.**

Kronos [MP] An unusual and majestic robot featured in the 1957 film *Kronos*. Kronos emerges from a flying saucer which crashes off the shores of Mexico. Rectangular and towering several hundred feet tall, Kronos has no limbs beyond its three pistonlike legs. First appearing on a beach, the robot begins to move, taking a step with its central leg, lowering the other two and withdrawing the first, then repeating the process. As it turns out, the automaton has come to earth to gather up energy for an alien race. Kronos attacks powerplants, absorbs the full force of an atom bomb—in short, proves utterly unstoppable. Finally, scientists find a way to turn Kronos' stored energy against the robot and melt it down. *Kronos* is also an accepted alternate spelling of *Cronus*, one of the foremost Greek Gods. see: **Cronus.**

Kubrick, Stanley [MP] A highly regarded film director with an affinity for the fantastic. Born in 1928 in the Bronx, Kubrick attended Taft high school. While still at Taft, he sold a photograph to *Look* magazine and continued peddling pictures to them for nearly five years. Kubrick's first love was movies, however, and his initial work was *Day of the Fight*, a short documentary made in 1950 about a boxer. His debut feature was *Fear and Desire* (1953). Of Kubrick's eleven pictures, four of the last five have been science fiction or fantasy. They are *Dr. Strangelove—Or—How I Learned to Stop Worrying and Love the Bomb* (1963), a comedy about World War III; *2001: A Space Odyssey* (1968), a tale of alien beings and a computer-gone-mad; *A Clockwork Orange* (1971), the story of teenage gangs and morality in the future; and *The Shining* (1980), a film version of Stephen King's best-selling novel about a young boy with supernatural abilities. see: **King, Stephen.**

Kukulkan [M] One of the most important of the Mayan gods. Pictured as a feathered serpent, Kukulkan was actually the chief god of many of the later Mayans. Originally viewed as the god of life, Kukulkan was refined in subsequent thinking, coming to personify the wind. Despite these magnificent personae, the deity is best known for having invented the calendar and teaching people how to use it.

Kull, King [L] A barbarian hero created by Robert E. Howard in 1929. The setting of the Kull stories are the environs of Atlantis at a time when the legendary continent was first developing into a magnificent empire. Sa-

vagery still reigns, a life for which the scarred and muscular ax-brandishing Kull is well suited. After adventures which include time spent as a galley slave, gladiator, and soldier, he settles on the European mainland, deposes the cruel King Borna, and becomes the ruler of Valusia, strongest of the seven empires and surrounded by such formidable lands as Kamelia, Grondar, Commoria, and Thule. Among Kull's many exploits are *The Shadow Kingdom* (1929), *The Mirrors of Tuzun Thune* (1929), and *The King and the Oak* (1939). see: **Conan; Howard, Robert E.**

Kzinti [TV] Alien beings created by author Larry Niven for his novel *Ringworld*, but best known through the animated "Star Trek" episodes "Slaver Weapon" and "Time Trap." Eight feet tall and powerfully built, with feline features and multi-colored patches and stripes, the Kzinti are skilled fighters. However, because they are aggressive beasts the Federation deprived them of weapons when the two groups signed a treaty of peace. Once the holders of a vast empire, these meat-eaters—who would just as soon eat human flesh as any—now hold twelve worlds including their native planet, Kzin. Each Kzinti has many hearts. see: *Enterprise, U.S.S.*

Lamas [F] One of the four djinn of ancient Chaldea who looked out for the welfare of humans. Also known as Nigal, this powerful spirit has a human head atop the body of a lion. The other djinn in this protectorate are Sed-Alap or Kirub, a bull with a human head; Nattig, a human-headed eagle; and the fully human Ustar. see: **Djinn.**

Lamia [M] A monster of Greek mythology. As a mortal, she was the Queen of Libya and beloved of Zeus. Indeed, as a show of his affection the king of the gods gave her the ability to withdraw her eyes from her head. If that were not a very practical gift, it was kinder than the one given Lamia by Zeus' wife, Hera. Jealous of the queen, she slew her children and changed her into a monster that was half-snake and half-woman. Hera then forced her to go out into the world eating any child she came across. Some tales say that Lamia's appetite extended all the way to young men, whom she seduced with her human half before eating.

Those of Lamia's children which Hera allowed to survive are known as *Lamiae.* Bloodsuckers, they are half-human and half-serpent, with the hindfeet of a goat and the forefeet of a cat. Other of her progeny are half-goat and half-horse. They live in isolated regions of the forest and nip at humans who pass by. The wound these creatures inflict can only be cured by hearing Lamia's bellowing.

In Hebrew legend, Lamia is a lovely seductress with long hair. She appears as a succubus, making love to men while they sleep. Some texts make the Hebrew Lamia one and the same with the lascivious Lilith, the first wife of Adam. see: **Hera; Zeus.**

Lao, Dr. [L] An ancient Chinese gentleman featured in the clever Charles Finney novel *The Circus of Dr. Lao* (1935). The 400-year-old proprietor of a traveling circus, Lao showcases such fantastic creatures as unicorns, a werewolf, a two-headed turtle, a sphinx, and a chimera. He also brings with him tales of the drought-stricken city of Woldercan, whose citizens made virgin sacrifices to the awful god Yottle in the hope of ending their strife. Stopping in the small town of Abalone, Arizona, Lao uses his monsters and legends to enlighten the drought-plagued Abalonians.

In 1964, George Pal produced a movie version of the Finney novel, with Tony Randall as the wispy Oriental *and* most of his attractions. Retitled *The Seven Faces of Dr. Lao,* the Oscar-winning film gave the circus

Lamia

164

such odd sideshows as the Abominable Snowman, Pan, Medusa, Merlin the Magician, the Loch Ness Monster, and Appolonius the Seer. see: **Abominable Snowman; Chimera; Loch Ness Monster; Medusa; Merlin; Pal, George; Pan; Sphinx; Unicorn; Werewolf.**

Laputa [L] In the novel *Gulliver's Travels,* Laputa is "an island in the air, inhabited by men, who were able . . . to raise, or sink, or put it into a progressive motion, as they pleased." Gulliver reaches this strange land in 1707, after his ship is beset by pirates and he is put adrift in a small canoe. Access to the surface of Laputa is had via stairs on the side of the island. These steps lead to galleries from which its citizens fish. Taken onto Laputa, whose name means flying or floating island in the native tongue, Gulliver finds their speech, "not unlike in sound to the Italian." However, he assesses their appearance as somewhat more bizarre. "Their heads were all reclined either to the right or the left; one of their eyes turned inward, and the other directly up to the zenith. Their outward garments were adorned with the figures of suns, moons, and stars, interwoven with those of fiddles, flutes, harps, trumpets, guitars, harpsichords, and many more instruments of music unknown to us in Europe."

As it turns out, the residents of Laputa are odder than their guest's first impressions suggest. Experts in math and music, they cut their food in the shape of flutes, fiddles, equilateral triangles, and the like. Architecturally, Gulliver quips, "their houses are very ill built, the walls bevel, without one right angle in any apartment; and this defect ariseth from the contempt they bear to practiced geometry, which they despise as vulgar."

Despite this attitude, they are excellent astronomers and canny busi-nesspeople. Their king collects tribute by hovering Laputa over select regions and blocking the sun until he is paid. If that doesn't work, rocks are heaved on the populace from the 10,-000-acre island. And if the people below still refuse to yield, the king drops his 300-yard-thick, 7,837-yard-diameter kingdom smack on top of them. Upon leaving this pleasant place, Gulliver is deposited upon a mountain in Balnibarbi. see: **Balnibarbi; Gulliver, Lemuel.**

Lee, Christopher [MP] A popular film star best known for his portrayals of great movie monsters. Born Christopher Frank Carandini Lee in London in 1922, the young man went to Wellington College where he became a classical scholar. But acting quickly tore this six-foot four-inch descendant of Charlemagne from his tomes, and he made his movie debut in *Corridor of Mirrors* in 1947. Lee appeared in many movies thereafter, usually in bit parts as a villain. However, with *Curse of Frankenstein* (1957) as the Monster, and *Horror of Dracula* (1958) as the Count, Lee became an international star. Since that time he has been featured as Sir Henry Baskerville in *Hound of the Baskervilles* (1959), as the bandage-swathed fiend in *The Mummy* (1959), as Professor Mesiter in *The Gorgon* (1964), as Fu Manchu in a trio of films about the Oriental megalomaniac, as the sanguinary Count Dracula in six sequels to his original vampire film, as the three-nippled Scaramanga in the James Bond film *The Man With the Golden Gun* (1974), and in dozens of other genre roles. Lee is married to the Danish Birgit Kroencke and they have a daughter, Christina. see: **Bond, James; Cushing, Peter; Dracula; Frankenstein Monster; Fu Manchu; Hound of the Baskervilles, The; Mummy, The.**

Lee, Hok [FT] The bandit of "Hok Lee and the Dwarfs," a Chinese fairy tale.

Pretending to be hard working and industrious, Hok Lee is actually a bandit whose evil deeds cause his face to swell. Visiting a doctor, Lee is told that he "has called down the anger of the spirits" with his life-style, and must pay the doctor handsomely for a cure. The thief hands over the fee and is told that on the first night of the full moon he must wait by a special tree in a certain wood. In short order dwarfs and sprites will appear and begin to dance, and Hok Lee must dance with them. If he frolics to their satisfaction, they will cure him. If not, they will punish him. The first time out Hok Lee dances poorly and his face is made to swell even further. Returning a month later, he makes merry to the imps' delight and his face is made normal. Abandoning outright banditry, Hok Lee becomes a wealthy man by charging huge sums to send other accursed people to the dwarfs.

Lee, Stan [C] A comic book writer and editor. Born Stanley Lieber in 1922, Lee went to work as an assistant editor for Timely (later Marvel) comics in 1939. Three years later he became editor-in-chief. While holding this title, Lee also did the bulk of the writing for such characters as Captain America, the Destroyer, and Jack Frost. In 1961, he and his top artists got together and created such heroes as Spiderman, the Fantastic Four, the Incredible Hulk, and others. Their success made Lee the most popular writer in the history of the medium. Today, he is the titular publisher of Marvel and his writing is limited to a monthly column which appears in the comics, and essays for book collections of his work. Lee is married to Joan Lee and they have a daughter Joannie. Lee's brother, Larry Lieber, is a comic book artist; their cousin Martin Goodman was Marvel's former publisher. see: **Captain America; Hulk, The Incredible; Kirby, Jack; Spiderman; Thor; X-Men, The.**

Leprechauns

Leprechauns [F] Fairy shoemakers. The most noted of the fairy tribes of Ireland, leprechauns are old men who wear a cocked hat, a lace coat, knee breeches, and shoes with silver buckles. Standing an average of two feet tall, they make their brogues in out-of-the-way places such as wine cellars. Extremely wealthy little people, leprechauns can be held by a mortal's stare and forced to reveal where their money is hidden. However, if the person's eyes are diverted even for an instant, the leprechaun will disappear.

The word *leprechaun* derives from Leith Bhrogan, the "one-shoe maker," as leprechauns diligently work on only one shoe at a time. Some leprechauns moonlight as helpers on farms and in homes, but most spend their leisure time smoking or drinking in cellars. One breed of leprechaun, the Clurichaun, lavishes most of its time in this pursuit. According to several accounts, modern-day fairies are most active not in Ireland but in Perthshire, Scotland.

Leshy [F] A powerful forest spirit of

Slav folklore. Tall as a tree in its natural state, this shape-changer can usually be found at wood's-edge—not as a giant but as an imp-sized being who greets travelers and leads them astray. Once a mortal has encountered a leshy, the only way to be free of it is to sit under a tree, strip, don your clothes backward, and put your shoes on the wrong feet. Possessing human features, the leshy has blue skin due to its blue blood, boasts a long green beard, and has green popeyes. It usually wears its shoes on the opposite feet and its clothes upside-down, inside-out, and front-to-back. The leshy dwells in small clans and are most visible in the spring but never in October, when they breed and die.

Leviathan [F] A great sea-beast of Biblical legend. Possessing fins whose radiance obscures the sun, and eyes so bright that they illuminate the sea, the fishlike Leviathan carries the world along the waters. A foul-smelling creature, it is described in some texts as the wife of the land beast Behemoth; other writings claim that it is male and that its mate was slain by God so that it can never reproduce. When Leviathan is hungry, its hot breath causes the sea to boil; only the tiny stickleback fish can control Leviathan, as in stopping it from snorting the ocean to oblivion. Eventually, Leviathan will be forced to battle Behemoth to the death, the loser's flesh being distributed by the Messiah to the righteous. see: **Behemoth.**

Lewton, Val [MP] A producer of high quality horror films. Born in Yalta, Russia, in 1904, Vladimir Leventon was the son of Nina and Maximillian Leventon. When his parents divorced, the young boy went to Berlin with his mother and sister, Lucy. The trio immigrated to the United States in 1916. After attending the New York Military Academy, Lewton settled in Connecticut and became a successful novelist, one of his books becoming

the 1932 Clark Gable-Carole Lombard film *No Man of Her Own.* In 1933, Lewton moved to Hollywood and became a screenwriter for producer David O. Selznick. After subsequently serving as a story editor, he accepted an offer from RKO in 1942 to produce his own films. Lewton gravitated toward horror and fantasy and among his most noted pictures are the classics *The Cat People* (1942), *I Walked With a Zombie* (1943), *Leopard Man* (1943), *Curse of the Cat People* (1944), and Robert Wise's brilliant *The Body Snatcher* (1945). Lewton's last film was *Apache Drums* released in 1951, the year of his untimely death. Lewton was survived by his wife, Ruth, whom he had married in 1929, and a daughter, Nina, born in 1930.

Ligeia [L] The subject of Edgar Allan Poe's 1838 short story "Ligeia." Described as a "tall, somewhat slender woman of ... rare learning," with black hair and a "placid cast of beauty," she is the wife of the story's narrator. Sadly, Ligeia falls ill and though she "wrestles with the shadow," she becomes horribly emaciated and dies. Soon thereafter the narrator weds the fair-haired and blue-eyed Lady Rowena Trevanion. However, after two months she becomes deathly sick. When the narrator fears that she too has passed on, he is amazed to see her corpse stir, "arising from the bed, tottering, with feeble steps," approaching him not as the Lady Rowena but as Ligeia. Whether or not this vision is the narrator's imagination is never explained.

In 1965, this tale was brought to the screen as *The Tomb of Ligeia* starring Vincent Price. The slightly altered scenario has the new wife of widower Price being haunted by his former spouse, Ligeia. see: **Poe, Edgar Allan; Price, Vincent.**

Lilith [F] The first wife of Adam. Originally the bride of Satan, Lilith proves wild and impulsive and leaves him for the First Man. But her stay with Adam is brief. Because they had both been created from the dust, Lilith demands equal rights. Adam refuses, they argue, and she leaves him. Upset, Adam asks God to retrieve her, and he assigns the task to the angels Senoi, Sansenoi, and Sammangelof. They catch up with Lilith and order her to return to her mate. But she resists and is punished by having 100 of her children die daily. In retribution, Lilith devotes her life to harming the offspring of others. She can only be driven off by a talisman inscribed with the name of the three angels. Ironically, after the expulsion of Adam and Eve from Eden, the couple is separated for 130 years—during which time Adam once again takes up with Lilith. The children born of this coupling become the demons and shedim which thereafter haunt humankind. Lilith is frequently identified with Lamia of Greek mythology. see: **Lamia.**

Lilliput [L] In *Gulliver's Travels*, a land of diminutive humans. Located southwest of Sumatra, Lilliput is visited by the storm-tossed Gulliver in the year 1699. Washing onto a grassy beach, Gulliver finds the Lilliputians to be not quite 6 inches high, with horses 4½ inches tall. Chained in a temple until the little people are certain of his peaceful intentions, Gulliver is called *Quinbus Flestrin*—"Great Man Mountain"—and eats the equivalent of food "sufficient for the support of 1,728 Lilliputians."

The Englishperson finds the political situation in Lilliput rather uneasy. The small nation is at war with Blefescu, their neighbor beyond a channel some 800 yards wide and 70 glumgluffs—6 feet—deep. The altercation grew over an argument whether eggs should be broken at the large or little end, a debate which Gulliver renders academic by towing away Blefescu's

fleet. But the hero's glory is short lived. Putting out a fire at court by urinating on it, and subsequently being accused of conspiring with the Emperor of Blefescu, Gulliver is sentenced to lose his sight, to which "twenty of his majesty's surgeons will attend . . . by discharging very sharp-pointed arrows into the balls" of Gulliver's eyes. The castaway chooses flight to blindness and takes to sea in a "prodigious vessel" he finds in Blefescu. He is rescued by an English merchantman.

Among the oddest customs found on Lilliput, or any of Gulliver's other stops, involves the burying of the Lilliputian dead, recounted here in full: "They bury their dead with their heads directly downwards, because they hold an opinion that in eleven thousand moons they are all to rise again, in which period the earth (which they conceive to be flat) will turn upside down, and by this means they shall, at their resurrection, be found ready standing on their feet." see: **Gulliver, Lemuel.**

Limbo [O] A region of rootless phantom beings. Traditionally, Limbo is the abode of spirits who are not entitled to enjoy the alleged wonder of Heaven, but do not deserve the steamy torment of Hell. Located on the border of these two afterlife extremes, Limbo is generally described by theologians as a home for unbaptized infants and good people who died before the coming of Christ. According to Dante Alighieri's epic poem *The Inferno*, shades can be summoned from Limbo to assist other beings. Not so on Krypton, the home planet of Superman, where Limbo is known as The Phantom Zone, a place to where convicted criminals are sent to exist as harmless, disembodied spirits. see: **Hell; Superman.**

Link, Adam [L] A popular robot of fiction. Created by author Eando Binder, Adam Link is built by Dr.

Charles Link. It takes twenty years to tool and encase the robot's sophisticated systems in a body crafted by skilled artisans. But when it is completed, Adam—with an iridium-sponge brain and photoelectric eyes—can both think and reason like a human, without knowing human pain. Unfortunately, Dr. Link's extensive plans for his creation go awry. When a loose angle-iron of a transformer falls from the wall and caves in the scientist's skull, Adam is accused of murder. The eight-foot-tall robot flees with Dr. Link's dog, Terry, although he is quickly captured, tried, and sentenced to die in the electric chair. Luckily, reporter Jack Hall proves Adam innocent and the powerful robot is released.

Requiring a new battery every forty-eight hours, Adam crams each two-day period with many adventures. Prominent among these is a battle with nine-foot-tall alien creatures who are a cross between a gorilla, an upright horned buffalo, and "a surrealistic statue representing a hunchback on whom a mountain has fallen." Throughout his adventures, Adam is constantly improving himself and, with the aid of friends, even builds a girl friend robot named Eve. Eventually, Adam and Eve tire of our inhospitable world and settle on the moon. The saga of Adam Link has also appeared in *Creepy* magazine, and on TV's "Outer Limits." see: **Creepy, Uncle; Outer Limits.**

Little Nemo [C] The young star of the comic strip "Little Nemo in Slumberland" created by Winsor McCay. Each night, Nemo is borne in dream to Slumberland, where he has surrealistic adventures with giants, monsters, and such characters as the green dwarf Flip, the cannibal Impy, Dr. Pill, Slumberland's King Morpheus, and Jack Frost. The first Nemo strip appeared in *The New York Herald* on October 15, 1905, and was published every Sunday in full color. Although each Little Nemo cartoon is self-con-

tained, they are all part of a continuing, if episodic, saga. Every installment concludes with Nemo awaking in bed, commenting about his dream. The strip was dropped by the *Herald* in 1911, ran in the Hearst papers for three years, and then was discontinued. It was revived briefly by the *Herald* from 1924–1927. see: **McCay, Winsor.**

Little Prince [L] A young boy who scours different worlds for the roots of human emotions. Created by author Antoine De Saint Exùpéry (1900–1944), this hero of the novel *The Little Prince* (1943) lives on the tiny asteroid B-612. In addition to three volcanoes—two of which are extinct—the small world boasts a flower. But the flower's very human pride disturbs the Little Prince, disrupting the tranquility of B-612. The young boy decides he must therefore meet other beings to understand what has happened. His early voyages take him to planets inhabited by a king, a businessperson, a historian, and others, all of whom are obsessed with their own problems. Finally, the Little Prince reaches earth. After adventures with a fox, snake, and lost pilot, the boy dies—but not before giving new meaning to the life of the pilot. In 1974, *The Little Prince* was filmed as an entertaining and underrated musical starring England's Stephen Warner as the prince and Richard Kiley as the pilot.

Little Two Eyes [FT] "Because Little Two Eyes did not look any different from other children, her sisters and mother could not bear her." Such is the lot of a Grimm Brothers heroine whose sisters are Little One Eye, with an orb in the center of her forehead, and Little Three Eyes, who has a trio of lids blinking from her face. Little Two Eyes is starved and overworked. Then, while she is tending the goats one day, a woman sits beside her. The newcomer teaches Little Two Eyes a chant to call food from the aether:

"Little goat bleat, little table appear." Thus is Little Two Eyes' life made tolerable. But her sisters spy on the suddenly contented girl and see her wish upon the goat. Furious, her mother slays the animal. Forlorn, Little Two Eyes is once again visited by the strange woman. This time she tells the girl to bury the goat's heart and, the next day, a tree has grown sporting leaves of silver and fruit of gold. Whenever anyone but Little Two Eyes approaches, the boughs move out of reach. One day, a knight happens by and offers the reward of any wish to whomever can pick the tree's wealth. Only Little Two Eyes succeeds. She asks the knight to marry her, which he does—the tree uprooting itself and following them to the warrior's castle. Years later, Little Two Eyes' sisters appear at their door as beggars. Little Two Eyes takes them in and they repent. see: **Grimm, Jakob and Wilhelm.**

Llarn [L] A world created by author Gardner F. Fox in 1966. Featured in a series of novels whose titles include *Warrior of Llarn* and *Thief of Llarn*, this alien planet hosts the adventures of Alan Morgan. An earthperson, Morgan is brought to Llarn to help Vann Tarr in his quest for a special red metal ball and green rod. The alien is a being known as an Ephelos, and these artifacts will permit Vann Tarr to move on to the next stage of existence. During the period of the search Morgan has many adventures, most notably rescuing Tuarra—the daganna (princess) of the great city Kharthol—from the blue men of Azorra, marrying her, and restoring the throne of Kharthol unto her father, Drakol Tu. see: **Kothar.**

Lobster-Quadrille [L] A dance in *Alice in Wonderland* (1865), explained to Alice by the Mock Turtle and the Gryphon. To do the Lobster-Quadrille, you form two lines of seals, turtles, salmon, etc. along the seashore. Then, "when you've cleared all the jellyfish out of the way," you take a lobster as a partner and advance twice. Then, you "set to partners, change lobsters, and retire in the same order, then you throw the lobsters as far out to sea as you can, turn a somersault in the sea, change lobsters again, back to land again, and that's all the first figure." Alice is unenthused by either the dance or its proponents. see: **Alice; Griffin; Mock Turtle.**

Loch Ness Monster [U] One of the world's most famous fantastic creatures. There is still no hard evidence to prove that the Loch Ness Monster exists—but neither is there any way to disprove that a large, possibly dinosaurian beast lurks at the bottom of the twenty-seven-mile-long, one-mile-wide Loch Ness in the Highlands of northern Scotland.

Reports of monsters reach back 1,-500 years, the earliest known sighting occurring when St. Columba chased a huge sea animal away from a bather. However, it wasn't until the government built a road around the lake in 1933 that the Loch Ness Monster became an international phenomenon. It was seen and photographed many times over, generally emerging as a large, worm or sluglike creature with humps on its back, a serpent's head, and flippers. As recently as the mid-seventies photographs of the monster's face, neck, and flippers were taken with underwater cameras. Alas, these pictures are hazy and inconclusive due to extremely poor visibility in the peat-filled loch. An expedition mounted by *The New York Times* in 1976 turned up little new evidence, and a search by camera-bearing dolphins is now being readied.

Scientists suggest that if there is a monster in Loch Ness, it is probably not one creature but a herd of them, only some of which are occasionally sighted. As for their identity, they may be prehistoric animals whose line escaped extinction when changing geography cut the lake from the North

Sea tens of thousands of years ago. Whether it *is* such an ancient creature—for instance, a plesiosaur which it closely resembles—or something as comparatively mundane as a large variety of long-necked sea cow, the Loch Ness Monster remains a formidable mystery. see: **Morag; Ogopogo; Worm of Lambton.**

Loki [M] An evil Norse god. The son of Laufey and the giant Farbauti—who ferries the dead across the waters of the underworld—Loki is the personification of fire as a tool of destruction. Extremely handsome, his most striking attribute is his cunning—a quality he uses in an unending effort to cause the downfall of the gods. Indeed, even the collapse of the universe will content Loki as long as his fellow deities fall with it. The father of Fenrir the wolf, the Serpent of Midgard, and Hel by the giantess Angurboda; and of the boys Nari and Vali by Sigyn, Loki commits many murders in the pursuit of his obsession. Several times the wicked god is caught and punished—one time being chained beneath a serpent whose poison dripping on Loki's head causes him to shake with such pain that the earth itself trembles. Ultimately, he is slain at the time of Ragnarok by the golden-toothed Heimdall, god of light, in a battle to reclaim a necklace stolen from Freya, the goddess of young love. Heimdall is also killed in the match. see: **Balder; Fenrir; Hel; Odin; Thor.**

Looe [O] A ghost which haunts Cornwall in England. A white hare, the Looe is frequently seen running along the roads and is said to be the ghost of a disconsolate girl who long ago took her life. More likely, however, the Looe is simply a rabbit to whom an occult nature was attributed by smugglers of yore who wanted to keep people from stirring about the coast at night. see: **Phouka.**

Looking Glass Insects [L] Creatures invented by author Lewis Carroll for his 1871 novel *Through the Looking Glass.* The first Looking Glass Insect met by Carroll's heroine Alice is a gnat the size of a chicken. Others include a rocking-horse fly—"It's made entirely of wood, and gets about by swinging itself from branch to branch"—which feeds on sap and sawdust; a snapdragon-fly—"Its body is made of plum pudding, its wings of holly-leaves, its head is a raisin burning in brandy"—which subsists on "frumenty and mince pie and ... makes its nest in a Christmas box"; and a bread-and-butter-fly, whose wings are "thin slices of bread and butter, its body is a crust, and its head a lump of sugar," and who lives on "weak tea with cream in it." see: **Alice.**

Looney, Matthew [L] A popular children's book character, created in 1961 by writer Jerome Beatty Jr. and artist Gahan Wilson. Residing on the moon, in a cave in the town of Crater Pluto, young Matthew lives with his father, Monroe, his mother, Diana, his sister, Maria, and his pet murtle. When we first meet the doughy moon beings, their scientific community is preparing an expedition to earth to see whether or not their hub world sustains life. Matthew's dream is to work as a cabin boy on the voyage, which will be commanded by his uncle, Capt. Lockhard Looney. But Monroe has his heart set on getting his son a job at the Mt. Pico Powder Works—where, since there is no erosion on the moon, every unwanted item has to be ground to dust. Naturally, Matthew gets his way and the first Looney novel, *Matthew Looney's Voyage to Earth,* tells of the spaceflight and its startling discoveries. Sequels to this volume include *Matthew Looney's Invasion of Earth, Matthew Looney in the Outback,* and *Matthew Looney and the Space Pirates.* The travels of Matthew's sister are recounted in *Maria Looney on the Red Planet* and *Maria Looney and the Cosmic Circus.*

Among the more interesting problems invented by Beatty for his lunarians are the disease cosmos, which is caused by exposure to the sun, changes the color of one's skin, and induces laziness; and velocipitis, the inclination to move too rapidly in the moon's low gravity and send yourself hurtling into the air.

Lorelei [F] A nymph of European legend. In life, Lorelei was a young girl who leaped into the Rhine and drowned after being spurned by her lover. Thereafter, assuming the form of a nymph—some say a siren or a mermaid—she haunted a rock on the right bank of the river. There she sits, running a golden comb through her hair and singing an alluring song. This melody is said to be so lovely that it causes those who are fishing or boating nearby to forget themselves and crash on the rocks or be caught in the swift river currents. Some tales say that those who hear Lorelei must stay by her side forever; those who see her lose their eyesight or their mind. Occasionally identified with Hulda, the queen of the elves, Lorelei is the subject of a poem written in 1800 by Klemens Brentano (1778–1842). see: **Mermaid; Nymph; Siren.**

Lorre, Peter [MP] An actor famous for his performances in horror films. Born in a small Hungarian village in 1904, Lorre worked in a bank before joining an acting troupe. He performed for many years in a variety of parts, but it was his first film, Fritz Lang's *M* (1931) which made Lorre a star. Playing a child killer, it also typecast him in maniacal roles. Lorre's first English language film was Alfred Hitchcock's 1934 classic *The Man Who Knew Too Much.* Among his most famous fantasy films are *Mad Love* (1935) as a lunatic surgeon; *The Face Behind the Mask* (1941) as a horribly disfigured watchmaker; *The Beast With Five Fingers* (1946) about a severed, murdering hand; *Twenty Thousand Leagues*

Under the Sea (1954) and *Voyage to the Bottom of the Sea* (1961); *The Raven* (1963) as the titular bird-man; and *The Comedy of Terrors* (1964) in which he plays an undertaker who decides to create a market for his services. Thrice married—to Celia Lovsky, Kaaren Verne, and Anna Marie Brenning (by whom he had a daughter, Cathy)—Lorre died in 1964.

Lovecraft, H.P. [L] One of the great names in fantasy fiction. Born in Providence, Rhode Island in 1890, Howard Phillips Lovecraft saw both of his parents die in an insane asylum. Living with two aunts, he began his writing career with an astronomy column penned for his own amusement. His first fiction sale was "The Alchemist," which was published in an amateur magazine in 1916. Professionally, he broke the ice with a series of stories entitled *Gruesome Tales* (1922). However, it was "Dagon" which appeared a year later in *Weird Tales* which brought him widespread and lasting fame. In fact, most of Lovecraft's fifty-two short stories would appear in the pages of that illustrious magazine—although he *did* supplement his income by editing the manuscripts of others and ghostwriting for Harry Houdini. Among Lovecraft's most famous short stories are "The Call of Cthulhu" (1927), "The Colour Out of Space" (1927)—filmed in 1965 as *Die, Monster, Die*—and "Cool Air" (1928). The reclusive Lovecraft was briefly married to Sonia H. Greene, and died of a kidney ailment in 1937. see: **Cthulhu; Kadath; Weird Tales.**

Ludovico's Technique [L] A controversial process of rehabilitation used in Anthony Burgess' 1963 novel *A Clockwork Orange.* After a drug is administered via hypodermic needle, a criminal is exposed to whatever habit is to be broken. In the case of protagonist Alex de Large, he is to be cured of his violent tendencies. Alex is shown films of beatings and rape, and because of the drug the scenes make him ill. Thereafter, whenever Alex even thinks about an aggressive act he doubles over with nausea. Oddly, as a result of Ludovico's Technique, the murderer Alex becomes a subject of massive public sympathy. This tampering with his free will is deemed un-Christian, so he is returned to his former frame of mind—and put to work as a high-salaried government official to placate the voters. In Stanley Kubrick's 1971 film *A Clockwork Orange*, Alex was played by Malcolm McDowell.

Luggnagg [L] A land located southwest of Balnibarbi and visited by Lemuel Gulliver in 1708. Gulliver reaches Luggnagg via sea, sailing up a river to the seaport town of Clumegnig. Traveling on to see the king, he takes the precaution of sending ahead a messenger to see when he "might have the honour to lick the dust before his footstool." It is well that Gulliver pays this courtesy, for the monarch is a nasty sort indeed. When he is affronted, he has the floor strewn "with a certain brown powder, of a deadly composition" which causes death within twenty-four hours.

Luggnagg is a land which harbors one of the most set-upon races in *Gulliver's Travels*, the Struldbrugs. These people are born with "a red circular spot in the forehead, directly over the left eyebrow, which was an infallible mark that it should never die." When the Struldbrug child is twelve years old the spot becomes green, then a deep blue at twenty-five and coal black at forty-five. There is no predictable pattern to Struldbrug generation; immortal children may be born to normal parents, and normal children to immortal parents. In either instance, it is a life which no one covets. Because of their immortality, this group of some 1,100 men and women is governed by special laws.

Their marriages are automatically terminated by the state when they reach eighty, the reason being that, "those who are condemned to a perpetual contrivance in the world should not have their misery doubled by the load" of a spouse. At this age, Struldbrugs are also declared officially dead. Their estates pass to heirs and they are allowed a pittance on which to live. They are not allowed to work. Ten years later, their teeth and hair fall out, their taste fades, and they can no longer read because memory "will not serve to carry them from the beginning of a sentence to the end." After 200 years, they cannot even hold a conversation and are ignored by most other Luggnaggians.

After a year in this impersonal land, Gulliver sails on to Japan. see: **Balnibarbi; Gulliver, Lemuel.**

Lugosi, Bela [MP] An actor best known for his portrayal of Dracula. Béla Ferenc Dezsö Blasko was born in Lugosi, Hungary in 1882. The son of Paula von Vojnics and Stephen Blasko, his brothers were László and Lajos, his sister Vilma. Young Béla studied at the Budapest Academy of Fine Arts and subsequently performed in stage plays throughout his country. In 1910 he began appearing in motion pictures, mostly one or two reel short subjects; eleven years later he came to New York and organized a Hungarian stock company. Though he made movies in the United States—his first was *The Silent Command* (1923)—the bulk of his work was on the stage, where he spoke English phonetically until he learned the language. Then came the Broadway edition of *Dracula* (1927)—and the character which was to haunt the rest of Lugosi's career. The continental actor recreated his role on the screen three years later, and was thereafter forced into an unbroken string of less prestigious roles. Among his better vehicles: *Son of Frankenstein* (1939) and *Ghost* *of Frankenstein* (1942) as the twisted Ygor; *The Wolfman* (1941) as a gypsy werewolf whose bite turns Lon Chaney Jr. into the featured monster; *Frankenstein Meets the Wolfman* (1943) as the former; *Abbott and Costello Meet Frankenstein* (1947) as Dracula. Sadly, Lugosi never saw any money from the millions of dollars

Lybbarde and Looe

made by licensing his image as Dracula.

Bela Lugosi died in 1956. Five times married, his wives were Ilona Szmik, Ilona von Montagh, Beatrice Woodruff Weeks, Lillian Arch, and Hope Lininger. His son, Bela Lugosi Jr., is a Los Angeles attorney. see: **Dracula; Frankenstein Monster, The; Wolfman, The.**

Lung [M] The Chinese dragon of the sky. Unlike most dragons, Lung serves rather than assaults humankind. The radiant, health-providing beast brings good luck to those who deserve it, causes it to rain at the proper time of year, watches that the winds don't blow too violently, and maintains the levels of the rivers. The counterpart of Lung is Le, the dragon of the sea. see: **Dragon.**

Lybbarde [F] A giant leopard of medieval folklore. Generally viewed as the spawn of a panther and a lioness, the lybbarde has been known to both aid and attack humans, depending upon the story being told. Regardless, the beast is noted for its courage and was popular in heraldic imagery as a representation of fortitude.

Mab [F] The United Kingdom's revered queen of the fairies. A popular literary figure of the sixteenth and seventeenth centuries, she is described in William Shakespeare's play *Romeo and Juliet* (1595) as a fairy who rides a coach pulled along by insects and serves as midwife to the birth of dreams. She is more prominently featured in Ben Jonson's *Entertainment at Althorpe* (1603) as a mischievous sprite. Mab's roots are thought to lie in the warrior-queen Maeve of Ireland. see: **Fairies; Oberon.**

MacCoul, Finn [F] Also known as Fionn, a hero of Irish legend. The grandson of the war god Tuatha De Danann, and the son of the giant Cumhal, Finn is raised by the peasants Bodmhall and Liath. Employed by the seer Finn Eger for seven years, the young man becomes all-knowing when he tastes the salmon of the Boyne River, a fish which had fed on the hazelnuts of wisdom. In addition to the vast knowledge he gains, Finn MacCoul has great strength. He uses this to battle the giant Fomors and is also said to have slain a dragon after being gobbled down, wielding a sword to slice his way out. The father of Fergus and Ossian, Finn is slain by an angry populace after jealously causing the death of his nephew Diarmait, a rival for the affections of the beautiful Grainne. Often identified with the sun, Finn has been seen from time to time throughout Ireland, inspiring his people in times of trouble. It is written that when Ireland most needs him, he will return in flesh as well as spirit. see: **Fomors; MacRoman, Caoilte.**

Maciste [L/MP] A strongman of Italian fiction and film. Though created by author Gabriele D'Annunzio for the novel *Cabiria*, Maciste is best known as the hero of many dozen screen adventures. In the 1914 film version of *Cabiria*, Bartolomeo Pagano starred as the first movie Maciste, the servant of a Sicilian girl. However, in later films Maciste became a demigod, a hero with powers to rival those of Hercules. Indeed, when many of these Italian-made pictures were shown in the United States, the name Maciste was changed to the more familiar Hercules, Samson, Atlas, or Goliath. Among these Maciste movies are *The Marvelous Maciste* (1915), *Maciste in Hell* (1926), *Maciste and the Vampires* (1961), *Maciste in the Land of the Cyclops* (1961), *Maciste and the Night Queen* (1961), and *Maciste vs. the Moon Men* (1964). see: **Hercules.**

MacRonan, Caoilte [F] A hero, soldier, and bard of Irish legend. Also known as the Thin Man, Caoilte is possessed of the spirit of the wind and is so fleet he can outrace anything. His most famous escapade involves a fairy who assumes the guise of a boar and terrorizes the countryside. Ruler Finn MacCoul offers a reward of any woman in the land to the warrior who can stop the creature. Caoilte catches and kills the boar and returns to collect his prize. Because his own wife is quite beautiful, Finn puts a bag over her head—but Caoilte selects her anyway. see: **MacCoul, Finn.**

Mafulke [M] In the mythology of Polynesia, an old woman who owns the underworld and serves as the goddess of fire. She is the ancestress of the shape-changer Maui, a Polynesian hero. In the most famous myth involving the goddess, Maui asks Mafulke for fire to bring to the surface world. The goddess hesitates, for it is a dangerous tool. But she capitulates and gives him one of her fingers. Tossing its sparks into a tree, Maui douses the remainder of the finger's fire in a stream. Returning to Mafulke, he complains that the flame went out before he could reach the world above. He asks for another finger, which she reluctantly hands him. The hero places its sparks in a tree, drowns the finger, and repeats the pattern until Mafulke has given him all of her fiery fingers and toes. When she realizes that she has been tricked, and that humans can now produce fire merely by rubbing two sticks together, she falls into a rage and sets the world ablaze. Observing what has happened, the gods send rain and snow to put out the fire—and they have been with us ever since.

Magician [O] In days of old, magicians were inquisitive, usually scholarly people who communicated with spirits. Most of this intercourse was undertaken merely to ask questions of the dead—the art of *sciomancy* as opposed to the reanimation of corpses or *necromancy*—or to learn more about God. Later magicians expanded these parameters to include the summoning of devils. This was conducted from within magic circles, and to step outside these protected regions was to be instantly ripped apart or carried into hell by the conjured demons. Some magicians went so far as to become *wizards,* gaining the complete cooperation of these underworld denizens by agreeing to serve Satan whenever the need might arise. Today, magicians are thought of more as illusionists than practitioners of sorcery. see: **Magus; Necromancy; Wizards.**

Magic Spindle [FT] An important artifact in the Grimm fairy tale "Spindle, Shuttle, and Needle." When a king's son decides to take a bride, he announces that "she shall be my wife who is at once the poorest and the richest." Riding out, he visits a fifteen-year-old orphan who makes her living by weaving. He leaves her, for though she is surely poor he does not see how she can be rich at the same time. But the girl, a generous miss who shares her meager earnings with the needy, has fallen hopelessly in love with the prince. Speaking to her spindle, she says, "Spindle, spindle, go and see, if my love will come to me." Immediately, the spindle leaps from her hand and catches up to the prince. Dancing before him, its golden thread dangling behind, the spindle silently convinces the prince to go back and give the young girl a second look. Meanwhile, she asks her shuttle to weave a lovely welcome mat, and her needle to sew elegant curtains and upholstery. When the prince arrives and sees the beautiful chamber, he realizes that he need search no further. They are wed, and the spindle, shuttle, and needle are placed in the royal treasury. see: **Grimm, Jakob and Wilhelm.**

Magic Tablecloth [FT] A miraculous fabric in the Russian fairy tale "The Stolen Turnips." When an old man's nagging wife decides that she must have turnips, he goes to plant them. Since there is no room in the garden he decides to grow them on the roof. Unfortunately, the best of these turnips are snatched—presumably by animals—and the old man's wife forces him to track them down. Heading into the forest, he finds a hut filled with imps. They confess to having eaten the turnips, and repay the theft by giving him a special tablecloth. This spread will magically create food by "flying into the air, rolling itself this way and that, and then suddenly laying itself flat on the table again, covered with bowls of soup, mushrooms, kasha, meat, cakes, fish, and ducks." Upon instruction, the tablecloth will flip over and the dishes will vanish.

The next day, more turnips are missing. The old man pays the imps another visit and this time, for having eaten his turnips, they give him a goat with a cold. But what a cold! Whenever the animal sneezes, gold flies from its body. The third time turnips are taken, the imps give the old man a flute which compels all who hear it to speak the truth. The forest-dwellers promise never again to steal his turnips, and he believes them.

Come morning, he goes to the roof and sees that they have spoken the truth. But his wife does not believe him and orders the old man to carry her to the roof that she may see for herself. However, the woman is heavy and, as they climb the ladder, she slips from her husband's arms and falls to her death. He lives happily ever after.

Magic tablecloths have appeared in many other Russian fables, including the saga of Ilya Murometz. see: **Imps; Murometz, Ilya.**

Magus, Simon [H] A sorcerer who lived during the second century A.D. Some say that Simon was the prototype for the legend of Faust; others say he was a sham. Whatever the truth, his story is a fascinating one. Living in Rome with his mistress, Helena, Simon was devoted to the occult. But he didn't let that stop him from becoming a Christian—not for religious reasons, but to learn how Christ worked his miracles. A favorite of both the emperor Nero and other people in the government, Simon was ultimately compared to god by his followers. Fascinated by the analogy, Nero insisted that Simon either prove or disclaim it. Simon elected the former, saying that he would rise from Rome's Forum to Heaven as an exhibition of his powers. However, no sooner had the sorcerer begun his ascent than the Apostle Peter arrived and began to pray. Moments later, Simon plummeted to earth. Though the great sorcerer died, would-be heirs called Ophites came along years later to carry on the traditions of Magus as our first *magicians.* see: **Faust; Magicians.**

Mahar [L] The cruel rulers of Edgar Rice Burroughs' Pellucidar, the world inside the earth. Resembling winged prehistoric creatures known as *pteranodons,* the Mahars are all females.

They lay eggs without fertilization and communicate through a form of telepathy—tossing their thoughts into another dimension from which other Mahars retrieve them. Served by apelike brutes called Sagoths, the scientifically advanced Mahars feed on human flesh and have the ability to instantly hypnotize other living beings. see: **Burroughs, Edgar Rice; Pellucidar.**

Manabozho [F] The Great Hare of Algonquin Indian legend. The creator of all life, Manabozho is the grandson of Nokomis, the earth. There are two accounts of the Great Hare's origin. Some tales say he is the son of Flint, who made a dish, used it to scoop up some earth, and dipped this earth in blood. The blood became Manabozho. Other tales have him as the twin brother of Chibiabos, with whom he argued while still in the womb. When Chibiabos emerges first, the vengeful newborn immediately slays their mother. But Manabozho manages to crawl from her corpse and, in retribution, kills his twin. In this way, the Great Hare becomes a bold warrior and the protector of life. Among the many services performed by Manabozho for humankind are the defeat of the murderous Great Fish, into whose mouth he crawls to plunge a spear through its heart; and the bringing of fire to his grandmother, Nokomis, after stealing it from a campfire in the far east.

Manda [MP] A giant monster featured in several Japanese science fiction films. Manda first appeared in the movie *Atragon* (1963), in the form of a sea serpent. Inhabiting the waters in the vicinity of the world of Mu, it attacks a supersub bound for the lost civilization. However, Manda's most famous screen appearance was in *Destroy All Monsters* (1969). Under the control of invading aliens called Kilaaks, it comes ashore and levels London. In the end, Manda joins Godzilla and other monsters in throwing off the Kilaak yoke and battling their sole remaining slave, Ghidrah. After the slugfest, Manda settles with its victorious cronies on Monster Island. see: **Ghidrah; Godzilla; Mu.**

Mandrake [C] A comic strip magician created in 1934 by Lee Falk (1912–   ). Having studied mysticism and legerdemain in Tibet, Mandrake uses his abilities to serve society. Though relying mostly on hypnotism to achieve his ends, Mandrake occasionally calls upon creatures of the supernatural to serve him. Wearing a red cape and top hat, he travels around the world and even into space. Ever at his side is his loyal aide Lothar, the king of an African tribe and a man of prodigious strength. Less visible is Princess Narda, Mandrake's lover. In 1939, Mandrake was featured in a motion picture serial. Warren Hull starred as the magician in a fight against the underworld forces of the Wasp. see: **Magician.**

Manipogo [U] A lake monster of Manitoba, Canada. First reported in 1909, Manipogo was described as over forty feet long and possessing three lumps on its slimy, yellow-brown body. Later sightings differed in that they gave the monster a horn on its flat head and made it a brownish-black or gray color. Many people believe that if such a creature does exist, it is related to Igopogo of Lake Simcoe near Toronto. That creature, first seen in 1952, has been pictured as thirty to seventy feet long, dog-faced with a thick neck, and a charcoal or slate gray in color. see: **Loch Ness Monster; Ogopogo.**

Manitou [O] An Algonquin Indian force for good and evil. All of the Indians believed in this nature spirit, although they called it different names. To the Sioux it was *waken*, to the Iroquois *orenda*, and to the Incas *huaca*. How-

ever, in each form it was considered the union of peoples' spiritual force, an invisible power which fills the world and both forms and guides life. Not thought of as a god, per se, the manitou is the proverbial Great Spirit. Able to assume a tangible state as an animal, it is in this guise that the manitou protects or harms individual mortals. Eastern manitous tend to be more mischievous than deadly, particularly in the Catskill Mountains of New York. Some manitous have favorite abodes and, whether forests, lakes, mountains, or rocks, these places were declared holy by the Indians. In 1977, a malevolent spirit named Misquamacus was the subject of Graham Masterton's best-selling novel *The Manitou*, which was released as a motion picture in 1978.

Manning, Col. Glen [MP] A soldier who becomes a monster and razes Las Vegas in Bert I. Gordon's 1957 film *The Amazing Colossal Man*, and who levels Los Angeles in Gordon's 1958 sequel *War of the Colossal Beast*. In the first film, Manning—played by Glenn Langan—runs onto a plutonium bomb test site to save someone's life. Caught in the blast, Manning is charred from scalp to foot. However, due to plutonium's strange restorative properties the colonel's skin heals overnight. Unfortunately, there is a side effect. Manning begins to grow at a rate of from eight to ten feet per day. Finally, when he is eighty feet tall, the beleaguered fellow loses his mind and goes on a destructive rampage. After crumbling a great many trees, cars, and buildings he is shot from atop Boulder Dam. But the fall only disfigures the giant and, in the second film, Manning—again actor Langan—is drugged and chained in a hangar at Los Angeles International Airport. Breaking free, he stomps through the metropolis. He realizes, however, that life as a savage giant is not worth living. Thus, turning from a busload of children he was about to crush, the Colossal Beast grabs a handful of power lines and electrocutes himself.

Manticore [F] Also called the mantichora, a lion with a sinister human face. Living in India it feeds on humans, chewing their flesh with the three rows of teeth set in both its upper and lower jaw. Though it's unlikely, if the manticore's mouth fails to stop its prey, its tail does not. Terminating in a scorpion's sting, the appendage also possesses barbs which can be launched to wound or kill. The manticore is sometimes shown as having horns and bat wings as well. According to Spanish legend, this creature is actually a form of werewolf, a human by day and a monster by night. The lore of other lands describe it not as a meat eater but as a vampire looking only for human blood. see: **Vampire; Werewolf.**

Manticore

Mara [O] An old English demon. Also known as Mera, this devil is generally thought of as female. She comes to men at night, usually adopting one of two forms. If she appears as a beautiful succubus, her victim will have erotic dreams. If she comes as a monster, they will have bad dreams. As Mahr, this entity is not a demon but a soul which its possessor sends on nighttime errands, usually to give an enemy a restless evening. If the sleeper happens to wake, its tormentor quickly transforms itself into a portion of the material from which the bed is made. Mahrs can also be the souls of girls who visit their lovers, stimulating them to nocturnal emissions. It is from the dark side of Mara and Mahr that we get the word *nightmare*. see: **Incubus; Lamia.**

Marduk [M] The eldest child of the grain goddess Hinlil and the water god Ea. Half-man and half-fish, and the chief deity following the fall of the old Babylonian gods, Marduk is referred to by the title Bel (Lord), for it was he who created the earth. He did this by engaging the dread Tiamat in battle, cleaving in two she who symbolizes chaos and fear. From her dual halves Marduk made the heavens and earth, chaining her pet dragons and using them to light what he had wrought. Referred to as the sympathetic god of wisdom and the spring sun, Marduk is married to Zarpanit and is the father of Nebo, the god of learning and the creator of writing. Some scholars believe that Marduk and Tiamat are comparable to the Biblical Leviathan and Behemoth, respectively. see: **Behemoth; Leviathan.**

Mares of Diomedes [M] Four horses who feed on human flesh. The object of the eighth labor of Hercules, the mares are owned by Diomedes, the son of Ares and Cyrene. King of the Bistones in Trace, Diomedes uses the mares to keep his kingdom peaceful; they eat any strangers who dare enter. Hercules' assignment is to capture the horses and bring them alive to his cousin Eurystheus. Snaring them is easy enough for the powerful Son of Zeus—although getting them out of the country is quite another matter. Met by an angry Diomedes and his army, Hercules leaves the mares in the care of his friend Abderus and takes on his foes. During the altercation, the horses turn on Abderus and eat him. Enraged, Hercules goes on to beat the king's soldiers and feeds the ruthless Diomedes to his own mares. Upon eating his flesh, the animals become calm vegetarians. After Hercules shows the beasts to Eurystheus, he sets them loose on Mt. Olympus— where the suddenly docile horses are attacked and consumed by wild beasts. see: **Hercules.**

Maria [L/MP] The heroine of Thea von Harbou's novel *Metropolis* and Fritz Lang's 1926 film version of this classic work. Set in A.D. 2026, *Metropolis* tells of the young girl's efforts to win rights for the downtrodden masses who live and work in subterranean Metropolis. The elite surface dwellers resent her efforts, and their leader, Joh Fredersen, contracts the mad scientist Rotwang to help them. Creating a mechanical duplicate of Maria— called both Parody and Futura—Rotwang kidnaps the Christ figure, sends his robotrix out to behave lasciviously in public, and thereby intends to erode her credibility. But his plan backfires, as the subterraneans revolt and force parity between the worlds. In Lang's film, both Maria and Parody/Futura were portrayed by Brigitte Helm.

Mar Jiryis [F] Called Eliyahu ha Navi in Hebrew lore, and El Khudr by the Moslems, this Christian saint long ago discovered the Fountain of Youth somewhere between the Red and Mediterranean Seas. Drinking of its waters, Mar Jiryis became eternally young and decided to use this new-found vigor to protect children and all who are weak. Usually invisible, the golden-robed and fully armored Mar Jiryis travels about the world on a white horse. When the saint pauses, it is usually at the Well of Solomon in Jerusalem or at the Well of Zemzem

in Mecca, to which the defenseless may come for aid. Prior to assuming this grand purpose, Mar Jiryis slew a dragon in much the same fashion as St. George. Whether this means that the legends have a common origin cannot be proven. see: **Fountain of Youth; George, St.**

Marley, Jacob [L] The chief spectre of *A Christmas Carol,* a novella written by Charles Dickens (1812–1870). The mortal Jacob Marley was a partner in the firm Scrooge and Marley, moneylenders and landlords. Dead seven years when the story begins, his ghost appears one Christmas to his miserly partner, Ebeneezer Scrooge. Standing before Scrooge, his body transparent and his eyes "death-cold," Marley shows his mortal partner other phantoms "wandering hither and thither in restless haste, and moaning as they went," all wearing chains and all denied eternal peace because of the cruelty they had exhibited in life. The grim visitor, whose hair and clothes

Jacob Marley

"were still agitated as by the hot vapor from an oven," tells Scrooge that this fate will also be his unless he mends his ways. To this end, the spirit's departure is followed by the coming of three other ghosts: the Ghost of Christmas Past, the Ghost of Christmas Present, and the Ghost of Christmas Yet to Come. Their portrait of the unhappiness Scrooge has fostered reforms the man—although the reader is inclined to believe that Marley and his spectral associates were but the inventions of a tortured conscience.

Mascot [F] An animate or inanimate object which brings good luck to its owner. The word derives from the French *mascotte* or "talisman," which itself appears to have come from the Latin *mascus* or "ghost." Originally, mascot was a term applied to a child born with the caul, a child destined to have luck and to bring good fortune to others. Today, a mascot is an animal or item adopted by an athletic team, military group, scientific expedition, or the like to bring the participants success.

Mataora [F] A figure in Polynesian folklore. One day, Mataora is visited by beings called Turehu, who hail from the underworld. Among their number is the beautiful Nuvarahu, whom Mataora marries. But she makes the mistake of showing affection for Mataora's brother, and her jealous husband beats her. She runs back to the underworld. Guilt-ridden, Mataora marks himself with ceremonial paints and follows Nuvarahu's trail. Reaching her realm, he is greeted with laughter. The Turehu tell him that his paints are for children, because of how easily they smear. The subterraneans show him how to make the designs permanent, in the form of tatoos. The process causes Mataora considerable pain, and he cries out. Nuvarahu hears him and hurries to comfort him. The lovers apologize and take up residence in the underworld. However, Mataora quickly becomes homesick and asks if they might return to the surface. Nuvarahu agrees, although the Turehu are upset that their hospitality has been refused. Thus, when Mataora and his wife depart, a guardian seals the entrance to the underworld. Since that time, only incorporeal spirits have been able to visit the domain of the Turehu.

Mather, Cotton [H] An American witchfinder. Born in Boston in 1663, the son of Increase Mather, Cotton graduated from Harvard and went on to become a churchperson. With witch hunts occupying everyone's attention, Mather took the stance that prayer rather than execution was the best way to treat a witch, and spent his early career pursuing that tack. However, harsh treatment was the vogue and Mather succumbed, hoping to win personal favors from the judges who advocated torture and death. He became a fanatic, often dragging innocent people before the courts—a public attitude which hardly reflected the private Mather, a student of science who wrote such books as *Wonders of the Invisible World* in 1693. Alas, when popular antagonism swung from the witches to their oppressors, Mather was a ready target. He was disgraced, and died so in 1728. see: **Hopkins, Mathew; Witch.**

Matheson, Richard [L] A prolific author of fantasy books and screenplays. Richard Burton Matheson was born in 1926 in Allendale, New Jersey, the son of Bertolf Mathieson and Fanny Svenningsen—both of Oslo, Norway. A graduate of the University of Missouri, Matheson's first sale was the short story "Born of Man and Woman"—later the title of his first anthology—which was published in *The Magazine of Fantasy and Science Fiction* in 1950. His first novel was *Someone is Bleeding* (1953), and his first film work consisted of adapting his novel *The Shrinking Man* into the 1957 motion picture *The Incredible Shrinking Man*. In 1958 Matheson wrote his first teleplay. Entitled "The Last Flight," it appeared on "The Twilight Zone" in 1960. Among Matheson's other film and TV work are episodes of "The Twilight Zone" entitled "Steel," "Nick of Time," "Death Ship," and "Third from the Sun"; the movies *The House of Usher* (1960), *The Pit and the Pendulum* (1961), *The Master of the World* (1961), *The Raven* (1963), and *Trilogy of Terror* (1974); and teleplays for "Star Trek" ("The Enemy Within"), "Thriller" ("The Return of Andrew Bentley"), and "Night Gallery" ("The Funeral"), among others. He has also scripted his novel *I Am Legend* for no less than three movies: *The Last Man on Earth* (1964), *The Omega Man* (1971), and an unrealized Hammer Films version. In recent years his most notable teleplays include the adaptation of Jeff Rice's novel "The Night Stalker" (1972) and "The Night Strangler" (1973). Matheson's screenplay for *The Legend of Hell House* (1973) based on his novel *Hell House* remains a cult fa-

vorite. Matheson is married to Ruth Ann Woodson and is the father of Richard, Alison, and Christian Matheson.

Mauthe Dhoog [O] A phantom hound which haunts the Isle of Man in England. Lurking principally about the environs of Peel Castle, it is particularly fond of one hallway which leads to the Guard Room. First seen in the seventeenth century, the Mauthe Dhoog is thought to have belonged to someone at the castle—perhaps a guard. Those who see this specter usually die within a week. see: **Black Hound.**

McCay, Winsor [C/MP] An American cartoonist and animator. Born in Spring Lake, Michigan in 1869, McCay had very little formal schooling. He chose, instead, to draw. Accordingly, at the age of seventeen he went to Chicago to do poster illustrations and at the same time pick up a few art lessons. In 1891 he moved to Cincinnati to work for the newspapers. At the age of thirty-four he created his first strip, "Tales of the Jungle Imps," and that same year went to New York and began several other comic strips. These included "Dreams of a Rarebit Fiend" for *The Evening Telegram*, "Little Sammy Sneeze" (1904)—about a boy with a hurricane-force sneeze—and "Little Nemo in Slumberland" (1905). In 1906, while he was still doing his newspaper work, McCay began drawing animated cartoons. The most famous of these is *Gertie the Dinosaur* (1906), about a trained brontosaur. McCay died in 1934, but much of what he did in terms of perspective, surrealism, action, droll humor, and outrageous fantasy remains unsurpassed. see: **Little Nemo; Rarebit Fiend.**

Medicine Bundle [F] A package of protective charms in the lore of the American Indian. On a day-to-day

Gertie (see Winsor McCay)

basis, Indians—particularly the Plains Indians—counted on dreams for spiritual guidance. However, when an Indian entered the teenage years it was time to seek a grand vision. This was done in an isolated location, the Indian usually enduring self-inflicted starvation and torture to accomplish the goal. If successful, the youth would be visited by a supernatural being who would stay on as a guardian. In addition to teaching its charge magic chants, the spirit would order the Indian to gather certain objects to serve as protective talismans. These sacred items were wrapped in animal skin and called a medicine bundle. They had to be present whenever the Indian sought counsel with the shepherding spirit.

Medusa [M] The one mortal Gorgon. The daughter of Phorcys and Ceto, and aunt of the hero Orion, Medusa lived with her sisters Stheno and Euryale on the shores of Oceanus near Tartarus. Originally a beautiful

Mauthe Dhoog

Medusa

woman, Medusa offended the goddess Athena who turned her most striking feature, her hair, into a teeming bed of snakes. According to some tales, Medusa was otherwise very lovely—save for feet and hands that had become talons, and her cold eyes—while other accounts say she had talons, yellow tusks, and bronze-scaled skin just like her sisters. Some tales also give her wings. Regardless of her monstrous accoutrements, to see Medusa was to be turned instantly to stone. The hero Perseus avoided this pitfall by gazing into a highly burnished shield while he moved in and lopped off her head. Upon her death, Medusa's blood mingled with the earth to bring forth the flying horse Pegasus—although some legends say that she bore the horse after mating with Poseidon. see: **Athena; Gorgon; Pegasus; Perseus; Poseidon.**

Medusans [TV] Alien beings featured in the "Star Trek" episode "Is There No Truth in Beauty?" Appearing as blobs of light when viewed through special lenses, the Medusans possess superb sensory faculties. They can communicate most effectively with other telepaths—such as Mr. Spock—and have a deep appreciation of things of beauty. However, in their natural form the Medusans are so ugly that to see them will drive a person mad. Technologically advanced, the Medusans are represented to the Federation by an ambassador named Kollos. see: *Enterprise*, **U.S.S.; Federation; Spock, Mr.**

Megalon [MP] A Japanese movie monster featured in *Godzilla vs. Megalon* (1973). Bipedal, with a tail, layered armor, a beetlelike head, two pincer-arms, and a wingback shell, Megalon is the slave of the Seatopians. Located under the Pacific Ocean, Seatopia is all that remains of the ancient civilization of Mu. Worried that nuclear tests will destroy their already depleted society, the submariners send forth Megalon to reduce the surface world to a realm of flint-chipping cave dwellers. Coming ashore, the huge Megalon is met by Jet Jaguar (also known as Robotman), a giant cyborg created by Professor Goro Ibuki. When it looks as though Megalon might be turned back, the Seatopians place a call to outer space. They summon the aid of the monster Gigan, who is experienced in attacking the earth, having cut his eyeteeth in *Godzilla vs. Gigan* (1971). Two-legged, with ivory arms and a body covered with scales, the beaked, fin-backed Gigan teams up with Mu's savior. Outnumbered, Jet Jaguar is badly battered and earth seems doomed. Not so. Followed by a mile-long wake, Godzilla comes thumping from the sea. Together, the monster-fest veteran and novice cyborg turn back the invaders. see: **Godzilla; Mu.**

Melange [L] The "spice of spices" harvested on the planet Arrakis in Frank Herbert's novel *Dune*. Slightly addictive in small doses—dangerously so when taken in amounts of more than two grams daily per seventy kilos of body weight, a quantity which turns the eyes blue—melange has medicinal properties. It also is rumored to inspire prophetic abilities. Fetching as much as 620,000 solaris a decagram, it is a fungusoid in its natural state, a growth which becomes melange after it has been exposed to water, sun, and air. see: **Fremen; Sandworm.**

Méliès, George [MP] A French producer of silent fantasy films. Born in Paris in 1861, the son of a well-to-do-bootmaker, Méliès was educated in England. Working as a newspaper artist—and signing his work George Smile—Méliès maintained a passionate interest in both magic and the ballet. So strong was his love for the former that he eventually abandoned drawing to purchase the Theatre Robert-Houdin. There he both exhibited and practiced magic. At about this

time, motion pictures came into being. They were particularly well received in France, where Méliès began presenting them at his showplace. By 1896 he was also making movies. But Méliès wasn't just filming seashores and other documentary sights. He was one of the first to use the camera to tell short stories, and he was *the* first to apply a magician's eye to film. The father of motion picture special effects, he created over 500 fantasy films between 1896 and 1914, including such titles as *The Haunted Castle* (1896), *The Man with the Rubber Head* (1901), and the classic *A Trip to the Moon* (1902). Represented by his brother, Gaston, many of Méliès' films were popularly received in the United States.

During World War I, Méliès' studio was taken over by the French government, and the filmmaker had to sell his equipment and movies in order to survive. Years later, he was discovered selling newspapers in a kiosk on the Gare Montparnasse. He died in 1938 in a home for destitute actors, survived by his second wife, Charlotte Faes.

Melsh Dick [F] A wood spirit in the folklore of England. In medieval times, nuts were thought to increase a person's fertility. Because of their tremendous value, they were protected by the Melsh Dick. The primary task of this demonic figure was to keep children from plucking the nuts unripe, but Melsh Dick also saw to it that animals did not consume more than their proper share. In those parts of the United Kingdom not serviced by Melsh Dick, nut-guarding was done by the sprite Churnmilk Peg. Legend also has it that because nut-gathering was so popular, the Devil set aside a full day—Sunday—to make the rounds of sinners who dared to go a-picking on the Christian Sabbath.

Melusina [F] A monster-girl of ancient

folklore. After his wife dies, King Elinas of Albania spends his time hunting. One day, he meets the fairy Pressina and proposes marriage. She agrees, as long as the king does not visit her when their children are born. But Pressina bears him triplets, daughters Melior, Palatina, and Melusina, and the monarch is so excited that he runs to see them. The mother and children immediately vanish, living in self-imposed exile in a distant land. One of the girls, Melusina, is so bitter about this that she encloses her father within his castle—for which disrespect Pressina turns her daughter's lower quarters into those of a serpent. In that form she must remain until she marries a man who will refrain from being with her on Saturdays.

Melusina finds such a man, the Frenchman Raymond of Poitou, and her human anatomy is restored for six days a week. However, when their children are born deformed, friends tell Raymond that his wife has had other lovers on Saturdays. Hiding near their home, the poor fellow watches, and sees that she becomes a serpent-woman. He says nothing, though when he slips and calls her a "pernicious snake," Melusina realizes that her secret is out. Turning to her husband she says, "I am condemned now to fly through the air in pain till the day of judgment." Since that time, she has appeared at the castle before the death of every owner. She comes in human form, and when she lands on the windowsill, her footprints always linger long after Melusina is gone.

Mephistopheles [O] A devil of German legend. Mephistopheles actually has two identities. To some scholars he is merely a subordinate devil; to others he is Satan himself. In the latter form he is handsomely dressed in red, wearing a starched cape, sporting a cock's feather in his hat, and carrying a long pointed sword. Regretting that he was forced to leave the good life of Heaven behind, Satan/Mephistopheles is a sad and mellow soul who commits only those acts of evil which are absolutely necessary. As a lesser demon, he is considered something of a familiar. A joker, he will tease mortals, appearing to them as a human or an animal; or else he will try to trick them out of their souls. Mephistopheles is most frequently the devil pictured in the tale of Faust. see: **Devil; Faustus; Satan.**

Merlin [F] A historical magician whose exploits have taken on the dimension of legend. Allegedly born from the union of an incubus and an unconscious nun, Merlin was saved from damnation by a priest who baptized him as soon as he was born. Studying under the magician Blaise of Brittany, Merlin was originally a resident of the court of King Vortigern. At the age of five, the brilliant young boy performed his first wonder. He figured out why each day's construction on a new fort was collapsing every night. The lad claimed that it could only be due to rumbling caused by a pair of dragons fighting in a nearby lake. Intrigued, the ruler ordered the body of water drained. Much to his delight, the monsters were found. One of them, a red dragon, was slain. The other, a two-headed white dragon, was chased from the kingdom.

After spending years with Vortigern, Merlin befriended Uther Pendragon. As a favor to the noble, the sorcerer and prophet made him look like Gorlois, Duke of Cornwall, so that Uther could make love to Gorlois' wife, Igerne. From this union came Arthur, the future king of England. Becoming Arthur's protector, Merlin helped him win and keep his throne. However, after years of sage counsel the magician's judgment finally failed him. He permitted himself to be seduced by the Lady of the Lake, a vixen who was jealous of the fame of the Knights of the Round Table. Merlin was not her first choice; he only assisted the round table. Arthur had made it the great body it was. But when Arthur spurned her, she settled for his magician, tricked him into teaching her a few magic spells, and quickly imprisoned him in an oak tree. There Merlin remains, to this day. see: **Arthur, King; Incubus; Lao, Dr.; Magician.**

Merpeople [F] Men and women who live in the sea. In folklore, merpeople traditionally have a human torso and the tail of a fish. Sometimes identified with sirens, they are generally less destructive—although often not as attractive. For example, some Irish mermen have green hair, small green eyes, and long red noses.

The most common tales of merpeople involve females of the breed who are anxious to mate with human males. Whether these mermaids genuinely love the men or are merely looking to lure them from their wives differs according to the individual incidents. However, if a mermaid decides to come and live with her husband on land, she can shed her tail—although she can never regain it.

Merpeople

Not that merpeople rush to exchange this useful appendage for legs. By draping themselves in clothing they can usually move unnoticed among humans. The only key to their identity is a damp spot which forms on the right side of the mermaid's clothes and on the left side of the merman's outfit.

The lore of merpeople differs from country to country. Among the many legends are that the children of human-merpeople couplings will be born with webbed hands and feet, their bodies covered with scales; that captured merpeople can be held from the ransom of a wish; that merpeople are the souls of people who have drowned; that they will shop only among mortals, since we offer better buys than seapeople; that a person soon to die by drowning will see merpeople dancing on the water; that mermaids fall in love only with human sailors; and that merpeople never commune with humans, throwing themselves quickly into the water when one approaches.

Realistically, merpeople are probably nothing more than mistaken sighting of seals, walruses, and other sea animals. Yet, some scientists *do* maintain that an aquatic branch of humans is not an impossibility, creatures evolved from apes who came from the trees and went directly to the ocean instead of settling on the land. see: **Blue Men of the Minch; Golden Mermaid; Lorelei; Sirens.**

Merripit Hill [O] A place in Dartmoor, England which is haunted by a most incredible ghost. Roaming the environs is a phantom sow and her litter. At the beginning of their trail, they ritualistically learn that there's a dead horse lying nearby. They hasten to eat it, but when the swine arrive they find naught but the animal's bones. Sulking back to Merripit Hill, the poor pig family begins the identical quest anew.

Micronauts [E] Top-selling robot warrior toys from Mego, whose popularity has earned them a spin-off adventure comic book. Traveling from inner space via microship, the tiny team consists of the Six Thousand series roboid with hydraulic limb-extensions Biotron, the mighty Acroyear, Microtron, and the comic book-created Marionette, the insectivorid Bug, and Commander Rann. The hated enemy of the Micronauts is Baron Karza, a black-armored villain of Homeworld in the subatomic universe. The Micronauts' primary transport on earth is the rocket-powered Astrostation. Other Micronaut figures in the toy line are the android horse Oberon, the time traveling Pharoid, the six-limbed Antron, Membros (whose brain glows!), and the winged Repto. A line of comedic Micronauts known as the Trons—Alphatron, Betatron, and Gammatron—has been added to the toy lineup but not to the magazine.

Midas [M] Probably an historical king of Phrygia to whom some rather fantastic things occurred. The most famous of these is the "Midas Touch." For respectfully receiving Silenus, the teacher and friend of Dionysos, the god gives Midas the power to turn whatever he touches into gold. Unfortunately, the king cannot eat, for the food in his mouth changes instantly to gold; so does Midas' daughter when he takes her in his arms. Begging the deity to retract his blessing, Midas is told to bathe in the river Pactolus in Lydia. Midas is cured, but the waters have ever since run gold.

In another story, Midas is elected to judge a musical contest between the satyr Pan and the god Apollo. When the king selects the goat-man as the winner, the furious Apollo changes Midas' ears into those of an ass—to match his taste. see: **Apollo; Dionysos; Satyr.**

Mighty Mouse [MP] A superpowered movie mouse created by writer-artist Isidore Klein and producer Paul Terry in 1942. Mighty Mouse's first appearance was in the animated cartoon *The Mouse of Tomorrow.* In that and two succeeding cartoons he was known as Super Mouse. He lived in a supermarket and became super strong by eating super foods. However, the Super Mouse name was allegedly an infringement on the copyright held by Superman, so the producers quickly dubbed their character Mighty Mouse. With the name change came a new identity. He was no longer a normally meek rodent who assumed great abilities when danger threatened—à la Clark Kent-Superman. He was always strong, always vigilant, looking after the oppressed from his stations on the moon, atop the Empire State Building, in the peaks of the world's tallest mountain, etc. Whenever mice, rabbits, or ducks were menaced by cats, wolves, or vultures, in he zoomed. He also turned his muscles, power of flight, and magical abilities against volcanoes, floods, hot-rodding mice in suburbia, and sundry monsters.

In his most popular cartoons, Mighty Mouse, along with his girl friend Pearl Pureheart and their nemesis Oil Can Harry, parodied Gilbert and Sullivan with all-singing adventures. These mini-operas are classics of action and deadpan humor, as well as brilliant spoofs of motion picture serials. Mighty Mouse's tenor cry of "Here I Come to Save the Day!" can still be heard in his syndicated television cartoon show. see: **Superman.**

Minnikin [FT] The twin brother of Pippin and the son of very poor parents in the fairy tale "Minnikin." Seeking to unburden their mother and father the boys leave home, going separate ways. On the road, Minnikin meets a hag whose one eye he steals—and then returns it in exchange for "a sword which is such a sword that it can conquer a whole army." Snatching a second hag's only eye, he returns it for "a ship which can sail over water, over high hills, and through deep dales," but which can otherwise fit in his pocket. From a third hag, he gains the recipe for a malt which will serve as many people as gather around the glass.

Traveling on, Minnikin meets a princess whose father has reluctantly given her to three trolls who possess five, ten, and fifteen heads respectively. The boy uses his magical tools to deliver her from the monsters, but the princess' guardian, Ritter Red, claims to have slain the creatures and forces his charge upon pain of death to lie for him. They return to the court and the grateful king grants the princess and half his kingdom to Ritter Red. But Minnikin plots revenge. Gaining access to a great palace feast by masquerading as a kitchen helper, Minnikin presents his case to the king. Ritter Red scoffs and shows his liege the trolls' lungs and tongues, which he had had the foresight to cut out. But Minnikin proves that he was in the trolls' lair by exhibiting silver and diamonds he had taken from them. The king believes Minnikin, gives him the princess and half the kingdom, has Ritter Red lowered into a pit of snakes, and promises the other half of his holdings to Minnikin if he will rescue his second daughter from different trolls. The boy saves her by involving the ogres with his delicious mug of malt, then turns over this princess and the reward to his brother Pippin. The twins' parents come to live with them and all live happily for many, many years.

Minotan [MP] A golden, mechanical minotaur seen in Ray Harryhausen's 1977 motion picture *Sinbad and the Eye of the Tiger*. Ten feet tall, the bull-headed robot is built by the sorceress Zenobia to singlehandedly row her huge barge from the Middle East to the Arctic, spear her foes with a golden lance, and perform other services. The Minotan is destroyed when it helps its mistress enter a huge, mystical pyramid located at the top of the world. Yanking out a huge block so that she may step inside, the robot stumbles from a ledge, pulling the great stone with it, and is crushed. Though the monster was brought to the screen using a miniature stop-motion model, it was played in several shots by actor Dave Prowse (Darth Vader) wearing a Minotan costume. see: **Darth Vader; Harryhausen, Ray; Sinbad.**

Minotaur [M] A creature which is half-man and half-bull. When King Minos of Crete—the son of Zeus and Europa—asks Poseidon to send him something to acknowledge his kingly authority, the sea god causes a white bull to rise from the waters. Minos is instructed to sacrifice this beautiful animal to the god as thanks for creating the symbol. However, Minos is so smitten with the handsome bull that he keeps it, substituting another. Poseidon is deeply insulted and, in retribution, causes Minos' wife, Pasiphae, to mate with the bull, then drives the animal mad—providing mythology with the Cretan Bull and Hercules with his seventh labor. The result of Pasiphae having coupled with the beast is the Minotaur.

Repulsed by the creature, Minos has the architect Daedalus build a labyrinth beneath the palace at Knossos, into which he places the bull-man. Minos' problem seems to dwindle—until he learns that the Minotaur will eat only human flesh. If it is not fed, it looses a roar so loud that the people of Crete freeze with fear. Hence, each year he sends seven youths and seven maidens into the maze. The Minotaur eventually finds and consumes the young people. Minos' sole consolation is they they all come from Athens rather than his own kingdom, as part of the tribute the mainland city must pay the king.

Finding grave fault with this arrangement, the hero Theseus offers to be one of the fourteen sacrifices. Entering the labyrinth—trailing a length of thread given to him by his lover, Minos' daughter Ariadne—Theseus waits until the monster is asleep and then slays him with his bare hands. The hero is then able to escape the maze by following the unraveled thread. see: **Cretan Bull; Daedalus; Hercules; Poseidon; Theseus.**

Minunians [L] Creatures created by Edgar Rice Burroughs for his 1924 novel *Tarzan and the Ant Men*, the tenth book in the Ape-Man series. The Minunians are eighteen-inch-tall people who dwell in beehivelike apartments. Riding a diminutive form of antelope, the tiny bronzed warriors live in the jungle where they are well versed in the use of swords, spears, and knives. These skills come in handy, since the land of Minuni is bordered by the realm of the Alali. Stone Age giants, the cannibalistic Alali are dominated by their women. Vicious fighters, it takes no less than 100 Minunians to fell a lone Alalus female. The little people are also at war with each other, ancient hatreds dividing the nations of Trohanadalmakus—ruled by King Adendrohahkis and his son, Komodoflorensal—and the evil Veltopismakus—led by Elkomoelhago and his daughter, Janzara. Tarzan rescues Komodoflorensal from an Alalus woman by firing an arrow through her heart, and is drawn into local politics when shrunk to Minunian size by the Veltopismakusians. Eventually, the Ape-Man escapes from these remarkably Lilliputianesque people and returns to his normal size. see: **Burroughs, Edgar Rice; Lilliput; Tarzan.**

Minya [MP] The son of Godzilla and his mate, Gojilla. Introduced in the 1968 motion picture *The Son of Godzilla*, Minya hatches from an egg on a time-forgotten island inhabited by giant mantises. Unlike his father, the pug-faced young monster is unable to launch a cloud of incendiary breath—he can manage to blow only smoke rings. Riding about on his father's tail, he is ever-anxious to learn the ways of a twentieth century dinosaur. His education is a harsh one. In his second film, *Destroy All Monsters* (1969), he joins Godzilla and an army of his giant comrades in their battle against Ghidrah and the alien Kilaaks. In *Godzilla's Revenge* (1969), a new side of the monster emerges. Befriending a small boy who flies to Minya's home on Monster Island, the son of Godzilla is able to converse with the lad and shrink from his normal towering height to the boy's own size. Like many other media characters, Minya appears destined to exist in perpetual preadolescence. see: **Ghidrah; Godzilla.**

Mr. Ed [TV] A talking horse and the star of the half-hour television comedy "Mr. Ed." When architect Wilbur Post (Alan Young) and his wife Carol (Connie Hines) move into a home in Los Angeles, they inherit a horse left behind by the previous owner. Wilbur decides to keep the animal and, while brushing it, learns that it can speak. The architect is the only one with whom Mr. Ed will converse, becoming close-mouthed whenever anyone else happens by—usually leaving Wilbur talking to himself. The program premiered in 1960 and ran for six seasons.

Mr. Terrific [TV] A superhero featured in the one-season (1966) CBS television series of the same name. In his civilian identity, Mr. Terrific is gas station owner Stanley Beamish (Stephen Strimpell). Employed by Barton J. Reed (John McGiver) of the Bureau of Secret Projects, Beamish also works for the government as the mighty Mr. Terrific. To become the hero, he merely swallows a power pill and—according to network press releases—

is immediately endowed with the strength of 100 elephants, the jumping power of 1,000 kangaroos, and a nose as sensitive as those of 500 bloodhounds. Donning goggles and a silver suit, Mr. Terrific gets about by flying—a state he achieves by flapping his arms.

Mr. Toad [L] The most popular character from the novel *The Wind in the Willows* by Kenneth Grahame (1852–1939). A wealthy, eccentric, and well-dressed frog, Mr. Toad lives in Toad Hall, an estate complete with a flower-decked lawn and a private creek. Headstrong and proud, he one day decides to take his friends on a trip beyond their cozy realm of Wild Wood, to show them the world. After many adventures, Mr. Toad steals a motorcar and ends up in jail. Eventually making his way back to Toad Hall, he is shocked to find that it has been taken over by gun-toting ferret soldiers and weasels. With the aid of his friends Mr. Badger, the Mole, and Water Rat, he is able to recapture the mansion. Mr. Toad is the star of a 1949 Walt Disney cartoon featurette, and is honored by an attraction at Disneyland entitled "Mr. Toad's Wild Ride." see: **Disney, Walt.**

Mjölnir [M] The magic hammer owned by the Norse thunder god, Thor. In reality, Mjölnir is a thunderbolt which, according to some tales, was forged into a hammer by dwarfs. When thrown, the mallet never misses its mark and always boomerangs back to Thor. No one but the thunder god can use it; not even the king of the gods, Odin, can raise Mjölnir. Thor also owns a belt which doubles his strength as well as a pair of iron gloves which he wears to protect his hands while using his hammer. In the comic book *Thor,* the god changes from a deity to his mortal identity of Dr. Don Blake merely by striking Mjölnir on the ground. It becomes an innocent walking stick, which Blake taps

against the firmament to transform himself into the thunder god. see: **Thor.**

Mock Turtle [L] A creature invented by Lewis Carroll for his 1865 novel *Alice in Wonderland.* A bizarre turtle-pig hybrid, the Mock Turtle is discovered by Alice and the Gryphon. It is sitting on a little ledge of rock, sighing, complaining that, "Once I was a real turtle." Though the Mock Turtle lectures Alice about math—ambition, distraction, uglification, and derision—and teaches her how to dance the Lobster-Quadrille, it never explains how it came to have the head and hind feet of a pig. However, the Mock Turtle does sing several choruses of "Turtle Soup"—during which Alice leaves to attend the trial of the Knave of Hearts. see: **Alice; Hatter, The; Lobster-Quadrille; Queen of Hearts.**

Mole People [MP] Hideous humanoids who live underground in the 1956 motion picture which bears their name. The crusty-skinned, pop-eyed Mole People are the slaves of albino Sumerians who settled underground in 3000 B.C. in a search for the sacred land of Ishtar. Ruled by King Chanau, these white-skinned ancients are visited by a scientific expedition headed by Dr. Bentley (actor John Agar) and Dr. Bellamin (Hugh Beaumont). After much reflection, the Sumerians vote to execute the visitors from the surface. But the newcomers had shown great kindness to the Mole people, who revolt against their frail taskmasters. The Sumerians are overthrown, the scientists return to their world, and a fresh earthquake shuts the million-year-old society of Mole People underground forever. The Mole People are no relation to the stars of the 1951 motion picture *Superman and the Mole Men.* The latter creatures were dwarfish beings who crawled from the center of the earth to protect their home from the ravages of the world's deepest oil well. see: **Ishtar; Superman.**

Moloch [M] An ancient god who stood for the sun in all of its destructive facets. Moloch was worshiped by the early Canaanites and various Semitic people. An enduring deity, it was still being honored as late as A.D. 100. Pictured as having a bull's head with huge jaws, Moloch also possesses long, muscular arms with which to grab and hold human victims. One of the most notorious of all the gods, Moloch demanded that only young children be offered as sacrifices. In the 1926 film *Metropolis*, the great machine run by the oppressed subterraneans was referred to as Moloch. see: **Maria.**

M113 Creature [TV] A fearsome alien seen in the "Star Trek" episode "The Man Trap." A native of the planet M113, this being has the ability to disguise its features. Killing scientist Nancy Crater, it assumes her identity and permits Nancy's husband, Robert, to live as long as he can supply the monster with what it needs to survive—salt. In its true form, the M113 Creature is covered with a full coat of matted hair, has small eyes, no nose, and a round mouth with sharp teeth. The last of its breed, the salt vampire boards the U.S.S. *Enterprise* and slays crewmembers—as well as Robert—by sucking sustenance from their bodies. The alien is slain by Dr. McCoy just as it is about to kill Captain Kirk. see: *Enterprise*, **U.S.S.; Kirk, Captain.**

Monongahela Monster [O] A sea serpent with excellent documentation. Seen by Captain Seabury and the crew of the whaling vessel *Monongahela* on January 13, 1852, the monster was harpooned and caught. With a diameter of over 50 feet, the monster was 103 feet long, its neck measuring 10 feet thick and 10 feet in length. Its head was like that of an alligator, filled with ninety-four teeth that were each three inches long and hooked back like those of a snake. The monster was of a brownish gray color with a three-foot-wide stripe of white running along the entire length of its underbelly. There were two air holes, and the creature propelled itself through the water with a knobby, fifteen-foot-long tail—although it had four "paws" which could be used for swimming. A picture of the creature was drawn, signed by all of the crew, and given to Captain Gavitt of the *Rebecca Sims* which passed on its way back to New Bedford. Captain Seabury discarded the monster's body but pickled its head, and the *Monongahela* pressed on with its whale hunt. Sadly, the craft was wrecked and the great head went down with it.

Monster of Glamis [O] A mysterious creature that haunts the huge estate of Glamis in Scotland. Only Lord Strathmore and his heirs are certain of the monster's true identity. That it exists is all anyone else knows. Among the surrounding villages, three stories about the monster's real nature seem the most popular explanations: that it is the ghosts of gamblers and party-goers who are trapped in the castle for having sinned, "condemned" to revel until judgment day; that it is the spirits of guests of Glamis who have starved to death or otherwise died on the estate; or that it is a vampire, which the Strathmores have been known to produce every four generations, imprisoned here to protect the populace. see: **Vampire.**

Moonbase Alpha [TV] The human colony on the moon in the television series "Space: 1999" (1975–1977). When accumulated energy from a nuclear disposal area on the moon explodes on September 13, 1999, the earth's only natural satellite is shoved from its orbit. Pinballing from galaxy to galaxy, it provides the 311 Alphans under Commander John Koenig (Martin Landau) with a chance to visit strange worlds and alien civilizations. Also along for the ride are the shape-changing extraterrestrial Maya (Catherine Schell) and Dr. Helena Russell (Barbara Bain).

Moonbase Alpha is composed of six sections, all of which were inaugurated in the middle of 1997: Environmental Control, Hydrophonics (cultivation of plants for food and atmosphere), Engineering and Technics, Research, Medical, and the nerve center Main Mission. Transportation about the moon and for a reasonable distance into space is provided by utility ships called Eagles. These come in four varieties: Transporter Eagles for ten passengers; Reconnaissance Eagles for scientific missions; Rescue Eagles; and Freighter Eagles. see: **Anderson, Gerry.**

Mooncalf [L] A food source bred by the Selenites in H. G. Wells' 1901 novel *First Men in the Moon*. Described as "animated lumps of provender," each mooncalf is an enormous, flabby creature with a girth of some eighty feet, its length nearly two hundred feet, and its skin "of corrugated white, dappling into blackness along the backbone." It has little intelligence, a

Mooncalf

"slobbering, omnivorous mouth," small nostrils, squinty little eyes, and it alternately bleats and bellows. The mooncalf moves along by heeling over, dragging forward along the ground, creasing its leathery skin, and rolling again. In Ray Harryhausen's 1965 motion picture, the mooncalf is portrayed as something of a giant centipede. see: **Harryhausen, Ray; Selenites; Wells, H. G.**

Morag [U] A monster that inhabits Loch Morar on Scotland's west coast. According to an old Scottish ballad,

Morag, harbinger of death,
Giant swimmer in deep green Morar,
The loch that has no bottom,
There it is that Morag the monster
*   lives.*

Although Morar isn't bottomless, it is over one thousand feet deep in parts. As for its monster, Morag is said to be a dark gray color, with a twining, five-foot-long neck, a small head, a humped back, and flippers. This description is similar to that of Morag's more famous Scottish cousin, the Loch Ness Monster. see: **Loch Ness Monster.**

Moreau, Dr. [L] The vivisectionist antagonist of H. G. Wells' horror fantasy *The Island of Dr. Moreau.* Approximately fifty years old, Moreau was forced out of England due to his cruel scientific practices. Setting up shop on a small South Pacific Island—probably Noble's Island—he humanizes animals through surgery in order to study "the plasticity of living forms." When we first meet Moreau in 1887, he has been in exile for eleven years. Described by Edward Prendick—a castaway late of the *Lady Vain,* and a horrified observer to the scientist's experiments—the silver-haired Moreau stands roughly six feet tall, "a powerfully built man with a fine forehead and rather heavy features." Moreau calls his experimental creations Beast

Men, proud of the fact that while each is humanoid in form it also preserves the quality of its particular species. Among their number are a Leopard Man, one that is half-hyena and half-pig, another that is a satyr-like ape-goat, a Swine Man, and an old woman who is part bear and part vixen. Moreau is most proud of his Puma Man; it is fitting that when the Beast Men revolt, this one slays its creator.

In the cinema, Moreau has been twice portrayed, and superbly so. Charles Laughton essayed the role in 1933 in *The Island of Lost Souls* and Burt Lancaster was the scientist in *The Island of Dr. Moreau* in 1977. see: **Wells, H. G.**

Morella [L] The eerie wife of the narrator in Edgar Allan Poe's short story "Morella." A student of German mysticism, Morella spends her time studying its literature. Her husband shares her interest at first—but his attention soon wanders, as does his affection. Morella dies giving birth to their daughter. The narrator remarks that the child, also named Morella, is extremely mature—so much so that "the lessons of experience fell from the lips of infancy." As the days pass, the young Morella comes to look exactly like her mother. Then, at her baptism, she dies. The grieving narrator goes to bury her and is deeply shocked "as I found no traces of the first, in the charnel where I laid the second, Morella." see: **Poe, Edgar Allan.**

Morgor [L] Incredible beings created by Edgar Rice Burroughs for his 1943 John Carter novella *The Skeleton Men of Jupiter*. Residents of the planet Sasoom (Jupiter), the Morgors are out to conquer Barsoom. Essentially, these creatures are living skeletons. They have black eye sockets, bony fingers, and no hair. Their parchmentlike skin has no cartilage or fat beneath and is stretched so tight as to be almost transparent; indeed, when they stand before a bright light their internal organs are visible. Hairless, they wear a G-string and a harness which holds a sword, dagger, and pouch. The Morgors speak in "graveyard tones." The creatures' capital city is Morgor City, which is walled, rectangular, and covers 400 square miles. see: **Burroughs, Edgar Rice; Carter, John.**

Mork [TV] A young alien played by Robin Williams in the television series "Mork and Mindy" which premiered in 1978. Hailing from the planet Ork, Mork arrives on earth in his spaceship the *Flying Egg*. Landing in Boulder, Colorado, he moves in with the only earthperson who knows his real identity, attractive music store employee Mindy McConnell (Pam Dawber). Orkans are a strange lot. They have no hearts or lungs; are all five-foot, five-inches; eat only flowers and coffee, and use their fingers—*bloinks* in the vernacular—to drink and iron clothes. While they also don't feel emotion or have a sense of humor, the madcap Mork—who wears shabby earth clothes instead of his red Orkan uniform—finds himself quickly assimilating these human qualities. Between shouts of "shazbot" (an alien oath) and "na-no, na-no" (Ork's counterpart for "greetings") and taking slang expressions literally, Mork reports to his superior, Orson, about his adventures on earth.

Morlocks [L] Monstrous humanoids in H. G. Wells' 1895 novel *The Time Machine*. Subterraneans of the far future, they are the viler of the two species into which humans have evolved. The others, the peaceful Eloi, are bred and eaten by the Morlocks. The fierce underground dwellers are described as apelike and of a dull white color, with large greyish red eyes and flaxen hair on their head and down their back. The Morlock civilization boasts great underground machines—an interesting contrast to their in-

Morlock and Minotaur

herently barbaric nature. see: **Eloi; Wells, H. G.**

Mother Goose [FT] A legendary character associated with nursery rhymes and children's stories. An old woman usually portrayed with a full dress and a bonnet, Mother Goose was popularized by author Charles Perrault in 1697. Perrault's prose volume *Tales of Long Ago with Morals* was subtitled inside as *Tales of Mother Goose,* named for his host-narrator. In 1780, London publisher John Newbery borrowed the character and identified Mother Goose with nursery rhymes, using her to introduce *Mother Goose's Melody—or—Sonnets for the Cradle.* The historical Mother Goose has traditionally been Boston's popular eighteenth century storyteller, Mother Vergoose. However, this does not explain Perrault's use of the name. More likely, Mother Goose originated with the mother of Charlemagne, Queen Goosefoot.

Mothra [MP] A giant insect featured in a series of Japanese motion pictures. In its first film, *Mothra* (1961), the

creature lies unhatched within a huge egg. Worshiped by natives on a primitive South Pacific Island, Mothra is served by a pair of six-inch-tall high priestesses. When these girls are abducted by a Japanese entrepreneur, Mothra hatches. It crosses the sea as a giant caterpillar. Upon reaching Japan, it pulls down the Tokyo Tower, spins a cocoon, and emerges as a giant moth. Mothra begins to level the metropolis, and the Japanese quickly arrange to bring the high priestesses to the airport. There, the tiny women are returned to their god.

Mothra returns in *Godzilla vs. The Thing* (1964) and is slain by the fire breather. But the insect's twin caterpillar offspring move in to defeat the giant. As caterpillars, one or the other of Mothra's web-spinning children are also on hand to battle the titular star of *Ghidrah, the Three-Headed Monster* (1965), and Ghidrah as well as alien invaders called Kilaaks in *Destroy All Monsters* (1969). see: **Ghidrah; Godzilla.**

M'Quhae, Peter [H] The captain of the ship *Daedalus* which, on August 6, 1848, sighted a sea monster in the waters off the West Coast of Africa. The creature was described as "an enormous serpent, with head and shoulders kept about four feet constantly above the surface of the sea." Over sixty feet long, the animal was brown with a yellow-white throat and a seaweedlike mane. It was clocked traveling at twelve-to-fifteen miles per hour. The entire crew claimed that the sighting was authentic; sworn statements were given to British Naval officers, a serious matter if proven to be a hoax. Authorities claim that what the captain and crew actually saw was a decorated native canoe in the tow of a harpooned sea creature. see: **Monongahela Monster.**

M'Ress, Lieutenant [TV] A crewmember of the U.S.S. *Enterprise* in the animated version of the "Star Trek" television series. Hailing from Cait, a planet in the Lynx constellation, the slight M'Ress has an orange-colored mane, gold eyes, the face, paws, and tail of a cat, and a purring voice provided by actress Majel Barrett. Her position on the starship is that of communications officer. see: *Enterprise, U.S.S.*

Mu [F] A legendary lost continent, thought by many to have been the Garden of Eden. The shores of Mu were located somewhere south of Hawaii and north of the Fijis and Easter Island, and its disappearance circa 12,000 years ago was concurrent with the alleged sinking of Atlantis.

Historians provide us with a fairly complete picture of what Mu—Lemuria, to some—was probably like. The continent itself stretched 5,000 miles from east to west, 3,000 miles from north to south, and was comprised of three land masses separated by narrow seas. There were no mountains, and the climate was tropical. In its prime, Mu had 64,000,000 inhabitants. They lived in ten tribes under one government, the Empire of the Sun, headed by King Ra Mu. There were seven major cities and an olive-skinned race was in the majority—although black, white, and yellow-skinned peoples coexisted without prejudice. The residents of Mu are said to have colonized the rest of the world, including Atlantis. While they were not a superscientific society, they possessed a glorious culture and dazzling architecture. Then, in 10,000 B.C., this seed civilization was destroyed literally overnight by volcanoes and earthquakes which sunk the continent.

There are hints of Mu in the lore of many other civilizations. For instance, to the Egyptians Mu was the personification of light. Most of what we know about this lost world comes from the work of James Churchward

(1852–1936). A British colonel, he researched Mu extensively and wrote such books as *Children of Mu* (1931), *The Sacred Symbols of Mu* (1933), and *The Cosmic Forces of Mu* (1934). see: **Atlantis; Ra.**

Mugato [TV] A giant apelike being featured in the "Star Trek" episode "A Private Little War." A native of the planet Neural, the white-furred creature has a ruddy face, hands, and feet, and an ivory horn which curves back from its head. The Mugato's fangs are poisonous, and infection can only be cured by the application of a mako root. Tall, powerfully built, and monogamous, these nomadic creatures are capable of harboring hatred. When the mate of one Mugato is slain, the affronted beast later returns to exact vengeance. see: *Enterprise, U.S.S.*

Mummy, The [MP] Historically speaking, a mummy is a bandage-swathed, embalmed or dried, usually gutted corpse. Cinematically speaking, a mummy is all of that and more—an historical mummy that has been reanimated. In most of its many motion picture incarnations, the mummy is brought back to life to protect a tomb from being defiled by archaeologists. According to the screen mythos, there are two ways of fanning the spark of life in these long-dead beings. The first is by reading from the Scroll of Thoth, and the second is by burning or liquifying Tana leaves—three every full moon simply to preserve life, and nine to give the mummy mobility.

Motion pictures have seen a great many mummies. The parent of them all is the rotting Im-ho-Tep, played by Boris Karloff in *The Mummy* (1932). He was followed by Tom Tyler's Kharis in *The Mummy's Hand* (1940); Lon Chaney Jr.'s Kharis in *The Mummy's Tomb* (1942), *The Mummy's Ghost* (1943), and *The Mummy's Curse* (1943); Eddie Parker's Klaris in

Abbott and Costello Meet the Mummy (1955); Christopher Lee's Kharis in *The Mummy* (1959); Dickie Owens' Ra-Antef in *Curse of The Mummy's Tomb* (1964); Eddie Powell's Prem in *The Mummy's Shroud* (1966); and others. A popular Mexican film series features a character called The Aztec Mummy, seen in such films as *Curse of the Aztec Mummy* (1959), *The Robot vs. the Aztec Mummy* (1959), and *The Wrestling Women vs. the Aztec Mummy* (1964). The most effective means of destroying these creatures are to summon the aid of an Egyptian god, lure them into quicksand, or set them on fire. see: **Thoth.**

Munchausen, Baron [L] A spinner of tall tales made famous by the works of Rudolph Erich Raspe. An actual person, Munchausen was the braggart Baron Karl Friedrich Hieronymous von Munchausen. Raspe merely pushed the baron's bold "autobiographical" tales of his exploits to their most impossible extremes. His efforts were published anonymously in 1785 as *Baron Munchausen's Narrative of His Marvelous Travels and Campaigns in Russia.* Other writers added to this germinative work and, before long, the name of Baron Munchausen was synonymous with fantastic adventure. Indeed, the second edition of his travels was appropriately entitled *Gulliver Revisited.* On the screen, the good baron has appeared in motion pictures produced as far back as 1909 and 1927, and as recently as 1962. However, the most famous of these films was made in 1943 starring Hans Albers and pitting him against human and monstrous foe alike. In German, the character is known as Baron Münchhausen. see: **Gulliver, Lemuel.**

Mundy, Talbot [L] The pen name of William Lancaster Gribbon, a popular writer of occult and adventure fiction. Born in Surrey, England in 1879, Mundy came to the United States in 1911 after working for the British government in Africa and India. One of his first works, and surely his greatest success, was *King of the Khyber Rifles* (1916), a nonfantasy action story. Later books were more in the realm of the supernatural, such as *The Nine Unknown* (1922), *Om: The Secret of Abhor Valley* (1924), *The Devil's Guard* (1926), and *Full Moon* (1935). His most popular creation in the fantastic milieu is Tros, a sword and sorcery hero who lives in the era of Julius Caesar. The Tros stories began appearing in *Adventure* magazine in 1925, and comprise a trilogy in book form: *Queen Cleopatra* (1929), *Tros of Samothrace* (1934), and *Purple Pirate* (1935). Mundy died in 1940.

Murometz, Ilya [F] One of the greatest heroes of Russian folklore. A peasant, Murometz spends the first thirty years of his life confined to bed, unable to use his hands or legs. Then, one day, he is visited by Jesus and two apostles. They restore life to Murometz's limbs and endow him with the strength of many men. He is told to use these abilities in the defense of Christian Russia. Saddling his horse, Cloudfall, Ilya rides out. The first person he encounters is the hero Svyatogor, who is as tall as the trees. Svyatogor gives him a mighty sword and Murometz presses on. During the course of his travels, he fights invading armies as well as many monsters. The most famous of the latter is the giant firebreathing bird Nightingale the Robber, whom he defeats. Murometz's last conflict is with the Oriental chief Kalin, whom the hero slays. This accomplished, Murometz turns to stone. Throughout these adventures, Murometz is accompanied by his aide, Alyosha Popovkin, himself a brave warrior and the killer of such monsters as the Dragon Man.

The saga of Ilya Murometz was told on the screen in the 1956 Soviet motion picture *The Sword and the*

Dragon. In it, the peasant-hero battles the Tugars under Kalin, along with their three-headed, flame-breathing dragon, Zuma. Murometz is excellently portrayed in the film by Boris Andreyev.

Muses [M] Nine young goddesses who serve Apollo. Daughters of Zeus and the Titaness Mnemosyne (Memory), they can usually be found on mountaintops and in forests where they inspire mortals in various fields of art and learning. The Muses and their specific fields are as follows: Thalia (comedy), Euterpe (music and lyric poetry), Erato (love poetry), Urania (astronomy), Terpischore (dance), Polyhymnia (sacred hymns), Melpomene (tragedy), Klei/Clio (history), and Kaliope/Calliope (epic poetry). see: **Apollo; Zeus.**

Mwuetsi [F] The first man, according to the Wahungwe Mgkoni tribe of South Rhodesia. In the beginning, the one god, Moari, created Mwuetsi, gave him a horn filled with ngona oil—a substance which could raise the dead, impregnate the living, and create fire or lightning—and placed him on the bottom of a lake. But Mwuetsi didn't like his wet and chilly home, so Moari let him move to earth. Complaining that the world was barren, Mwuetsi was given a wife named Massassi. During their first night together, Mwuetsi moistened his finger with ngona oil and touched his mate. The next day she bore foliage. He did not touch her again, and after two years Maori took Massassi from the first man and gave him the harlot Morongo. She told her husband to smear their loins with the magic oil and then make love to her. He did, and the following day she gave birth to chickens, goats, and sheep. A second bout of lovemaking brought forth cattle, and a third gave Mwuetsi and his wife human children.

Satisfied that the world was complete, Maori forbade further intercourse. However, the lusty Mwuetsi disobeyed and Morongo brought forth snakes, lions, scorpions, and the like. Swearing off his wife, Mwuetsi had intercourse with his daughters. The children they mothered made him patriarch of a great nation. Unfortunately, Morongo sought solace by sleeping with a snake. When Mwuetsi came upon them, the serpent lunged and bit him. The land was immediately swept with plague, and Mwuetsi's children were told that the only cure was to kill their four-year-old father and return him to the lake bottom. When this was done, the flush of good health returned to the earth.

Mxyzptlk, Mr. [C] A foe of the comic book hero Superman. Mr. Mxyzptlk is a sprite from the fifth dimensional land of Zrfff, and when he comes to earth it is with his almost limitless magical powers. A jester in his home plane, Mr. Mxyzptlk visits our world by muttering a pair of (unnamed) words which he plucked from the library of a Zrfffian scholar. Cocky and egocentric, the yard-high imp dresses in a bowler, gloves, boots, and high-hemmed dirndl. Mr. Mxyzptlk first appeared in September of 1944 and has returned frequently throughout the years. His expressed goal is not really to harm anyone, but to embarrass Superman whenever possible. The only way to force the taunting fellow back to Zrfff is by tricking him into saying his name backwards. That pronouncement will keep him there for a minimum of ninety days. see: **Superman.**

Myrmidons [M] A group of people in Greek mythology with a very strange genesis. When the Island of Aigina is crippled by plague, most of its population dies. Dumbstruck, the religious King Aiakos calls upon Zeus. The monarch laments that he has honored the king of the gods, and deeply loves him; why, then, has this disaster been permitted? Zeus explains that lessons in life and death are often for the ages, not merely the present. However, the deity does not want Aiakos to suffer. Thus, he transforms an ant heap into humans and calls these new subjects Myrmidons, from *myrmix* meaning "ant." Ultimately, these people follow the king's descendant Peleus to Pythia, and then his son Achilles into the Trojan War. see: **Zeus.**

Mysterians, The [MP] A race of alien beings in the 1959 Japanese motion picture *The Mysterians*. Faced with extinction, these humanoid beings from the planet Mysteroid look for fertile creatures with whom to mate. Landing on earth's moon, they study our world and decide to use human women to help repopulate their ranks. The vanguard of their invasion is a huge robot who fires a destructive green ray from its eyes. When the rampaging robot is finally destroyed—blown up while crossing a booby-trapped bridge—the golden-spacesuited extraterrestrials attack the earth themselves. They are defeated when earth scientists develop equipment able to turn the aliens' death ray back on its source. In Japan, this motion picture is known as *Earth Defense Forces.*

Nagaq [F] The name of a snake which lives on the Malayan Peninsula, and of a dragon that dwells in its lakes. According to ancient legends, the lakes were created by an old man—also named Nagaq—who drove his staff into the ground and created holes from which water rose. Monsters living in the area were trapped by the flood, and inhabit the lakes still. People who have seen Nagaq the dragon say that it is slate-colored, has a long neck and a flat snakelike head, and stands as tall as a palm tree.

Napier, Carson [L] Author Edgar Rice Burroughs' blond, twenty-five to thirty-year-old Californian who decides to seek adventure in outer space. Building a rocket on Guadalupe Island off the coast of Baja, California he heads for Mars. Rather naively, however, he forgets to consider the tug of the moon when plotting his course, and its gravity swings his spaceship from the Red Planet toward Venus. Reaching the cloud-enveloped world, Napier encounters a variety of monsters such as a giant spider called the targo, amoeba people, lionlike tharbans, bisonlike basto, and flying humanoids known as klangan. He also meets, falls in love with, and marries the very human Duare, janjong (princess) of Kooaad in the kingdom of Vepaja. Napier learns that the Venusians call their world Amtor, takes an injection of immortality serum, leaps inside an anotar (airship), and with Duare swashbuckles his way through

five novels: *Pirates of Venus* (1932), *Lost on Venus* (1933), *Carson of Venus* (1938), *Escape on Venus* (1940), and *Wizard of Venus* (1941). see: **Burroughs, Edgar Rice; Korva.**

Narayana [M] In the legends of the lost continent of Mu, a seven-headed serpent. Also known as the Supreme Spirit, the Creator, and the Great Self-Existing Power, Narayana has a vast intellect which was used to create everything in the universe. Humans are a part of the tapestry woven by the serpent, although Narayana made them unique since they are the only entities endowed with the capacity to think. see: **Mu.**

Narcissus [M] A handsome Greek youth whose vanity causes the downfall of himself and the oreade (mountain nymph) Echo. Echo is not the cleverest of creatures. At the request of Zeus, she keeps his wife, Hera, occupied while the king of the gods dallies with the other nymphs. When Hera learns of Echo's part in the deception, she punishes her. Henceforth, the oreade can speak only by repeating sounds made by others. Wandering lonely through a forest one day, Echo sees Narcissus. She becomes immediately enamored and goes up to him. Affronted by her aggressiveness, the youth departs—leaving Echo so embarrassed that she hides in caves and valleys until all but her voice has wasted away. As for Narcissus, his pride and rudeness toward Echo are dealt with in time. While gazing into a pool, the gods cause him to fall in love with his own reflection. Mesmerized, Narcissus eventually pines away and is transformed into the flower which bears his name. see: **Hera; Zeus.**

Narnia [L] A world beyond the closet doors of an English estate. Created by author C. S. Lewis in 1950, Narnia is a land which lies between a lamppost near the wild woods of the West, and the great castle of Cair Paravel on the shores of the Eastern sea. It is home to many strange creatures, from the very polite Tumnus the Faun, to nymphs, to wild Red Dwarfs, to the White Witch who holds Narnia within her cruel grip. There are seven Narnia novels in all. In *The Lion, the Witch, and the Wardrobe*, Aslan the brave lion overthrows the White Witch and liberates Narnia. In *Prince Caspian* the titular noble leads his army of Talking Beasts to victory over the Telmarines. *The Voyage of the Dawn Treader* is the saga of Caspian's journey to the end of the world, while *The Silver Chair* is the story of Prince Rillan's flight from the subterranean realm of the Emerald Witch. In *The Horse and His Boy*, a talking steed and a young lad thwart an invasion of Narnia, while *The Magician's Nephew* is the story of how Aslan first created Narnia and empowered all of its animals with speech. Finally, in *The Last Battle* Aslan conquers all evil and leads his followers to Paradise.

Nautilus [L] The supersubmarine created by Jules Verne for his novels *Twenty Thousand Leagues Under the Sea* (1873) and its sequel *Mysterious Island* (1875). Inspired by submarines such as Robert Fulton's *Nautilus* of 1797 and the *Monitor* and *Merrimack* of the American Civil War, Verne's electrically powered *Nautilus* is commanded by the scientific genius Captain Nemo. At first, the world believes that the warship-destroying submarine is a sea monster. However, when a group sent to investigate the creature is taken onboard, they learn its true nature. As Nemo states, the craft is "an elongated cylinder with conical ends. It is very much like a cigar in shape. The length . . . is exactly 232 feet, and its maximum breadth is twenty-six feet." He also quotes its area as 6,032 square feet, its contents approximately 1,500 cubic yards, and its weight 1,500 tons. Structurally, the

submarine is composed of two steel hulls, one inside and the other outside, joined by T-shaped irons for added strength. The vessel is steered horizontally by a rudder, and vertically by "two inclined planes fastened to its sides, opposite the center of flotation (and) worked by powerful levers from the interior."

In *Twenty Thousand Leagues Under the Sea*, the submarine's purpose is explained as antiwar; Nemo uses its power to destroy the tools of battle. Alas, this vessel which was built in secret on a desert island in the Pacific is dragged to the ocean floor and crippled by a whirlpool located between the isles of Ferroe and Loffoden. While it returns in *Mysterious Island*, the craft is no longer seaworthy. Located in a harbor of Lincoln Island—where Nemo managed to guide it after he escaped the maelstrom in Norway—the craft was subsequently trapped there by the rising of basalt due to volcanic action. In the novel's climax, the steel ship is sunk to the bottom of the lake at Nemo's request, where it serves as the captain's tomb. see: **Nemo, Captain; Verne, Jules.**

Necromancy [O] Broadly, the art of contacting the dead; specifically, the magic of reanimating a corpse for mercenary ends. Originally, necromancers—or their spirits—would fly to the afterlife to converse with the deceased. However, this proved a difficult road for mortals to travel. Thus, rituals were devised to bring the dead to our own sphere. Sometimes this was (and is) worked through intermediaries; demons if the purpose is evil, angels if the purpose is good. Usually, this communication is held not for destructive reasons but to learn the location of treasure or seek information about the future.

The most common auditorium for necromancy is a graveyard or a ruined church. Reaching one of these sites, the necromancer will draw a magic circle by moonlight, step inside and, if a demon is being summoned, remain there until it has departed—or risk being dragged to the underworld. Sometimes a corpse must be present, which the spirit will enter to speak with its solicitor. To assure the constant cooperation of the hell-bound dead, many necromancers take the precaution of signing a contract with the Devil.

Since necromancy is not always used for nefarious ends, it appears without disfavor in such God-fearing works as the Bible. In one famous Old Testament incident Saul speaks with the Witch of Endor, a necromancer, to learn what will happen if he goes to war against the Philistines. He is told that he will be defeated—but attacks just the same, loses, and is slain. see: **Devil; Witch.**

Nemean Lion [M] A ferocious lion of Greek mythology. The offspring of Typhon and Echidna, the feline has a skin so sturdy that no weapon can harm it. For years, the creature roams the Valley of Nemea in Argolis, killing all who enter. Hercules' cousin Eurystheus knows of the lion and, as the first of the twelve labors he will impose on the demigod, orders him to slay the beast. Tracking it, Hercules attacks with club and arrows but to no avail. Finally, he confronts the lion and strangles it with his mighty hands. Then, using one of the animal's own claws, he skins it and dons the hide. Running up to Eurystheus on all fours, he terrifies his cousin—who instructs him to tell the tale of his conquest from a distance. see: **Hercules; Typhon.**

Nemo, Captain [L] The hero-villain of Jules Verne's novels *Twenty Thousand Leagues Under the Sea* (1873) and *Mysterious Island* (1875). The commander of the submarine *Nautilus*, Nemo was once Prince Dakkar of India, son of the rajah of the territory of Bundelkund. Born in 1818, he was sent at the age of ten to Europe to be educated. Nemo returned to India twenty years later where he married and fathered two children. By 1857, he had become embroiled in the anti-British Sepoy Revolt and, before long, he found himself the sole surviving member of his race. Then, "overcome with disappointment ... disgust for all human beings ... and hatred of the civilized world," he used his fortune and scientific knowledge to construct the *Nautilus*. Its purpose: to rid the world of warships and other aggressive weapons.

Nemo's voyages under the sea have increased his wealth many times over. He classifies himself as "immensely rich, sir; and I could, without missing it, pay the national debt of France." Physically, he is tall, has a large forehead, black eyes, a straight nose, a "clearly cut mouth," and beautiful teeth. Although he also boasts "self confidence, energy, and courage," he is characterized as having "a highly nervous temperament."

By the end of the nearly eight months covered in *Twenty Thousand Leagues Under the Sea* (early November of 1866 through June of 1867), Nemo is sixty years old. His submarine is crippled and, six years later, in the closing chapter of *Mysterious Island,* he dies, his life "simply fading out." A group of escaped POWs from a Confederate prison land by balloon on Nemo's Lincoln Island and sink the *Nautilus* with its creator still inside—a permanent tomb for a misunderstood genius. On the screen, Captain Nemo has been played by such actors as James Mason in *Twenty Thousand Leagues Under the Sea* (1954), Herbert Lom in *Mysterious Island* (1961), Robert Ryan in *Captain Nemo and the Underwater City* (1970), and Jose Ferrer in the television mini-series "The Return of Captain Nemo" (1978). see: *Nautilus;* **Verne, Jules.**

Nereids [M] Early Greek sea nymphs.

Nereids

Nautilus

Depending upon the account one chooses to believe, there are between fifty and two hundred nereids, all of them fathered by the oceanid Doris and Nereus, the seaweed-haired, trident-carrying Old Man of the Sea. Extremely beautiful and generous to humans, the nereids ride through the ocean on tritons—which are half-man, half-fish—and on dolphins. They are usually naked or draped in a flimsy garment, and always come to the assistance of sailors in distress. The most famous of these nymphs are Amphitrite, the wife of Poseidon and Queen of the Sea, and Thetis, the mother of Achilles by Peleus. see: **Poseidon.**

Nibelungen [F] Subterranean elves of German and Scandinavian folklore. Also known as Folk of the Mist, they are descended from the dwarf Nibelung and spend their days robbing treasure and hiding it underground. Their gold is used to make rings of fertility, which are highly prized by mortals. Characters in the Scandinavian *Volsunga Saga* and the late twelfth century German epic *The Nibelungenlied,* they gained their greatest fame as foils for Siegfried in Richard Wagner's twelve-hour opera *Ring of the Nibelungs,* written from 1848–1874. see: **Siegfried.**

Night Gallery [TV] A three-season television series hosted by Rod Serling and featuring stories about the occult. Among the ninety plays presented between 1970 and 1973, were many adaptations of classic works—such as H. P. Lovecraft's "Pickman's Model" and August Derleth's "The Dark Boy"—as well as tales written by Serling, Richard Matheson, and others. Of this latter group, the most popular are Serling's Emmy-nominated "The Messiah of Mott Street" starring Edward G. Robinson and "They're Tearing Down Tim Riley's Bar." Among the noted actors who appeared on "Night Gallery" were Ray Milland, Raymond Massey, Leonard Nimoy, Vincent Price, Carl Reiner, Laurence Harvey, and Joan Crawford (in a segment directed by Steven Spielberg, who went on to helm *Jaws* and *Close Encounters of the Third Kind*). Each segment of the series was introduced by a painting which symbolized its motif or moral. see: **Matheson, Richard; Serling, Rod.**

Nixie [F] A German mermaid, the female counterpart of a nix. The most famous legend of a nixie is included in the works of the Brothers Grimm. In "The Nixie of the Mill Pond," she is pictured as having long hair "which fell down on both sides and covered her white body," as well as a sweet voice. Appearing to a poor miller, she offers him great wealth for "the young thing which has just been born in thy house." Thinking that she means a kitten, he agrees and rushes home to tell his wife. Much to the man's chagrin, he finds her cuddling their newborn son.

The riches come as promised, and over the years the miller tells his boy to stay away from the pond. However, one day, shortly after his marriage, the young man kneels by the waters to wash his hands. The nixie bursts from the pond and grabs him. His wife is horrified and consults a sage old woman. The white-haired hag gives her a golden comb, a flute, and a spinning wheel, and instructs her to place them in the water on succeeding nights. The girl does as she is told, and each night more of her husband appears atop the lapping waves. Finally, with the surrender of the spinning wheel, the young man is able to leap from the lake. Taking on a life of its own, the pool surges after them "with a frightful roar." The wife calls upon the old woman for help, and the couple is immediately transformed into a pair of frogs. They ride the flood and, when it subsides, are returned to normal. However, the waters carried them so far from one another that it is years before the couple is reunited.

Generally, nixies have the torso and head of a woman and the tail of a fish. Not all of them drive as hard a bargain as the Grimm character. see: **Grimm, Jakob and Wilhelm; Merpeople.**

Noggle [F] A rural sprite who can usually be seen roaming about in the form of a small gray horse, accoutered with a bridle and saddle. The noggle takes its greatest pleasure in two acts of mischief: stopping mills from running; and appearing at a stream or pond, urging a passer-by to mount, dashing into the water, and turning into a cloud of blue flame, giving the rider an unexpected swim. The one way to distinguish a noggle on sight is by the way its tail swings up over its back. It can be chased away only by plunging a long, steel knife or a flaming brand through the venting hole of the mill.

Nomad [TV] A murderous space probe seen in the "Star Trek" episode "The Changeling." Sent from earth in August of 2002, its mission is to search for life forms in outer space. Struck by a meteoroid, it strays off course and loses contact with its home world. In time, it meets the alien probe Tan Ru, whose objective is to sterilize soil samples. The two robots combine to form Nomad, their respective missions being garbled in the process; the hybrid views as its purpose the sterilization of all that is imperfect. After destroying four billion inhabitants in the Malurian system, the five-foot-tall, floating Nomad is taken aboard the U.S.S. *Enterprise.* But the crew is not without its flaws, and the probe plans to destroy the starship. Luckily, before it can do so, Nomad mistakes Captain James Kirk for its creator Jackson Roykirk. When Nomad is shown the mistake it has made, the probe self-destructs for being imperfect. see: ***Enterprise,* U.S.S.; Kirk, Captain James.**

Norka [FT] A huge monster in the fairy tale "The Norka." A serpent with webbed claws and the face of a cat, the Norka dwells in a world that lies beneath a large white stone. Following the Norka underground, a prince named Ivan finds a richly bedecked horse and mounts. They ride to a palace made of copper, and Ivan finds a lovely lady locked therein. Traveling on, Ivan comes to another of the monster's sisters living in a silver palace, and yet another in a golden palace. Then, finding the Norka asleep by the sea—where its snores shake the water for seven miles around—Ivan smites it. The three sisters pack their palaces within eggshells and travel to the surface world with Ivan. They are met by the prince's two elder brothers, who help the girls from beneath the stone—but push Ivan back inside.

Meanwhile, the sisters have been forbidden from telling the king where his third son is. However, they put off the two brothers' advances by refusing to marry until they have clothes *exactly* like those they had in the land of the Norka. The princes fail, but Ivan does not. Escaping from the pit and arriving in such an unkempt condition that no one recognizes him, he opens the eggshells and pulls out the castles—along with the girls' clothes. At this, Ivan reveals his identity as well as his brothers' treachery. Yet, he forgives them, and a triple wedding is held soon thereafter.

Norns [M] The three Norse goddesses of fate. Giants, their job is to weave the web of destiny, water the sacred ash tree Yggdrasil—whose three roots reached to the sphere of the mortals, the realm of the giants, and Niflheim (the Land of Mist)—and to keep Yggdrasil healthy by constantly nourishing it with fresh soil. By name, the Norns are the kindly Urda and Verdani, and the cruel Skuld. They represent the past, present, and future, respectively. In addition to their other tasks, the three norns cast lots over the crib of every newborn. Urda and Verdani try to bless the child, and bestow it with many gifts; Skuld seeks to curse it with bad luck.

Nosferatu [MP] A motion picture vampire patterned after Count Dracula. Nosferatu, "the Undead," is actually the evil Count Orlock (referred to as Count Orlof in some prints of the original silent film). Leaving his Carpathian castle in 1838, he heads for Bremen, Germany, to seek fresh blood. Following him, wherever he travels, is an army of rats. Yet the plague they bring pales to insignificance beside that of the vampire. Pursuing one girl in particular—the lovely Ellen Hutter—Orlock is destroyed when she sacrifices her life to keep him by her side until dawn. Struck by the sun's purifying rays, the bloodsucker evaporates.

First filmed in 1922, *Nosferatu* starred Max Schreck—whose surname means "terror"—and was directed by F. W. Murnau. The popular 1979 remake featured Klaus Kinski in the title role under the direction of Werner Herzog. Both incarnations picture the vampire as bald, with pointed ears, large fangs, and clawed fingers.

That Nosferatu was created at all can be attributed to Murnau's desire to film Bram Stoker's novel *Dracula*—without paying a fee for the then-copyrighted work. see: **Dracula; Vampire.**

Nostradamus [H] An astrologer, alchemist, and physician born at St. Remy de Provence in 1503. Bearded, with dark curly hair, intense eyes, and a strong nose, Michel de Nostre-Dame—popularized as Nostradamus—is best remembered today as a prophet, whose predictions appear to embrace such figures as Napoleon, Hitler, Kennedy, and others. Much of anyone's belief in Nostradamus depends upon whether or not they accept Annemarc as Princess Anne and Mark Phillips, Hister as Hitler, and so on. Nostradamus' most famous work is *The Centuries,* penned in 1555—eleven years before the seer's death. In modern times, Nostradamus is also the name of a vampire played by German Robles in a series of Mexican films. Among their titles are *The Curse of Nostradamus* (1960), *Nostradamus and the Genie of Darkness* (1960), and *Nostradamus and the Destroyer of Monsters* (1962). see: **Vampire.**

Nuckelavee [F] A sea monster of Scottish legend, and one of the foulest beasts alive. Half-man and half-horse, with fins growing from its legs and a truly enormous mouth, Nuckelavee lacks an outer layer of skin. Its flesh is red, raw, and dripping, with black blood pumping through yellowish veins. Panting poisonous, vaporous breath, the sea creature exudes a sickening odor and lurks in all but fresh or running water—to which it is allergic. Fulfilling its mission to visit evil upon the world, Nuckelavee travels about

Nuckelavee

killing crops, slaughtering cattle and other livestock, and murdering any humans it meets. Once sighted, the only way to escape a Nuckelavee is to cross a running stream.

Nutcracker [E] The featured article of fantasy in the tale "The Nutcracker and the King of Mice" by Ernst Hoffman (1776–1822), and *The Nutcracker Ballet* by Peter Tchaikovsky (1840–1893). Carved in the figure of a man, the titular nutcracker comes to life on Christmas Eve as a dashing prince. In this form, the nutcracker escorts his owner, young Clara, on a series of adventures involving magic and fanciful beings. Among their escapades are a battle with an army of mice led by the Mouse King; a trip to the magic land of the Sugar-Plum Fairy; and dances with Russian dolls, Arabian girls, and a silken Chinese fan. see: **Odette.**

Nymphs [M] Beautiful female divinities of nature in Greek mythology. Among the most populous breeds of nymphs are the sea nymphs known as oceanids; the mountain nymphs or oreades; the wood nymphs called dryads; nymphs of the rivers and springs or naiads; and tree nymphs referred to as hamadrayads. Valleys, meadows, gardens, flocks, and other things of nature all had their own nymphs. Many of these breezy creatures were also responsible for attending a superior deity.

Oannes [F] Fish beings from another world. According to the more imaginative proponents of alien visitation on earth, the Oannes allegedly presented themselves to the ancient Sumerians. Remaining for several generations, they instructed the terrestrials on the correct way to build a civilization. All of this is said to have taken place on the Persian Gulf, in the city of Eridu, circa 4000 B.C.

Oberon [F] The king of the fairies. Most scholars trace Oberon's roots to Alberich, a German dwarf. Anglicized as Auberon and then Oberon, the pixie potentate can grow no taller than a three-year-old child, due to an ancient curse placed on him by an evil fairy. The king's queen is Titania. Far more stately than Mab, her flighty counterpart in many legends, she is portrayed as constantly at odds with Oberon. The couple's most famous bout is chronicled in William Shakespeare's 1596 play *A Midsummer Night's Dream*. In it, Titania refuses to give Oberon a changeling boy. As a result, through magic, the queen is made to fall in love with the mortal Bottom, who has been saddled with the head of an ass. By play's end, the fairy lovers have stopped their bickering—temporarily—and leave the woods arm-in-arm. see: **Bottom; Changeling; Fairy; Mab; Puck.**

O'Brien, Willis [MP] A stop-motion animator. Willis Harold O'Brien was born in Oakland, California in 1886, the son of William and Minnie Greg O'Brien. During his youth, he worked as a boxer and stonecutter before discovering that clay models could be set in different poses before a motion picture camera; and that, if these incremental movements were each exposed to one frame of movie film, the model would seem to be alive. Raising the money to shoot an experimental short subject, O'Brien pitched his concept to Thomas Edison. The renowned inventor commissioned a series of brief prehistoric era comedies, the first of which was *The Dinosaur and the Missing Link* (1917). Because clay had a tendency to droop and melt under hot movie lights, O'Brien began making his models from sturdier stuff, such as rubber, molding this around strong ball-and-socket jointed skeletons. Much of this work was done in conjunction with sculptor Marcel Delgado.

Moving on to feature films, O'Brien created such stop-motion classics as *The Ghost of Slumber Mountain* (1919); *The Lost World* (1925); the immortal, original *King Kong* (1933); *The Son of Kong* (1933); the special effects Oscar-winner *Mighty Joe Young* (1949); *The Black Scorpion* (1957); *The Giant Behemoth* (1958); and others. His last film was a 1960 remake of *The Lost World*—budget cuts forcing O'Brien to use live lizards rather than dinosaur models. O'Brien died in 1962, survived by his second wife, Darlyne Prenett. His first wife, Hazel Collette, had shot their two sons, Willis Jr. and William, before taking her own life. see: **Giant Behemoth, The; Harryhausen, Ray; King Kong; Young, Mighty Joe.**

Odette [E] A young girl transformed into a swan by a wicked sorcerer in Peter Tchaikovsky's 1877 ballet *Swan Lake*, which is based on both an ancient legend and an 1871 work by the composer. Odette must remain a swan until a man falls in love with only her.

Unhappily, the prince who fulfills this provision is misled through magic into loving the girl's nasty double. The real Odette dies and, realizing his blunder, the prince takes his own life. However, the two spirits renew their affections in the hereafter—the tangible benefits of which are elusive. The sorcerer also perishes.

Odin [M] The white-bearded king of the Norse gods. The grandson of Ymir (some tales say Bure, the fire god from whom we get "burn" and "burnish"), and the son of Bor, Odin is the god of war, wisdom, poetry, and magic. Handsome, brave, and well spoken, he is always dressed in a shining breastplate and a helmet of gold, and is never without his mighty dwarf-forged spear Gungnir. Odin holds court in Valhalla, and when he travels it is always on the back of the eight-hooved horse Sleipnir, the swiftest animal in all of creation. Among Odin's other kingly attributes are his great knowledge, gained from drinking the waters of the fountain of Mimir; a magic ring known as Draupner; the ravens Hunin and Munin, who sit on Odin's shoulders and are sent from his palace daily to see what is going on in the world; and the ability to change into any shape he wishes.

Odin is married to Frigg, the goddess of love and of the home, and is the father of Thor, Balder, Hoder, Vithar (the strongest god after Thor), Bragi (a god of wisdom), and Tyr (the god of athletics). Remarkably, the king of the gods has only one eye. The other he gave to his nephew, Mimir, to keep in a well in exchange for draughts from the fountain of wisdom.

Odin is also known as Wotan and Woden, from which Woden's day or Wednesday derives. Friday is Frigg's day. see: **Balder; Loki; Thor; Valhalla; Valkyries; Ymir.**

Odysseus [L] Known as Ulysses to the Romans, one of the great adventurers of Greek literature. Odysseus' exploits are chronicled in two epic poems written by Homer circa 800 B.C., *The Iliad* and *The Odyssey*. The son of Laertes and Anticleia, and the husband of Penelope, Odysseus is a clever, brave, and merciless man described as "a worthless-looking runt" by the cyclops Polyphemus. Though the hero *is* short—shorter by a head than Agamemnon—he is extremely broad of chest and shoulders.

After ending the decade-long war with Troy by conceiving of the Trojan Horse (*The Iliad*), Odysseus begins a ten-year-long journey from Troy to his home in Ithaca (*The Odyssey*). During his voyage he has many fantastic adventures. Among the most challenging are encounters with Polyphemus, whom Odysseus blinds, earning the wrath of the cyclops' father Poseidon; the Lotophagi or Lotus-eaters, who make the hero's men so lethargic that he has to drag them to the ship and lash them to their benches; Circe on the island of Aeaea, where the enchantress turns the Greeks into swine; the Sirens, whose song drives mortals mad; Scylla and Charybdis, a huge monster and a whirlpool respectively; trips to the land of the Cimmerians and to Hades—the latter to consult with the blind prophet Tiresias; the inopportune opening of a bag of wind given to Odysseus by the king of the winds Aeolus, which blows the sailors backward; and the slaughter of the black oxen of Helios at Thrinacia, which drives Zeus to strike Odysseus' boat with lightning, drowning all hands save for the hero.

Thus far, two years have elapsed. The next eight are spent with the nymph Calypso, a daughter of Atlas, whom Odysseus meets upon reaching land. He finally gets around to building a raft and sailing to the Phaeacian isle of Scheria, ruled by King Alcinous. Obtaining a ship, Odysseus goes home. In the meantime, his wife has kept suitors from her bed by saying that she will not remarry until she has finished weaving a garment for Laertes. Each night, Penelope unravels what she has done during the day, thus postponing matrimony. Upon Odysseus' arrival, his dog Argus is so excited that it dies of joy, and the hero's son Telemachus helps him find a way to rid his home of suitors. To this end, the lad announces that whoever can string the bow of his father and shoot an arrow through the holes in twelve axe blades will win Penelope. Only the disguised Odysseus is able to perform the feat—after which he shoots every one of the suitors. see: **Atlas; Charybdis; Cimmeria; Circe; Cyclops; Poseidon; Scylla; Sirens; Zeus.**

Ogaloussa [M] A figure in Liberian mythology. When Ogaloussa fails to return after a hunt, his wife and three sons think nothing of it. Months later, Ogaloussa's fourth son, Puli, is born. Looking around he asks, "Where is my father?" No one can tell him. The boy is shocked by this irresponsible answer, embarrasses his brothers for their lassitude, and makes them go out and search for Ogaloussa. After traveling for several hours, they find their father's scattered bones. The first son puts them back together; the second restores the flesh and muscle; and the third places breath into the body. The group then returns home. When they arrive, Ogaloussa asks which of his sons did the most to return him to life. Puli steps forward, and Ogaloussa rewards him by giving the boy his prize possession, a cow-tail switch. The moral: "No one is ever really dead until they are forgotten."

Ogopogo [O] A monster that dwells at the bottom of Lake Okanagan in British Columbia. Pictured as seventy feet long and having whiskers, a goat's head (some witnesses say that it is more like that of a cow, horse, or sheep), a snakelike neck, a humped back, and flippers, Ogopogo was first described by the Okanakane Indians

as an evil god named N'ha-a-itk. So fearful were they of this creature that the Indians always placed a pig or a dog alone in a canoe before they themselves crossed the waters. That way, if the monster appeared, its attention would be drawn to the sacrifice and not the natives. The name Ogopogo was coined by whites in 1926. Though Ogopogo is the most famous of the Canadian monsters, it is by no means the only one. Other such lake dwellers include Tazama, Tsinquaw, and Pohengamok. see: **Loch Ness Monster; Manipogo.**

Ogres [F] A particularly nasty breed of giants in European folklore. Unlike run-of-the-mill giants, who are powerful and usually very selfish, ogres are genuinely wicked. In almost every legend they feast exclusively on the flesh of humans, and will go out of the way to eat children where their parents can see. Always ugly or deformed, ogres are sometimes pictured as nonhumanoid monsters, or as human-sized cannibals. In addition to being fierce and cruel, all ogres are extremely sloppy. see: **Giants.**

Ogre and Odysseus

Oleg [H] The Prince of Kiev, son of Vladimir, and first Christian ruler of Russia. Though Oleg actually lived, his brush with the fantastic is probably apocryphal. According to a nineteenth century poem by Alexander Pushkin (1799–1837), on his way to battle the Hazars in Crimea, Oleg met a necromancer. The ruler asked to be told the future. The seer said Oleg would win all of his battles and never be harmed by any weapon—but that his horse would be responsible for killing him. As a precaution, Oleg immediately put the animal out to pasture. Years later, he asked what had become of the horse. An aide told him that it had died, and the prince grinned. Deciding to pay his respects to the poor beast, Oleg went to visit its bones. While the ruler was standing beside the skull, a snake shot suddenly from within and bit him. Before the day had ended, Oleg was dead—thus fulfilling the prophecy. see: **Necromancy.**

Olympus [M] The dwelling place of the Greek gods. Olympus is actually a mountain in Thessaly, standing 10,000 feet tall and designated the home of the gods simply because of its size. From its summit, the giant but human-shaped deities could see all which transpired among the mortals. To protect this abode from invasion, the entrance was barred with clouds and guarded by the Hours, the goddesses of order, justice, and peace who also saw that the seasons of earth came when they should. Later tales located Olympus in the heavens rather than at the top of a mountain. In both places, the gods lived in palaces made of bright metal and traveled about in chariots drawn by celestial steeds or via golden shoes. see: **Zeus.**

Omniont [M] A giant snake worshiped by the Huron Indians. Apart from its incredible size, Omniont was famous for a huge, sharp horn which grows from its head. Durable enough to cut a path through mountains and trees, the horn was also able to ward off evil. To have a part of it was considered the strongest of all good luck charms, and many primitive shamans held their authority by claiming to own such a relic; odd, since the horn was said to be unbreakable. It was the greatest dream of every Indian just to see Omniont, although its exact whereabouts could never be known by any mortal. see: **Shaman.**

One Ring [L] The foremost Ring of Power featured in J. R. R. Tolkien's *Lord of the Rings* trilogy. Forged by Sauron in the fires of Sammath Naur, the One Ring is to be used by the evil tyrant to gain control over others who hold lesser rings. But the simple band of gold is taken from Sauron, and passes in turn from Isildur to Déagol to Gollum to Bilbo Baggins to Frodo Baggins. With the help of Gollum, Frodo destroys the ring in the exact same spot where it was created, thus keeping it from Sauron and preventing him from obtaining its attendant powers—not that the One Ring works only on behalf of the bearer. Though it gives some of its owners long life and invisibility, it is Tolkien's symbol for greed and makes its possessors avaricious and suspicious. Its inscription can only be read when the band is heated. see: **Bilbo Baggins; Frodo Baggins; Gandalf; Hobbit; Sauron; Tolkien, J. R. R.**

One Step Beyond [TV] A television series featuring half-hour-long occult dramas. Hosted by Cincinnati-born actor-director John Newland, the program premiered in 1959 and ran for three seasons. It presented allegedly factual stories about extrasensory perception, ghosts, and other supernatural phenomena. Among the many noted performers who appeared on the ABC series are Cloris Leachman, Jack Lord, Charles Bronson, Warren Beatty, Christopher Lee, and Louise

Fletcher. The program returned to the air in 1978 as the syndicated "The Next Step Beyond," featuring all new stories and Newland once again starring as our guide to the beyond.

Oni

Oni [O] Evil spirits of Japanese lore. Grotesque-looking creatures, the Oni are green or red and have the head of an ox or horse atop a human torso. Most can change their shape or become invisible. The cruelest of the Oni are those who service the underworld. Their job is to nab sinners and bear them to hell in a flaming chariot. These demons also spread sickness and steal the souls of the newly deceased—the latter by assuming the guise of a relative and approaching the fresh corpse. Not that all Oni inflict suffering without being forced to endure an agony or two. Many are made to go without food or water, and as a result move through their wicked paces with perpetually bloated bellies.

Opar [L] A legendary walled city created by Edgar Rice Burroughs for his Tarzan novels. Introduced in *The Return of Tarzan,* the second book of the series, Opar is 10,000 years old and is located in a desolate valley in Africa. Ruled by the high priestess La, it has wide roads, tapering towers, huge domed buildings, and temples with pillars of gold—all of it overgrown with vegetation. Originally, La was a haven for sun worshiping Atlanteans. However, when Atlantis sunk the Oparians were stranded and quickly fell to savagery. Indeed, they went so far as to mate with apes producing shaggy male children but still-beautiful females. Weak males or ugly females were (and are) destroyed. Stumbling upon Opar, Tarzan uses its wealth to build himself a huge estate in Africa. Other novels in which the Ape-Man has adventures in Opar are *Tarzan and the Jewels of Opar* (book number five), *Tarzan and the Golden Lion* (book number nine), and *Tarzan the Invincible* (book number fourteen). see: **Atlantis; Burroughs, Edgar Rice; Tarzan.**

Orion [M] A magnificent giant of Greek mythology. His origin is confused. Some accounts say he is the son of Poseidon and Euryale, while others claim that he grew from the ground where the skin of a cow had been buried by Zeus, Hermes, and Poseidon. In either case, Poseidon was in some measure responsible for Orion's birth and, paternally, gave him the ability to walk on or through water. Sadly, everything which follows Orion's birth is downhill. Falling in love with Merope, he asks her father, Oenopion, for permission to wed. This is granted, but Orion can't wait and tries to rape his bride-to-be. As a result, Oenopion has him blinded. Apollo restores the giant's sight, at which point he takes up with the god's sister, Artemis. Apollo is outraged and plots vengeance. He challenges his sister to an archery contest, the target being an object bobbing about in a lake. Artemis does not know that this is the back of Orion's head, and slays him. To compensate for her blunder, she places her lover in the sky as a constellation. Orion's dog, Sirius, was transformed into a star and follows its master through the sky. see: **Apollo; Artemis; Hermes; Poseidon; Zeus.**

Orlac [L/MP] A pianist whose soul is corrupted in a bizarre operation. When Stephen Orlac's hands are amputated after an accident, a surgeon grafts on a new pair—the hands of a murderer. In short order, Orlac himself begins to manifest the skills and moral degeneracy of the killer. Whether the possession is actual or psychological is never resolved. This tale by Maurice Renard has been thrice filmed: as *The Hands of Orlac* in 1925 and 1964 (in the latter, the hand transplant turns out to have been a hoax) starring Conrad Veidt and Mel Ferrer respectively, and in 1935 as *Mad Love* with Colin Clive as the pianist and Peter Lorre as the surgeon, Dr. Gogol. see: **Lorre, Peter.**

Orpheus [M] A legendary poet. The son of Oeagrus, the King of Thrace, and the muse Calliope; the historical Orpheus lived in the era before Homer. Of this actual person we know very little. Of the mythological Orpheus it is said that the music he created on his golden lyre—a gift from Apollo—was pure enchantment. Trees, rocks, and animals followed him around, rain and winds ceased when he played, and even Hades allowed his tormented souls to rest when Orpheus' notes reached his realm. So lovely were his melodies that the mortal Orpheus was permitted to visit Olympus and move among the gods.

Sailing with the Argonauts, Orpheus' lyre saved them from the lure of the Sirens, when his songs proved lovelier than theirs. Following the Argosy, Orpheus married the nymph, Eurydice. One day, however, the poor nymph was accosted by Aristaeus, the god of the bees. Fleeing his unsolicited advances, Eurydice was bitten by a snake and died. Heartbroken, Orpheus went to Hades and pleaded for the return of his wife. The god agreed—as long as the poet did not look back en route to the surface. The trek went well, until Orpheus was mere yards from journey's end. Unable to wait any longer, he spun about; Eurydice vanished with a cry. Sitting by the river Strymon, Orpheus took neither food nor drink. Eventually he was ripped to pieces by maenads, attendants of Dionysos, when he refused their seductive wiles. Zeus recovered Orpheus' lyre and placed it in the sky as the constellation Lyra. An opera entitled *Orpheus in the Underworld* was written in 1858 by Jacques Offenbach (1819–1880). Its overture contains the melody popularly known today as *Can-Can.* see: **Apollo; Dionysos; Hades; Muse; Zeus.**

Orthos [M] A two-headed Greek dog. The son of Typhon and Echidna, and the brother of the three-headed hound Cerberus, Orthos is the companion of the giant Eurytion. Together, they guard the red cattle owned by the monster Geryon. Like his brother, Orthos pits his might against Hercules, whose tenth labor is to capture Geryon's herd. Unlike his brother, Orthos is clubbed to death by the hero, rather than captured. In occult circles, Orthos is also a term used to describe the spirit world. It is a word which the spirits themselves coined and passed on. see: **Cerberus; Geryon; Hercules; Typhon.**

Osiris [M] The Egyptian Judge of the Dead. The son of Keb (earth) and either Nut (sky) or Neph (world-ocean), depending upon the myth, Osiris is the brother of Set (the god of evil), the brother-husband of Isis, and the father of Horus. In early legends, Osiris was known as Busiris. The name change occurred when many Egyp-

Osiris Constellation of Orion

tians elevated him to the level of a sun and moon god equal in rank to Ra. Then came the fall and apotheosis. Set slew his brother, cutting his body to pieces and spreading them throughout Egypt. Isis reassembled her husband and, with the help of Thoth (the secretary of the underworld), and an assist from Set's wife, Nephthys (the goddess of the dead and of dusk) and the murderer's son, Anubis (the god of the dead and of embalming), resurrected Osiris through magic rites. The revived god became a deity of eternal life and the judge of the underworld before whom all souls come upon dying. His duties are outlined in *The Book of the Dead*, which describes the travels of the soul after death, the hearing before Osiris, and the Osirian scheme for immortality. see: **Anubis; Horus; Isis; Ra; Thoth.**

Ouija Board [O] A small wooden board which serves as a medium for messages from the beyond. Ouija comes from the French and German words

for "yes": *oui* and *ja*. To use the Ouija—which is actually a *planchette*, a usually heart-shaped platform with a pointer—one simply places it upon a surface decorated with the alphabet and numbers. The participant's hand is placed lightly on the planchette and the Ouija proceeds to move from letter to letter spelling out communiques from the spirit world. Used since the era of Pythagoras—circa 540 B.C.— the Ouija is now popularly employed as a means of peering into the future.

Outer Limits, The [TV] A science fiction television series. Created by Joseph Stefano, the program premiered in 1963 and ran for two seasons on ABC. With monsters from space or another dimension featured in most of the forty-nine episodes, "The Outer Limits" was nonetheless literate and often moving. Among the most famous episodes are "I, Robot," the saga of robot Adam Link; "The Zanti Misfits" about antlike criminal aliens; "The Galaxy Being," the show's premiere episode about a creature teleported to earth from the Andromeda Galaxy; and "Demon with a Glass Hand," the story of a man who carries a tape transcript of all of humankind within his artificial hand. "The Outer Limits'" roster of distinguished guest stars include Martin Landau, Robert Culp, Cliff Robertson, Bruce Dern, William Shatner, Leonard Nimoy, and Robert Duvall. see: **Link, Adam; Zantis.**

Ovions [TV] Antlike creatures seen on "Battlestar Galactica." Ruled by Queen Lotay, the four-armed, five-foot-tall aliens are a female-dominated race, the males used solely for labor and propagation. They live below the surface of Carillon where they mine the petrol ore tylium. Long ago subjugated by the Cylons, the greenish creatures work with their conquerors to destroy humankind. The harp-playing Ovions do this by *eating* humans, fattening them up in a resort on the planet's surface, then storing them within huge honeycomblike coffins. During a climactic battle between Cylons and crewmembers of the *Galactica*, the tylium walls of the Ovion chambers catch fire and cause Carillon to explode. see: **Cylon; Galactica.**

Oz [L] A fantasy land created in 1900 by author Lyman Frank Baum (1856–1919) in *The Wonderful Wizard of Oz*. This land over the rainbow is the setting for the adventures of young Dorothy Gale and her dog, Toto. Carried to Oz by a tornado, Dorothy hopes the wizard can return her to Kansas and seeks him out in his Emerald City headquarters. On the way, she befriends a Scarecrow who wants a brain, a Tin Woodman who wishes a heart, and a Cowardly Lion who dreams of courage—all of whom go off with her to see the wizard. Their path—a yellow brick road—is fraught with curios and danger. There are good witches (from the north and south) and bad witches (from the east and west); little people called Munchkins; Kalidahs with the bodies of bears and the heads of tigers; aggressive trees; winged monkeys; yellow-skinned Winkies who serve the Witch of the West—whom Dorothy melts with water when Oz orders her to kill the wicked woman to gain his favor; and a land of china people and nasty Hammerheads. Among their allies are field mice and happy people called Quadlings. The Quadlings are ruled by the kindly Glinda, the Witch of the South. It is Glinda who shows Dorothy how to get home using magic silver shoes the girl took from the Witch of the East, whom she also slays.

Oz is divided into four regions, each area represented by a different color. It is a land where magic is studied as a science, and ingenuity is prized above all. Among the many sequels written about this region are Baum's *The Marvelous Land of Oz* (1904), *Ozma of Oz* (1907), *Dorothy and the Wizard of Oz* (1908), *The Road to Oz* (1909), *The Emerald City of Oz* (1910), *The Patchwork Girl of Oz* (1913), *Tik-Tok of Oz* (1914), *The Scarecrow of Oz* (1915), *Rinkitink of Oz* (1916), *The Lost Princess of Oz* (1917), *The Tin Woodman of Oz* (1918), *The Magic of Oz* (1919), and *Glinda of Oz* (1920). Nineteen additional Oz volumes were written by Ruth Plumly Thompson following Baum's death.

In the cinema, the first Oz book was brought to the screen in 1908, 1910, 1924, with Dorothy Dwan as Dorothy and Oliver Hardy as the Tin Woodman, and in 1939 starring Judy Garland. Other Oz movies are *The Patchwork Girl of Oz* (1914), *The Magic Cloak of Oz* (1914), *His Majesty the Scarecrow of Oz* (1914), the cartoon *Journey Back to Oz* (1971) featuring the voice of Liza Minnelli, and *The Wiz* (1978) based on the all-Black 1975 musical play of the same name. see: **Emerald City, The.**

P

Padfoot [O] An English boogey. Sometimes visible and sometimes not, Padfoot usually stalks a traveler from afar; then creeps alongside the person and screams horrendously, frequently jangling a great chain. The same size as a goat, with long hair and huge eyes, Padfoot will occasionally curl into a ball, bounce about the woods or along byways; then suddenly roll beside a victim and roar. Under no circumstances must Padfoot be touched, or bad luck will ensue. Many people consider the boogey to be an omen of death.

Pal, George [MP] A fantasy film producer born in Cegled, Hungary in 1908. The son of George and Maria Pal, young George studied to be an architect. He moved into film when the market for buildings evaporated. Moving to Berlin, he opened his own studio in 1932 but abandoned it when the Nazis came to power. Pal and his wife, Zsoka Grandjean, came to the United States in 1939. Establishing a new studio, Pal began filming animated Puppetoons for Paramount Pictures. These fantasy short subjects were all shot using wooden puppets, a different one being carved for each incremental movement, the figures being replaced between frames. Pal made forty-one Puppetoons before releasing his first feature motion picture, *The Great Rupert* (1949). This story of a superintelligent squirrel was filmed using a poseable stop-motion model for Rupert, his movements being nursed along a fraction of an inch per frame of film.

Pal's filmography is an impressive one. His subsequent films were *Destination Moon* (1950), *When Worlds Collide* (1951), *War of the Worlds* (1953), *Houdini* (1953), *The Naked Jungle* (1954), *Conquest of Space* (1955), *Tom Thumb* (1958), *The Time Machine* (1960), *Atlantis the Lost Continent* (1960), *The Wonderful World of the Brothers Grimm* (1962), *The Seven Faces of Dr. Lao* (1964), *The Power* (1968), and *Doc Savage* (1975). Many of these have won special effects and/or make-up and other technical Oscars. Pal and Zsoka have two children, David and Peter. see: **Atlantis; Grimm, Jakob and Wilhelm; Lao, Dr.; Savage, Doc; Tom Thumb; Wells, H. G.**

Pandora [M] The first woman in Greek mythology. Manufactured from clay by Hephaestus, the lovely Pandora is created to plague humankind. Prior to being placed among men, the girl is given a box and told never to open it. Then, box in hand, she is brought by Hermes, at Zeus' instructions, to Prometheus. Since Prometheus had helped men by giving them fire, he deserves the honor of presenting them with this cursed new being. But Prometheus refuses, and Hermes carries Pandora to the fire-bringer's brother, Epimetheus. Taken with her beauty, and considering the many things he can do with this Pandora, Epimetheus accepts the girl as his bride. After they have been married some time, Pandora is overcome with curiosity about the contents of the box. She opens it, and out flits a horde of demons, every ill which would ever after bother mortals. Startled by the buzzing, darting evils, Pandora manages to shut the lid in time to lock in Hope—which has remained with humankind ever since. see: **Hephaestus; Hermes; Prometheus; Zeus.**

Paracelsus [O] A Swiss physician and alchemist. Born Philippus Aureolus

Theophrastu Bombastus von Hohenheim in 1493, Paracelsus was the first doctor to try to treat the complete human being—the mind and soul as well as the body. A student of chemistry, biology, astrology, and philosophy, he coined the term *Sylphs* for "invisible spirits" which he believed inhabited the air, and is said to have created a living, "artificial being" or *homunculus.* Paracelsus detested fraudulent occultists and alchemists, and fought to expose them until the time of his death in 1541. see: **Homunculus; Sylph.**

Paul, Frank R. [I] One of this century's outstanding fantasy and science fiction illustrators. Frank Rudolph Paul was born in Vienna, Austria in 1880. Although he trained as an architect in Europe and then in the United States, he ultimately diverted his talent for design into painting. His first work was for Hugo Gernsback's science oriented *Electrical Experimenter* and *Science and Invention* magazines. The artist's first fiction illustrations were published in the seminal science fiction periodical *Amazing.* All of the covers from its April 1926 debut issue through June 1929 were Paul's. In that latter month, Gernsback founded *Science Wonder Stories* for which Paul rendered every cover from the first issue to the March 1936 edition, when the magazine became *Thrilling Wonder Stories.* In addition to his popular "Stories from the Stars" series in *Amazing*—February 1943 to August 1946—Paul created imaginative back cover illustrations for both *Amazing* and its companion magazine *Fantastic Adventures.* He also painted four covers for the short 1953 run of Gernsback's last science fiction magazine *Science Fiction Plus.* Though Paul died in 1963, many of his covers were reprinted in *Amazing* and *Fantastic* through 1968. He was the Guest of Honor at science fiction's first annual fan convention, the Worldcon of 1939.

Pecos Bill [F] The most famous cowboy in all the tall tales of cow country. The inventor of roping, Pecos Bill was able to loose his lariat and nab an eagle in flight. A gracious man, he was hard-nosed and adventuresome. He once won a Stetson by betting that he could lasso and ride a cyclone. For an encore, he roped a bolt of lightning and rode it over Pike's Peak. In keeping with his bold image, Bill owned a wild horse named Widow Maker. He boasted that it saved him a lot of shooting because he had no trouble keeping other people off. To wit, Widow Maker once bucked a friend of Bill's to the top of Pike's Peak. Bill lived in Arizona, which he is said to have fenced-in early-on for use as a calf pasture. However, perhaps Bill's most noteworthy achievement is the ending of a terrible drought by digging a huge trench and filling it with water from the Gulf of Mexico. Today, we call this gully the Rio Grande.

Pegasus [M] The flying horse of Greek mythology. The daughter of Medusa—either by the horse-lover Poseidon or by the blood of the Gorgon spilled by Perseus—Pegasus appears in a number of myths. Apart from creating the Fountains of Hippocrene by stamping the ground with her foot, the winged horse is most famous for her part in the story of Bellerophon. Taught by Athena how to tame the mare, Bellerophon tries to ride her to the summit of Olympus. For this act of insolence, Zeus sends an insect to sting Pegasus and throw her rider to his death. As for the horse, she continues her majestic flight to become a constellation in the night sky. see: **Athena; Bellerophon; Gorgon; Medusa; Perseus; Poseidon; Zeus.**

Peg O'Nell [O] A specter of English legend. At one time a maid of Waddow Hall, Peg had the misfortune of arguing with the lady of the estate. As the servant left to get water, her mistress said she hoped she broke her neck. Crossing the grounds, Peg happened to slip on a patch of ice—and did just as the lady had wished! Returning to Waddow Hall as a ghost, she made it known that once every seven years she would return to claim a victim for the River Ribble, to which she had been headed when she fell. Thus, if a cat or dog were not drowned in the river each seventh anniversary of Peg's death, she claimed a human victim. Although the spirit never announced plans for committing other crimes, the death of local children and livestock has been blamed on Peg O'Nell.

Pellucidar [L] Author Edgar Rice Burroughs' world on the shell of the inside of the earth. Because its land masses coincide with bodies of water on the surface, there is more dry land in Pellucidar than without. Lighted eternally by a miniature sun which hangs at the center of our globe, there is no night and hence no measure of time. Burroughs' inference is that time is more illusion than fact. For example, in Pellucidar one can go hunting and return to find those left behind aged decades. Conversely, one can undertake an odyssey in the time another would use to nap.

The sun of Pellucidar boasts a satellite called the Pendent World. Because it revolves in tandem with earth's rotation, the small moon always bathes one small section of Pellucidar in darkness. This region is appropriately known as the Land of Awful Shadows. Another peculiarity of this inner world is that its horizon turns up into the sky. Only the brightness of the sun prevents Pellucidarians from seeing the land above their heads. These inner earth denizens are primarily Stone Age humans and incredible monsters. However, there are also the Mahars, a breed of supremely intelligent and powerfully winged creatures who hold much of Pellucidar in cruel fiefdom.

The novels in Burroughs' Pellucidar saga are *At the Earth's Core* (1913), *Pellucidar* (1915), *Tanar of Pellucidar* (1928), *Tarzan at the Earth's Core* (1929), *Back to the Stone Age* (1935), *The Land of Terror* (1939), and *Savage Pellucidar*—a compendium issued in 1963 containing four novelettes written in 1942: *The Return to Pellucidar*, *Men of the Bronze Age*, *Tiger Girl*, and *Savage Pellucidar*. Recently, author John Eric Holmes has continued the series with his books *The Mahars of Pellucidar* and *Red Axe of Pellucidar*. see: **Burroughs, Edgar Rice; Innes, David; Mahars; Perry, Abner.**

Peris [M] Good djinn or angels of Persia, as opposed to the evil deev (also known as daevas). Dwelling in the mountains of Kaf in Jinnistan, both breeds were born in fire and wage perpetual war against one another. Subsisting on the scent of exquisite perfumes—an odor which repulses the unrefined deev—the beautiful peris are less powerful than their ugly, long-horned, fanged, shape-changing foes. Thus, they do not hesitate to give mortals amulets, magic weapons, or fantastic creatures like the simurgh to aid them in the cause. It is alleged that the peris even created the stars to assist them in the struggle. The respective leaders of this war are the cruel Angra Mainyu (also known as Ahriman and Druj) and the king of the Persian gods, the Lord of Wisdom Ahura Mazda (also known as Ormazd). see: **Djinn; Simurgh.**

Perrault, Charles [FT] A collector of fairy tales and the man who immortalized Mother Goose. Born in Paris in 1628, Perrault was a high-ranking government worker who believed that the lore of his country was greater than that of ancient Greece or Rome. To prove his point, he gathered such tales as "Cinderella," "Puss 'N' Boots," "Tom Thumb," and "Sleeping Beauty" and published them in 1697. The volume was called *Tales of Long*

Ago with Morals and subtitled *Tales of Mother Goose*, and appeared under his son's name. Not a creator, Perrault is nonetheless as important to fairy lore as the Brothers Grimm. He died in 1703. see: **Cinderella; Grimm, Jakob and Wilhelm; Mother Goose; Puss 'N' Boots; Sleeping Beauty; Tom Thumb.**

Perry, Abner [L] An amateur paleontologist featured in Edgar Rice Burroughs' Pellucidar series. The inventor of the Iron Mole, he convinces his young backer, David Innes, to travel with him inside the earth. Perry's Iron Mole is a remarkable invention; jointed so it can bend while its revolving drill chisels through the various strata, the craft is a 100-foot-long steel cylinder. It has more power per cubic inch than any other engine has to the cubic foot. Though it is a great achievement, the Iron Mole is not the limit of the talent possessed by this "old fellow." Once he and David become established in the society of Pellucidar, Perry constructs an airplane and by series' end fully intends to build a submarine. see: **Burroughs, Edgar Rice; Innes, David; Pellucidar.**

Persephone [M] The wife of the Greek god Hades. Known as Prosperina to the Romans, Persephone is called the virgin goddess. The daughter of Demeter and Zeus, she is also the victim of one of mythology's great injustices. Promised to Hades by Zeus, Persephone has no knowledge of the arrangements. She is, therefore, rather surprised one day when, while she is out picking daffodils, the ground opens up and she is seized by the god of the underworld. Meanwhile, Demeter is so upset by these events that she leaves Olympus. Wandering aimlessly about the earth, she is a pitiful figure. Showing a rare edge of pity, Hades decides to allow Persephone to leave the underworld for eight months out of every year. When this happens, the world is warm and fertile; when she leaves, winter rules. see: **Demeter; Hades; Zeus.**

Perseus [M] One of the greatest of the Greek heroes. A son of Zeus, Perseus has a most unusual adolescence. His mother is Danaë, daughter of King Acrisius of Argos. When an oracle tells the ruler that one of his daughter's sons will kill him, he puts Danaë and Perseus in a wooden box and tosses it into the sea. Zeus guides the chest to the Isle of Seriphos in the Aegean Sea, where the fisher Dictys finds it and escorts the castaways to King Polydectes. The monarch falls in love with Danaë, and to monopolize her affections orders her son to fetch him the head of Medusa.

Realizing he will need help, the young man travels to see the Graiae. Grabbing the one eye and tooth they share, he says he will return it in exchange for magic arms. The sisters capitulate, turning over winged sandals for speed, the helmet of Hades for invisibility, and a strong sack for Medusa's snake-haired head. The gods add gifts of their own. Hermes presents Perseus with a sickle and Athena gives him a mirror-shield, since to gaze upon Medusa will turn a person to stone. Locating and slaying the fiend, Perseus eludes the other Gorgons and heads for home. En route, he pauses in Ethiopia. There he finds Andromeda, the daughter of King Cepheus and Queen Cassiopeia, chained to a rock as an offering to a sea serpent. Killing the monster and marrying Andromeda, the hero enrages her uncle Phineas to whom the princess had been engaged. Phineas plots to kill Perseus, but is turned to stone for his scheming efforts.

Returning to Seriphos, Perseus finds Polydectes still chasing his mother. He ends that one-sided romance by flashing Medusa's head before the potentate. His trial ended, Perseus gives Hermes his enchanted tools and makes a gift of the Gorgon's head to Athena, who places it on her breastplate.

Perseus fathers a flock of noted children: a daughter, Gorgophone;

and the sons Alcaeus; Sthenelus—the father of Eurystheus, the designer of the twelve labors of Hercules; Perses—the patriarch of the Persians; and Electryone—whose daughter Alcmene becomes the mother of Hercules by Zeus. The one stunning tragedy in this noble life is Perseus' accidental slaying of his grandfather, Acrisius, wrought with a tossed discus during athletic games. The saga of Perseus' journey is told in the motion picture *Clash of the Titans* (1980). see: **Athena; Gorgon; Graiae; Hermes; Hercules; Medusa; Zeus.**

Peter Pan [L] The hero of *Peter Pan and Wendy*, a fantasy novel written in 1911 by James Matthew Barrie (1860–1937). A boy who never grew up, Peter Pan is "a lovely boy, clad in skeleton leaves and the juices that ooze out of trees." Still possessing his baby teeth, Peter and his fairy aide, Tinker Bell—who speaks via golden bells, the language of fairies—drop in one night on the Darling children, Wendy, John, and Michael. Teaching the children to fly ("You just think lovely wonderful thoughts and they lift you up in the air"), Peter takes them to Neverland. They arrive "after many moons" not due to Peter's expert guidance but because "the island was out looking for them." Landing, they meet the pirates of Capt. Hook, mermaids, Indians, and others magical and menacing. When the quartet returns to England, Mrs. Darling tries to convince Peter to stay with them—but the thought of going to school to "learn solemn things" and then taking an office job is "repugnant." Peter leaves—but returns years later to visit Wendy's daughter Jane, and then Jane's daughter Margaret.

The genesis for the 1911 novel was Barrie's 1902 tale *The Little White Bird*, and a five-act children's play he wrote two years later. Peter Pan's most famous media appearances were in the brilliant 1952 Walt Disney car-

toon and the popular Mary Martin television special in 1955. see: **Disney, Walt.**

Pew Mogel [L] The fiendish villain of Edgar Rice Burroughs' 1941 novelette *John Carter and the Giant of Mars.* Created by the scientific genius Ras Thavas, Pew Mogel is rather misshapen. His left eye keeps falling out, his skin is pale, tongue thick, lips thin, cheeks hollow, teeth yellow, and lidless eyes close set. His torso is crooked, his arms are of unequal length, his hands are clawed, and one foot is longer than the other. Pew Mogel also has an extremely small, bald, bullet-head—although his intelligence is vast. He studied with Ras Thavas in his laboratories at Morbus, learned a great deal, and now wishes to rule the planet. Among the tools which the platinum and diamond-clothed Pew Mogel brings to bear in this dream are the 130-foot-tall artificial monster Joog, built from the gut and sinew of 10,000 Barsoomian red men and white apes. But Joog is of no help to Pew Mogel during his duel with John Carter. The hero decapitates the would-be tyrant; his head and body live on but they cannot work together. Thus, Pew Mogel's body tumbles helplessly from a precipice and John Carter flings the head after it. see: **Barsoom; Burroughs, Edgar Rice; Carter, John; Ras Thavas.**

Pfall, Hans [L] The hero of Edgar Allan Poe's science fiction tale "The Unparalleled Adventures of One Hans Pfall." Five years before the narrative begins, Pfall had left his wife, Grettell, by flying off in a balloon made of newspaper. A mender of bellows, he had run into hard times and was looking to escape his creditors. Purchasing a book on astronomy, he conceived of flying to the moon and selling for a profit the details of his discoveries. Now, returning in that same balloon is

Hans Pfall   Phoenix

a two-foot-tall, earless, speechless man who claims to come from the moon. His gray hair in a queue, his chin and cheeks doubled with flab, his nose crooked and his hands huge, he certainly looks the part. According to the written story he brings to Pfall's home in Rotterdam, the earthling's trip took nineteen days and brought him to a crowd of "ugly little people" on the moon, such as the one who has returned to earth with the balloon. Pfall explains that earth's satellite is extremely hot or cold, changing every fortnight—but that is all he will reveal. In exchange for further information he wants a reward as well as a pardon for "accidentally" killing three of his creditors upon takeoff. The government refuses to honor his demands, and the moon-dweller takes off. Those who have heard the story

feel that it is a hoax, an opinion buttressed by reports from a nearby city saying that a short conjurer who had his ears cut off for a crime had been missing for several days. Poe takes no one's side, and the reader must draw her or his own conclusions. see: **Poe, Edgar Allan.**

Phantom [O] An apparition or spectral figure. A phantom is one of three closely related but distinct occult figures. It exists with transparent substance, as opposed to a *phantasm*, which is an illusion; and *phantasmata*, intangible clouds of thought which can communicate with humans. see: **Ghost.**

Phasers [TV] Weapons used in the television series "Star Trek." The phaser's beam can be used to vaporize a foe or stun by striking at the nervous system; it is also capable of seering holes or warming objects to radiate warmth. A phaser permitted to overload will explode and destroy everything else in its immediate vicinity. There are four different types of phasers. The hand phaser is worn on a crewperson's belt. The more powerful pistol phaser has a power source in its handle; this firearm can be adapted to the third kind of phaser, a rifle base which greatly boosts its power. The fourth and most potent of the phasers is the starship unit which is fired by the helmsperson from the vessel's saucer section. The craft's navigational systems are used to direct the beam to its target. see: *Enterprise*, **U.S.S.**

Phibes, Dr. Anton [MP] The deranged antagonist played by Vincent Price in the motion pictures *The Abominable Dr. Phibes* (1971) and *Dr. Phibes Rises Again* (1972). The day after his wife, Victoria, dies on the operating table, the distraught Phibes has a car accident. Though he is thought to have perished, he in fact survives—horribly disfigured but alive. Able to speak only via an electrical plug in his neck,

Phibes spends the first film avenging his wife's death by setting about to kill all of London's physicians. His methods are most unusual; he commits his crimes according to the plagues of the Old Testament's tale of the Exodus. In the sequel, he tries to bring Victoria back to life. Journeying to Egypt, he searches for an Elixir of Life—in the end, we see him barging down a sacred underground river within sight of his goal. see: **Price, Vincent.**

Philosopher's Stone [O] A substance allegedly able to change base metals into gold, among other wonders. Though it was sought primarily by alchemists, the Philosopher's Stone is said to have been used by Noah to provide light and heat in the ark. According to scholars, the Philosopher's Stone was created from many of the same elements which make up the Elixir of Life, a legendary powder which chases away death. see: **Phibes, Dr. Anton.**

Phoenix [F] A fabulous bird the size of an eagle and a near-golden yellow in color. First worshiped by the ancient Egyptians, the phoenix dwells in Paradise on a branch overlooking the Fountain of Youth. After from five hundred to one thousand years, the bird leaves Paradise. Making a pyre of spices in a desert palm tree, it waits until the sun rises and then burns itself to ashes. As the fire builds the phoenix sings, its song becoming lovelier by the moment. Upon its death, a worm creeps from the blackened pyre. After three days it has become a fully grown phoenix. Gathering its parent's ashes, the new phoenix brings them to Heliopolis—the Egyptian City of the Sun—then wings on to Paradise. The land of its death-to-life ritual is Phoenicia, named for its legendary martyr. see: **Fountain of Youth.**

Phouka [F] An Irish pixie. Sometimes compared to the English Puck, the phouka is a mischief-maker. Most of its frolics revolve around its ability to alter its shape. Fond of disguising itself as a horse, the phouka pretends to be tame—until a rider mounts, at which time it bucks wildly. Phoukas can also be found masquerading as an eagle, a bat, or a rabbit. In the play *Harvey,* the titular phouka is a six-foot-tall white rabbit; in the film *Darby O'Gill and the Little People* (1959) it appears as an iridescent horse which knocks O'Gill into a well. see: **Harvey; Puck.**

Piast [F] A sea serpent of Ireland. Piast spends most of its time in the water, specifically Lough Ree, one of the three Shannon lakes. A comparatively small six-to-ten feet long, Piast has a serpentlike head capping a two-foot-long, four-inch-diameter neck. The humpbacked creature moves about the twenty-fathom-deep (120 foot) lake propelled by flippers. Some eyewitnesses say that Piast also has a matted mane. Many local legends make the creature more like a dragon, one who comes ashore for an occasional meal.

Pied Piper [F] A character of German folklore. When big black rats invade the town of Hamelin, its residents panic. The rodents are everywhere, biting children, snatching food, and sneering at the cats, traps, poison, and prayer used against them. In the midst of this invasion, the populace is visited by a ratcatcher called the Pied Piper. He is described as "a great gawky fellow, dry and bronzed, with a crooked nose, a long rat-tail moustache, two great yellow piercing and mocking eyes, under a large felt hat set off by a scarlet cock's feather." As for his garb, he is dressed "in a green jacket with a leather belt and red breeches, and on his feet are sandals fastened by thongs passed round his legs."

Contracting to liberate the town for a tidy sum, the Pied Piper employs his bagpipes—a flute in some versions of the tale—to play a tune which draws all 999,999 rats into a whirlpool where they drown. However, the people refuse to pay the piper as they had promised. Thus, while they are all at church their savior uses his music to lure away Hamelin's children. While their parents mourn, the youngsters follow their leader to Transylvania, where their descendants live still.

Pinocchio [L] A living wooden puppet featured in the novel *Pinocchio* by C. Collodi (pen name for Carlo Lorenzini). Pinocchio is carved from a piece of talking wood by the yellow-wigged Geppetto, the poor man hoping to teach the puppet "how to dance, to fence, and to leap like an acrobat." The two would then "travel about the world to earn a piece of bread and a glass of wine." When Pinocchio is completed, the stringless marionette begins to move of its own volition. A snide, prank-playing fellow, he meets the Talking Cricket who counsels him on right and wrong, neglects his studies, falls in with the evil Fox and Cat, goes to prison, meets a Fairy and a Serpent, visits the Island of the Industrious Bees, goes to the land of Cocagne and becomes a donkey, rescues Geppetto from a giant dogfish, and is transformed by the Fairy into a real boy. Apart from footsteps which make "as much chatter as twenty pairs of peasants' clogs," Pinocchio has a nose which grows every time he tells a lie. Beyond the countless editions of the novel, Pinocchio's most famous incarnation is as the star of Walt Disney's 1940 feature length cartoon. The voice of this famous screen Pinocchio was provided by Dickie Jones. see: **Cockaigne; Disney, Walt.**

Piscas [O] Demons of Hindu lore. Dwelling in the water supplies of towns and cities, these unthinkably ugly creatures seek out corpses to drink their blood and eat their flesh. Nor are the piscas above murdering to sate their appetite. They are especially anxious to sup on the bodies of fathers. In a great Hindu tale, a huge, yellow pisca is destroyed by the thunder god Indra.

Pixies [F] Sprites who delight in waylaying travelers. Not as delicate as fairies, pixies are often the same size as humans. However, the two can be distinguished since all pixies have red hair, pointed ears, and turned-up noses. They are usually dressed in green and frequently squint. One of the favorite recreations of pixies is stealing horses and riding them about in *gallitraps,* "the pixy version of fairy circles." A human who sets one foot within a gallitrap will be able to see the prancing pixies; place two feet within and one becomes a prisoner of the little people. According to legend, pixies are either the souls of unchristened children, non-Christians, or those who died before the coming of Christ and while not bad enough for hell are thus "unfit" for heaven. Like fairies, pixies can be driven off by iron, a cross, bread (the symbol of life), or the chanting of hymns. In certain dialects these imps are also known as pigsies and piskies. see: **Fairies.**

Planet of the Apes [L/MP] A world where apes are the articulate masters and humans the mute savages. In Pierre Boulle's 1963 novel, astronauts discover this society on Soror, a world orbiting the giant star Betelguese. After a series of adventures—which Boulle uses to spin metaphors about human ego and vanity—the space traveler Ulysse, his Sororian wife, Nova, and their son, Sirius, return to earth to find it run by apes.

In the 1968 film *Planet of the Apes,* and its sequels *Beneath the Planet of the Apes* (1970), *Escape from the Planet of the Apes* (1971), *Conquest of the Planet of the Apes* (1972), and *Battle for the Planet of the Apes* (1973), the mythos is slightly different. Dogs and cats are killed in 1982 by a space plague, apes are domesticated and turned into slaves, the monkeys revolt, and after many years they become the rulers of earth. However, a war erupts between the apes and mutated, telepathic humans which results in the detonation of the Doomsday Bomb. An all-powerful nuclear device, its explosion destroys earth—the Planet of the Apes.

Plastic Man [C] Jack Cole's comic book hero who is able to stretch and reshape his puttylike body. In a dramatic about-face, Plastic Man was once criminal Eel O'Brien. Wounded during a robbery, he falls into a vat of acid and is left behind by his cohorts. Found and cared for by a monk, Eel discovers that the acid has given him remarkable elastic properties. Leaving the monastery, reformed by his experience, Eel dons a red stretch-suit and sunglasses, arrests his old gang, and goes to work for the FBI. Plastic Man and his aide, Woozy Winks, first saw the comic book light of day in *Police* #1, August 1941. In the sixties, the Plastic Man supporting cast was changed, the erudite Gordon K. Trueblood replaced Woozy, and the hero dated wealthy Micheline De-Lute III. Other heroes with stretching abilities include Elastic Lad, Jimmy Olson's sometimes alter ego; Mr. Fantastic, the leader of the Fantastic Four; Ralph Dibny, the Elongated Man; and Rita Farr, the Elasti-girl of the Doom Patrol. see: **Doom Patrol; Fantastic Four, The.**

Poe, Edgar Allan [L] One of the great short story authors. Born in Boston in 1809, Poe was orphaned at the age of two. Adopted by Mr. and Mrs. John Allan of Richmond, Virginia, he left home when Mrs. Allan died and her wealthy husband disowned Edgar. A failure in school—he dropped out of West Point—Poe entered the working world where things were not much better. He was unable to hold any po-sition due to his short temper, drinking, and inability to work with other people. His only joys in what he once described as a life that was "insane, with long intervals of horrible sanity," were his cousin-wife, Virginia Clemm, and his writing. Paying to have many of his works published in book form, Poe died poor in 1849—too soon to see the great respect that would later gather round his writings. Among Poe's most important short stories— there were sixty-seven in all—and poems are "Morella" (1835), "Ligeia" (1838), "The Fall of the House of Usher" (1839), "The Masque of the Red Death" (1842), "The Black Cat" (1843), "The Tell-Tale Heart" (1843), "The Raven" (1845), and "The Cask of Amontillado" (1846). see: **Fortunato; Hopfrog; Ligeia; Morella; Pfall, Hans; Prospero, Prince; Usher, Roderick; Wilson, William.**

Polevik [F] A protector of the fields in Russian lore. Pictured as either a white or black-draped figure, the polevik has clumps of grass for hair, different colored eyes, and an unbearably ugly countenance. A strict guardian, it admits into the field only people who plan to work. All others,

Polevik

Poe

as well as trespassers, are tripped, misled, beaten, or otherwise turned back. Slothful drunkards who come by are strangled. A family spirit, the polevik puts its children to work catching birds who light in the field and preparing them for supper. The only way to cross the polevik's realm without working is to leave an offering of an old rooster and a pair of eggs.

Poltergeist [O] A silent, trick-playing entity which throws objects around, lights fires, and is responsible for other forms of mischief. Poltergeists usually haunt people who are near the age of puberty, sticking tenaciously by them as though launched on a vendetta. The presence of other persons affects poltergeists in different ways, causing some to be still and others to step-up their activities. The spirit's tantrums are always spontaneous and quite violent, and the thrown articles rarely follow a normal trajectory. The poltergeists' favorite playthings are stones, which they heat and hurl at people and their possessions.

Pooh, Winnie The [L] A bear featured in the novels of Alan Alexander Milne (1882–1956). Pooh is based on a toy bear owned by Milne's son, Christopher. When the boy was very young, he had a pet swan called Pooh. But the swan flew off one day, so Christopher changed the name of his bear from Edward to Winnie the Pooh. By his own admission, Pooh is "a bear with no brain at all." In such books as *Winnie the Pooh* (1926) and *The House at Pooh Corner* (1928) he shares adventures with the equally dull Tigger, Piglet, Kanga and Baby Roo, a Heffalump, and the donkey Eeyore—whose tail is attached to his body with a nail. All are based on toys owned by Christopher—who appears in his father's stories as Christopher Robin. As pictured in the famous "decorations" by Ernest H. Shepard, Pooh is tan-furred and pudgy. The bear has been featured in two very popular Walt Disney cartoon featurettes, *Winnie the Pooh and the Honey Tree* (1966) and *Winnie the Pooh and the Blustery Day* (1968). see: **Disney, Walt.**

Popeye [C] A mighty sailor-man created by Elzie Chrisler Segar (1894–1938). Popeye first appeared in the newspapers in "Thimble Theatre" on January 17, 1929, endearing himself with characteristic mispronunciations such as "hooman," and "irriktating." Not a wealthy man, Popeye lives on prize money he earns from boxing, or on treasure uncovered in an adventure. What makes him different from other Depression era figures is that the tough-chinned sailor becomes supertough when he gobbles down spinach—strong enough to lift a house or bend steel in his bare hands. Among the many supporting characters in Popeye's world are his girl friend, Olive Oyl; her brother, Castor, and their parents, Cole and Nana; the nefarious 800-year-old Sea Hag; hamburger fiend J. Wellington Wimpy; King Blozo of Nailia; Popeye's father, Poopdeck Pappy; the sailor's adopted son, Swee'Pea; and the fourth-dimensional Eugene the Jeep.

From 1933 to 1957, Popeye was featured in a superb series of cartoons produced by animation pioneer Max Fleischer for Paramount Pictures. Today, less extraordinary Popeye cartoons are being made by Hanna-Barbera. The live-action musical film *Popeye* (1980) stars Robin Williams as the thick-armed, pipe-smoking hero. see: **Fleischer, Max.**

Poppins, Mary [L] A rather amazing nanny created by Australian-born author Pamela L. Travers (1906–   ). Dropping in—literally, on an open umbrella and a strong East Wind—at number seventeen Cherry Tree Lane, Ms. Poppins replaces Katie Nanna as the nanny for young Jane, Michael, John, and Barbara Banks. Thin, with shiny black hair, small blue eyes, and large feet and hands, Mary is very strict and very strange. She carries a carpet bag, inside of which the children see nothing—though it produces a stream of articles from soap to a chair. The young Banks find that they instinctively obey the woman, for she is "frightening, and at the same time most exciting."

During Mary's stay, she partakes in many unusual escapades. These range from the modest—sliding *up* a bannister—to the incredible. In one of this latter grouping, she and the matchman, Bert, jump into a picture he has drawn on the sidewalk, and roam through a fantasy land. Alas, when the West Wind comes whistling down Cherry Tree Lane, Mary flies away on her parrot-handled umbrella. However, though the adventure *Mary Poppins* (1934) is concluded, the nanny returns in *Mary Poppins Comes Back* (1935) at the end of a kite string, *Mary Poppins Opens the Door* (1943) returning via rocket, and *Mary Poppins in the Park* (1952). In 1964, Walt Disney brought *Mary Poppins* to the screen in the person of Julie Andrews. This Oscar-winning picture was a huge box office attraction. see: **Disney, Walt.**

Portunes [F] Tiny English fairies. Roughly ½ inch tall, portunes are agricultural sprites. They labor on farms during the day and, at night, catch frogs. When everyone is asleep in the household, they enter, build a fire, and cook and eat the frogs. Described as very old men with wrinkled skin and patchwork clothes, portunes are rarely nasty. Once in a while they *will* mislead a traveler—but that is a habit fairly ingrained in fairy stock! see: **Fairy.**

Poseidon [M] The Greek sea god. Known as Neptune to the Romans, Poseidon is the son of Cronus and Rhea and the brother of Zeus. He shares his golden palace under the sea with his nereid wife, Amphitrite, the daughter of Nereus and Doris. The couple has three children: Triton, who is half-man, half-fish; Benthesikyme; and Rhode (or Rhodos), after whom the isle and Colossus of Rhodes are named. By Chione, the philandering Poseidon fathered a son Eumolpus; by Gaea, the wrestler Antaeus, who is slain by Hercules; by Medusa, the winged horse Pegasus, Chrysaor, and Echidna; by Thoösa, the cyclops Polyphemus; by Princess Aethra, the hero Theseus (although some accounts make Theseus the son of King Aegeus of Athens); and by Demeter, the talking horse Arion.

The god of horses as well as of the sea, Poseidon invented the animal by jabbing his trident into the ground. He himself owns a splendid team to draw his chariot, horses with bronze hooves and golden manes. The Ocean Lord is also the god of earthquakes, which he creates by striking the firmament with his trident. Poseidon appears in many, many myths, from an attempt to overthrow Zeus— worked with Athena and Hera to no avail—to helping the Greeks during the Trojan War, to trying to destroy Odysseus for the Greek hero's blinding of Polyphemus. see: **Athena; Cronus; Demeter; Hera; Hercules; Medusa; Odysseus; Pegasus; Rhea; Theseus; Zeus.**

Possession [O] The surrender of one's body and will to the spirit of another, either living or dead. Possession is often confused with subconscious personation, in which someone acts or sounds possessed but isn't really. The distinguishing feature is that knowledge hitherto unknown is brought to the individual through possession. Though possession is a blanket term, the takeover of a being by the Devil or another evil entity is technically called *obsession.* In these cases, a spirit will enter the body through a medium such as a Ouija Board or even a piece of fruit. Nuns and young children are favorite victims of the Devil, and their takeover is manifest by rolling and twitching about on the floor, speaking in a strange tongue, and regurgitating unusual items such as nails, cloth, glass, and wood. The obsessive spirit can only be driven out by scourging the bare skin, prayer, religious services dedicated to the sufferer, or the placing of the Devil's pawn on a large wheel and spinning it until the demon flies out. Often, these possessions are worked through intermediaries such as witches. see: **Devil; Witch.**

Potentilla [FT] The heroine of the old French fairy tale "Prince Narcissus and the Princess Potentilla." Jealous of the princess' beauty, her mother, Queen Frivola, locks her in a house near the palace. She tells everyone that the girl is too ugly to be seen, and promises to decapitate anyone who tries to see her. Protected by the fairy Melinette, Prince Narcissus comes to the court of Frivola and her husband, King Cloverleaf. Donning a cloak of invisibility he visits Potentilla. The prince goes to her house each day— until a powerful rival appears. The one-eyed, long-toothed enchanter Grumedan escapes from the stone under which he'd been imprisoned by the fairy queen and happens upon the princess. Melinette warns him that if he wishes to win her, he must do so without the use of magic. He tries: he has frogs sing a five-hour opera he composed, has 1,000 oysters drop pearls at her feet, creates a volcano, and sings himself "with a voice like a screech-owl's." Failing all, he asks Frivola and Cloverleaf for her hand and they give the marriage their blessings. At the ceremony, Melinette and Narcissus make a dramatic entrance. She grabs the giant by the eyelashes and imprisons him in a crystal ball for 1,000 years, and the prince weds Potentilla. Further, Melinette gives them the kingdom, deeming the king and queen unfit to rule.

Potter, Beatrix [L] The creator of Peter Rabbit and other anthropomorphic animals. Born in London in 1866, Potter lived most of her seventy-seven years in the English county of Cumbria. There, she became enamored of animals and, indeed, owned most of the creatures about which she wrote. Among these figures are the aforementioned Mr. Rabbit, created in 1902, plus the indomitable Squirrel Nutkin, the flighty Jemima Puddle-Duck, Mrs. Tiggy-Winkle the hedgehog, Jeremy Fisher the frog, and Mrs. Tittlemouse. A few of the over twenty titles Potter both penned and illustrated are *The Tale of Peter Rabbit, The Tale of Benjamin Bunny, The Tale of Johnny Town-Mouse, The Tale of Tom Kitten, The Tale of Pigling Bland, The Tale of the Flopsy Bunnies,* and *The Tale of Timmy Tiptoes.*

Price, Vincent [MP] A distinguished fantasy film actor. Born in St. Louis, Missouri in 1911 to Vincent and Marguerite Cobb Wilcox Price, Vincent Leonard Price acted throughout his early youth. However, school-play experience was no help in the professional world and, after graduating from Yale, Price drove a bus, taught art, and worked other odd jobs while looking for work. He failed, and decided to go to London in 1935. There, he landed two bit-roles in the play *Chicago.* Returning to America that same year, he appeared on Broadway with Helen Hayes then toured the northeast with stock companies. His

first film role followed in 1938 in the picture *Service Deluxe.* Two years later Price performed in his first horror vehicle, *The Invisible Man Returns.* Among his more notable efforts in this genre have been a cameo reprise as the Invisible Man in *Abbott and Costello Meet Frankenstein* (1948), *The House of Wax* (1953), the devil in *The Story of Mankind* (1957), *The House on Haunted Hill* (1958), *The Fly* (1958), *The Tingler* (1959) about a parasite which feeds on fear, *The House of Usher* (1960), *The Pit and the Pendulum* (1961), *The Raven* (1963), *Theatre of Blood* (1973) with Diana Rigg and Coral Browne, and many others. Price has been three-times married: to Edith Barrett, by whom he had a son, Barrett; to Mary Grant, with whom he parented Mary Victoria; and to Coral Browne. see: **Castle, William; Griffin, Dr.; Lorre, Peter; Phibes, Dr. Anton; Usher, Roderick.**

Pringle [O] A Scottish ghost. Inhabiting the environs of Galashiels in Selkirkshire, Pringle is especially visible at Buckholm Tower in June. He is doomed to roam the mortal sphere for having slain a pair of covenanters—the murder site still stained with their blood. Pringle's mission is to search out another spirit, the ghost of a man who used to set his killer dogs on innocent villagers. Whenever spectral baying is heard in this region—Pringle is sure to follow. see: **Black Hound.**

Prisoner, The [TV] The "Everyman" of television, the protagonist of the seventeen-episode 1968 cult hit "The Prisoner." After resigning from a government job, a man (played by Patrick McGoohan) is gassed when he enters his apartment. Awaking some time later, he finds himself in the Village—a placid resort from which there is no easy escape. Everyone is called by a number—our hero is Number Six—and all are docile about their fate.

Only Number Six is constantly trying to flee, always stopped by Village emissaries or by a huge white balloon which induces unconsciousness. Meanwhile, Village chief Number Two is perpetually pressing Number Six to reveal unspecified information, leading the viewer to speculate that the Prisoner is privy to top-secret information. Indeed, "The Prisoner" hints at being a sequel to McGoohan's previous series "Secret Agent," which would make that show's John Drake and Number Six one and the same. In the program's final episode, Number Six does indeed escape—although as he enters his London flat the door opens automatically, just as it did in the Village. Thus speaks Everyman: we are *all* prisoners! see: **Everyman.**

Prometheus [M] The Greek Titan who gave fire to mortals. The son of the Titan Iapetus and the oceanid Clymene, Prometheus is brother to Atlas, Epimetheus, and Menoetios. Sage and kind—his name means forethought— Prometheus is assigned by the gods to tender abilities and attributes to the creatures of earth. The Titan does well by the animals, but somehow manages to leave men—there are not yet any women—naked and without speed or strength. To compensate for this oversight, he steals fire from the gods and gives it to men. Since earth is perpetually temperate and peaceful, Prometheus does this more to assuage his own feelings of guilt than to help the humans. But Zeus doesn't care. Only immortals are permitted to have fire, and since it is too late to take it back he makes its presence on earth a necessity. The world becomes alternately dark and cold, and no longer a paradise.

After several other run-ins with Zeus, the king of the gods chains the Titan to Mt. Caucasus. There, an eagle eats out his liver by day, only to have it grow back during the night. Prometheus is finally liberated by Hercules. The firegiver is said to have

been married to either his mother Clymene, Hesione, or Asia—one of which bears him a son named Deucalion, the father of Hellen and the ancestor of all the Greeks (Hellenes). see: **Atlas; Hercules; Pandora; Zeus.**

Prospero [L] A magician in *The Tempest* (1611), the last play written by William Shakespeare. The rightful Duke of Milan, Prospero's lands are stolen by his brother Antonio and the King of Naples. The Duke and his daughter, Miranda, are set adrift in a boat and eventually reach a desolate island. There, Prospero watches his enemies—and waits. Then, when Antonio, the king, and the king's son, Ferdinand, go to sea he causes a tempest which wrecks them on his shores. Prospero torments the castaways, and finally offers a truce *if* they will return all which belongs to him. They agree, and Prospero also permits Ferdinand to marry Miranda. As Prospero leaves his land of exile, he breaks his magic wand and forgoes the occult ever after—which most scholars read as Shakespeare's own farewell to the theater. see: **Ariel; Caliban.**

Prospero, Prince [L] The corrupt ruler in Edgar Allan Poe's short story "The Masque of the Red Death" (1842). With his kingdom half-dead from plague, the decadent Prospero calls 1,000 knights and dames to court. Though many think him mad, he holds a masked ball—during the midst of which something eerie occurs. In walks a new presence, "tall and gaunt, and shrouded from head to foot in the habiliments of the grave." Its vesture is dabbed in blood and it is wearing the mask of a corpse. Stalking among the waltzers, the figure enrages Prospero with its arrogance and "blasphemous mockery." The prince goes to stab the newcomer—and he himself perishes. The visitor is revealed as the Red Death, and it takes the lives of the revelers, a debt too long borne only by the poor. see: **Poe, Edgar Allan; Price, Vincent.**

Ptath [M] The Egyptian world-ocean and seat of all creation. Also known as Neph, Nu, Cnouphis, Cenubis, and Num, Ptath made the world and everything in and around it, including the gods. Usually pictured as having a ram's head and sitting behind a potter's wheel, he is also described as a mummy wearing a skullcap, a pygmy, or a dwarf. Ptath is married to the goddess Auka. Some legends say that Ptath worked through the god Khepera, who rose from the world-ocean. see: **Khepera.**

Puck [F] One of the most famous sprites in folklore. In early legend, puck was a general term used to describe a devil. Later, it became a specific being, slightly larger than an adult mortal and able to change into any person or animal he wishes. Usually naked in his normal form, Puck is prominently featured in William Shakespeare's 1596 play *A Midsummer Night's Dream*. The jester to King Oberon, he spends much of the piece playing pranks on his human co-stars—although he does have a soft spot for lovers. Shakespeare also refers to the magic-maker as Robin Goodfellow.

In Welsh lore, a figure closely related to Puck is Pwca. Described as having the body of an elf and the head of a bird, it serves humans for the modest wage of a bowl of milk. see: **Bottom; Oberon; Robin Goodfellow.**

Puddocky [FT] A magic frog in the German fairy tale which bears her name. Because a poor woman cannot feed her daughter, Parsley, she sends her to live with a well-to-do witch. One day, three princes happen by and duel for the hand of the maiden. When the witch sees what strife Parsley has caused, she changes her into a frog. With the girl gone, the brothers become friendly once more. Returning to court, they are called before their father. The king announces that he wishes to see which of his sons is worthy of succeeding him. To this end he assigns them three tasks: to bring him a piece of linen that is 100 yards long but fine enough to pass through a golden ring; a dog small enough to fit in a nutshell; and the fairest maiden to be his daughter-in-law. The princes set out and, before long, the youngest encounters a frog named Puddocky. The animal pulls the requested linen from her swamp, gives the prince a hazelnut containing a tiny dog, and joins him as his wife—asking the prince to trust her in this last matter. When the couple reaches the palace, the enchanted Puddocky becomes the lovely Parsley, and the youngest prince becomes his father's heir.

Punch and Judy [F] Puppet characters of the Italian stage. Punch—short for Punchinello—is a hunchback with a long nose. Wily and rather hot-tempered, he strangles his child in a moment of rage, and Judy hits him with a club. Grabbing a bludgeon of his own, Punch kills her and hurls her body

Punch and Pixie

into the street. It is discovered by a police officer who goes after Punch and arrests him. Tried and sentenced to be hanged, Punch tricks the executioner into placing his own head in the noose and releasing the trap door. Fleeing, Punch is met by the Devil. However, through quick thinking the vicious Punch convinces Satan to leave without taking his soul.

Purple People Eater [E] An alien creature created by singer Sheb Wooley for his hit 1958 record "The Purple People Eater." The extraterrestrial is described as short, pigeon-toed, having one big eye, and sporting a detachable horn on its head—which, when played, sounds remarkably like a trumpet. The visitor speaks in a high-pitched voice, is able to fly, and has an aversion to eating tough-skinned or non-purple people. When all is said and done, the Purple People Eater admits having come to earth not to perch on trees, or eat tender purple flesh, or look at girls in "short-shorts," but to play its horn in a rock and roll band.

Puss 'N' Boots [FT] A heroic cat of lore. When a miller dies, he leaves his three sons the mill, an ass, and a cat. The young men feel that the last is useless and plan to dispose of him—but the cat argues against this. He asks for and is given a pair of boots and a bag to allow him to prove his worth. Leaving the mill, he brings gifts of game to the king. The Puss informs the monarch that he serves the Marquis of Carabas, whom the king says he would like to meet. Organizing a cortege, the ruler rides out—and Puss rushes ahead. He tells his favorite of the three brothers to jump into a river along the route of the procession. When the king comes upon him, Puss explains that robbers stole the marquis' carriage and tossed him into the water. While the king helps the soaked "noble," Puss presses on and asks the local peasants to salute his master as the marquis. They agree, and Puss runs to a castle owned

by an ogre. He casts aspersions on the giant's fabled ability to change his shape. Angered, the ogre becomes a lion. Puss teases that it's easy to become a large animal, so the ogre makes himself a mouse—and the feline eats him. When the king's party arrives, Puss welcomes his master as though the castle were his. The monarch is so impressed that he gives his daughter and a dowry of great wealth to the marquis—all thanks to Puss 'N' Boots!

Pyrrha [M] A Greek matriarch. The daughter of Pandora and Epimetheus, she marries Deucalion, the son of Prometheus. Just before Zeus sends a flood to destroy the crude and wicked human civilization, the couple is advised by Prometheus to build an ark. They do, finishing the job just before the deluge. After nine days and nights, the vessel lands on Mt. Parnassus. When the waters recede, the unwilling mariners exit. Upon Zeus' instructions they begin throwing stones. The pebbles tossed by Deucalion become men, and those thrown by Pyrrha become women. They have a son, less immaculately conceived, named Hellen. The father of Greek civilization, Hellen sires Doros and Ion (the root of the terms Doric and Ionic), Aeolus, Xathos, and Achaeus. see: **Pandora; Prometheus; Zeus.**

Python [M/O] The Greek dragon whose name now signifies a species of large constrictor. In mythology, Python is a huge female serpent sent by Hera to plague Leto as she is in labor with Apollo and Artemis—the children of Hera's husband, Zeus. After performing her task, Python slithers off to Mt. Parnassus where she makes her home in a cave. Years later, Apollo tracks down the creature and slays her for having caused his mother grief.

Python is also an occult term signifying a spirit, or a person possessed by this spirit, which is able to foretell the future. see: **Apollo; Hera; Possession; Zeus.**

Quatermass, Professor [L/MP] A hero of British science fiction. Created by writer Nigel Kneale for a BBC radio series, Professor Bernard Quatermass went on to star as a character in a trio of highly regarded science fiction films. In *The Quatermass Xperiment* (sic) (1955; United States title *The Creeping Unknown*), Quatermass battles an astronaut who was contaminated during a space flight by living energy and is slowly becoming a killer blob. In *Quatermass II* (1956; United States title *Enemy from Space*), the scientist pits his skill against aliens who are taking over humans preparatory to an invasion of earth. And in *Quatermass and the Pit* (1967; United States title *Five Million Years to Earth*), Quatermass fights a Martian life force which threatens to destroy the earth after being released from a long-buried spacecraft. Brian Donlevy portrayed Quatermass in the first two films; Andrew Keir played the scientist in the third movie.

Queen of Hearts [L] A shrill-voiced, bespectacled tyrant in Lewis Carroll's novel *Alice in Wonderland.* Alice has a dramatic run-in with the Queen at the trial of a knave who is accused of having stolen some tarts. With a jury of animals and the White Rabbit as the trumpet-tooting herald, the proceedings get underway. The Queen proves herself a volatile sort. Characteristic is the way she receives a minor bit of rudeness from the Dormouse with a cry of "Behead the Dormouse!"—although she has a change of heart and orders instead, "Off with his whiskers." Bill the lizard also endures her wrath when, in a rage, she hurls an inkstand at him. When Alice intercedes on behalf of the knave, the plump, scowling, heart-sceptered Queen orders the girl's head removed. Happily, Alice begins to grow to her normal height in this shrunken land and is spared. The Queen's card subjects fly at her and, as Alice wakes from her dream visit to Wonderland, she finds fallen leaves blowing all over. In Alice's next adventure, *Through the Looking Glass*, she meets two more queens: the Red Queen and the White Queen, belonging to a living chess set. see: **Alice; Hatter, The; White Rabbit.**

Questing Beast, The [F] A monster that prowled the kingdom of King Arthur. With the body of a lybbarde, the hindquarters of a lion, the feet of a deer, and the head of a snake, the Questing Beast can roar as loud as forty hounds. In fact, its name comes from the baying of dogs as they hunt, their crying also known as *questing*. In legend, the monster is pursued by Sir Palomides of the Round Table; in T. H. White's novel *The Once and Future King*, it is chased by King Pellinore. see: **Arthur, King.**

Questing Beast

Quetzlcoatl [M] The Aztec god of the sun and air, the son of the war god Camaxtli and Chimalman, and the inventor of the calendar. The name *Quetzlcoatl* means "the serpent dressed with green feathers," the god using these feathers to hide his ugly features. In his secondary capacity as the god of wisdom, Quetzlcoatl is also pictured as a man with a long beard, a white robe, and a walking staff. After being defeated in battle by the magic of his mortal enemy, the supreme god Tezcatlipoca, Quetzlcoatl hurls himself on a funeral pyre. His heart rises from the ashes to become the morning star. When the Spanish explorer Cortéz arrived in Mexico early in the sixteenth century, he convinced the Aztecs that he was Quetzlcoatl, using the god's good name to win influence among the people.

Quetzlcoatl

Ra [M] The Egyptian sun god. Self-created, he is the guardian of Egypt's kings, and they used his name before their own to signify such. Represented as having a man's body and the head of a hawk, Ra wears a red disk atop his head to symbolize his might and importance. During the day he travels the waters of the skies in a great boat, sailing at night into Tuat, the realm of the dead. As the rising sun he is frequently referred to as Mentu; as the setting sun as Atmu, Atem, or Temu. Only at midday is he truly Ra.

The husband of Maut—who has the head of a lioness and the headdress of a vulture—Ra fathered Athor, the goddess of the sky; Maat, the goddess of truth; Mu, the personification of light; Shu, the personification of solar light; and Keb (or Seb), the god of earth. Ra's long rule loses some of its luster when the goddess Isis fashions a serpent from dust mixed with the old god's dribble. The snake bites him and Isis agrees to tender an antidote only if he will surrender some of his powers of light to her son, Horus. Ra yields, losing substantial credibility as a viable sun god.

Another name for a solar deity of Egypt is Amen-Ra, a hybrid intended to elevate the popular god Amen. see: **Amun; Horus; Isis.**

Raggedy Ann [L] A rag doll character created by political cartoonist and author Johnny Gruelle (1880–1938). Raggedy Ann is based on a rag doll found by Gruelle's daughter Marcella in the attic of their Connecticut home. It had been made by the author's grandmother. In the first Raggedy Ann book, the figure comes to life when "one day the dolls were left all to themselves." Raggedy Ann's comrades include the Tin Soldier, French Dolly, Indian Doll, and Jumping Jack. None ever stirs until their owner is out of the room. However, the two most popular of Raggedy Ann's companions are a dog based on Marcella's pet, Fido, and Raggedy Andy, inspired by another doll in the Gruelle attic. Among the fanciful, fairy-filled books written and illustrated by Gruelle and featuring his floppy heroes are *Raggedy Ann Stories, Raggedy Ann and Andy and the Camel with the Wrinkled Nose,* and *Raggedy Ann and the Wonderful Witch.*

Rakshasah [O] "The Destroyer" of ancient myth, an evil spirit with the ability to change into human, quadruped, or vulture form. The powers of the Rakshasah build as evening nears, reaching their zenith at midnight and vanishing come the dawn. In their natural shape, these extremely ugly demons have bloated bellies, long tangled hair, five feet, and fingers set backward upon their hands. Also known as Yatudhanas, the Rakshasah eat women, appearing to them as a lover, husband, or relative. The females of the breed, Rakshasis, eat only men after first seducing them with their sensual beauty. The Rakshasah have appeared in the work of H. P. Lovecraft, which inspired their use in the "Horror in the Heights" episode of television's "The Night Stalker." see: **Lovecraft, H. P.; Kolchak, Carl.**

Rapunzel [FT] The long-haired heroine of the fairy tale "Rapunzel." For trying to steal from the garden of the witch Gothel, a man is forced to give the hag his first born. Named Rapunzel—after the rampion her father had been pilfering—the girl is placed in a high tower with no doors and only one window. When Gothel wishes to enter she merely says, "Rapunzel, Rapunzel! Let down your hair!" and the girl spills her golden tresses to the ground. Overhearing this ritual, a prince calls to Rapunzel one night and climbs her locks. The couple falls in love, and the prince visits her every night thereafter. Alas, Rapunzel slips and tells the witch of the romance. Gothel cuts off the girl's hair, lowers it when the prince calls, and blinds him when he reaches the summit. The prince remains sightless for years. Then, one day, while roaming aimlessly, he comes across Rapunzel with their twin children. When the girl sees her lover she cries; her tears fall on his eyes and his sight is restored.

Rarebit Fiend [C] A fantasy character created by Winsor McCay for his comic strip "Dreams of the Rarebit Fiend." Actually, the Rarebit Fiend is a different individual in each installment, one who eats Welsh Rabbit and has an incredible nightmare. Statues come to life, people grow giant, old men become babies, cannibals buy and sell human meat, and so forth. The strip began as a one-shot cartoon about a tobacco fiend who couldn't find a cigarette in the Arctic. McCay's editor suggested the segue into rarebit, and the dreams ran regularly in *The New York Telegram* from 1904–1907, and semiregularly for seven years more. Because he was under contract, McCay signed his creation Silas—named after a garbage collector. The artist created an animated version of the strip in 1917. Called *The Adventures of a Rarebit Eater*, it is much less remembered than Edwin S. Porter's 1906 live-action classic *The Dream of a Rarebit Fiend*. see: **McCay, Winsor.**

Ras Thavas [L] A character created by Edgar Rice Burroughs for his series of Martian novels. Ras Thavas is his world's greatest surgeon. A noble of the city of Toonol, he dwells on his large family estate. When we first meet him, he is an old, wrinkled man with a hearing aid and thick-lensed glasses. An expert in limb and organ transplants, he is also filled with grand dreams. He has been able to put half a human brain in an animal's body, a woman's brain in the body of a man, and so forth; his plan is to create life. Before he can do this, the scientist is driven from his home by Vobis Kan, the Jeddak (Emperor) of Toonol. Setting up a laboratory in the ancient, deserted city of Morbus on the border of the Toonolian Marshes, Ras Thavas manufactures a race of synthetic beings called hormads. However, these nearly-human creatures would rather lead than follow. Turning on Ras Thavas, they force him to build a hormad army bent on conquering Barsoom. Eventually, John Carter arrives on the scene, rescues Ras Thavas, and destroys Morbus. The surgeon thereafter settles in Helium. Among his other accomplishments are the building of Pew Mogel and the discovery and domesticating of giant birds called Malagors, which had long been thought extinct. see: **Barsoom; Carter, John; Pew Mogel.**

Rath [L] A bizarre creature invented by Lewis Carroll for *Through the Looking Glass*. The rath is described by Humpty Dumpty as "a sort of green pig." In his interpretation of the poem "Jabberwocky," where the olive swine is introduced, Dumpty says that the rath have lost their way home. Their anxiety over this fact is manifest by "outgrabing"—which, according to the egg, "is something between bellowing and whistling, with a kind of sneeze in the middle." see: **Alice; Humpty Dumpty.**

Ravana [F] A Hindu demon who battles Rama, an *avatar*, "reincarnation," of the great god Vishnu. The son of King Dasaratha, Rama is banished by Queen Kaikeyi who wants the kingdom to pass to her own son. Accompanied by his wife, Sita, and brother, Lakshmana, Rama settles in a cave in the woods. One day, the demoness Surpanakha visits the men and asks each in turn to marry her. They refuse, so she attacks Sita. Lakshmana leaps to her defense, slashing off the ears, nose, and breasts of the evil being. Surpanakha goes crying to the castle of her brother, Ravana. Disguising his aides as golden deer, the demon lures the brothers from the cave, then goes to Sita disguised as a hermit. Once inside, he assumes his natural form as a ten-headed monster. Grabbing the girl in one of his thousand hands, he makes off with her in his chariot. Meanwhile, a vulture informs Rama of what has transpired. Joined by Hanuman, general to the king of the monkeys, Rama journeys to Ravana's island fortress. After the ape-warrior causes various mischief in the demon's realm, Ravana meets Rama in combat. However, each time Rama decapitates his foe a new head takes its place. Eventually, Rama flings the mighty sword Astra into Ravana's heart and the demon perishes. see: **Hanuman.**

Raymond, Alex [C] A renowned comic book artist. Born in New Rochelle, New York in 1909, Alexander Raymond studied at the Grand Central School of Art in New York. In 1934 he made comic strip history by creating "Flash Gordon," followed by "Jungle Jim" and "Rip Kirby." In the thirties he also drew "Secret Agent X-9," a strip scripted by Dashiell Hammett. The artist turned his characters over to assistant Austin Briggs in 1944 so that he could join the Marine Corps. Raymond died in a car accident in 1956, leaving behind an immortal legacy of action-filled, realistic art. see: **Flash Gordon.**

Redcap [F] A goblin who visits scenes of violence, especially in northern England. A dwarflike man with long fingernails, fangs, and hair reaching to the middle of his back, he wears a cap which is red from constant dipping in human blood. Redcaps aren't above killing for even more blood, which is why it is dangerous to loiter about a battlefield, the site of an accident, or someplace where a murder has been committed. The red-eyed goblin can only be chased away by religious symbols; one thrust in his face will cause him to shriek and vanish, leaving behind one of his carnivorous teeth. Sometimes used as familiars, redcaps usually live in the ruins of castles, revelling in the decay. In certain lands, such as Holland, redcaps are much less dangerous. see: **Familiar.**

Reëm [F] A monster of Hebrew lore. Standing 4 parasangs (14 miles) tall at birth—its horns alone stretching 100 ells (375 feet) in length—there are only two Reëm at any given time. One is male, the other female, and they mate once every seventy years. After coupling, the female mauls the male and he dies. She carries for the next twelve years, in the last year of which the pregnant Reëm is so heavy that she can't move. If it weren't for her spittle falling to earth and bringing forth nourishment, she would die. Finally, the Reëm's belly bursts and twin creatures crawl forth—always a female and a male. One goes east and the other heads west; after seven decades they meet and the process begins anew.

Reeves, Steve [MP] A popular movie strongman. Born in Glasgow, Montana in 1926, Reeves worked as a newspaper boy until he began entering —and winning—body-building contests. Among the titles he copped were Mr. Pacific, Mr. America, Mr. World, and in 1949 the coveted Mr. Universe. Moving from weights to the stage, Reeves appeared in such plays as *Kismet* and *Wish You Were Here;* he made his screen debut in *Athena* (1954). However, it was *Hercules* in 1959 which made Reeves a superstar.

A few of the other epic fantasies in which he has appeared are *Hercules Unchained* (1959), *Goliath and the Barbarians* (1960), and *Duel of the Titans* (1962) as the legendary Romulus. The wealthy, six-foot one-inch star now resides in Berne, Switzerland, with his second wife/business-manager, Aline. see: **Hercules; Romulus.**

Remora [F] A huge fish of legend. According to eyewitnesses, Remora roams the seas with the Biblical giant Leviathan. If it is hungry, Remora will not hesitate to sink a ship and feed upon its crew. Conversely, if it is fed, it will actually help a vessel in distress. Its most noted attribute is its ability to cause a vacuum which will hold a ship steady in a storm. Tales of Remora were especially popular in the time of Columbus. see: **Leviathan.**

Remus, Uncle [F] A black folklorist created by reporter Joel Chandler Harris. The stories of old Uncle Remus began appearing in the Atlanta *Constitution* in the late 1870s. An exslave living on a plantation, Remus spins mesmerizing tales in dialect—usually to prove his side of an argument or teach an important lesson to the son of his former master. According to Harris, Remus is a composite of three elderly black men that he knew, and his stories are all rooted in actual black lore. Filled with truth and whimsy, these tales are mostly about animal characters and appeared in book form as *Uncle Remus, His Songs and Sayings* (1880), *Nights with Uncle Remus* (1883), *Uncle Remus and his Friends* (1892), and *Told by Uncle Remus* (1905). In the 1946 Walt Disney film *Song of the South*, Uncle Remus was played by James Baskett. see: **Br'er Rabbit; Disney, Walt.**

Reptilicus [MP] A monster who razes much of Copenhagen in the 1961 motion picture *Reptilicus*. While drilling for copper in the Sulit Mountains of Lapland, miners uncover a large piece of flesh. A scientist brings it to the Copenhagen Aquarium—where it regenerates into a complete creature over 100 feet long. Serpentine, with small legs and arms, scales, and huge fangs, Reptilicus goes on a destructive rampage. Guns are no match for its suffocating white expectoration, and artillery cannot pierce its skin. With two wings beginning to bud from its shoulders, Reptilicus is forced into the sea by flame-throwers. There, a depth charge blows off one of its feet—and Reptilicus heads back to the land. Eventually, a narcotic is placed on the tip of a rocket and fired into the monster's mouth. Reptilicus passes out, and scientists leisurely search for a way to destroy it. Meanwhile, the leg torn from the animal begins to grow a new lizard. . . . *Reptilicus* was directed by Sidney Pink, and a novel based on the film was written by Dean Owen.

Rhedosaur [MP] A fictitious dinosaur seen in Ray Harryhausen's 1953 motion picture *The Beast from Twenty Thousand Fathoms*. Frozen in a glacier, the rhedosaur is roused from eons of hibernation by nuclear tests in the Arctic. Making for its ancestral grounds in the submarine canyons off the coast of New York, this amphibious giant levels coastal towns, sinks ships, and decimates Manhattan on its way home. The fifty-foot-tall monster presents a particular problem because it must be destroyed in one piece; its blood carries prehistoric germs against which modern antibiotics are helpless. This feat is accomplished when a radioactive isotope is fired into a wound in the creature's neck, roasting it from the inside out. see: **Harryhausen, Ray.**

Rhodan, Perry [L] The Peacelord of the Universe. Created in 1960 by authors Walter Ernsting and Karl-Herbert Scheer, one-time test pilot Rhodan is the commander of the spaceship *Stardust*, the first moon rocket. Reaching our natural satellite, the Major discovers a race of superbeings called the Arkonides. Crashed on the moon, the extraterrestrials hail from a distant solar system. Using the aliens' advanced technology—knowledge gained through "hypnoschooling"—Rhodan returns to earth and sets up a base in the Gobi Desert, an outpost dedicated to unifying humankind and ridding the galaxies of evil. Lean and tall, with a narrow and angular face, Rhodan travels about the earth and space on missions of peace and justice. Along for the benevolent ride are the mouse-beaver Pucky, the platinum blonde Arkonide Thora, Rhodan's friend Reginald Bell, and Arkonide genius Khrest. Over 500 Rhodan novels have appeared in the authors' native Germany; slightly more than 100 of these have been published in the United States. In the 1968 film *Mission Stardust,* Rhodan was played by actor Lang Jeffries.

Rhossili [O] A village in Wales. In the moors behind Rhossili, 600 feet above the sea, visitors report feeling a frightening sense of eternity and dread. This almost tangible fear which fills the air is said, by villagers, to be the spiritual presence of Stone Age peoples who once inhabited this region. It is not known whether some terrible evil smote them all, or whether they were a tribe whose cruelty has doomed them to linger forever on earth.

Roaring Bull of Bagbury [O] An English monster. The Roaring Bull is the soul of a man who was wicked in life, and thus transformed into a raging beast. Prowling about farms and other out-of-the-way places early in its career, the Bull would bellow so loud that nearby structures would shake or collapse. Fed up with the animal's assaults, one dozen parsons pursued the Bull and cornered it in a church. There, they prayed until the creature began to shrink. After a while it was

small enough to be placed inside a snuffbox. The imprisoned Bull asked for a tiny boon, and the clergy agreed to hear him out; he asked to be put beneath a local bridge so that he could howl at night and cause pregnant women or animals which passed overhead to miscarry. Needless to say, the parsons refused the request, and instead had the snuffbox flung into the Red Sea.

Robby the Robot [MP] A popular automaton created for the 1956 film *Forbidden Planet.* Designed by a long-extinct race of aliens called the Krel, Robby was tinkered together by linguist Dr. Morbius, one of the earthpersons who traveled to the alien world Altair IV as a colonist. Robby speaks many languages, is able to sense the approach of animals and other objects, can synthesize gems, foods, fabric, alcohol, and other substances, and is incredibly strong. It

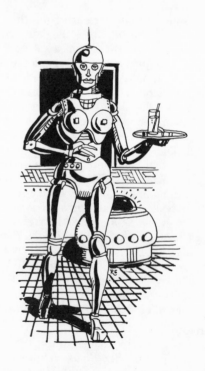

Robby Robot

barely strains the robot to raise a ten-ton weight in one three-fingered hand. Yet, Robby is programed never to harm a human being. When Morbius decides to destroy Altair IV and its dangerous store of Krel knowledge, Robby travels to earth. There, he is brought from the future and, in the 1957 motion picture *The Invisible Boy,* is subjugated by an evil computer. The robot—though not Robby of *Forbidden Planet,* per se—has made many other film appearances, most notably in the 1964 "Twilight Zone" episode "The Brain Center at Whipple's." see: **Id, Monster from the.**

Roc

Roc [L] A huge bird of Middle Eastern legend. Some scholars say it may really have been a strain of giant eagle—though no eagle comes to mind which could have carried off an elephant in its talons as the roc is alleged to have done. Generally pictured as having the body of a bird and the head and tail of a lion, the roc gained fame as a recurring foe of Sinbad the Sailor. In the hero's second voyage, he is stranded on an island and spots a great white dome. Nearing, he finds that it's an egg fifty paces around. When the parent birds arrive, Sinbad uses his turban to lash himself

to a leg as thick as a tree trunk. When the bird flies off, Sinbad rises with it. After soaring so high that the earth vanishes, the bird lands to eat a huge serpent, and Sinbad dismounts.

The sailor's next encounter with the roc is during his fifth voyage. Hungry, Sinbad's merchant friends break a roc egg and dine on the baby. When the mother and father birds return, they begin to pluck up huge boulders and drop them on the sailors and their ships—one of which is sunk.

In Ray Harryhausen's 1958 motion picture *The Seventh Voyage of Sinbad,* the adventurer battles a two-headed roc, while Popeye the Sailor roasts the giant bird in the classic 1936 Max Fleischer cartoon *Popeye Meets Sinbad the Sailor.* see: **Fleischer, Max; Harryhausen, Ray; Popeye; Simurgh; Sinbad.**

Rodan [MP] A Japanese movie monster. Actually, in the 1957 film *Rodan* there are two creatures, one male and the other its female mate. When the world's deepest mine shaft disturbs their eons-old eggs, the pteranodon-like giants with wingspans of several hundred feet hatch, feed on monster insects which live inside the earth, and take to the air. Flying at supersonic speeds, the Rodans level several Japanese cities. They are eventually scalded to death when a rocket barrage reduces their mountain home to a volcanic inferno. However, one Rodan returns in *Ghidrah the Three Headed Monster* (1965), its physique amended to include a chest quilled with spikes. In that film, Rodan, Godzilla, and Mothra are called upon to battle the titular monster from space. Rodan and Godzilla go it alone against Ghidrah in *Monster Zero* (1965), but return with an army of titans to battle the three-headed alien in *Destroy All Monsters* (1969). In Japan, Rodan is known as Radon. see: **Ghidrah; Godzilla; Mothra.**

Rogers, Buck [L] The hero of Philip

Nowlan's 1928 science fiction novel *Armageddon, 2419 A.D.*, Buck Rogers (real name: Anthony Rogers) was born in 1898. Twenty-nine years later, while he is exploring a mine for the American Radioactive Gas Corporation, leakage of said gas puts him to sleep for 492 years. Upon waking, he climbs from the shaft to find the world of 2419 far different than the one he left behind. There are domes of metalloglass, radios that turn energy into matter, the antigravity element Inertron—and, above all, the nefarious Killer Kane, who is intent on subjugating the entire planet. In the end, Buck, his love interest, Wilma Deering, and their beleaguered allies defeat the cruel dictator.

Although a popular novel, *Armageddon, 2419 A.D.* did not bring Buck his most enduring fame. It was a comic strip which first appeared on January 7, 1929, and a twelve chapter motion picture serial released in 1939 and starring Buster Crabbe that made the character a household word. Crabbe, who had already been seen on the screen as Tarzan and Flash Gordon, magnificently personified Buck's jut-jawed nobility. In a minor break with the Nowlan tale, the movie had the twentieth century Buck crashing a dirigible in the Arctic and being felled for 500 years by Nirvano gas.

Buck returned to the screen in 1979 in the person of Gil Gerard. However, in a major alteration of the legend, William "Buck" Rogers is an astronaut who, while on a space mission in 1987, is exposed to strange meteoric gases. They put him to sleep for five centuries, during which time his ship tumbles aimlessly about the solar system. It is ultimately retrieved by Killer Kane, and their perennial battle begins anew.

Romulan [TV] Warlike aliens in the television series "Star Trek." Frequent allies of the sadistic Klingons,

the Romulans are vicious fighters who take no prisoners in combat. However, unlike the swarthy Klingons, the Romulans are content to live in peace with humans wherever possible. A Vulcan race which separated from the main body before logic became the dominant trait, the Romulans live in a binary star system defined by the primary sun, Romulus, and its secondary companion, Romli. see: *Enterprise, U.S.S.*; **Klingon**; **Spock, Mr.**

Romulus [M] The first—probably legendary—ruler of Rome. The son of Mars and Rhea Silvia, he is the twin brother of Remus. Set adrift in a basket, the two babies are found and raised by wolves. In time they organize a group of warrior shepherds who found a city on the spot where the boys had been discovered by the animals. Shortly thereafter, Remus and Romulus argue over the interpretation of an omen—a quarrel which escalates to blows and ends with the slaying of Remus by Romulus. The new city is named Rome in honor of the victor, who invites thieves and murderers to settle in the area. His thinking is to breed a population of bold citizens, despite their questionable moral fiber. After the death of Romulus, his mantle is assumed by Numa, who benefits from the divine guidance of his nymph wife, Egeria. see: **Nymph**; **Reeves, Steve.**

Rook, The [C] A time-traveling hero created by Bill DuBay. The Rook first appeared in *Eerie* magazine #82, March 1977. A master inventor, the Rook is really young Restin Dane, whose one dream was always "to escape the greatest prison ever to incarcerate humankind: *time* itself!" Constructing a time machine in the shape of a huge chess piece—hence his nickname—Restin goes century-hopping in search of adventure. On one of his first trips into the past, he visits the old west and saves the life of his great great grandfather, Bishop

Dane. The scruffy elder Dane now lives with Restin in the present, frequently partaking in his adventures. Also along for the ride every now and then is Restin's cultured but timorous robot-servant, Manners, and the semicomical mechanical being, Bolts. see: **DuBay, William B.; Eerie, Cousin.**

Rosanella [FT] The heroine of an old French fairy tale which bears her name. The daughter of King Barandon and Queen Balanice, Rosanella is so named because of a little pink rose which grows on her throat. Concurrent with the princess' birth, the queen of the fairies falls ill. Wishing to appoint a successor, she decides that the fairies Paridamie and Surcantine are equally qualified. To simplify the difficult choice, the queen orders Paridamie to raise a princess so charming as to make anyone fall instantly in love with her, and Surcantine a prince who is utterly inconstant. Stolen from the cradle and reared by Paridamie, Rosanella one day meets Surcantine's charge, the flirtatious Prince Mirliflor. The princess is so beautiful and poised that Mirliflor eventually abandons his random ways to marry her.

Rossum [L] The patriarch of robots in the 1921 play *R.U.R.* Written by Karel Capek (1890–1938), the father of Czechoslovakian theater, *R.U.R.*—which stands for Rossum's Universal Robots—introduced the word robot, derived from the Czech word *robota* meaning "forced labor." In the play, *Rossum* is an old inventor whose name means "intellect." Wishing to prove that God is both unnecessary and ridiculous, he decides to create a supply of thinking robots. His son is less concerned with metaphysics than with the smooth operation of the robot factory, since people are paying $150 per mechanical being. Ultimately, the project backfires as the robots overthrow human domination, and the fertile automatons Helena

and Primus become the progenitors of a robot race.

Rotwang [L/MP] An eccentric scientist in Thea von Harbou's novel *Metropolis*. Living in a house that is ugly and dark, "a blot and an annoyance . . . to the cleanly town" of A.D. 2026, the white-haired inventor has "eyes smouldering of a hatred which was very closely related to madness." One-armed due to an accident, he creates a robotrix for the ruler of Metropolis, an artificial woman intended to impersonate and thereby undermine the power of Maria, a spokesperson for the oppressed masses. In the 1926 motion picture, Rotwang was played by Rudolf Klein-Rogge, a black mechanical arm giving an ominous flavor to the character's visualization. see: **Maria.**

R2-D2 [MP] A squat, bullet-shaped droid. In addition to its primary functions as an R2 unit—"thermocapsulary dehousing assistance" (computer repair and information retrieval) and use as a plug-in computer aboard X- and Y-wing spacecraft—R2-D2 is employed by Princess Leia Organa to smuggle technical schematics of the Death Star to Jedi Knight Obi-Wan Kenobi. Accomplishing this, the droid becomes the property of Luke Skywalker, helping him in his fight against the Galactic Empire. In the climactic Battle of the Death Star, R2-D2 is disabled by an energy burst from the pursuing Darth Vader. After the strife, R2-D2 is repaired. R2-D2 can locomote either as a biped or by using an extendable tripod leg. It communicates in the electronic pips and queeps of robot language. see: **C-3PO; Darth Vader; Death Star; Droid; Kenobi, Obi-Wan; Skywalker, Luke.**

Rubáiyát [L] A work of truth and fantasy written by the Persian poet-astronomer Omar Khayyám (c. 1050–1123). *Rubáiyát* means "quatrains," and in his 1,200 quatrains—only 500 of which are known to be authentic—the poet uses metaphor and symbol to illustrate the wonder of life. Omar Khayyám's emphasis is on the mortal sphere rather than the hereafter, and in the unrelated thoughts of his work he cautions against greatness, points out the danger of intimacy, warns of the instability of fortune, and the like. Among the fantastic elements in the *Rubáiyát* are the Bird of Time, magic, the Throne of Saturn, Destiny playing games with human pieces, incredible journeys, etc.

Rumpelstiltskin [FT] A character in a fairy tale of the Brothers Grimm. When a poor miller tries to impress the king by lying that his daughter can turn straw into gold, the monarch locks her in a room and orders her to spin gold by morning or die. Left alone, the girl begins to cry. Suddenly, a little man appears. He says he'll work the magic if she'll give him her necklace. She agrees, he spins the gold, and the king doubles her quota for the next night. The dwarfish man returns and helps her out, this time in exchange for the girl's ring. On the third night, the king says he'll make the prisoner his queen if she can produce but one more batch of gold. The imp poses a steeper price. He demands the girl's first born when she marries. She has no alternative but to comply.

After a year, the little man comes to collect the child. The queen pleads with him, and the dwarf promises her a reprieve by guessing his name. For two days the queen gives names, but none is correct. Then, with only one day left, a young man passing through the woods comes upon "a comical little man" dancing about a fire. He is

singing a curious ditty in which he refers to himself as Rumpelstiltskin. The young man passes this information on to his queen. On the third day, the dwarf comes to her and she gushes, "Your name is Rumpelstiltskin!" Shocked, the little man stamps so hard that his right leg sinks into the ground up to the knee. Bracing his left foot, Rumpelstiltskin pushes with such fury that he rips himself in two and dies.

In addition to this Grimm version of the tale, there are various provincial editions. In England he is Tom Tit Tot; in Wales, Trwtyn Tratyn; in Scotland, Whuppity Stoorie; in Austria, Kruzimügeli; in France, Robiquet; in Hungary, Panczumanczi; in Iceland, Gilitrutt; and in Russia, Kinkach Martinko. see: **Grimm, Jakob and Wilhelm.**

Rusalka [O] The spirit of a drowned girl. The rusalka differ slightly from country to country. For example, in the region of the Danube they are pale, lovely sirens whose song lures people to a watery grave. In Russia they are the corpses of the drowned, reanimated in order to drown others. Generally, however, they haunt the water and wait for victims. If none is to be had, they will steal, break mill wheels, poke holes in dams, and so forth. Only during one week per year do they venture onto land, hiding in trees and calling to one another as they watch for passers-by. The only value of the rusalka to humans is that wherever these grim beings tread, the ground is made fertile. The love of a mortal prince for one of these accursed creatures is the subject of the opera *Rusalka* by the Czechoslovakian composer Anton Dvorák (1841–1904).

S

Sabbat [O] A gathering of witches to honor the Devil and various aspects of their beliefs. Rooted in pagan fertility rites, the witches celebrate evil rather than the old gods. The traditional Sabbat begins at 10:00 P.M. on Sunday night—preferably at some isolated locale and in the presence of monoliths, the traditional representation of God. After a lavish meal, the witches partake in frenzied dancing and usually sex. Familiars attending in the form of goats, sheep, cats, frogs, or dragons frequently partake in the goings-on. New witches are made to step on a cross and then receive the Black Baptism, a dousing with dirty water. If the Devil is present, the novice is forced to kiss his buttocks, after which the other witches often fornicate with him. Though this last is considered an honor, it is said to be quite painful, since the Devil's penis is scaly and his semen intensely cold. The Sabbat always disburses at sunrise. Four times each year the witches also hold Grand Sabbats, on February 2, June 23, August 1, and December 2. *Not* conducted at a Sabbat is the casting of spells, the discussion of coven finances, and other nonritual business. This is taken care of at a meeting called an Esbat. see: **Black Magic; Coven; Devil; Witch.**

Sadko [F] A fabled Russian musician. Born in Novgorod, Sadko makes his living performing at royal feasts. But hard times befall him, so he just sits by a lake and plays a harp. One day, he is startled when up rises Tsar Vodyanoi, king of the water. The lord thanks Sadko for entertaining the lake people, and tells him how he might become a wealthy man. He's to go to a feast and bet the nobles that he can catch three golden fish living in the lake. They take Sadko up and, with Vodyanoi's help, he catches the fish. Now quite rich, Sadko becomes a merchant. This pleases the sea king Tsar Morskoi—who becalms the ocean and demands tribute before he will allow Sadko's vessels to move. The neophyte merchant dumps the cargo of one ship overboard. When Morskoi says that isn't enough, Sadko jumps into the water. The sea lord tells him that he wants the musician to choose a wife and remain in the submarine kingdom. Sadko reluctantly accepts. But the sympathetic tsaritsa says that if he doesn't kiss the bride, he will automatically be returned to the surface. Sadko does as she suggests and is sent home. He retires to a small village, content with the quiet life it offers.

Salamander [F] A fabulous creature said to live in fire—no relation to the modern-day amphibian. In their earliest

Salamander

241

form, salamanders were thought to have the ability to put out a fire merely by stepping inside of it. Later, they became the patron of blacksmiths and could usually be found in their forges. When the salamanders were content, the fires burned full and hot; when they were disturbed or sad, the flames flickered and died. Salamanders possess the body of a cat, with wings and a serpent's tail. Asbestos is said to be made from their skin, and their bite is alleged to be lethal.

Sandman [F] A benevolent old man who puts children to sleep either by sprinkling sand in their eyes or passing a magic wand over their faces. According to Hans Christian Andersen, "When it is evening and children are sitting around a table or in a corner on a stool, then he comes sneaking up the stairs; he walks on his stocking feet and makes no noise." After tossing his sand, the sandman "blows softly down their necks; and their heads seem, oh, so heavy!" This nocturnal visitor wears strange clothes. His suit is silk

Sandman

and it changes color from moment to moment. Under each arm he carries an umbrella. One is covered with pictures, and he puts this on the headboards of good girls and boys so that they will have pleasant dreams. Naughty children get the umbrella without pictures, which causes them to toss all night and have nightmares.

Sandpeople [MP] Also known as Tusken Raiders, human-sized nomadic bandits. The Sandpeople prowl the deserts of the planet Tatooine in the 1977 motion picture *Star Wars*. Their bodies are completely concealed beneath layers of clothing—which protects them from the fierce heat of the planet's double sun—and their faces are shielded by characteristic facial grid-sandfilters, goggles, and aural receptors. Skittish, strong, and vicious, they keep an uneasy peace with the inhabitants of the planet. Their guttural tongue consists mostly of consonants, and they are said to be distant relatives of Jawas. Luke Skywalker, C-3PO, and R2-D2 are attacked by a band of Sandpeople in the Jundland desert shortly before meeting Obi-Wan Kenobi. Sandpeople wield large, "bi-blade axes" called *gaderffii* and ride "shaggy creatures" called *banthas*—always in single file to conceal their numbers from trackers. see: **C-3PO; Jawas; Obi-Wan Kenobi; R2-D2; Skywalker, Luke.**

Sandworm [L] A breed of huge monster which dwells on the desert world Arrakis in Frank Herbert's novel *Dune*. Also known as Shai-Hulud, "Grandfather of the Desert," and "Old Father Eternity," the scaly, segmented, glistening sandworms grow to awesome size, many reaching over 1,300 feet. These giants are long lived unless slain by another sandworm, electrified, felled by an atomic blast—the only kind of explosion which can destroy every one of their ring sections—or exposed to water, an element which is lethal to them. The creeping sandworms are a menace to miners and are responsible for having created most of the sand on Arrakis. see: **Fremen, Melange.**

Sanford Orcas [O] A manor in Somerset, England, inhabited by no less than fourteen ghosts! Among the spirits which haunt Sanford Orcas are the Lady in Green, the Lady in Red Silk—who stirs just before midnight and sometimes appears as nothing more than a chill breeze—a black hound, a monk, the spirit of Sir Hubert Medlycott—a former owner—a rake who committed suicide in the manor gatehouse, a woman in Elizabethan garb who drifts about the courtyard, and the specter of a seven-foot-tall rapist who is manifest only when a virgin is present. This latter is thought to have been a footman who began his career by seducing the maids at Sanford Orcas.

Santa Claus [F] A jolly old man who, at Christmas time, mounts a reindeer-driven sleigh to bring people gifts manufactured by elves at the North Pole. The real-life model for Santa Claus is St. Nicholas, a fourth century bishop who lived in Turkey and suffered under the rule of Emperor Diocletian. The patron saint of children, Nicholas is famous for helping fathers pay their daughters' dowries. This he did by coming to their home at night and tossing gold into the window. One time he pitched a bag of money into a sock which was drying over the fireplace—thus giving birth to the Christmas stocking and the notion of Santa sliding down the chimney.

The evolution of the St. Nicholas character into our contemporary Santa Claus came from many different quarters. In Holland, for example, St. Nicholas had nothing to do with Christmas. He was called Sinter-Klaas and was celebrated with a Feast Day on December 5. At this time children were given gifts in his honor. The Dutch carried their tradition to the New World and, when English colonists settled beside them, Sinter-Klaas was melded with the British Father Christmas. Author Washington Irving described this new character as extremely rotund and jolly in *Knickerbocker's History of New York* in 1809, Clement Clark Moore added a few touches with his 1822 poem *A Visit From St. Nicholas*—popularly known as *The Night Before Christmas*—a fur suit was borrowed from the German imp Pelz Nichol, and cartoonist Thomas Nast put it all together in his famous illustrations of Santa Claus in *Harper's Weekly* in the 1880s. Other trappings came from the German Christkindl —better known as Kriss Kringle— the patron of the Little Christ Child.

Sargasso Sea [F] A mysterious, oval-shaped region of the North Atlantic. Located between the twentieth and fortieth parallels of the north latitude, and between the thirty-fifth and seventy-fifth meridians west of Greenwich, the center of the Sargasso Sea is some two thousand miles west of the Canary Islands. It is recognizable by the tangle of plants which float about its surface, by excessive saltiness, and by a very deep blue color. Named after *sargaço*, the Portuguese word for "seaweed," the Sargasso Sea is essentially a sector of slow ocean currents surrounded by swifter ones. It was first sounded by Christopher Columbus in 1492. Thereafter legends of this quiet, ominous area grew. The seaweed was said to net ships and hold them firm, creating a fleet of ghost ships run by skeleton crews and restless spirits. Large islands inhabited by monsters were reported, along with tales of treasure accumulated from the snared vessels. In fact, the Sargasso Sea is uncanny since its plant life probably originated in the West Indies, became trapped, and mutated to fit a new life-style in the open sea. Tangentially, many small animals have also adapted to existence among the mesh of weeds. see: **Bermuda Triangle.**

Sasquatch

Sasquatch [U] An ape-human of North America. Also known as Bigfoot, the creature walks on two legs, weighs approximately three hundred pounds, is covered with short brown hair—except on its face, which is bare—and stands from seven to nine feet tall. Legends of shaggy humanoids are quite ancient, and Sasquatch is believed to be a holdover of dawn people. The Greek god Silenus and the earlier Phrygian forest spirits, or sileni, looked not unlike Sasquatch, and there is a striking similarity between this beast and the Russian Almas, the Indonesian Orang Pendek, and the Himalayan Yeti. Indeed, it is thought that Sasquatch may have crossed to the North American continent from Asia, using the land bridge which once existed between Russia and Alaska.

Sasquatch has been photographed—most notably on twenty-eight feet of motion picture film by Roger Patterson and Bob Gimlin in Bluff Creek, California on October 20, 1967—and people claim to have spent time with Sasquatch tribes. More un-usual are sightings of Sasquatch in places like Staten Island, New York, where they are thought to be biological robots dropped by UFOs for purposes of exploration. see: **UFO; Yeti.**

Satan [O] The Devil; prince of hell and of the fallen angels. In heaven, Satan was Sammael, one of the seraphim—the highest order of angels—with twelve wings. Second in power only to God, Sammael became greedy and fostered an uprising. He was bested in battle by the Archangel Michael and, with the rest of his rebellious host, was pitched from heaven. In hell, Sammael became Satan, the Angel of Death and the executioner of the human race. However, Satan carried his duties one step further, plotting the fall of humankind because of his hatred of God and pining for lost Paradise. Arousing the passion of Adam and Eve, he caused them to be driven from Eden. Yet, God saw a benefit to be had in all of this. He decided thereafter to use Satan to tempt

Satan

mortals to see if they were noble or base.

Legend has it that there are four crown princes of hell, of which Satan is Lord of the Inferno and Adversary of God, located in the south. In the north is Belial, who represents Baseness of the Earth; in the west is Leviathan, the Serpent from the Deep; and in the south is the glorious Lucifer, the Bringer of Light and Knowledge. In Christian lore, the second coming of Jesus will begin one thousand years of triumph over Satan. Battling this belief are the Satanists, a religious faction formed in the latter half of the eighteenth century and dedicated to the spread of evil and obscenity. see: **Black Magic; Devil, The; Leviathan; Mephistopheles.**

Satyr [M] Hybrid creatures who attend Dionysos, the Greek god of wine. Originally, satyrs had human bodies with the face of a goat and the tail of a horse. However, the image of the popular centaur was later fused to the satyr leaving them with the torso and face of a human but the lower quarters and horns of a goat. Minor gods, the satyrs represent both the strength and lushness of nature. They love to drink, can become quite rowdy, and frequently have their way with willing—and sometimes unwilling—nymphs at the orgies of Dionysos. The leader of the satyrs is the Arcadian Pan, the son of Hermes and a nymph. The curly-haired god of the countryside and patron of shepherds, Pan—whose name means "all"—is an excellent musician, particularly on his reed pipes. His sister, Daphnis, is the inventor of pastoral poetry. The Roman counterpart of satyrs are fauns. see: **Midas, King; Nymphs.**

Sauron [L] An evil being in author J. R. R. Tolkien's Ring trilogy. A one-time aide to the evil Morgoth, Sauron spends hundreds of years building his own cruel might. Forging the Rings of Power, he plans to conquer all of

Satyr

Middle Earth. The wars rage for hundreds of years, the inventor of the Black Speech seeking to assure victory by obtaining the all-powerful One Ring. But the artifact is destroyed, along with Sauron's nine slaves called the Nazgûl—and the tyrant becomes so weak that his corporeal form dissipates. A spirit, Sauron no longer poses a threat to the security of the hobbits and their kin. see: **Frodo Baggins; Gandalf; Hobbit; One Ring; Tolkien, J. R. R.**

Savage, Doc [L] A pulp magazine hero created by Lester Dent (1904–1959) (writing under the pen name of Kenneth Robeson). The son of Clark Savage, Clark "Doc" Savage Jr. was raised from the age of fourteen months to be physically and mentally perfect. The foremost expert in most fields of human endeavor, Doc still works two hours per day to improve on his phenomenal abilities. With bronze-hued skin, slightly darker hair, and flake-gold eyes, the wealthy Savage travels the world helping those in need. From his headquarters on the eighty-sixth floor of the Empire State Building, and a hideaway in the Arctic called the Fortress of Solitude, Doc is in constant touch with his five aides: chemist Monk (Lt. Col. Andrew Blodgett Mayfair), lawyer Ham (Brig. Gen. Theodore Marley Brooks), engineer Renny (Col. John Renwick), geologist and archaeologist Johnny (William Harper Littlejohn), and electrical marvel Long Tom (Maj. Thomas J. Roberts). A sixth associate is Doc's beautiful bronze-haired cousin Pat Savage.

Doc's first adventure was published in *Doc Savage Magazine* in 1933, and was followed by 180 others in which the superhero battles foes ranging from shaman to dinosaurs. Nearly 100 of these tales have thus far been reprinted in paperback. In 1975, George Pal produced a motion picture called *Doc Savage,* starring Ron Ely as the Man of Bronze. see: **Pal, George; Superman; Zarkon.**

Savitiri [F] A clever girl of Hindu legend. The only child of an Indian king, she falls in love with Prince Satyavan. Savitiri makes plans to marry the young man—even though her father's seer, Narada, says that he will die in one year. Sure enough, after a year of bliss the couple is visited by Yama, the god of death. Yama places Satyavan's soul in a noose and leads him away. The god orders Savitiri to bury the body—but she refuses saying that since the soul is her husband, and not the body, she will accompany them. Pleased with this loyal response, Yama grants her one wish—exclusive of the life of her husband. She asks that the sight of her blind father-in-law be restored, and the god complies. Immediately afterwards, announcing that she really enjoys the deity's company, Savitiri is rewarded with a second wish on the same terms. This time she asks for her father to be able to sire a child to replace her, and it is done. Still

later in the journey, Savitiri exclaims that there is truly much she can learn from the wise Yama, and the god grants her a third conditional wish. Savitiri says she wants to bear 100 sons and the god tells her she shall. Soon, Yama remarks again how faithful Savitiri is to accompany her husband in death. The woman says she is indeed faithful—so much so that she will never sleep with any other man, not even to have the 100 sons Yama has promised. The god stops short. Realizing the trap that's been sprung, Yama is forced to return Satyavan's life for as long as it takes him to father 100 children.

Saynday [F] A sage leader in the lore of the Kiowa Indians. Saynday's first great accomplishment is to lead humans from the dark within the earth, through a massive tree trunk, to the surface world. Once there, he must find a way to feed his hungry people, and thus invents hunting. To this end, he converses with trees to learn what material is best for use in making bows and arrows. After eating, Saynday creates clothing—not only for warmth, but for modesty. After all, it had been black underground and the people could not see one another. In the light of day it was a different matter. Once the Kiowa civilization has been established, Saynday serves as the Solomon of his tribe, designing tools, settling disputes, and planning a culture.

Scalosians [TV] Beings from the planet Scalos in the "Star Trek" episode "Wink of an Eye." Extremely advanced entities, the Scalosians are plagued with males rendered sterile by radiation released from great volcanoes. This radiation has also boosted the Scalosian metabolism to a point where they move so quickly as to appear invisible, and sound like buzzing insects to whomever they address. When the U.S.S. *Enterprise* answers a distress call from Scalos, some of the ship's male crewmembers are accelerated to mate with the females. The Scalosians' Queen Deela has her eye on Captain Kirk, and he too is sped up. Eventually, Kirk is able to inform Mr. Spock and Dr. McCoy of his predicament and an antidote is found. The fate of the Scalosians is unresolved, although it is assumed that they will be given the antidote and assisted in their hour of need. see: *Enterprise, U.S.S.*; **Kirk, Captain.**

Scheherezade [F] A legendary storyteller. Scheherezade is the alleged author of the tenth century masterpiece *The Arabian Nights Entertainments.* She came to compose this collection in a most unusual fashion. Because the first wife of the sultan Schahriar was unfaithful, his lordship takes a new bride each night and strangles her in the morning. Scheherezade, the daughter of Schahriar's Grand Vizier, determines to put a stop to this. She does this by marrying the sultan and, each night, attended by her younger sister Dinarzade, spins wondrous tales. In order to hear a new story every eve, the sultan does not kill Scheherezade and his storm of vengeance is ended. Among the characters created by Scheherezade are Sinbad and Aladdin. see: **Aladdin; Sinbad.**

Schlauraffen [F] A land of luxury and idleness. According to a plotless tale—indeed, merely a tour guide—collected by the Brothers Grimm, a visitor sees amazing sights in Schlauraffen. Among them are a man without feet outrunning a horse; a sword cutting through a bridge; an ass with a silver nose; hot cakes growing on lime trees; a plough ploughing by itself; honey flying like water; two crows mowing a meadow; gnats building a bridge; a pair of doves tearing a wolf to pieces; a snail slaying two lions; a barber shaving a woman;

two goats beating a stone; and so on. This land probably exists only in the narrator's dreams, since the recitation ends with a cock-a-doodle-doo. see: **Grimm, Jakob and Wilhelm.**

Schwägel, Anna Maria [O] The last European to be tried and executed as a witch. A servant, Anna Maria was seduced by a coachdriver who was heavily involved with the occult. The girl went to Sabbats with her lover, and eventually renounced Catholicism. That's when she learned that her friend was married, and left him. By this time Anna Maria had lost her job and survived by begging. She was quickly picked up and placed in a Bavarian insane asylum. Mentioning her woeful story to one of the inmates, Anna Maria found herself hauled from her cell, tried for witchcraft, and beheaded. A few months later, circa mid-1775, witchcraft was reduced from its status as a capital crime—a positive step, but one which came too late to help Ms. Schwägel. see: **Sabbat; Witch.**

Scott, Gordon [MP] A popular motion picture strongman. Born Gordon M. Werschkul in Portland, Oregon in 1927, Scott served in the infantry and, upon his discharge, held odd jobs as a cowboy, salesperson, and fire fighter. In 1953, while working as a lifeguard in Las Vegas, the six-foot three-inch Scott was discovered and featured in a Tarzan film entitled *Tarzan's Hidden Jungle* (1955). Several other Tarzan pictures followed, after which Scott went on to appear in *Duel of the Titans* (1961) as Remus to Steve Reeves' Romulus, *Goliath and the Vampires* (1961), *Hercules vs. Moloch* (1963), *Samson and the Seven Miracles of the World* (1961), and as Hercules in a television pilot entitled "Hercules and the Princess of Troy" (1966). Scott has a son, Mike, by his third wife, Vera Miles. see: **Hercules; Reeves, Steve; Romulus; Tarzan.**

Scylla [M] A monster of Greek mythology. Before becoming a much-feared creature, Scylla was a beautiful maiden who angered Glaucus, one of Jason's Argonauts, by spurning his advances. The offended sailor retaliated by convincing the wicked sorceress Circe to enchant the waters in which Scylla regularly bathed. Circe's potent magic transformed the girl into a huge six-necked snake. Horrified, Scylla slithered off to a cave on the coast of Sicily where she joined forces with the whirlpool Charybdis, and spent the rest of her woeful days feeding on seafarers caught in the rushing waters. see: **Charybdis; Circe; Jason; Odysseus.**

Seal Maidens [F] Sea creatures of English lore. Also known as Selkies and the Roane, the seal maidens are beautiful girls who live within seal skins. These sleek hides permit them to travel easily through the water, though they are air breathers and cannot long stay submerged. When the mood strikes them, they leave the water completely, crawl from their skins, and dance about on the land. If the skin is stolen, they can never return to the sea. A seal maiden can be persuaded to marry a mortal, although children born of such a union will have small horns between their fingers. Nonetheless, these youngsters are considered lucky because their mother will give them the wisdom of the ages as it is known only to those of the sea. see: **Merpeople.**

Seaview [MP/TV] A nuclear submarine featured in both the motion picture *Voyage to the Bottom of the Sea* (1961) and the four-season run (1964–1968) of the TV series based on the film. The mission of the *Seaview* is to conduct underwater research and protect the United States from enemies. This second group includes both foreign agents and aliens from space. In command of the *Seaview* is Capt. Lee Crane (Michael Ansara in the film;

David Hedison on television) with retired Admiral Harriman Nelson (Walter Pidgeon; Richard Basehart) along for the ride. The blue-gray *Seaview* is 400 feet long and features huge bay windows on its bridge. It carries onboard a yellow disklike Flying Sub which can be launched underwater and flown by a crew of two.

Sehlat [TV] A huge bearlike creature in the animated "Star Trek" episode "Yesteryear." One of these furry brutes belongs to young Spock on the planet Vulcan. Its name is I-Chaya, and it is seen protecting its master from a vicious le-matya, a tigerlike creature with poisonous claws. The le-matya is stopped, but I-Chaya is mortally wounded, and the seven-year-old Spock elects to put the animal out of its misery. Though the sehlat has fangs nearly six inches long and is quite a violent animal, it can be domesticated and makes a devoted pet. see: **Spock, Mr.**

Selenites [L] Moondwellers in H. G. Wells' novel *First Men in the Moon.*

Selenite and Seal Maiden

Nearly five feet tall, they are described by earthperson Bedford as having "much of the quality of a complicated insect," with whiplike tentacles and an arm projecting from a shining, cylindrical body case. Their clothes are "garments of some leathery substance"; they wear helmets to prod mooncalves, headpieces with many spikes, and a pair of goggles with dark glass. Naked, the lunarians have "very short thighs, very long shanks, and little feet," and step in a noiseless, birdlike walk. The Selenite face has no nose, two bulging eyes at the side, and a down-curved mouth. Along the crest of the head is a low ridge of whitish spines, with a much larger ridge curved on each side over the eyes. The neck is jointed in three places, and the skin is hard, shiny, and hairless. Bedford characterizes the voice as consisting of "reedy tones ... that seemed to me impossible to imitate or define." see: **Mooncalf; Wells, H. G.**

Serling, Rod [TV/MP] A highly respected telescripter who specialized in fantasy and science fiction. Born in Syracuse, New York in 1924, Serling graduated from Antioch College in 1950. Working in radio and then in television as a continuity writer, he quit to become a freelancer. His first television script was an adaptation of Pat Frank's science fiction novel *Forbidden Area*. It was presented on "Playhouse 90" in 1958. A year later Serling created the fantasy omnibus program "The Twilight Zone," following that with "Night Gallery" in 1971. Serling was the on-camera host for both. During the course of his career, Serling won six Emmy Awards and authored the renowned play "Requiem for a Heavyweight." In 1968 he wrote the plotline—though not the dialogue—for the theatrical motion picture *Planet of the Apes*. Serling died in 1975, survived by his wife, Carolyn—whom he wed in

1948—and two daughters, Nan and Jody. see: **Night Gallery; Twilight Zone, The.**

Seuss, Dr. [L] An author of fantasy books for children. Born in Springfield, Massachusetts in 1904, Theodor Seuss Geisel graduated from Dartmouth in 1925, then studied at Oxford. After serving in the army and working in advertising—where he coined the slogan, "Quick, Henry! The Flit!"—Geisel created the character Gerald McBoing-Boing for animated cartoons (1950). During this period, Geisel wrote books to amuse himself. He also illustrated them, although he had no formal art training. Much to his pleasure and surprise, one of these volumes was published in 1937, *And To Think That I Saw it on Mulberry Street*. A year later *The Five Hundred Hats of Bartholomew Cubbins* appeared, followed by *Horton Hatches the Egg* in 1940. However, Geisel's greatest success was enjoyed by two books issued in 1957: *The Cat in the Hat* and *How the Grinch Stole Christmas*. Dozens of books have followed, most of them bearing Geisel's trademark of a rhyming presentation with a moral.

Seven League Boots [F] Footwear with a most unusual property. Either manufactured or enchanted by fairies—their origin differs from culture to culture, along with their properties—the seven league boots enable the wearer to travel just such a distance in a single stride. They are used by imps to round the globe, heroes to escape villains, or villains to pursue heroes. In Oriental lore, these boots are frequently capable of spanning several thousand leagues per step. They are often used to follow a rainbow to the pot of gold which lies at its end.

Shadow, The [L] One of the twentieth century's first and greatest superheroes. In the late 1920s, mystery stories were being read on the radio, verbatim, from magazines published by Street and Smith. To give the tales a dash of melodrama, the narrator called himself the Shadow, a character described by the catch-phrase, "Who knows what evil lurks in the hearts of men?" As the popularity of this resonant-voiced figure grew, Street and Smith decided to make him a crimefighter and the star of his own mystery magazine. The first tale was printed in April 1931. Entitled *The Living Shadow,* it was written by Walter Gibson—alias Maxwell Grant—who eventually wrote 280 Shadow adventures. Wearing a slouch hat and cloak, the Shadow has the ability to cloud people's minds, control his involuntary bodily functions—he survives being buried alive by cupping air in his armpit and drawing upon it for several hours—become invisible, and pass through solid objects such as doors. He is fond of sticking to swirling fog.

The hawk-nosed hero operates under not one, but several, secret identities: Lamont Cranston, a millionaire playboy; Fritz, a janitor at police headquarters; pilot Kent Allard; and others. The Shadow's aides in his battle with the underworld are Harry Vincent; communications coordinator Burbank; reporter Clyde Burke; criminal imposter Cliff Marsland; Mann, the broker; cab driver Moe Shrevnitz; and his personal assistant Margo Lane.

On the radio, the Shadow was played by Hardy Andrews, Orson Welles, and Bret Morrison; in the movies he has been impersonated by Rod La Rocque, Victor Jory, and Kane Richmond. Several dozen of the Shadow's pulp magazine adventures have been reissued in paperback, and Gibson wrote a handful of new stories in the mid-1960s

Shaman [O] An Indian medicine man, an individual with strong occult powers. Able to cure the sick, shaman

Shaman

also held congress with spirits. This consisted of wishing for luck in the hunt, war, or farming; summoning a demon for some vile purpose; or asking for details of future happenings. Shaman also presided over religious ceremonies and, while the chief led the tribe, few made decisions without first consulting their shaman. Even white settlers trusted these people as physicians for the body and soul. Not that all medicine men were legitimate. Many were out-and-out fakes who could throw their voices, cause illusions, create awesome chemical displays, and the kind. The shaman ultimately became so powerful that many tribes outlawed their "guild," a group known as Midewiwin.

Many Indian cultures had witch doctors instead of shaman. The responsibilities of these occult personalities were less broad than those of shaman. Their principal duties were to exorcise evil spirits and detect witches. In many modern-day countries, shamans and witch doctors are still potent influences, even casting spells at soccer matches.

Shamir [F] In Hebrew lore, a creature made at the very end of the sixth day of Creation. Actually, the Shamir is a form of Salamander, born in a fire of myrtle wood that kept burning for seven years. No larger than a mouse, the wormlike creature dwelt in Paradise until it was captured by an eagle sent by Solomon. Because it could slice through stone or metal, the king wanted it to cut the building blocks of his temple. Among the Shamir's other properties are the use of its blood as a lotion of invulnerability, and the employment of its web as protection against fire. Indeed, one of the reasons God is said to have sent a flood rather than flame was to circumvent this property of the Shamir. Although this animal can even eat through diamond, it is unable to penetrate a wool cloth filled with barley corn and placed in a lead basket. see: **Benaiah; Salamander.**

Shangri-La [L] A village of peace, love, and long life. Nestled in the towering mountains of Tibet, this mythical land was created by author James Hilton for his 1933 novel *Lost Horizon.* When a plane crashes near Shangri-La—*la* meaning "mountain pass"—Messrs. Conway, Barnard, Mallinson, and Miss Brinklow are brought to the temperate utopia. As it turns out, their plane had been swung from its course by an Oriental pilot, the passengers kidnapped so that Conway could be brought to Shangri-La. The reason? The Briton has been selected by Father Perrault, the High Lama of Shangri-La, to succeed him—the same Perrault who was born in 1681 and founded this retreat in 1734, 200 years before the time of the narrative. After four months of reflection, Conway decides not to accept the post and reluctantly leaves Shangri-La.

According to the party's host, Chang, Shangri-La is perfect without being sterile. Its citizens believe in moderation of all things, including virtue, and there are no sexual distinctions. Physically, Shangri-La has "a dreamlike texture, matching the porcelain blue of the sky." In its monastery are treasures "that museums and millionaires alike would have bargained for," all of it housed with impeccable taste in places where delicate perfection seems to have "fluttered into existence like petals from a flower." All about are courtyards, lotus pools, statues—of dragons, lions, and unicorns—open pavilions, and excellent libraries, all presenting themselves with harmony and "a gradual revelation of elegance."

Shangri-La was brought to the screen in two film versions of *Lost Horizon,* one in 1937 and another in 1973.

Shannara [L] A noble name in Terry Brooks' best-selling 1977 fantasy novel *The Sword of Shannara.* The sword itself is the only weapon which can be used against the Warlock Lord who is plotting to destroy the world. Originally, the weapon is given to the Elfin king Jerle Shannara by the Druid Bremen for use against trolls. The blade renders Jerle invincible, as it does all who wield it. Upon Jerle's death, the sword passes to the Druid Council at Paranor; it is set in a large block of Tre-Stone and secured within a vault. The story proper relates the sword's use by the half-elfin Shea Ohmsford—Jerle's one heir and the only being who can raise the blade—against the Warlock Lord Brona. In the final confrontation, the truth-revealing weapon destroys the villain by disclosing that his corporeal form ceased to exist long ago, and his present spiritual incarnation is an impossible lie. After saving the world, the sword is jabbed blade-down into red marble and placed in a vault in Callahorn.

Shedim [O] One of the four groups of Hebrew demons, the others being

Roukhin, Mazikin, and Lilin. In three ways these beings are like humans: they reproduce, they must eat, and they die. Likewise, they share a trio of attributes with angels: they have wings, they can travel anywhere, and they know the future. The four breeds of demon can assume any form they wish, and have the ability to turn their heads completely around. Stirring from their homes in places avoided by mortals—such as ruined buildings, deserts, and swamps—the Shedim and their fellows are most visible on the eves of Wednesday and Saturday. Vulnerable only to the presence of God's spoken name, they are nonetheless powerless to affect anything which is sealed, tied up, counted, or measured.

Shock [O] An English boogy. Usually appearing as a horse or an ass, and sometimes as a dog or a calf, the shock can be distinguished from real animals by their bulging saucer eyes and excessively hairy mane. The ghosts of impudent mortals, these creatures enjoy frightening people, but nothing more. If anyone tries to touch a shock, it will bite the bold rascal and then disappear. The scar is one which will remain for the rest of that person's life.

Shogun Warriors [E] Giant Japanese robots who can rearrange their body components to become aircraft, land-vehicles, submarines, or any manner of machine required for a specific task. Gaining fame as a cartoon program and as Mattel toys, the Shogun Warriors consist of a veritable army of robots—the axe-wielding Dragun, the sword-swinging Great Mazinga, the arrow-firing Raydeen, plus Combatra, Dangard Ace, Gaiking, Posiden, Grandizer, and Raider. Now the stars of a popular comic book, the Oriental titans battle many faces of evil. The stars of the magazine are Raydeen, Combatra, and Dangard Ace. In the comic book mythos, all are com-

manded by the humans Richard Carson, Genji Odashu, and Illongo Savage from Shogun Sanctuary in the mountains of Japan.

Sidhe [F] The nobility among Scottish and Irish fairies. Handsome sprites— so much so that humans are forbidden from gazing upon them—the sidhe are the largest, oldest, and most powerful of all the fairies. Oddly, though, the sidhe do not live like gentry. They look after their animals, play incredibly beautiful music, and subsist primarily on milk and whiskey. Their touch can drive a mortal mad or cause grave illness, and their arrows kill instantly. If a human strikes the fancy of a sidhe, he or she is captured, kept as a slave or lover, and eventually released. However, such mortals are never again quite the same. They either go insane or become prophets. The sidhe do not tolerate any affront. see: **Fairy.**

Siegfried [M] A hero whose epic adventures appear in the Teutonic *Nibelungenlied* (*Lay of the Nibelungs*) and the Norse *Saga of the Volsungs*, in which Siegfried is known as Sigurd. The son of Sieglinde and Siegmund—who died before his son's birth—Siegfried is raised by the dwarf Mime. Since this guardian is an avaricious sort, he gives Siegfried Siegmund's sword, Gram, and urges him to slay the dragon Fafner, who looks after a great treasure. Mounting his horse, Grani—of Sleipnir's stock—Siegfried kills the monster and bathes in its blood. This makes the young man invulnerable and enables him to understand the language of birds. What he hears from a flock of the creatures is that Mime cares for nothing but the treasure—so Siegfried hastens home to murder him.

Moving on, Siegfried comes to a hill on which Brünhilde, the most beautiful of the Valkyries, lies sleeping within a ring of fire. It is the work of

Odin, and his edict is that Brünhilde can only be rescued by someone brave enough to enter the flames. This Siegfried does, and he falls in love with the Valkyrie. However, he elects to press on to the land of the Nibelungs. There he is given a potion which causes him to forget his affection for Brünhilde. Instead he marries Kriemhild and, donning Tarnkappe—a cloak of invisibility—helps her brother Gunther rescue the trapped Valkyrie. Brünhilde comes to court to wed her noble savior; however, at a great feast the spell cast on Siegfried wears off. He recalls his love for the Valkyrie, which causes Kriemhild to grow jealous. She tells Brünhilde about Siegfried's clandestine role in helping Gunther, which humiliates the bravery-conscious woman. Seeking retribution, she has Kriemhild sew Siegfried a garment with a cross on the spot where a fallen leaf prevented the dragon's blood from coating him fully. In the meantime, the Valkyrie mixes a will-sapping drug from wolf's flesh and serpent's venom, feeds it to Gunther's brother Hagen, and commands him to slay her former lover. When Siegfried stoops by a stream to draw water, Hagen draws his bow and shoots the hero. In a sudden surge of conscience, Brünhilde takes her own life.

In the Norse legend, Sigurd is raised not by a dwarf but by the blacksmith Regin, eats the dragon's heart, and is stabbed while he is sleeping by the doped Hagen. The names, too, are different: Brünhilde is Brynhild, Kriemhild is Gudrun, Gunther is Gunnar, Hagen is Guttorm, Sieglinde is Hjordis, and Siegmund is Sigmund. see: **Fafner; Nibelungen; Odin; Valkyries.**

Silky [F] The female counterpart of a brownie. Most silkies are domestic sprites. Dressed in silk, they do household chores, as well as work nasty mischief on wives, daughters, or servants who are idle. Sometimes silkies appear as ghosts—their natural form, since they are spirits of the dead—or else as petite little ladies. When not at work in someone's home, they spend their time sitting in trees. Certain silkies take other forms—for example, as seals—and live for pleasure or to pull pranks. see: **Brownies; Seal Maidens.**

Silmarils, The [L] A trio of jewels holding the essential Light of the Two Trees of Valinor—destroyed by the first of the Dark Lords, Morgoth, who set the jewels in his crown. They are featured in J. R. R. Tolkien's novel *The Silmarillion.* As Tolkien's *Ring* Trilogy is an account of events transpiring during the Third Age of the World, so *The Silmarillion* is a chronicle of the history of the First Age, "the Elder Days" of Middle Earth. The main body of the book, the "Quenta Silmarillion," is concerned with a narrative of rebellion and war, seen by and large from the viewpoint of Fëanor, creator of the Silmarils. The volume also contains four shorter, only partially related works forming the links between this "prequel" and the remainder of the mythos embodied in *The Hobbit* and *The Lord of the Rings:* the "Ainulindalë," the "Valaquenta," the "Akallabêth," and "Of the Rings of Power." see: **Hobbit; One Ring; Tolkien, J. R. R.**

Silver Surfer [C] An incredible antihero created by writer Stan Lee and artist Jack Kirby. The Silver Surfer was originally Norrin Radd of the planet Zenn-La. When the giant alien Galactus came to sap the planet's energy, Radd offered to become his herald, seek out uninhabited worlds, if he would spare Zenn-La. Galactus agreed, encasing Radd within glistening galactic matter which sustains his life in the void of space. Traveling about on a thought-controlled board, the mighty Surfer soon found himself beset by moral qualms. He felt he had to do right rather than simply follow orders, and for questioning his master was exiled to earth. Though the Surfer feels trapped on our world, between his complaints and intellectual musings he manages to help us battle the many forms of evil. The Silver Surfer first appeared in 1966 and starred briefly in his own magazine. Today he is a frequent guest star in the Marvel line of comic books and, in 1978, was featured in a popular illustrated book entitled *The Silver Surfer*. see: **Lee, Stan; Kirby, Jack.**

Simeli Mountain [FT] A mountain in a story from the Brothers Grimm. The tale concerns two brothers, one wealthy and one not, the latter scratching out a living by selling corn. One day he sees twelve wild men ride up to a mountain in the forest. When they scream "Semeli Mountain open!" it splits down the center, they ride in, and emerge carrying riches. The dozen men order it to close, after which they gallop off. Walking to the magic peak, the poor man repeats their call and the mountain opens for him. Stealing a few of the gems he finds within, the intruder departs, feeds his family, and distributes the remainder of the riches to other needy souls. Whenever he runs out of money, he simply borrows a bucket from his brother and returns to the mountain. Curious as to what his poverty-stricken sibling is up to, the rich man coats the bucket with pitch. When he finds a pearl stuck in the bottom, he forces the secret from his brother by threatening to have him arrested for robbery. Rushing to Simeli, the greedy man enters, stuffs his pockets with jewels—but forgets the phrase which will reopen the mountain. When the wild riders return, they find the frightened man, say they are glad to finally catch the fellow who has been stealing from them, and lop off his head. see: **Grimm, Jakob and Wilhelm.**

Simurgh [F] An incredible, all-knowing bird of Middle Eastern lore. The simurgh dwells on Gaokerena, looks much like a roc, has seen the world destroyed three times, and possesses profound prophetic powers. It also grows feathers which, when stroked upon any wound, cause it to heal instantly. In the Persian story of Creation, the simurgh created all plants by shaking their seeds from a huge tree in which it roosted. These were gathered and planted by its servant-bird the camrosh. Legend has it that this winged wonder is pleased to raise human children among its own nestlings. see: **Roc.**

Sinbad [F] A hero of the Arabian Nights. Sinbad dwells in the Bagdad of Caliph Haroun-al-Raschid. Inheriting a great deal of money from his parents, Sinbad squanders it all. He uses what little remains to join a company of merchants. Landing upon various shores, he has a series of adventures. On his first of seven voyages, he beaches his boat on an island which turns out to be the back of a very angry whale. On the second, he has trouble with a roc and giant serpents; and on the third, with a cyclops. On the fourth voyage, Sinbad survives cannibals as well as being buried alive. On the fifth voyage, he battles more rocs and a goblin called the Old Man of the Sea; and on the sixth, he is shipwrecked on an island belonging to a race of wealthy and sophisticated blacks. On his seventh voyage, Sinbad tangles with elephants. The active sailor makes back his fortune early in his career, but keeps at it because he detests inactivity.

Sinbad tells the story of his life to Hindbad, when he hears the jealous porter complaining that his life is harsh while that of Sinbad has been easy. Sinbad gives him a great deal of wealth, and the porter regrets his harsh words.

On the screen, Sinbad's adventures have been recounted in such films as

Sinbad the Sailor (1947) starring Douglas Fairbanks, *The Seventh Voyage of Sinbad* (1958) with Kerwin Mathews, *Captain Sinbad* (1963) featuring Guy Williams, *The Golden Voyage of Sinbad* (1973) with John Phillip Law, and *Sinbad and the Eye of the Tiger* (1977) starring Patrick Wayne. see: **Cyclops; Roc; Scheherezade.**

Singing Bone, The [FT] A fairy tale from the works of the Brothers Grimm. With a brutal boar goring his subjects, a king offers his daughter to whomever slays the creature. Two brothers, one innocent and the other crafty, undertake the task. When the naive one kills the boar, his brother murders him, tosses his corpse into a stream, and carries the boar to the king. Years later, a shepherd finds a bone jutting from the stream. Unbeknownst to him, it belongs to the dead brother. The shepherd uses it to make a mouthpiece for his horn. As soon as he begins to play, the instrument sings the song of what happened to the innocent brother. The young man plays the horn for the king; the monarch is intrigued, and sends a handful of soldiers to dig up the river bed. There they find the skeleton of the innocent lad. Gathering his remains, they bury them in a churchyard. As for his ruthless brother, he is tied in a sack and drowned. This tale, with variations— the quarry is a dragon, and the innocent brother is brought back to life— was presented in George Pal's motion picture *The Wonderful World of the Brothers Grimm* (1962). Otto Krueger played the king, Terry-Thomas the cruel Ludwig, and Buddy Hackett the kindly Hans. see: **Grimm, Jakob and Wilhelm; Pal, George; Transparent Apple.**

Sirens [M] Maidens who live near the sea and lure sailors to their death with an irresistible song. Pictured as having a woman's body with the lower quarters and feet of a bird, the sirens are the daughters of the river god Achelous and a muse—either Calliope or Terpischore, depending upon the account. Scholars are also divided as to just how many sirens there are. Some say that there are only two, Aglaiophemi (Clear Speaker) and Thelxiepeia (Magic Speaker). Others claim that there are three sirens, Leukosia, Ligeia, and Parthenope, who play the lyre, pipes, and sing, respectively. Among the sirens' most famous prey are the sailors of Jason's Argosy and Odysseus' Odyssey. It is said that after they failed to draw Odysseus' men to their shores, the sirens flung themselves into the sea where they became rocks. The sirens were heard—though not seen—in the 1958 motion picture *The Seventh Voyage of Sinbad* and in *Hercules* one year later. see: **Jason; Muses; Odysseus.**

Six Million Dollar Man [TV] A half-man, half-robot featured in the television series which bears his name. Based on Martin Caiden's 1972 novel *Cyborg*, "The Six Million Dollar Man" stars Lee Majors as Lt. Col. Steve Austin, astronaut. The youngest human ever to walk on the moon, Austin loses an arm, an eye, and both legs when the M3F5 airplane he's testing crashes. Scientists replace Austin's missing parts with plastic and computer substitutes. This makes him a cybernetic organism or cyborg, able to run sixty miles-per-hour, vault thirty feet in the air, lift great weights with his artificial arm, or spy on distant objects with his twenty-to-one zoom eye. Austin goes to work for Oscar Goldman (Richard Anderson) of the governmental agency OSI (Office of Scientific Investigation), and when his show is a hit, pretty young tennis pro Jaime Sommers (Lindsay Wagner) loses an arm, an ear, and both legs in a skydiving accident, is rebuilt, and takes to the airwaves as "The Bionic

Woman." A cyborg boy and dog are later added to the series, which run for five and three seasons, respectively.

Skrimsl [F] A legendary Scandinavian sea serpent. Skrimsl's presence has been reported as far back as 1345, most of these sightings coming from serious-minded fishers who are not prone to fancy. Generally, Skrimsl is said to have a seal or horselike head, a long neck, two or three humps on its back, and a pair of powerful paddles. It is reported to be a very swift swimmer. Over the years, huge hulks and skeletons have washed ashore, which local residents identify as Skrimsl. see: **Loch Ness Monster.**

Sleeping Beauty [FT] A popular fairy tale character. When a king and queen have their long-wanted daughter, they name her Rosamond and invite twelve wise women to a feast. Eleven bring gifts of beauty and virtue. However, before the twelfth can offer her attribute, the evil and uninvited thirteenth wise woman storms into the banquet hall. She declares that "in the fifteenth year of her age the princess shall prick herself with a spindle and shall fall down dead," then departs. Fortunately, the twelfth woman is able to amend the curse with her own bestowment, saying that Rosamond shall not die, but sleep for 100 years.

The king and queen order all spindles burned—yet on her fifteenth birthday the princess finds an old woman spinning in an ancient tower of the castle. Touching the spindle out of curiosity, Rosamond pricks her finger and falls asleep. So does everything else in the palace, from her parents to the dogs and horses, to the fire and wind. Thorns grow round the grounds, and over the years many princes try and fail to pierce them. Finally, one prince decides to get through come what may. Coincidentally, when he arrives the 100 years are just ending. The thorn hedge turns to flowers, which part to admit him. He finds the princess, kisses her, and everything in the palace is reborn. Shortly thereafter, the prince and Rosamond are wed.

In Walt Disney's feature-length 1959 cartoon, Sleeping Beauty is called Aurora, the prince is named Phillip, and true love's first kiss—not 100 years—is all it takes to wake the princess. There are three good fairies and one evil—Maleficent—who becomes a dragon and is destroyed by the prince after he hacks his way through the thorn forest. see: **Disney, Walt.**

Smaug [L] A great dragon in J. R. R. Tolkien's *The Hobbit*. Nearly 200 years before the period of the novel the monster had gone to the mountain Erebor, razed the human city of Dale on the peak's southern slopes, driven away the dwarfs from the Kingdom Under the Mountain, and taken great treasure. Now, dwelling in the Ered Mithrin—the Grey Mountains, and lair of many lesser dragons—Smaug is challenged by Thorin and Company who seek to recover both the wealth and Thorin's title of King of Durin's Folk at Erebor. However, Smaug is not the kind of dragon to tolerate impudence, and decides to attack the human city of Esgaroth. The decision proves to be a hasty one, as the monster is met and slain by Bard the Bowman. Smaug's gold is used to reconstruct the devastated realm. see **Hobbit; Tolkien, J. R. R.**

Smith, Clark Ashton [L] A fantasy author whose words and imagery were sheer poetry. Born in Long Valley, California in 1893, Smith left school at the age of fourteen. He picked up the bulk of his education from books. Although Smith's first sale was a poem—"Moonlight," which appeared in the western magazine *Overland Monthly* in 1910—he abandoned his early desire to be a poet exclusively and turned to fiction. His first publication in the fantasy genre was *The Ninth Skeleton* in 1928, but it was *The Last Incantation* in 1930 which established him among the leading figures in the field. Writing about imaginary gods such as the three-horned Tolometh; about Atlantis; about the distant past and future; about the Arctic world of Hyperborea; and about his mythical land of Zothique, Smith produced 110 stories in all. Most of these were written prior to 1936. Smith married his wife, Carol, in 1954 and died seven years later. Many of his tales are available in anthologies, and the bulk of story fragments he left behind have been completed by Lin Carter. see: **Carter, Lin; Zothique.**

Smith, Dick [MP] One of the cinema's great make-up artists. Born in 1922, Smith became fascinated with fantasy film faces after seeing Charles Laughton as *The Hunchback of Notre Dame* in 1939. After spending time in the army, Smith landed a job doing make-up for NBC television in New York. After working for other networks on such programs as Roald Dahl's occult series "Way Out" (1961), Smith transferred his talents to the big screen. Among his many genre credits are *The House of Dark Shadows* (1970), *The Exorcist* (1973), *Exorcist II: The Heretic* (1977), and *The Sentinel* (1977). He also did the make-up for *Little Big Man* (1971) and *The Godfather* (1972). Smith and his wife, Jocelyn, have two sons, Douglas and David.

Smith, Valentine Michael [L] In Robert A. Heinlein's novel *Stranger in a Strange Land* (1961), a survivor of the eight crewmember spaceship *Envoy*. Raised by Martians after his parents are killed in an attempt to land on the Red Planet, the young, babyfaced Smith is returned to earth a quarter-century later by the Federation Ship *Champion*. Legally the owner of

Mars, the innocent Smith falls in with a nurse, a reporter, and a sharp author-lawyer-philosopher who tries to keep him from being used by the greedy government. Not that Smith needs other than legal protection. When threatened, he can will an object to disappear. Eventually, Smith founds a religion based on the sharing of water as a sacred act and on "the ability to comprehend all things fully" or *grok*. Alas, for preaching that people and God are one and the same, Smith is soon thereafter shot and bludgeoned to death. Ascending to a heaven which proves that he was correct, Smith plans to continue his dispensation from above.

Smith, Wayland [F] A magical sprite of English legend. The son of a sailor and a mermaid, Smith is the king of the elves and the manufacturer of such items as a boat made of feathers, a coat sewn from wings, and swords whose users can never be defeated. All of Smith's brothers are married to Valkyries, although these unions are not permitted to last for more than nine years. The most famous tale of Smith involves his capture by King Nidudr (also Nidung) of Sweden. The elf's feet are mauled and he is forced to serve as a slave. Smith eventually escapes by donning his winged garment, after which his vengeance is sure and severe. He kills Nidudr's sons and rapes his daughters. Then he sends the king a clutch of presents: golden skulls, eyes inset with gems, and jewelry made of teeth. Only when the gifts have been accepted does Smith send word that they were made from the remains of his sons. The imp's favorite pastime is shoeing horses, which he will do quickly and for a pittance provided the owner doesn't watch. In France, Smith is known as Gallans; in Germany as Wieland; and in Norse legend as Volund or Volundr.

Snake Leaves [FT] Enchanted objects in

the Grimm fairy tale "The Three Snake Leaves." A poor young man painstakingly distinguishes himself in battle and, after a time, has risen in rank sufficiently to marry the king's daughter. The only catch: if she dies first, the young man must promise to be buried alive with her. Needless to say, the princess passes on and the couple is entombed. While the young man sits mourning his wife and his lot, in squirms a snake. The young man slays it. Later, a white snake bearing three leaves enters the tomb. It uses the leaves to revive the first snake, after which the young man applies them to the princess. She awakens, and they leave the mausoleum. The couple decides to take a cruise. Sadly, with her new life the princess has lost all love for the young man. She finds a new lover in the ship's captain and, together, they toss the young man overboard. His servant quickly launches a boat, pulls him from the foaming sea, and uses the snake leaves to revive him. They return to the kingdom. When the princess and the captain reach shore, they tell the king that his son-in-law died of illness and was buried at sea. But the king has already spoken with the young man and learned the truth. He orders his thankless daughter and her paramour set asea in a boat filled with holes, and they drown in short order. see: **Grimm, Jakob and Wilhelm.**

Snark [L] A creature described in Lewis Carroll's poem "The Hunting of the Snark." The work tells of a strange group of people who set sail to go Snark hunting. Their prey is a most incredible beast. It gets up very late and eats breakfast at 5:00 P.M. It is slow at taking a jest, loves to bathe, and is very ambitious. Though it tastes "meagre and hollow," it is crisp and especially good if served with greens. The Snark can also be used for striking a light. Some Snarks have feathers and bite, some have whiskers and scratch,

Snow Queen

but most will not harm humans—unless it is a Boojum. This breed of Snark causes people to vanish. As it turns out, the Snark pursued by the heroes of Carroll's poem is a Boojum.

Snow Queen [FT] An evil character in the work of Hans Christian Andersen. Described as the queen bee of the white swarm, this empress of snow never lies down like the other flakes. When the winds die, she simply flies toward the clouds. In Andersen's tale, two children are menaced by the queen. One, the boy Kai, happens to look out of his window and sees her form from flakes. "Her clothes looked like the whitest gauze. It was made of millions of little star-shaped snowflakes. She was beautiful but all made of ice." The Snow Queen spirits the boy away, and his playmate Gerda sets out to rescue him. Eventually, she reaches the ice being's palace. Lighted by the northern lights, it has over 100 snow halls with windows made of sharp wind. In one of these halls are mutated porcupines, snakes, and bears who serve as the queen's guard; in another is a great frozen lake and the throne of the Snow Queen. Gerda bides her time and, when the chill ruler leaves to annoy the warmer countries, she rescues Kai. see: **Andersen, Hans Christian.**

Snow White [FT] Also known as Snow-Drop, a character in the tales of the Brothers Grimm. For years, a magic looking glass tells an evil queen that she is the fairest woman of all. However, when her stepdaughter, Snow White, reaches the age of seven, the mirror revises its opinion—to the detriment of the queen. Her majesty is furious, and orders one of her hunters to cut the lung and liver (or heart, depending upon the version of the story) from the ebony-haired Snow White and bring them to her. Instead, the hunter tells Snow White to run away and gores a boar. Snow White hurries deep into the woods, where she takes up residence with seven mine dwarfs.

Meanwhile, when the magic mirror pronounces Snow White still the fairest of all, the queen dresses as a peddler and crosses the seven mountains to the home of the dwarfs. There, she presents Snow White with lace. The girl puts it on and it begins to suffocate her; fortunately, the dwarfs return home in time to loosen it. The queen tries again, this time offering Snow White a bite of poison apple. As soon as the girl's lips touch the fruit, she falls lifeless to the ground. The dwarfs return and find her dead, though the pink of life still blushes her cheek. Thus, rather than "hide her away in the black ground," they place her in a glass coffin.

Soon thereafter, a prince passes through the wood. Struck with Snow White's beauty, he asks for the body. The dwarfs give it to him, but no sooner is it moved than the bit of apple falls from Snow White's mouth. She awakens and marries the prince.

Furious, the wicked queen pays her stepdaughter yet another visit. This time, however, she enters the court and is arrested, fitted with iron shoes which are heated red hot, and made to dance until she falls down dead. see: **Disney, Walt; Grimm, Jakob and Wilhelm.**

Snuff Box [FT] A wish-granting object of lore. In a famous French fairy tale that bears its name, the snuff box is discovered by a man who asks for gold and a splendid palace near that of the king. When the potentate pays his new neighbor a visit, he is so impressed by what he sees that he gives the man his daughter in marriage. The princess is also impressed; so much so that she steals the snuff box and orders it to carry her, her father, and her husband's palace far away. Left out in the cold, our despondent hero travels to the moon to ask the all-seeing orb if it happened to notice just where his wife went. The moon says that it has no idea, a situation echoed by the sun. Fortunately, the wind has seen them and gives the man directions. He journeys to the castle where he gains employment as a gardener. Sneaking inside one day, he finds the box and orders it "to go with the palace to the old place, and for the king and his daughter and all their servants to be drowned in the Red Sea." It is done, and the man lives happily for the remainder of his days.

Sojarr [L] A literary hero created by author Manly Wade Wellman and his editor, Mort Weisinger, for the March 1941 edition of *Startling Stories*. The saga of Sojarr is set 1,000 years in the future. By this time, most of the worlds in our solar system have been colonized. The one shining exception: Saturn. A large reward is offered to whomever makes a successful journey to the planet, and adventurer Pitt Rapidan and his three-year-old son Stuart give it a go. But Rapidan crashes in a jungle on the ringed giant, and his last words to Stuart are to be "a good soldier." The tad creeps from the wreckage and, mincing his father's dying pronouncement, calls himself Sojarr. The boy learns to speak by tuning in the rocket radio, and grows to literate and powerful manhood. Battling four-armed humanoids known as Truags as well as many strange monsters, Sojarr also becomes adept at using a sword as well as a pistollike weapon which is fired by an explosive substance called tuvo. The exploits of Sojarr are considered prime entertainment among the many such works inspired by the writings of Edgar Rice Burroughs. see: **Burroughs, Edgar Rice.**

Sokurah [MP] The evil magician played by Torin Thatcher in Ray Harryhausen's 1958 motion picture *The Seventh Voyage of Sinbad*. Bald and black-robed, Sokurah lives in a castle on monster-infested Colossa Island. When Sinbad rescues Sokurah from a pursuing cyclops, the magician loses his magic lamp to the one-eyed monster. Sinbad refuses to return to Colossa, so the magician shrinks the sailor's fiancée, Parisa, to doll size. He thereupon informs her lover that she can be restored only by a potion prepared in his castle. Sinbad reluctantly sails to Colossa where, in the course of his adventures, he finds the magician's lamp. However, he refuses to hand it over until Sokurah releases Parisa from her enchantment. This is done— but Sinbad does not trust the magician. Besides, if the lamp is tossed into lava its occupant, Barani, will be freed from mystic servitude, something the genie much desires. Thus, Sinbad flings the lamp into boiling mud. Enraged, Sokurah orders the dragon-protector of his castle to murder the lovers and their crew. Fortunately, Sinbad had had his men assemble a giant crossbow which they fire at the dragon. The fire-breather falls dead, crushing its cruel master in the process. Among the wonders worked by Sokurah during the film are reading live coals to tell the future, bringing a human skeleton to life, and uniting a snake and a woman into a slithering hybrid creature. see **Colossa; Genie; Harryhausen, Ray; Magician; Sinbad.**

Sola [L] A green woman of the Thark tribe in Edgar Rice Burroughs' John Carter of Mars novels. After Carter's arrival on the Red Planet, this four-armed daughter of the noble prince Tars Tarkas and the late Gozava becomes the earthperson's teacher and custodian. Unlike most Tharks, Sola is neither wicked nor lacking in emotion, and she is one of Carter's genuine allies on this hostile world. The olive-skinned creature is only eight feet tall, not yet having reached her full maturity. Carter describes her as his "fair companion," and a lucky one at that; she knows who parented her, a rarity among Tharks. see: **Barsoom; Burroughs, Edgar Rice; Carter, John; Thark.**

Son of Kong [MP] The twelve-foot-tall, white-furred offspring of King Kong. Featured in the 1933 motion picture *The Son of Kong*, the ape is an even-tempered berry-eater. Rescued from quicksand on Skull Island by Carl Denham—the entrepreneur who carried King Kong to New York—the gorilla later saves Denham and his lady friend, Hilda Peterson, from dinosaurs, helps them locate the treasure of the island, and rescues Denham when an earthquake sinks Skull Island, holding him above the waves until a rowboat arrives. Alas, after releasing Denham poor Kong is dragged underwater, his foot caught between two masses of shifting rock. The amiable ape was animated by Willis O'Brien. see: **O'Brien, Willis.**

Sorcery [O] In its purest form, sorcery is a means of controlling nature as well as spirits both benign and evil. Though sorcery can be used for good or black purposes, the church defines it as the summoning of demons to tap Satan's powers; this a careful counterpoint to witchcraft, which is the calling up of demons or spirits to work deeds which are in direct violation of God's laws. Sorcery also embraces fortunetelling, prophecy, and the casting of spells. A practitioner of sorcery is called a *sorcerer*. see: **Satan; Witch.**

Sord [TV] A six-foot-tall lizardlike creature seen in the animated "Star Trek" episode "Jihad." Powerfully built, it joins Captain Kirk, Mr. Spock, the human Lara, the winged humanoid Prince Tchar of Skorr, and a small and shaggy alien thief called Em/3/Green on a quest to retrieve the Soul of Skorr. In this hallowed sculpture are recorded the brain waves of the revered teacher Alar. If Alar's followers, the Skorr, were to learn of the theft, they would launch a holy war—precisely what was planned when the traitorous Tchar stole it! The artifact is recovered before the jihad can erupt. see: *Enterprise,* **U.S.S.; Kirk, Captain; Spock, Mr.**

Spectre, The [C] A "dead" superhero. The Spectre was created by writer Jerry Siegel—the co-creator of Superman—and artist Bernard Bailey, and premiered in the fifty-second issue of *More Fun Comics.* In his mortal identity, the Spectre is police chief Jim Corrigan. Investigating a robbery committed by the Gat Benson gang, Corrigan is nabbed, placed in a cement-filled barrel, and dropped into the river. He dies, but a voice in the afterlife tells Corrigan his job is not yet done. The law officer is sent back to earth as a costumed ghost called the Spectre. In this form, Corrigan wears a white body leotard and a green hood, trunks, and cloak. He can fly, become invisible, walk through objects, work magic, grow to the size of a galaxy, cause time to stand still, and the like. When the Benson gang is

Sphinx

apprehended, Corrigan is offered the option of eternal peace or an eternity of crimefighting on earth. He chooses the latter. The Spectre is permitted to retrieve his body and reanimate it. The hero now inhabits Corrigan's mortal form, emerging as needed. see: **Superman.**

Sphinx, The [M] A creature appearing in several mythologies. In Egypt, the Sphinx is a gracious creature which personifies the food-producing aspects of the earth. She is also the goddess of wisdom, represented as having wings, the head and breasts of a woman, and the body of a lion. She is sometimes pictured with the head of a hawk or jackal. Regardless, a sphinx was located in front of every Egyptian temple. In Greek mythology, the Sphinx is a beast sent by Hera to punish the city of Thebes for its wanton worship of Dionysos. This Sphinx has the head of a woman, the wings of a great bird, and the chest, limbs, and tail of a lion. Its job is to sit on a hill outside the city and pose the following riddle created

Spiderman © *Marvel Comics Grp.*

by the Muses: "Who is it that walks first on four feet, then on two feet, and then on three feet?" All who cannot answer are eaten. Eventually, young Oedipus correctly responds "a man," and the Sphinx is recalled to Olympus (some tales say she flung herself from a cliff and died). see: **Hera; Muses; Olympus.**

Spiderman [C] A popular superhero created by Stan Lee and artist Steve Ditko. Spiderman first appeared in *Amazing Fantasy* #15, August 1962.

The original story tells of how high school student Peter Parker is bitten by a radioactive spider and inherits many of the creature's abilities. He has the proportionate strength of an arachnid, is able to crawl up sheer walls, and develops a "spider sense," a strong intuition which warns him when danger is near. A proficient student of science, Parker designs a web-shooter to complement his abilities, a finger-activated unit which fires a strand, mesh, or blob of strong webbing. He also builds tiny "bugs," tracers in the shape of spiders. When not running around as Spiderman in his red and blue costume, Parker works as a freelance photographer for the *Daily Bugle* newspaper. Nicholas Hammond portrays the New York based wall-crawler in the CBS television series. Among the comic book character's most nefarious foes are Dr. Octopus, the Green Goblin, the Kingpin, and the Vulture. see: **Lee, Stan.**

Spirit, The [C] A hero created by Will Eisner for a weekly seven-page feature in Sunday newspapers. Famous for its cinematic lighting, angles, and atmosphere, the series ran from June 1940 to September 1952. It revolved around the Central City adventures of criminologist Denny Colt. When Colt is thought to have been killed, he keeps up that facade to enable himself to work clandestinely against the forces of evil. Donning a mask, business suit, and trenchcoat, and setting up headquarters in Wildwood Cemetery, he becomes the Spirit. In the course of his many adventures, he battles such foes as Powder Pouf, Mortimer J. Titmouse, Sparrow Fallon, and others. His sidekick is young Ebony White, and his girl friend is lovely Ellen Dolan, the daughter of Police Commissioner Dolan.

Spock, Mr. [TV] An alien being played by Leonard Nimoy and featured in the "Star Trek" television series. Born in the city of ShiKahr on the planet Vulcan, Spock is the first officer and chief science officer of the starship U.S.S. *Enterprise*. Spock looks entirely Vulcan, being humanoid with arched eyebrows, a heart in his lower abdomen, greenish skin—due to his green, copper-based blood—sleeping with his eyes open, having a pulse which throbs 212 times per minute, and boasting sharply pointed ears. However, Spock is a half-breed, the son of the Vulcan Sarek and the human woman Amanda Grayson. His diverse roots are especially evident when Spock tries to be exclusively logical like most Vulcans; once in a while human emotions do creep into his bearing. In common with other Vulcans, however, Spock is extremely powerful. He can also communicate telepathically by touching another being, and has the ability to render humans insensate with the Vulcan nerve pinch. Spock's serial number is S179-276SP and he has been an officer with Star Fleet for eighteen years. Prior to serving with Captain Kirk, he was assigned to the *Enterprise* under the command of Captain Christopher Pike. see: *Enterprise*, **U.S.S.; Kirk, Captain; Sehlat.**

Spriggans [O] The ghosts of English giants. Though usually quite small, spriggans have the ability to grow to the huge size they enjoyed in life. Extremely ugly, they act as servants to fairies and guardians to hidden fairy treasure. Spriggans are also frequently responsible for kidnapping mortal children and leaving changelings in their place. When they have a free moment, spriggans love to work a bad deed or two of their own invention, such as causing foul weather, destroying crops, or stealing from mortals. However, these spirits will rarely hurt a human being. see: **Changeling; Fairy.**

Squarefoot, Jimmy [A] An English monster—a large man with the head of a black pig and the upturned tusks of a boar. In early legends, Jimmy Squarefoot was actually a great swine on whose back sat a giant. As the pig waddled about the land, the giant tossed stones at people—especially at his spouse, with whom he was forever arguing. When the giant's wife finally ran off, the big fellow stopped both throwing rocks and riding Jimmy Squarefoot. He began walking behind the huge swine and, eventually, the two creatures merged into one. Some legends say that Jimmy Squarefoot can change to all-giant or all-pig at will.

Starr, Lucky [L] A space hero created by author Isaac Asimov (writing as Paul French). In the far future of A.D. 6945, when the solar system has been long-colonized, the "tall and rangy" Lucky Starr is a representative of earth's Council of Science. This group is above the government, and its members are identified by special wrist markings—oval spots with yellow stars in the pattern of the constellations Orion and the Big Dipper. The brown-haired, brown-eyed Starr is one of the most powerful members of the Council of Science. Aided by the five-foot two-inch John Bigman Jones, our hero uses the spaceship *Shooting Starr* to battle enemies of earth within and without the solar system. Among the titles in this series of novels are *David Starr, Space Ranger* (1952), *Lucky Starr and the Pirates of the Asteroids* (1953), *Lucky Starr and the Oceans of Venus* (1954), *Lucky Starr and the Big Sun of Mercury* (1956), *Lucky Starr and the Moons of Jupiter* (1957), and *Lucky Starr and the Rings of Saturn* (1958). see: **Asimov, Isaac.**

Steele, Barbara [MP] The queen of the 1960s horror film. Born in Birkenhead, England in 1937, Steele studied dance and acting upon graduating from school. She starred in English stage plays throughout the early and mid-fifties, and made her screen debut in *Bachelor of Hearts* in 1958. Her first horror film was the classic Italian production *Black Sunday* (1960), in which Steele played a vampire-witch. It was followed by *The Pit and the Pendulum* (1961), *The Horrible Dr. Hichcock* (1962), *The Ghost of Dr. Hichcock* (1965), *Terror Creatures from the Grave* (1965), *Nightmare Castle* (1965), and *The Crimson Cult* (1968) co-starring Boris Karloff and Christopher Lee. Steele still makes a movie every now and then, such as *Pretty Baby* in 1978, though few are in the fantasy milieu. see: **Karloff, Boris; Lee, Christopher.**

Stone, Jabez [L] Satan's victim in the classic short story "The Devil and Daniel Webster" by Stephen Vincent Benét (1898–1943). Stone lives in Cross Corners, New Hampshire, and is rather unlucky at farming. With his family starving, he says that he'll sell his soul to the Devil for other than ill luck. The next day, a dark-suited gentleman with pointed teeth arrives. He presents Stone with a contract, and the farmer signs in blood—his soul in exchange for seven years of good fortune. Stone prospers, and after six years he is visited by the Devil. The Dark Lord is out collecting other souls—they look like little moths—and stops to remind Stone to ready his. The frightened man gets a three year extension, but realizes that a good lawyer would be even better still. Thus, he contacts Daniel Webster (1782–1852) who takes the case.

When the time comes for the Devil—called—Scratch—to collect his fee, Webster meets him at Stone's home and requests a trial. Scratch agrees, summoning twelve evil men from his realm, including the pirate Teach and the strangler Reverend John Smeet. Presiding is the long-dead witchfinder Justice Hathorne of Salem. Upon their arrival, the room fills with "the blue mist of evil." But Webster is not deterred. He speaks to them about Stone's failings and needs, the wants of all people, and asks if damnation is a proper way to deal with these. The specters identify with Stone, and find against the Devil. As terrorist-juror Walter Butler points out, "Perhaps 'tis not strictly in accordance with the evidence, but even the damned may salute the eloquence of Mr. Webster." The ghosts leave in a puff of smoke and, for losing, Scratch must do as Webster bids. The defense attorney forces him to draw up a paper promising never again to bother Stone or any one else from New Hampshire, then orders the Devil out.

Benét's sequel to this tale, "Daniel Webster and the Sea Serpent," never achieved the recognition of its predecessor. see: **Devil.**

Strange, Adam [C] A comic book hero who first appeared in *Mystery in Space* #53, August 1959. Created by writer Gardner Fox and artist Carmine Infantino, Adam Strange is an earth scientist who is hit by a Zeta Beam and transported to the planet Rann in the Alpha Centauri galaxy. There he falls in love with the raven-haired beauty Alanna, dons a red and white suit and crash helmet, and becomes a rocket-powered superhero. Adam's beat is the entire universe, which he protects from evil both human and alien.

Strangelove, Dr. [MP] The somewhat manic German genius played by Peter Sellers in Stanley Kubrick's *Dr. Strangelove or How I Learned to Stop Worrying and Love the Bomb* (1964). A man who is known personally to very few people, scientist Strangelove holds considerable sway with the defense policies formulated by President Merkin Muffley. A cynical man, Strangelove is bitter over the fact that he is bound to a wheelchair—an unfortunate result of the British bombing of Peenemünde where he was working on V-2 rockets. The raid also cost him his right hand, its prosthetic replacement always sheathed within a black glove and frequently jerking out of control. The scientist wears bifocals and speaks with great precision. He is busy plotting the relocation of himself and other high government officials to mine shafts when World War III breaks out destroying their plan—along with the rest of humankind.

Stymphalian Birds [M] The subjects of the fourth labor of Hercules. The Stymphalian Birds are creatures whose wings, beaks, and claws are made of brass (some stories say iron). Raised by Ares, they dwell in the swamp near Lake Stymphalis and eat human flesh. There are so many of these birds that when they take to the air the land is darkened by their shadow. They can fire their feathers like arrows. Hercules' task is to rid Arcadia of these frightful animals. Hiding beneath his impenetrable lion skin, the Greek hero sneaks into the marshland. Shaking a brass rattle given to him by Athena, Hercules drives the birds into the air. As each animal rises, the adventurer unquivers an arrow and kills it. see: **Ares; Athena; Hercules.**

Styx [M] The eldest daughter of Oceanus and the Greek goddess of the river which bears her name and circles Hades. All who enter the region of the dead—Erebus as opposed to Tartarus, the deeper part—must first cross these waters. Styx is the river by which the gods swear great oaths. Breaking such a vow, a god must repent by lying still for a year, neither speaking nor being attended by other deities. It is in the Styx that Achilles is dipped by his sea-goddess mother Thetis. The hero is thereby made invulnerable—except in the heel by which she holds him, and through which he is ultimately slain. see: **Hades; Tartarus.**

Submariner [C] A comic book character, created by Bill Everett, who first appeared in *Marvel Comics* #1, November 1939. The Submariner is Prince Namor, an undersea monarch with green trunks, upswept eyebrows, pointed ears, and wings on his feet. The son of an American sailor and Princess Fen of sunken Atlantis, he possesses great might, has the ability to fly, and can communicate with fish. Harboring a great hatred for surface dwellers and their pollution of land and sea alike, he wages unofficial war with all of humankind. The traditional foe of this watery antihero is the fiery Human Torch, an artificial man who can turn his body into a mass of flame.

Today, a somewhat reformed Submariner is a member of the Invaders, a group of superheroes who battle wrongdoers. His peers in this justice league are the Human Torch and Captain America. see: **Aquaman; Captain America.**

Superchicken [TV] A mighty pullet of television cartoons. In his secret identity, our hero is wealthy playchick Henry Cabot Henhouse III. However, when his lion aide, Fred, serves him his supersauce, the frail Henhouse metamorphoses into the caped, plume-hatted, sword-swinging, superpowered Superchicken. Soaring through the skies in his eggshaped Supercoop, the fearless foul engages such foes as the Zipper, Dr. Gizmo, the Oyster, and the Noodle. Among the crimes he foils are the theft of Rhode Island and the winterizing of India by sending all of its elephants to the equator. Created by Jay Ward, Superchicken clucks in triumph after each victory, and is constantly reminding the nonsuper, oft-beleaguered Fred, "You knew the job was dangerous when you took it!"

Superchicken

© *Jay Ward Productions*

Superman [C] The first comic book superhero. Superman was created by writer Jerry Siegel and artist Joe Shuster, and premiered in *Action Comics* #1, June 1938. On his native world Krypton, Superman is Kal-el, the son of scientist Jor-el and his wife, Lara. When Jor-el discovers that Krypton is soon to explode, he places his infant son in a rocket and sends him hurtling to earth. On our world, Kal-el is discovered and adopted by Jonathan and Martha Kent. Away from the red sun of Krypton, and subject to the less inhibitive properties of earth's yellow sun, Kal-el becomes superstrong, incredibly swift, able to fly, and nearly invincible. Among his lesser powers are X-ray, micro-, and heat vision, extremely sensitive hearing, and the like.

Posing as mild-natured Clark Kent, Kal-el grows to manhood and takes a job with the *Daily Planet*, a newspaper based in the city of Metropolis. His boss is editor Perry White, and his friends are reporter Lois Lane and Jimmy Olsen. Working for the tabloid keeps Kent in touch with fast-breaking news, and allows him to save lives as Superman. In this identity, he wears a red, yellow, and blue uniform and a red cape made from the invulnerable blankets in which he was swaddled by Lara. The costume was knit by Martha Kent, the threads cut by her boy's heat vision. In addition to natural catastrophes, Superman faces a variety of recurring foes, from the scientific genius Lex Luthor to the fifth dimensional imp Mr. Mxyzptlk, to the Bizarro Superman, to the brilliant green-skinned Brainiac. The Man of Steel is vulnerable only to the rays of a red sun, to magic, and to kryptonite. This latter is a variety of irradiated fragments from his home world. They come in five colors: green, which can kill Superman; red, which causes weird and unpredictable effects; gold, which will permanently rob our hero of his powers; blue, to which only Bizarro creatures are susceptible; and white, which affects only vegetation. Superman has a secret hideaway called the Fortress of Solitude, located in the Arctic, which is also used by the two other superbeings from Krypton: Krypto, a dog Jor-el had sent to earth in an experimental craft; and Superman's cousin Kara, also known as Supergirl, whose family had survived in a domed section of Krypton which had been blasted into space.

Superman has appeared in every medium, from comic strips to novels. On the radio he was impersonated by Bud Collyer; Kirk Alyn portrayed the alien being in the screen series *Superman* (1948) and *Atom Man vs. Superman* (1950); George Reeves was television's Superman from 1953 to 1957; Bob Holliday starred in the moderately successful Broadway musical *It's a Bird, It's a Plane, It's Superman;* and Christopher Reeve played the Man of Steel in the 1978 film *Superman.* see: **Bizarro; Mxyzptlk, Mr.**

Sylph [F] A delicate, slender female sprite alleged to inhabit the air, with origins in Greek mythology. The sylph's counterparts in the other three elements that were once thought to make up the physical world are the female salamanders who live in fire; the earth-dwelling gnomes; and the water lassies called nymphs. The term sylph was coined by the alchemist Paracelsus, and comes from the word sylvan which describes any denizen of the forest. see: **Gnome; Nymph; Paracelsus; Salamander.**

Symplegades [M] The Clashing Islands of Greek mythology. Huge cliffs made of rock, they crush to pieces any boat or being caught between them. The Symplegades are best known for their role in the saga of Jason. In exchange for ridding the seer Phineus of the wicked harpies, Jason is rewarded with a clue on how to pass safely through the islands. Releasing a dove, Jason watches as it darts unscathed between the peaks. This tells him just how much time he has to make the passage. Driving the Argonauts to ply their oars, he rushes his vessel from one side of the Symplegades to the other before they close in. Once Jason has made the passage, the Clashing Islands are thereafter tamed. In the Ray Harryhausen film *Jason and the Argonauts* (1963), Jason tosses a charm belonging to Phineus into the water. Moments later the sea god Triton rises and holds the cliffs apart. See: **Harpy; Harryhausen, Ray.**

T

Tai-Yo-Al-La-Ne [M] Thunder Mountain in an old Zuni myth. Long ago, these North American Indians were a cruel people. Warnings from the gods proved fruitless, so the deities sent two great floods. One came from above and one from below (and are residual today in the form of rain and rivers), forcing the Zunis to flee to the peaks of Tai-yo-al-la-ne. The waters kept rising and, though the priests prayed for an end to the flood, their chants went unheard. Finally, the gods told the Chief of the Priests that only the Zunis' repentance and the sacrifice of the fairest maiden and choicest brave would assuage their anger. The couple was found, tossed into the waters, and the deluge ceased. After many weeks, the ground was dry once more.

Talbot, Lawrence [MP] The mortal identity of the Wolfman, played by Lon Chaney Jr. We first meet Talbot in *The Wolfman* (1941) as he returns to Talbot Castle in Wales after an eighteen-year tour of the United States. When he is bitten by a werewolf—the hirsute, quadrupedal form of a gypsy played by Bela Lugosi—Talbot becomes the shaggy Wolfman. Stalking on two legs after human flesh whenever the moon is full, he is vulnerable only to silver. Talbot is destroyed by his father, John, who beats him to death with a silverheaded cane. In *Frankenstein Meets the Wolfman* (1943) Talbot is revived when his body is struck by moonlight. He perishes in a flood only to return in *House of Frankenstein* (1944), where he is thawed from a block of ice and eventually done-in with a silver bullet. In *House of Dracula* (1945) he inexplicably returns and is *cured* of his affliction—although Talbot is once again accursed in *Abbott and Costello Meet Frankenstein* (1947). When last seen, he is plummeting from a terrace into the ocean. see: **Chaney, Lon Jr.; Dracula; Frankenstein; Werewolf.**

Talos [M] A bronze man of Greek mythology. Built by Hephaestus at the order of Zeus, Talos is a gift to King Minos of Crete. Invulnerable save for a vein in his ankle, Talos sits within a fire, becomes red-hot, then cordially greets sailors. By embracing them, the bronze figure burns them to death. When not sitting in flame, Talos strides about Crete, crossing it twice a

Talos

268

year. Talos is destroyed when he pursues Jason; the hero's lover, Medea, implores spirits of the underworld to steer the man of bronze toward a rock. Scraping his ankle, Talos bleeds to death. In the Ray Harryhausen picture *Jason and the Argonauts* (1963), Talos is pictured as the six hundred-foot-tall guardian of the treasure of the gods. When Hercules steals a huge broach pin to use as a javelin, Talos comes to life and destroys the *Argo*. Jason stops the marauder by loosening a plug in his heel and draining the giant's ichor. see: **Hephaestus; Hercules; Jason; Olympus.**

Tane [M] The god of light and of the forest in New Zealand Maori mythology. Tane is one of four sons of the sky, Rangi, and the earth, Papa. His brothers are the god of war, Tu, the god of farming, Rongo, and the god of sea beasts, Tangaroa. Unfortunately, when the four gods are born none can move, since Rangi and his wife are still coupled. Tu tries to slash a path to freedom but fails. So Tane puts his shoulders against the ground and his feet to the sky and pushes them apart. Then he mixes clay with the blood of Ranti, drawn by Tu's blade, and forms the woman Hine-ahu-one. They make love and produce a daughter named Hine Titama, whom Tane marries. The pair has many children. However, when Hine Titama learns that her husband is also her father, she is repulsed. The girl flees to Papa far underground; since then all humans have paid for Tane's sin by following her in death.

Tangor [L] The hero of Edgar Rice Burroughs' 1940s science fiction novelettes "Beyond the Farthest Star" and "Tangor Returns"—both published in book form as *Tales of Three Planets* (1964). Tangor is an earthperson, although his terrestrial name is never revealed. After being shot in the heart during a World War II dogfight, the pilot is mysteriously transported to the relatively modern planet Paloda. There, he takes the name *Tangor*, which means "from nowhere," and finds himself right in the middle of a century-old war. He sides with the people of Unis in their battle against the dictatorial state of Kapara.

Paloda is but one of eleven worlds circling the sun Omos. The others are Antos, Rovos, Vanada, Sanada, Uvala, Zandar, Wunos, Banos, Yonda, and Tonos. All are in roughly the same orbit and share a single doughnut-shaped ring of atmosphere. Unlike Burroughs' earlier heroes, Tangor detests war. This attitude no doubt reflects the author's own sentiments about the World War being waged at the time. see: **Burroughs, Edgar Rice.**

Tantalus [M] The King of Corinth (some tales say Phrygia) and one of the great losers in Greek mythology. The husband of Dione, daughter of Atlas, Tantalus is the father of Pelops, King of Pisa. Possessing a warped sense of curiosity, Tantalus dices and cooks his son and serves him to the gods. Why? To see whether they can distinguish between human and animal meat. At his great feast, the deities push away their plates—all save Demeter, who is still in a daze from the loss of Persephone. The goddess eats a shoulder before she realizes what's been served. Hermes rebuilds the lad and restores his life; Demeter replaces the consumed shoulder with one of ivory. This replacement has the ability to heal the wounds or sickness of anyone who touches it. As for Tantalus, he is sent to Hades and there cursed with constant thirst and hunger. The king is placed in the middle of a lake, where the waters withdraw whenever he stoops to drink. Nearby are delicious fruits, budded from trees the branches of which withdraw whenever Tantalus reaches for them. Suspended over his head is a huge rock which ever threatens to crush the sadistic monarch. It is from Tantalus' troubles that we get the word *tanta-lize.* see: **Demeter; Hermes.**

Tara [L] The daughter of John Carter and Dejah Thoris in Edgar Rice Burroughs' Barsoom series. With the beauty of her mother and the tenacity of her father, Tara is introduced in *The Chessmen of Mars.* This novel finds her captured by the kaldanes of Bantoom, creatures whose heads can separate from their bodies. Escaping with the help of the brave Gahan and the kaldane Ghek, Tara goes on to enjoy many other adventures. Jed (prince) Gahan of Gathol eventually marries Tara and they have a daughter, Llana. Tara's brother is Carthoris. see: **Barsoom; Burroughs, Edgar Rice; Carter, John; Carthoris; Thoris, Dejah.**

Tarans [O] In Scotland, the ghosts of babies who died before they could be baptized. Also known as Spunkies, they are destined to wander the earth until Judgment Day. They can be saved only if an aged fisher blesses a pail of water, makes a cross in the air, and says, "I christen you John if a boy, and Jean if a girl." When not hovering about piers searching for salvation, Tarans can be found flitting about the forest and other isolated places, not quite understanding what has happened to them. Sometimes they can be heard to wail in tiny, pain-filled voices. They are truly among the most tragic of all spirits.

Tarantula, The [C/MP] A comic book hero created by writer Michael Fleisher and artist Pat Boyette. The Tarantula is actually Count Eugene Lycosa, the eleventh in his line to inherit the curse of a cult of spider worshippers. The curse has its roots in the Dark Ages, when an earlier Lycosa had ended the evildoers' devilish cult. Now Eugene suffers by becoming a green, humanoid tarantula whenever he is enraged. However, Lycosa has turned the bane into an asset by working with the police to hunt down criminals—whom he subsequently devours.

The Tarantula is also the subject of a 1955 film entitled *The Tarantula,* in which a mad scientist creates a 100-foot-tall spider that ravages the southwestern United States before being fire-bombed to death.

Tarot [O] The predecessor of contemporary playing cards, and an ancient form of fortunetelling. The seventy-eight cards are divided into two *arcanas,* the major with twenty-two cards and the minor having fifty-six. The minor arcana is subdivided into four suits: wands (modern-day clubs), swords (spades), cups (hearts), and money (diamonds). Each suit is composed of ten numbered cards, from ace through ten, with four court cards—a king, queen, knight, and page. The cards in the major arcana are numbered from one through twenty-one and are decorated with characters representing the elements, virtues, vices, nature, etc. The twenty-second card in the major arcana is the madman (our current joker) and is not numbered. Tarot

Taran

cards were first introduced in Italy during the twilight of the fourteenth century, probably brought from the Far East by Crusaders. see: **Divination.**

Tarzan [L] Edgar Rice Burroughs' classic jungle hero. Tarzan is actually John Clayton, Lord Greystoke. His father, John, and his mother, Alice, had set sail from England in May of 1888. Put ashore in Africa by a mutinous crew, the Claytons live bare, primitive lives. Alice dies shortly after John is born, and the elder Lord Greystoke is killed when their little hut is attacked by apes. However, the she-ape Kala has recently lost her child and takes the human baby as her own. Young Tarzan (which means "white skin") is reared as an ape. However, he finds books in the cabin and teaches himself to read. Years pass, and history repeats itself when a rebellious crew puts Professor Archimedes Q. Porter, his daughter, Jane, and their associates ashore. Tarzan falls in love with the lovely girl from Baltimore, and the two eventually wed. Although Tarzan makes frequent trips to Europe—he speaks English, French, German, and many other tongues, and is a member of the House of Lords—he spends most of his time on their plantation in Africa. Tarzan and Jane have a son, Jack (also known as Korak).

The first Tarzan novel, *Tarzan of the Apes,* was Burroughs' second novel. It was published in 1912, followed one year later by *The Return of Tarzan.* Burroughs wrote twenty-four Tarzan novels in all, as well as two novels for children. In addition to a TV series starring Ron Ely, a long-lived comic strip, and hundreds of coloring books, puzzles, games, and the like, there have been nearly forty Tarzan films. Among the actors who have starred as the screen ape man are Elmo Lincoln, Jock Mahoney, P. Dempsey Tabler, Buster Crabbe, Lex Barker, Gordon Scott, Mike Henry, and Johnny Weissmuller. see: **Burroughs, Edgar Rice; Korak; Opar; Scott, Gordon.**

Teenie Weenies [C] Little people created in 1914 by William Donahey for his newspaper comic feature "The Teenie Weenies." It was Donahey's desire to present a meaningful fantasy strip for children, rather than the sight gags which abounded in other features. Thus, his characters were placed in situations with which readers could identify: celebrating holidays, skipping school, making a meal, and the like. Among the characters he introduced were the four-inch-tall giant Paddy Pinn, the Poet, the Old Soldier, the Clown, the Dunce, the Scotchman, Grampa, and others—including mice, rabbits, and animals which appear giant to the Teenie Weenies. Donahey's efforts were manifest not in a comic strip, per se, but one illustration accompanied by several paragraphs of copy. "The Teenie Weenies" was finally discontinued in 1969.

Terrible Wild Monster [F] A creature who lurked outside of Jerusalem in the early 1700s. With the head of a lion, a beak like an eagle, elephant's

Terrible Wild Monster

ears, sharp teeth, and a four-foot-long scorpion's tail, the Terrible Wild Monster was as large as a horse and covered with scales made of mother-of-pearl. Wings, a spiny ridge along its back, and mighty talons completed the portrait. Born from the blood of people who had been murdered nearby, and powered by their spirits, the Terrible Wild Beast perpetuated itself by drinking the blood of people, horses, and cattle in the Forest Mountain region. Its average tally was fifty killings per month. Finally, in 1725, a bold warrior was able to run his lance down the creature's throat.

Tezcatlipoca [M] The Aztec god of the wind and air who later became the chief deity. Capable of being either good or evil, Tezcatlipoca both gives and takes away the breath of life. One-legged, from the time the gates of the underworld had snapped shut on him, Tezcatlipoca carries a great, burnished shield which allows him to see what mortals are up to. A rival of Quetzlcoatl, whom he vanquishes with magic, Tezcatlipoca also controls the weather, and thus the fate of the all-important Aztec agriculture. see: **Quetzlcoatl.**

Thanator [L] The setting of Lin Carter's Jandar novels. Known as Jupiter's moon Callisto to earth scientists, Thanator is not unlike earth in many ways. Though its skies are amber due to a golden mist which infuses its atmosphere, its gravity is only slightly less than that of our own world, and the climate is generally temperate. Thanator is inhabited by humanlike beings—people with a sophisticated culture which includes such verse dramas as *Parkand and Ylidore.* Geographically, the globe has two poles, between which are such landmarks as the great sea Corund Laj, the smaller sea Sanmur Laj, the plains of Haratha, the White Mountains, the Grand Kumala, and so forth. Only in its secondary life forms is Thanator truly unusual. Roaming the world's red grasses are creatures like the dragon-cat or yathrib, the seven-foot-tall mantis people known as yathoon, the wingless bird-horse called thaptor, the two-foot-long red-furred tiger or deltagar, and the flying reptile known as zell. see: **Carter, Lin; Jandar.**

Thark [L] Green giants in Edgar Rice Burroughs' Barsoom novels. Standing from twelve to fifteen feet tall, the olive-skinned Tharks have four arms, two legs, no hair, a pair of upturned tusks, two independently working eyes, antennalike ears, a love of war, and a deep hatred of all other beings. The two notable exceptions to the traditional Thark aggression are John Carter's allies Tars Tarkas and Sola. Thark is also the name of the land ruled by these green people. Most of this territory is desert sandwiched between a pair of fertile bands. The approximate population of Thark is thirty thousand, which is distributed among twenty-five separate villages. Thark is also the name of an ancient Barsoomian seaport. The mortal enemies of the Tharks are the savage green Warhoons. see: **Barsoom; Burroughs, Edgar Rice; Carter, John; Sola.**

Therns [L] White-skinned priests of Issus on Edgar Rice Burroughs' Barsoom. The Therns are descended from the Orovars, the former rulers of the planet and a very advanced people. Their main stronghold is within and upon the Otz Mountains. However, the Therns have temples in a great many of the world's major cities, since most Barsoomians hold Issus sacred. Indeed, when the 1,000 year lifespan of each Barsoomian is nearly over, she or he sails down the River of Iss to what they believe is heaven. What *really* awaits them is death or enslavement at the hands of monsters or the Therns—the latter believing that only they are fit for heaven. But the joke is on the priests, for it turns out that

Issus is not a goddess but a bald, old hag. The leader of the Therns is the Holy Hekkador Matai Shang. see: **Barsoom; Burroughs, Edgar Rice.**

Theseus [M] A historic Greek hero born in Argolis, the son of King Aegeus and Queen Aethra of Athens. Although Theseus is best known for his slaying of the Minotaur, his life is woven through with bold deeds. As a youth, he slays Periphates (also known as Corynetes), the monstrous son of Hephaestus, and keeps his iron club as a souvenir. Bitten by the bug of righteousness, Theseus goes on to kill Poseidon's son Sinis, whose hobby is tearing people apart; the mad sow Phaea; and Sciron, a thief who feeds his victims to an enormous tortoise. Seeking to end the sacrifices made to the Minotaur, he also ventures to Crete, does away with the man-bull, and flees with King Minos' daughter Ariadne. But Theseus proves a fickle lover. When Ariadne becomes seasick he strands her on the island of Naxos—where she dies awaiting his return. The hero goes on to serve with the Argonauts and journeys with Hercules to the land of the Amazons. There he weds Antiope, the sister of Queen Hippolyte. Other adventures carry Theseus to hell, see him marry Ariadne's sister Phaedra, and have him kidnapping Helen of Troy years before she becomes the spark which ignites the Trojan War. Theseus is eventually slain by Lycomedes, king of the Dolopians, who dumps the hero's body into the sea. However, Theseus' spirit returns whenever his good right arm is needed by his people. Most notably, he was seen leading Athenian soldiers against the Persians at the Battle of Marathon in 490 B.C. see: **Amazons; Argonauts; Hephaestus; Hercules; Minotaur; Poseidon.**

Third Eye [O] A psychic organ located in the forehead. Though the Third Eye is more developed in some people than in others, we all have the capacity to use it as a tool of unspoken communication and as a window into the spirit world. According to many scholars, the Third Eye is actually one with the pineal body, a vestigial sensory organ situated in the brain of all vertebrates. Some even believe that it is the home of the human soul, though this is disputed by those who believe that the soul, if it exists, is not an eye but an exact duplicate of the mortal body.

Thirteen [O] An unlucky number. The number thirteen is actually a two-pronged threat. Because there are twelve months in a year, twelve hours in the day and twelve in the night, and twelve items per dozen, thirteen is deemed beyond completeness, more than the proper parameters and therefore unlucky. It was also the number of people who sat down to the Last Supper—one of the less fortunate events in history. Today, when thirteen people gather round a table, the first or last person to rise will die within the year—not unlike Judas, who was the first to leave Jesus' side. Adding to the contamination of thirteen is the fact that twelve witches and the devil usually attend a coven. These notions are crystalized in the concept of the Baker's Dozen: thirteen objects which, in truth, have nothing to do with confections. It is actually the Boucca's Dozen, boucca being an obsolete term for a ghost. The only time thirteen is lucky is when one views it as the Trinity added to the Ten Commandments. see: **Coven.**

Thoat [L] A Barsoomian mount created by author Edgar Rice Burroughs. The gray-skinned, white-bellied thoat boasts eight legs; has a flat tail that tapers toward the animal; possesses a thick neck and a massive slash of a mouth; has padded, yellow feet whose toes lack nails; and wears shiny, hairless skin. Thoats can live for long periods without water, most of which they get from feeding on Barsoomian mosses. Though the rider uses a saddle, the beast is guided telepathically. The largest thoats, standing ten feet tall at the shoulder, are ridden by the green giants of Barsoom. Red people ride smaller, horse-sized thoats, while nobles move about on an albino strain. In some parts of Barsoom, thoats are raised for food. see: **Barsoom; Burroughs, Edgar Rice.**

Tholians [TV] Especially bizarre creatures seen in the "Star Trek" episode "The Tholian Web." Red and gold creatures with a crystalline structure and diamondlike eyes, the Tholians use their spaceships to weave a web around the U.S.S. *Enterprise.* The cause of this action is the invasion of Tholian space by the *Enterprise,* which is on a mission to aid the Federation vessel *Defiant.* The Tholian leader, Loskene, claims the *Enterprise* in the name of the Assembly, the Tholian government. However, Captain Kirk and his crew are able to sneak the starship into a space warp and away from the Tholians. see: *Enterprise,* **U.S.S.; Federation; Kirk, Captain.**

Thongor [L] A popular sword and sorcery hero created by author Lin Carter. A warrior of Lemuria, Thongor has golden eyes, bronzed skin, and long black hair. Born in the year 6982 (circa 493,000 B.Ç.) to Thumithar of the Black Hawk people, Thongor becomes a nomadic adventurer at the age of seventeen. Eventually, this youth from Valkarth in the Northlands rises to Lord of the Three Cities and ruler of Lemuria. His wife is the beautiful Princess Sumia, by whom he has a son, Thar.

In addition to many human foes Thongor faces in this civilization founded by the children of Nemedis, there are many breeds of monsters extant. Included in their number are the

long, killer worm or xuth; the black-furred lion or vandar; the rhinoceros-like beast of burden or zamph; and the twenty-foot-long zemadar, the most feared creature in Lemuria, with three rows of foot-long fangs, poison saliva, and red skin. Only in its yellow eyes is the zemadar vulnerable.

Among the many novels featuring Thongor are *Thongor and the Wizard of Lemuria* (1965), *Thongor and the Dragon City* (1966), *Thongor Against the Gods* (1967), *Thongor in the City of Magicians* (1968), *Thongor at the End of Time* (1968), and *Thongor and the Pirates of Tarakus* (1970). see: **Carter, Lin.**

Thor [M] The Norse god of thunder and war, whose bequest to the modern world is the name for Thursday. A simple, often abrasive god whose red beard symbolizes lightning, Thor is second in power and authority only to Odin, the king of the gods. The son of said ruler and the mountain goddess Jord (also known as Fjorgyn), Thor is

Thor

an ally to mortals and a brave warrior. His weapons in peace and war include the magic hammer Mjölnir, a belt which doubles his power, and a goat-drawn chariot which carries him from his palace, Bilskirnir, to the scene of a battle. Thor's most famous fight is his struggle with the giant Hrungnir, whose heart and head are made of stone. After the giant's defeat, his rocky members fall on Thor and pin him; only the thunder god's son, Magni, is able to move them. During Ragnarok, the altercation which destroys the Norse gods, Thor is slain by Thiassi, the god of winter. Most accounts refer to Thor's wife as Sif, although the golden-haired giantess Jarnsaxa is also sometimes mentioned.

In the top-selling comic book *The Mighty Thor,* the god is shown as having blond hair and a secret mortal identity of Dr. Don Blake. This inventive restructuring of mythology was the work of writer Stan Lee and artists Larry Leiber and Jack Kirby. see: **Lee, Stan; Kirby, Jack; Odin.**

Thoris, Dejah [L] The wife of John Carter of Mars and princess of Helium. Dejah Thoris is the daughter of Jed (King) Mors Kajak of Lesser Helium, and the granddaughter of Jeddak (Emperor) Tardos Mor of the nation of Helium—Helium being both the nation and a capital city thereof, consisting of Greater and Lesser Helium, two walled divisions seventy-five miles apart. Hers is a royal line which spans 10,000 rulers reaching back to the building of the very first Martian canal. Like most humanoid Martians, Dejah Thoris is oviparous rather than viviparous. Since humans are constantly on the move, nature made them egg-layers as an alternative to carrying around the extra weight of a growing fetus. Dejah Thoris is the mother of Tara and Carthoris, and the grandmother of Llana. see: **Barsoom; Burroughs, Edgar Rice; Carter, John; Carthoris; Tara.**

Thoth [M] The secretary of the Egyptian underworld. When the newly dead come before the god Osiris, it is the job of Thoth to weigh their souls, record their worth, and then pass them on to Osiris for judgment. As secondary duties, Thoth is god of the moon and a great magician. Indeed, it was he who helped Isis raise her husband Osiris from the dead, using his far-reaching occult abilities. This grim deity is pictured as having a human body with the head and beak of the storklike ibis. see: **Isis; Osiris.**

Thoth

Thumbelina [FT] Also known as Inchelina, a character from the imagination of Hans Christian Andersen. Wishing for a child, an old woman gives a witch twelve pennies in exchange for a grain of barley. She plants it, and from the seed blooms red and yellow petals with Thumbelina sitting inside. Because the girl is only inches tall, her excited mother is able to make her a cradle from a walnut shell and a small lake from a bowl of water. However, the old woman's happiness is short-lived because Thumbelina is abducted by a toad who wants her to marry his son. Escaping on a raft made from a leaf, Thumbelina is again kidnapped, this time by a May bug. Happily, the insect lets her go when its fellows complain, "no antennae and a thin waist, how disgusting!" Thumbelina lives alone in the forest, surviving the summer and fall without hardship. But the winter proves harsh, so she moves in with a field mouse, keeping its hole tidy in return for shelter. In time, the girl becomes engaged to a mole whom she does not love, and rescues a swallow who has been smitten by winter's icy breath. When the swallow's health returns, it spirits the girl away from unwanted matrimony and brings her to the ruins of an ancient temple. There she finds flowers inhabited by tiny, nearly transparent winged beings. One of these sprites, the King of the Flowers, asks Thumbelina to become his wife. She accepts, is given the new name Maja, and spends the rest of her days in contentment. see: **Andersen, Hans Christian; Tom Thumb.**

Thunderbird [M] A figure of American Indian mythology. Named Wauhkeon by the Dakota Indians, the thunderbird is quite huge, the flashing of its eyes causing lightning, its wings flapping thunder, and its cry summoning the rain. Wauhkeon is perpetually at odds with Unktahe, the god of the waters and a practitioner of witchcraft. The weather changes as the pendulum of victory swings from one god to the other. The thunderbird is frequently impersonated by Indians in religious ceremonies.

Tiana [L] The Highrider of Reme, a lady pirate created in 1978 by authors Andrew J. Offutt and Richard K. Lyon. The illegitimate daughter of a duke, she is captain of the plundering vessel *Vixen*. Not averse to using her exquisite body to distract enemies in battle or influence their opinions in private, the red-haired lass is equally proficient with a sword. Her foster father is named Caranga and her cat is Rarn. Among Tiana's opponents in the War of the Wizards trilogy is Lamia; a giant bat; murderous plants; and sundry sorcerers and demons.

Tiger-lily [L] A character in Lewis Carrol's *Through the Looking Glass.* Tiger-lily dwells in the Garden of Live Flowers, which is visited by heroine Alice. As the young girl quickly learns, these flowers can talk—but only "when there's anybody worth talking to." Nor will they speak unless first addressed, since it isn't polite. The Tiger-lily is the first to talk to Alice, followed by a rose and a very nasty violet in a conversation riddled with insights into the life of flora. For example, Alice learns that in times of danger a tree can bark "bough-wough" and that daisies are the rudest of all flowers, talking on and on. The Tiger-lily also explains that the only reason she is so astute is because the ground in which she's planted is so hard. If it were soft, she would fall asleep and miss a great deal. After listening to dubious counsel and a great deal of bickering between the blossoms, Alice moves on. see: **Alice.**

Tigerman [C] A superhero created by writer Gabe Levy and artist Ernie Colon. Tigerman first appeared in *Thrilling Adventure Stories* #1, February 1975. In his nonheroic identity, Tigerman is physician Lancaster Hill. Working in Zambia, he spends his spare time performing harmless experiments on a tiger from India. His preoccupation is in isolating the chromosomes which make the creature so fleet and powerful. Accomplishing this, Hill injects himself with the animal's essence. Later, when the tiger breaks loose, the doctor is able to kill it bare-handedly. He realizes that he has inherited the senses, speed, and strength of a tiger and decides to use his powers to fight crime. Presented with the tiger's skin, a gift from the local chieftain Jnuka, Hill dons a tiger mask and metal claws to make the disguise complete. Returning to the United States, he joins the staff of Harlem Hospital in New York and subdues wrongdoers in his spare time.

Tir Nan Og [F] The Land of Beauty in Celtic lore, thought by many scholars to be that culture's vision of heaven. Located to the west of the sea, it is a place where time stands still; where there is perpetual sunshine, music, and festivals; where fruit, drink, and meat is bountiful; and where warriors can struggle to their hearts' desire. Anyone who is slain in battle returns to life the following day. People who go to Tir Nan Og and elect to leave are not permitted to discuss what they have seen with anyone. If they do, the time they spent in this paradise—be it a day or a century—catches up with them in an instant. Some peoples referred to Scathach as the counterpart of Tir Nan Og, a place of darkness, pestilence, and famine.

Titans [M] The offspring of Uranus and Gaea. Originally, there were only twelve Titans. Led by Cronus and his sister-wife, Rhea—the youngest of their breed—they are Oceanus the sea, and the oldest of the Titans; Tethys the provider; Coeus and Phoebe, the lights of dusk; Creus, the power of the ocean; Iapetus, the creator of humankind and the father of Atlas and Prometheus; Themis, the mother of the Hours and the mistress of law and justice; Mnemosyne or memory, the mother of the Muses; Hyperion, an early sun god; and Hyperion's sister-wife, Thea. The number of Titans grew over the years to encompass many of the descendants of these divine beings. Many of these revered figures participate in a ten-year war against Cronus' son Zeus and his army of giants and cyclopes. The prize: supremacy over all of creation. Zeus wins, and most of the Titans are banished to Tartarus (some stories say they are sent to England). The word *Titan* is taken to mean "achiever or exerter," which these ill-fated Greek figures surely are. see: **Atlas; Cronus; Cyclops; Gaea; Muses; Rhea; Zeus.**

Tlaloc [M] The Aztec god of thunder and rain. Tlaloc is married to the Emerald Lady Chalchihuitlicue, with whom he parented the clouds. They live together in Tlalocan, the Aztec Paradise, to which only victims of drowning or lightning go and dwell in perpetual bliss. People who die of other causes are sent to the black and unpleasant Tlalxicco, where the afterlife is without pleasure or purpose. This dreary realm is ruled by Mictlan, the god of death.

Tobor [MP] One of the first movie robots, the star of the 1954 motion picture *Tobor the Great.* Invented by Dr. Nordstrom (Taylor Holmes), Tobor is designed to respond to telepathic impulses. What's more, the mechanical being has emotions! Tobor is particularly fond of its creator's grandson Gadge (Billy Chapman). Built to help the American space program—its artificial body able to withstand the rigors of interstellar travel—Tobor is sidetracked when he rescues Gadge and Dr. Nordstrom from foreign spies. In the end, the ten-foot-tall Tobor does indeed pilot a jet plane beyond the stratosphere.

Tolkien, J. R. R. [L] One of the world's most respected fantasy authors. Born John Ronald Reuel Tolkien in Bloemfontain, South Africa in 1892, Tolkien moved with his family to England four years later. In due course, he graduated from Oxford, married Edith Bratt, served in the military, and in 1921 went to work as a professor at the University of Leeds. Then, inspired by Scandinavian lore and by the conviction that fairy tales are really written for adults, he began penning *The Hobbit.* This saga of dwarfs, heroism, friendship, and simple pleasures was published in 1938 with Tolkien's own illustrations. His other major works are the *Lord of the Rings* trilogy—consisting of *The Fellowship of the Ring* (1954), *The Two Towers* (1954), and *The Return of the*

King (1955), 600,000 words in all—
and *The Silmarillion* (1977), which
was edited by the author's son Christopher. Other books include *Farmer
Giles of Ham* (1949), *The Adventures
of Tom Bombadil* (1962), and *Smith of
Wootton Major* (1967). Tolkien died in
1973. His other children are Michael,
Priscilla, and John. see: **Hobbit; One
Ring; Silmaril.**

Tom Thumb [FT] The hero of the
Grimm Brothers' "Tom Thumb" and
"Tom Thumb's Travels." Born to a
woodcutter and his wife, Tom is "perfect in all his limbs, but no bigger than
a thumb." In "Tom Thumb," two
greedy men see Tom directing his father's horse by sitting in the animal's
ear. They make a deal to buy the lad
for a while. However, once the trio
has journeyed some way, the impish
Tom flees into a mouse hole. After a
subsequent tilt with a pair of thieves,
Tom is swallowed by a cow. He cries
out, the cow is thought to be enchanted, and the beast is butchered.
But the stomach is tossed aside, Tom
is locked within, and is eaten by a
wolf. The lad calls to the carnivore
and says that in exchange for his freedom he'll lead him to a great store of
food. The wolf agrees and Tom takes
him to his father's house, where the
canine is slain.

By the time of "Tom Thumb's
Travels," the tiny man has become a
tailor. Deciding to see the world, he
joins a band of thugs who are planning
to rob the king. Tom crawls through
the treasury keyhole and helps with
the crime, then takes his share and
strikes out on his own. Unable to find
work as a tailor, he takes a job at an
inn. There, the maids and servants
come to hate Tom because he can see
all that they do. They feed him to a
cow, but Tom eventually emerges
from a pie made of the animal's meat.
Leaving the inn he is gobbled up by a
fox, promises the Reynard his father's
hens for his freedom—and, surprisingly, keeps his bargain!

Older versions of Tom Thumb
make the little man a creation of
Merlin the Magician and place him in
the court of King Arthur. Given
amazing powers by fairies, Tom can
suspend pots from sunbeams and survive without food. Russ Tamblyn
played Tom in George Pal's 1958 film.
see: **Arthur, King; Grimm, Jakob and
Wilhelm; Merlin; Pal, George;
Thumbelina.**

Topper, Cosmo [L/MP/TV] A proper
English gentleman who is bothered by
ghosts. Created by novelist Throne
Smith, banker Cosmo Topper earned
his greatest fame as the haunted hero
of three films and a television series.
In *Topper* (1937), we see how a young
husband and wife and their dog are
killed in an automobile accident. Sur-
facing as ghosts, they must remain on
earth until they have done someone a
good turn. They choose Topper, much
to his chagrin. The spectral young
woman is still with him in *Topper
Takes a Trip* (1938), and a new spirit
assists the henpecked mortal in *Topper Returns* (1941). Roland Young
played Topper in all three films. On
television, Leo G. Carroll essayed the
part, haunted by the ectoplasmic remains of George and Marion Kirby
and the St. Bernard, Neil. This time,
an avalanche in the Swiss Alps was responsible for dropping spooks on Topper's doorstep. see: **Ghost.**

Totem [F] An Algonquin word which
means "brother." Totem was a term
directed at any animal or product of
nature which the Indians construed as
a benefactor. The tribe would take the
object's name as its own, and thus be
entitled to its protection and guidance.
This was especially the case with
Indians of the Northwest, who went
so far as to carve these guardians'
likenesses into wood or sometimes
stone. These large icons, with several
figures often posed one atop the other,
are called *totem poles.* see: **Mascot.**

Tourneur, Jacques [MP] A revered
director of fantasy films. The son of
noted moviemaker Maurice Tourneur

Triffid Totem

(1876–1961) and actress Van Doren, Jacques was born in Paris in 1904. Moving to California in 1913, he worked for his father, went back to Europe to direct, then returned to the United States in the mid-thirties. Jacques' first assignment at the helm of a motion picture was the 1931 French film *Tout Ca ne Vaut Pas L'amour.* His first American film was *They All Come Out* in 1939. However, Tourneur is best known for his classic horror-trio made under the aegis of producer Val Lewton: *The Cat People* (1942), *I Walked with a Zombie* (1943), and *The Leopard Man* (1943). All are famous for their subtle depiction of terror rather than literal presentation of grisly horror. Later Tourneur works include the brilliant *Curse of the Demon* (1958), *Comedy of Terrors* (1963), and *War Gods of the Deep* (1965). see: **Lewton, Val; Lorre, Peter; Price, Vincent.**

Toves [L] Creatures in Lewis Carroll's poem "Jabberwocky." According to fanciful-animal expert Humpty Dumpty, "toves are something like badgers—they're something like lizards—and they're something like corkscrews." They make their nests under sundials and subsist on cheese. "Jabberwocky" describes them as "slithy," which Dumpty defines as "lithe and slimy." Toves are four-legged—though they can walk on two—possess a long tail, can use their trunk to drill into the ground, and have a thick mane. see: **Alice; Humpty Dumpty; Jabberwock.**

Transparent Apple [FT] A fantastic fruit in the Russian fairy tale "The Silver Saucer and the Transparent Apple." The merchant father of Little Stupid honors his daughter's request and brings her a transparent apple and a silver saucer from the market. Placing the fruit in the dish, the girl spins it and asks to see Moscow and the Czar therein. The apple obliges, fanning the jealousy of Little Stupid's sisters; they had asked for nothing more than a necklace and a new dress. When Little Stupid refuses to trade her treasure, the girls axe her to death and bury her in the forest. They tell their father that she was eaten by a wolf. Much to the girls' annoyance, the saddened man reacts by locking away the apple and saucer "in memory of my poor little daughter."

Months later, a shepherd finds a reed growing from Little Stupid's grave. He makes a flute from the reed, and when the instrument is played it sings the story of the girl's murder. The shepherd plays the flute for Little Stupid's father, and it explains that only water from the well of the Czar can restore the victim. The merchant hurries to court and the Czar agrees to lend out his water. A pailful is poured over Little Stupid's grave and, sure enough, within moments she has clawed from within. The reunited family is called to the palace, where the Czar falls in love with Little Stupid and makes her his wife. At the request of the new Czaritza, her devious sisters are pardoned. see: **Singing Bone, The.**

Tribbles [TV] Aliens created by writer David Gerrold for the television series "Star Trek." Small, furry, pastel-colored creatures, tribbles squirm along on their belly with constricting, wormlike motions. Their gentle purring is quite relaxing to humans and other beings, although they screech whenever a Klingon approaches. The dislike is mutual. Tribbles reproduce rapidly, giving merchant Cyrano Jones a great many to sell in the live-action episode "The Trouble with Tribbles," and causing problems on the U.S.S. *Enterprise* in the animated segment "More Tribbles, More Troubles." see: *Enterprise*, **U.S.S.; Klingons.**

Triffid [L] Giant plants committed to world conquest, created by author John Wyndham for his 1951 novel *The Day of the Triffids.* After a shower of comet debris blinds most of the earth's population, a curious form of plant life begins creeping about our planet. According to sighted hero William Masen, no one paid any attention to the triffids when they first appeared. The plants took root in gardens and in the wild, the result of what Masen refers to as "accidental biological meddlings." They grew from seven to ten feet in height and proved to be extremely sensitive to nearby movement. Following the comet disaster they began to move, walking "like a man on crutches" via three blunt root-legs—hence the "tri" prefix. The triffid body proper consists of a straight stem, a funnellike cup on top, leathery green leaves, and stinger tentacles which whip out with lethal results. These appendages kill or welt any human they touch. Carnivorous creatures, the triffids are equally at home eating insects or people. Fortunately, the plants can be destroyed by fire, and at the end of the novel humankind is struggling toward reci-

vilization, flamethrowers in hand. Wyndham's chilling monsters were brought to the screen in the 1962 motion picture *The Day of the Triffids.*

Troglodyte [MP] A generic term for a cave-dweller or hermit, used specifically as the name of two different movie monsters. In the 1970 motion picture *Trog,* Joe Cornelius played a short, powerful, apish figure frozen since the Ice Age. Revived, his mind probed by an anthropologist (played by Joan Crawford), he finds it difficult to adjust to the twentieth century. After committing several murders and sundry acts of mayhem, the prehistoric man is sealed inside a cave. In Ray Harryhausen's 1977 release *Sinbad and the Eye of the Tiger,* a ten-foot-tall, inarticulate troglodyte joins the Arabian adventurer in his quest for a mystic pyramid. The horned, club-carrying giant dies battling a sabre-tooth tiger. see: **Harryhausen, Ray.**

Trolls [F] Primarily Scandinavian beings, alternately identified with giants (in their most ancient form) or dwarfs (a more modern guise). As

Troll

giants, they guard treasure, have the capacity to change their shape, and are regarded as figures of fertility. As dwarfs, trolls are roughly human-sized, hunchbacked with red hair and misshapen features. They wear dark clothing and a bright red cap, and generally dwell in caves, hills, or even human abodes. Their favorite pastimes are dancing, stealing, and leaving changelings in the place of mortal babies. Possessing supernatural powers, most trolls are more mischievous than evil. An exception are certain fairy tale trolls, such as the multi-headed creatures in the saga "Soria Moria Castle." On June 28 of each year, St. John's Eve, trolls venture forth in their greatest numbers. see: **Changeling; Dwarf.**

True Thomas [F] The hero of a fourteenth century romance and ballad. The story of True Thomas is based on the alleged experiences of the thirteenth century prophet Thomas Rymour. Lying on a grassy bank one day, Thomas is visited by "a ladie gay" astride a milk-white steed. She is dressed in grass-green silk and fifty-nine silver bells hang from her horse's mane. The woman introduces herself as the Queen of Elfland, and asks Thomas to serve her for seven years. He accepts her offer and climbs on her horse. The couple rides for forty days and nights until they reach a beautiful garden before the gates of Elfland. Here, Thomas goes to pluck a fruit—but is stopped by the queen's admonition that "all the plagues in Hell light on that fruit." After seven years of devoted service, Thomas is returned to earth, a seer.

Tweedledum and Tweedledee [L] "They were standing under a tree, each with an arm round the other's neck. . . . " It is in such a posture that Alice first encounters Tweedledum and Tweedledee in Lewis Carroll's *Through the Looking Glass.* Fat little men who remind Alice of "a couple of

great schoolboys," the twins have an annoying habit of each presenting a point-of-view opposite from the other. After a while they begin to dance and tell Alice a very long poem. Actually, all the girl had required was directions out of the wood—but she is forced to listen to the woeful saga of "The Walrus and the Carpenter," the story of how the titular characters lure a clutch of trotting oysters to their death. Following the poem, Tweedledum and Tweedledee explain to Alice why they dare not wake the sleeping red king—they are all a part of his dream and would vanish—after which the twins argue over a toy rattle. They elect to settle the dispute in combat, and Alice helps dress them in armor made of blankets, saucepans, rugs, and coal scuttles. As the twins prepare to do battle, Tweedledum brandishing a sword and Tweedledee an umbrella, a monster crow appears and the portly pair runs off. see: **Alice.**

Twilight Zone, The [TV] A fantasy series which ran for five seasons on CBS television. Created by Rod Serling, "The Twilight Zone" premiered in 1959 with the episode "Where Is Everybody?" During the course of its run, the program dealt with such diverse subjects as devils, aliens, magic, angels, nightmares, and hallucinations—a bevy of topics which won host and frequent writer Serling three Emmy awards. Other writers included Charles Beaumont and Richard Matheson. Among the many fine guest stars were Gig Young, Cliff Robertson, Robert Redford (as Death!), Earl Holliman, Buster Keaton, Ed Wynn, William Shatner, Ida Lupino, Burgess Meredith, and Martin Balsam. There are 151 episodes of "The Twilight Zone," 18 of which—the entire fourth season—ran for one hour. see: **Matheson, Richard; Serling, Rod.**

Twitchett, Old Mother [FT] A fairy tale figure described in the following rhyme:

Old Mother Twitchett,
She had but one eye,
And a long tail which she let fly.
Every time she went over a gap
She left a piece of her tail
in the trap.

As the ditty implies, Old Mother Twitchett is the personification of a needle. She appears in the lore of many lands: in Haiti she is described as "very small, but she makes the length of the President"; in Yugoslavia she sings, "The farther I go the shorter my tail"; and in Turkey she is referred to as "a little naked creature who dresses others." Regarding which came first, the needle or the Twitchett, it was the former. Early needles looked something like human figures, with a slender body and a "face." A prick from Old Mother Twitchett is said to cause warts to vanish, while carrying her on your person will bring good luck.

Typhon [M] One of the most famous giants in Greek mythology. The son of Tartarus and Gaea, he is a grotesque, red-eyed brute with a loud, rattling voice and the heads of 100 snakes budded from his lower quarters. Married to Echidna, the daughter of the winged horse Chrysaor, Typhon is the father of the Hydra, the multi-headed dogs Cerberus and Orthos, the Nemean Lion, the Sphinx, and the Chimera. His most famous role in mythology is his battle with Zeus. After the king of the gods has defeated the Titans in battle, Gaea convinces Typhon to try and overthrow him. Zeus and the giant meet in Syria, where Typhon moves close to his foe and traps him in the mesh of snakes. Then, grabbing a sickle, he cuts the muscles from Zeus' hands and feet, wraps them in a bearskin, and leaves them in the care of the dragon Delphyne. But faithful Hermes finds the parcel and returns it to Zeus. The angry lord of Olympus corners Typhon and throws Mt. Aetna on top of him—where the giant occasionally makes his presence known by spitting forth the fires of indignation. see: **Cerberus; Chimera; Gaea; Hermes; Hydra; Nemean Lion; Orthos; Sphinx; Tartarus; Zeus.**

Uffington White Horse [F] A mysterious design etched on Dragon Hill in Berkshire, England. Cut through the surface to underlying strata, the "horse" is 2,000 years old and lies near the spot where St. George slew the dragon. It is thought that the figure—which some insist is a dragon and not a horse—was carved by blood drawn from the monster. One section is particularly barren, the eye of the creature, where if a person stands and makes a wish it will come true. see: **George, St.**

UFO [U] An Unidentified Flying Object, referred to in the vernacular as a "flying saucer." UFOs became preeminent in the public mind on June 24, 1947. On that date Kenneth Arnold, piloting his private plane, saw nine disklike objects over the skies of Washington. Arnold described them as saucers, and a reporter covering the story coined the term *flying saucer*. Not that this was the first sighting of a UFO. Columbus saw one during a voyage to America, and sightings have been reported in every succeeding century. Arnold's encounter merely brought

UFO

UFOs to the fore, an awareness enhanced by the Air Force's UFO research program Project Bluebook, begun in 1948, ended in 1969, and stocked with 13,000 individual entries. Motion pictures such as *Earth vs. the Flying Saucers* (1956), *The UFO Incident* (1975), and *Close Encounters of the Third Kind* (1977) have also done their part to fire the imagination.

Today, the study of UFOs is something of a calculable science. There are categories of contact: a Close Encounter of the First Kind is a sighting at close range, usually from a few hundred feet away; a Close Encounter of the Second Kind is a sighting followed by the discovery of physical evidence, such as marks on the ground or charred earth; a Close Encounter of the Third Kind is seeing or contacting the occupants of a UFO; and a Close Encounter of the Fourth Kind is a journey on an alien vessel. The fact that an object is a UFO does not automatically make it a flying saucer. As contrasted with an IFO, an Identified Flying Object, it merely merits further study.

Ulios [L] The hero of Edmond Hamilton's genuinely bizarre 1935 short story "The Vengeance of Ulios." The greatest scientist in all of ancient Atlantis, Ulios is also the Guardian of the Force, a rod which taps the power of the volcanic fires beneath the continent. The middle-aged Ulios has recently developed a technique of transplanting the human brain, and his wife Etain asks him to put her brain into a more youthful body. Her husband refuses. However, Ulios' sly aide, Karnath, agrees to perform the operation if the woman will run off with him. She agrees, and the two depart in a flyer—unleashing the full power of the Force before they go. Ulios and his servant Sthan set off in pursuit just as the Force causes Atlantis to sink. Thus begins a chase which lasts for centuries. Karnath and Etain constantly place their brains in fresh bodies, as do Ulios and Sthan who have a devil of a time keeping track of them. Our heroes follow their foes through Egypt, Babylon, Rome, France of the Revolution, London during the Blitz—where Sthan is killed by a sniper—and finally to New York of the 1960s. There, Ulios traces the billionaire Karnath to a luxurious penthouse and heaves him from a window. Then, with a divine streak of sadism, our hero takes poison and leaves his once-beloved Etain to mourn for this, her final life. see: **Atlantis.**

Ultraman [TV] A superhero created for Japanese television. In the twenty-first century, the aircraft of Science Patrol member Iota is struck by a vessel from Nebula M-78 in the Fortieth Galaxy. Iota dies—but the alien visitor Ultraman revives him by merging their bodies. Everafter, Iota can become Ultraman merely by exposing the alien's cylindrical Beta Capsule. However, the flying giant can only surface for a short while. A flashing light on his red, blue, and silver costume signifies when his stay is near its end. Ultraman's first foe was the monster Bemla, who has been followed by a parade of city-destroying brutes.

Umkovu [O] A hideous creature of African lore. A servant of the supernatural, the umkovu is traditionally a corpse revived by witches to serve as their familiars. They are the principal reason that darkness is a time of evil. Stirring from their mistress' abode, they work spells or feed poison to enemies. After performing their nefarious deeds, they scream and yell horribly. Umkovu are also thought of as spirits who cause strong winds and destructive storms. see: **Witch; Zombie.**

Underdog [TV] A cartoon superhero created in 1964 for NBC television. Dressed in a red shirt with a large "U" monogram, black boots, and a flowing cape, the airborne, superpowered Underdog is actually a mild-mannered shoeshine boy. With his voice provided by Wally Cox, he takes to the skies of Washington, D.C.—usually to rescue TV reporter Sweet Polly Purebred. The floppy-eared Underdog's most formidable foe is the evil scientist Simon Bar Sinister.

Undines [F] Female water sprites of European folklore. Undines are creatures who lack souls, although it is something they can obtain by bearing the child of a mortal man. However, there is danger for the male in this process. If he is in the water with an undine and angers her, she will leave him at once. If the man goes after her, she will kill him. Some people, such as the Finns, believe that undines are water musicians. Humans are able to learn their beautiful melodies by sitting on a rock surrounded by water and tying themselves to the undine. If these bonds are loosely done and the human escapes, he or she becomes an incomparable musician who can force people to dance and make an instrument play by itself, even if it is broken. In some cultures, undines are synonymous with nymphs and merpeople. see: **Merpeople; Nymphs.**

Unicorn [F] Usually pictured as a petite white horse with a lush mane and a coiled horn jutting from its forehead. The unicorn was first mentioned by Ctesias the Greek circa 500 B.C. He described the animal as having white skin, a purple head, solid blue eyes, and an eighteen-inch horn that is white at the root, black in the middle, and red at the top. Pliny the Elder pictured it with a horse's body, a deer's head, the feet of an elephant, a boar's tail, and a yard-long horn. Emotionally, these early unicorns were evil beasts with a piercing whinny and a horrible temper. However, because its beauty was so intense and its horn a cure for disease and poison, its disposition softened. It

Unicorn

gained fame for its paradoxical traits of bravery and shyness and came to be considered the most chaste and gentle of all creatures.

Feeding on dry grass, living for thousands of years, and singing an incredibly melodious tune upon death, the unicorn has but one mortal enemy, the lion. It is the feline's devious way to trick the animal into charging, burying its horn in a tree, and singing helplessly as the lion tears bitter-tasting bites from its bones. In fact, because the unicorn suffers so greatly before all predators—including humans—it has for centuries been the traditional representation of Jesus in art. The only living creature the unicorn will trust implicitly is a virgin. The horned animal recognizes these by the pleasant odor they exude. In China, the unicorn is called Ki-lin and, like the dragon, phoenix, and tortoise, is a figure of good luck. Some five thousand years ago, from the markings on the back of one of his pet unicorns, the emperor Fu Hsi was inspired to create writing. see: **Dragon; Phoenix.**

Uranus [M] The Greek personification of the heavens, known as Coelus to the Romans. The husband and son of Gaea, Uranus fathered the Titans, the cyclopes, and the Hecatoncheires. Alas, so horrified is he by these latter hundred-handed monsters that upon birth he tosses them into Tartarus. This horrifies their mother, Gaea, who talks the Titans into rebelling against their father. Only Oceanus does not partake in the revolution. The youthful Titan Cronus is bold enough to attack his sire's person directly, goring him with a sickle; from the blood which drips upon the earth rises the Furies and giants, and from the drops which fall upon the sea grows Aphrodite. Upon the overthrow of Uranus, the Titans free their brothers and elevate Cronus to supreme ruler of the gods—whereupon he flings his ugly siblings right back into Tartarus. see: **Aphrodite; Cronus; Cyclops; Furies; Gaea; Hecatoncheires; Titans; Tartarus.**

Urisk [F] A hirsute, Scottish imp. Living alone by ponds or inside waterfalls, the urisk is a half-human and half-goat who pleasures in scaring those who

Urisk

move abroad at night. Sometimes identified with both brownies and Roman fauns, the urisk labors by day on human farms, gathering crops and tending livestock. They restrict their movements to certain geographical areas, but can usually be seen in Perthshire, Scotland, and other traditional homesteads throughout that country. see: **Brownies; Satyr.**

Ursus [L/MP] A mighty hero of literature and film. Ursus first appeared in the novel and film versions of *Quo Vadis?*, a companion to the trouble-plagued heroine Lygia. Described as "tall and broadshouldered," his most impressive feat of strength is barehandedly killing a bull and rescuing his charge, who has been lashed naked to a stake. On the screen, there has been a series of Italian-made films based loosely on this character from the work of Polish author Henryk Sienkiewicz. Among their titles are *Ursus in the Valley of the Lions* (1961) starring Ed Fury, *Ursus in the Land of Fire* (1963) also starring Fury, *Hercules, Samson, Maciste, and Ursus* (1964), and its sequel *Battle of the Giants* (1966). A 1973 novel entitled *Ursus of Ultima Thule* by Avram Davidson has a more ancient Ursus moving through a sword and sorcery adventure set in the Arctic long before it was covered with ice. see: **Hercules; Maciste.**

Usher, Roderick [L] The doomed hero of Edgar Allan Poe's 1839 short story "The Fall of the House of Usher." Usher is a long-time friend of the tale's narrator. After a lengthy period during which the men were out of touch, Usher writes and asks his friend to come by. The narrator makes the journey and is shocked to find his host dramatically changed, "wan . . . cadaverous of complexion; an eye large, liquid and luminous beyond comparison; lips somewhat thin and very pallid." Usher's skin is ghastly white, his hair unkempt, and his spirits on-edge. There is something in the offing. During the course of the narrator's stay, Usher's sister, Madeline, wastes away. Roderick and his guest place her body in the vault, soon after which her brother becomes hysterical—and with good reason. The corpse of Madeline, bloody from clawing at her tomb—had she been buried comatose?—appears at the door. She grabs her brother and bears him dead to the floor. The narrator screams and prudently flees—moments before a storm brings down the house. In the 1960 film *The House of Usher*, the tormented Roderick was played by Vincent Price. see: **Poe, Edgar Allan; Price, Vincent.**

Ushnishaltatapatra [F] A Bodhisattva, a world savior whose very being is wisdom and who stands on the verge of becoming a Buddha. As a rule, a Bodhisattva has a purple and gold body and is dressed in 8,000 rays which represent the perfect state of beauty. The palms of this gold-faced entity are colored with the dyes of 500 lotuses, each fingertip bears 84,000 signet marks, each of these marks is composed of 84,000 colors, and each color radiates 84,000 beams which touch all things in heaven and earth. Ushnishaltatapatra is slightly different from the run-of-the-mill Bodhisattva, having 117 heads which are symbolic of her influence in various levels of existence. In her left hand she holds the protective World Umbrella, and in her right hand the Wheel of Law. To one day become a Buddha—like the original Buddha (566–489 B.C.), founder of Buddhism—Ushnishaltatapatra must, like any Bodhisattva, first reach complete enlightenment.

Utnapishtim [L] The ancestor of Gilgamesh, and a blessed being who now "shares unending life with the gods." When Gilgamesh decides to learn the secret of eternal life, he sets out to consult Utnapishtim. Locating the Sea of Death, Gilgamesh is borne across by Utnapishtim's ferrier, Ur-Shanabi. Entering Paradise, our hero locates his ancestor who tells him a pertinent story. It is the tale of the great flood sent by the water god Ea to destroy evil humankind. Only Utnapishtim and his family survived, having built an ark and thereby weathering the seven-day deluge. Ultimately, because they were good people, Utnapishtim and his wife were deified by the earth god Enlil. This explains why *he* is immortal—and why he is not at liberty simply to hand out the boon of unending life. However, Utnapishtim's wife takes pity on Gilgamesh, who is both jealous and angry at the turn of events. She reveals where the adventurer can find the plant of life, and he departs—even though his mission is destined to end in failure. see: **Enkidu; Gilgamesh.**

Valiant, Prince [C] A sword-swinging comic strip hero created in February of 1937 by Hal Foster (1892–). Valiant is the only son of King Aguar of Thule. When Aguar is deposed by the evil Sligon, he and his faithful attendants take refuge in the fens of Great Britain. There, young Valiant has run-ins with dragons, the fairy Morgana, an ogre—whom he bests by posing as a demon—King Arthur, Merlin, Sir Lancelot, and others. Armed with his enchanted blade, the Singing Sword, Valiant becomes a knight in short order. Married to Princess Aleta, our hero has four children. The oldest of these is Arn, the current star of the strip. In the 1954 film *Prince Valiant*, Robert Wagner played the title character.

Valkyries [M] Beautiful Norse women who live in Valhalla, Odin's court and the hall of dead heroes. Thirteen in number, they ride invisibly through the air on majestic horses, observe the progress of battle, and choose which warriors will fall. When their victims die, the armored Valkyries become visible to them, gallop to their side, kiss them, and escort their souls to Valhalla. Here, they are greeted by Bragi, the god of wisdom and poetry, are served endless food and drink by the Valkyries, and are permitted to fight over and over their final struggle, the contest which brought them eternal glory. Formidable fighters themselves, the Valkyries often partake in the matches on earth and in Asgard.

Though the bold warrior-women are permitted to marry, their work is their life, and their spouses are forced to leave them after nine years. see: **Odin.**

Valley Forge [MP] The featured Space Freighter in Douglas Trumbull's dire look at the future, *Silent Running* (1971). Lovingly run by ranger Freeman Lowell (Bruce Dern), the Valley Forge is a vessel on which earth's last remaining trees and plants are kept alive in huge domes. When the leaders of the deflowered earth order Lowell to destroy his precious cargo and return home, he kills his crewmates and, aided by a trio of three-foot-tall robotic Drones, takes the Valley Forge into deep space. When rockets from earth follow the ecologist to Saturn, he decides to leave a dome in the care of the one Drone who has survived the tribulations of space travel. Lowell thereupon jettisons the repository, perishing in the process.

Vampire [O] An occult bloodsucker, one of the walking dead. The notion of drinking blood has long haunted humankind. For thousands of years it was thought that feasting on the blood, flesh, or organs of a respected enemy would transfer his or her attributes to the victor. This practice crossed from reverence to sadism with the gruesome maimings perpetrated by the fifteenth century Prince Vlad Tepes of Transylvania—the model for Dracula—and the draining of virgin blood practiced by the sixteenth century Countess Elizabeth Bathory who bathed in the substance to preserve her youth. Along the way, these brutal habits shaded to the supernatural and emerged as the vampire.

Legend, vampire fiction, and vampire movies have created a wealth of lore surrounding these creatures. In general, they stir only between sundown and sunrise; drink life-giving blood through puncture wounds in the throat; can transform themselves into a bat, wolf, or mist; cast no reflection in mirrors; must retire to a coffin which contains soil from their native land; and can be repelled by a religious symbol, wolfbane, garlic, or a wild rose. Both sunlight and a stake in the heart are fatal to a vampire, although cutting out the fiend's heart and burning its remains will also do the trick. Lesser known legends claim that a vampire caught in a hawthorn bush cannot escape; that vampires sleep with their eyes open and can ride on moonbeams in the form of dust; and that smoking tobacco at a vampire's grave on the anniversary of its demise will prevent it from stirring during the coming year. Anyone who is bitten by a vampire will become one of the undead—unless the wound is immediately purified by a holy icon. (Cf. the recent novel by Anne Rice, *Interview with the Vampire*.) see: **Bathory, Elizabeth; Collins, Barnabas; Dracula; Nosferatu; Vampirella; Varney; Yorga, Count.**

Vampirella [C] A comic book vampiress. Created by author Forrest J. Ackerman and publisher James Warren, Vampirella hails from the planet Drakulon. After feasting on the members of an expedition from earth, she uses their ship to travel to our world. Upon landing, the scantily clad, raven-haired bloodsucker takes a job as assistant to the drunken illusionist Mordecai Pendragon—where her ability to change into a bat is one of the sot's finest "illusions." Occasionally crossing swords with vampire hunter Conrad Van Helsing, Vampirella is deeply in love with his handsome son Adam. Shortly after the debut of *Vampirella* magazine in September 1969, the toothsome lady began taking a blood substitute; this to keep her from putting the bite on too many mortals. Today, Vampirella is something of a superheroine, battling supernatural evil with the aid of Pendragon and her sister Pantha from Drakulon, a girl who has the ability to transform herself into a panther. Six Vampirella novels written by Ron Goulart were published in 1976; a motion picture starring Barbara Leigh was announced but never filmed. see: **Ackerman, Forrest J.; DuBay, W. B. Warren.**

Varan [MP] A mythological lizard-god featured in the 1958 Japanese motion picture *Varan the Unbelievable.* When Commander James Bradley (Myron Healy) arrives in the Japanese Archipelago to head a program of water desalinization, Varan rises from a bottomless lake to halt the project. After trashing most of the countryside, the awesome beast is driven back into the water by a massive dose of the desalinization chemicals. The filmmakers skirt the issue of whether Varan is dead—or merely waiting for a sequel. The froglike giant was called "Baran" in the original Japanese release, and was also able to fly. This latter ability was left on the cutting room floor when the film was tailored for American release.

Varney [L] The vampire featured in Thomas Preskett Prest's massive, 868 page novel *Varney the Vampire or the Feast of Blood* (1847). Written before *Dracula, Varney the Vampire* is the story of Sir Francis Varney. With eyes that resemble "polished tin" and teeth "hideously, glaringly white and fang-like," Varney is so emaciated as to be almost skeletal. After 220 chapters of bloodletting, the fiend dies by tumbling into the yawning crater of Mt. Vesuvius. see: **Dracula; Vampire.**

Vedala [TV] Creatures in the "Jihad" episode of the animated "Star Trek." Instrumental in summoning the U.S.S. *Enterprise* to avert a religious uprising, the Vedala have had the ability to commute through space for longer than most any other race. Bent and catlike, the white-furred beings live inside a silvery green asteroid, which they hollowed out and made capable of supporting life. Very strong, the Vedala can teleport living creatures or other matter across great distances. see: *Enterprise,* **U.S.S.**

Verne, Jules [L] One of the greatest science fiction writers of all time. The son of Pierre and Sophie Verne, Jules-Gabriel was born in Nantes in 1828. Working in the theater and as a stockbroker, he turned to writing in 1851 with the publication of his novella *The Mutineers.* His first science fiction work was another novella, *Doctor Ox's Experiment* which first appeared in 1854. Very concerned about world affairs, a staunch opponent of slavery, and a great fan of technology, Verne used fantastic literature as vehicles for these preoccupations. Among his more popular such works are *Journey to the Centre of the Earth* (1864), *From the Earth to the Moon* (1865)—with its prophetic launch from Florida and landing at sea—*Twenty Thousand Leagues Under the Sea* (1870), and its sequel *Mysterious Island* (1875). Verne married his wife, Honorine, in 1857 and had a son, Michel. He died in 1905. see: *Nautilus;* **Nemo, Captain.**

Viracocha [M] The Mayan god of water and the Universal Father. Viracocha is also one of the more benign and reasonable gods, asking for neither gifts nor sacrifices since, as the lord of all creation, he has everything he needs. In the beginning of time, Viracocha rose from Lake Titicaca and made the sun and the moon. Then he carved human figures from stone and brought them to life. He taught his children how to grow crops, how to pray, and how to nurture a culture—afterwards returning to the waters of Titicaca. He resides there still, occasionally sending forth a bolt of lightning to calm some volatile, potentially dangerous aspect of earth or its weather.

Virgilius [H] A priest of early eighth century Bavaria—though whether or not he was ever ordained remains a question. At a time when St. Boniface was working hard to convert the pagan peoples of this area, Virgilius was busy preaching rather unusual dogma. He maintained that there were people living inside our world, men and women who probably were not descended from Adam. Boniface complained to Pope Zachary, who responded thusly: "If it be true that he teaches that beneath the earth there is another world and other men, excommunicate him." The fate of Virgilius is not known, although some records suggest that he may have changed his name and ultimately become the Bishop of Salzburg.

Viswamitra [M] An incredible yogi of Hindu lore. When King Trisanku decides to try and reach heaven in body as well as in spirit, a horrified priest punishes him by reducing the sinful ruler to the humblest of castes. Looking for someone to vindicate him, the king stumbles across Viswamitra. It so happens the yogi is looking for a challenge worthy of his skills, and agrees not only to restore the king's standing but to send him to heaven as he desires. Viswamitra fasts and meditates for ten days, after which the king begins to rise. Reaching heaven, he is turned away by chief god Indra. Trisanku returns to earth and Viswamitra is outraged. His response is to make *another* heaven for the king—the stars, of which Triskanu is now one, twinkling in the night sky.

Vlad Tepes [H] Vlad the Impaler, a prince of Wallachia (modern-day Romania) and the model for Bram Stoker's Dracula. Born in 1431, the son of Vlad Dracule—a surname which means "Dragon"—Vlad the younger became known as Dracula, the Son of the Dragon. Dracula lived in a castle which bordered Transylvania. Here, tainted by a life of warfare and captivity, the prince treated his subjects and visitors to all manner of torture. His favorite spectacle was impaling people on huge stakes, though he also enjoyed feeding human flesh to guests or spilling blood any way possible. Twice wed—his first wife threw herself from a tower—Dracula fathered a son named Mihnea. The Impaler died in battle in 1476. see: **Dracula.**

Vodyany [F] Undersea imps in Slav lore. Extremely ugly, humanlike creatures, the Vodyany have long green hair, red eyes, weeds tangled about their person, horns on their head, tails, and paws. The males have beards which change color as the moon moves through its phases. The Vodyany dwell at the bottom of ponds and lakes in palaces made of crystal, decorated with treasure gleaned from sunken ships, and lit by a magic stone which shines more brightly than the sun. They keep human souls as slaves, souls which become theirs when they cause a bather, boater, or the like to drown. Enthralled by running water, the Vodyany are fond of destroying dams and causing other similar mischief.

Voltaire, François [L] A brilliant French author. Born in 1694, Voltaire became a writer when his father wished him to become a lawyer. He began attracting attention while he was still in his twenties, although much of it was negative. Because much of his work poked fun at leading figures of his day, Voltaire spent most of his professional life outside of France. He died in Paris in 1778.

Among Voltaire's works with fantasy content are the philosophical tale "Micromegas" (1752), about the titular figure, a young giant from "one of those planets that revolve around the star named Sirius"; "Candide" (1759), which includes a metaphysician hero named Candide, a trip to the wondrous land of El Dorado, and prayers to prevent earthquakes; and "Zadig" (1747), with a basilisk search and hermit-angel. see: **Basilisk; El Dorado.**

Voodoo [O] A branch of the occult with roots in Africa. It was carried to Cuba, Haiti, Trinidad, and Jamaica due to slave trade. The practice of voodoo is controlled by its priests—houngans if male and mambos if female. It is their job to raise zombies, cause injury, cure sickness, commit murder—provided they have the hair, nails, or a skin sample from the would-be victim—fan the flames of love, and otherwise influence human affairs through spells and enchantment. The mambo is also something of a seer. Sitting on a box which contains a snake—symbolizing the spirit of Damballa—she can tell fortunes when the serpent's spirit enters her body. During the course of voodoo rituals, goats and roosters are slain and their blood touched to the

Vodyany

lips of those present, forming a pact with the worshipers. These ceremonies are rather frenetic, pounding drums representing the voices of attending spirits and sexual intercourse frequently capping the event. see: **Zombie.**

Vritra [M] In Hindu folklore the Obstructor, a demon created by an offended priest to destroy the chief god Indra. So huge that the top of its head scrapes the sky, Vritra swallows Indra and turns to bellow at the other gods. When it does so, its quarry darts to freedom. The two battle long and hard, Indra aided by the storm gods Maruts and Rudras. Finally, a stalemate is declared and a bargain struck. Indra agrees not to attack Vritra and the demon promises to leave the gods alone. Vritra adds that Indra must never come at it with any material from which weapons are forged. Indra agrees, but the suspicious demon forgets the powers of a god. As soon as Vritra turns to go, Indra orders the four-handed god Vishnu to become a pillar of magic foam. Attacking the demon, Vishnu smothers it in short order.

Waff [O] A person's ghostly double—with a single-minded mission. The waff is filmy-white and appears when its mortal twin is about to die. At this time, it is seen either by the person or by a close friend. Once a waff comes calling, the only way to stem the coming of death is to yell at the double. Embarrassed that it was unable to strike terror into its companion's heart, the waff will evaporate. It will not reappear for some time thereafter. see: **Doppelgänger.**

Wainamoinen [F] A great Finnish hero. The son of the Sea and of Ilmater, the virgin daughter of the air, Wainamoinen first gains fame by defeating the mighty Youkahainen in battle. As a corollary to the victory, Wainamoinen is promised Youkahainen's sister Aino in marriage. However, she so detests the hero that she runs off, drowning in the process. Her bones become the first reeds, her hair seaweed, and her flesh fish. Mounting an eagle, Wainamoinen flies to Pohjola, the cold country of the north. There he tries to win the Maid of the North by performing great deeds—such as building a magic mill for her mother, Louhi—but the girl chooses Wainamoinen's aide and brother, Ilmarin, instead. As it turns out, the Maid is evil and must be destroyed. But the brothers remain in Pohjola, since the magic mill grinds out sacks of food and gems and has made it a happy land. However, when they try to ···rest it from Louhi's absolute control,

she puts up a fight. The wicked woman steals the sun, the moon, and fire and hides them in a cave guarded by snakes. In short order Wainamoinen locates the cache, slays the serpents, and restores the light of day and night to the world. By this time, Wainamoinen is old. Thus, it is with great joy that he learns of the maiden Marjatta who, after eating cranberries and crawling into a stable, gives birth to a new hero. Wainamoinen sails west in a copper ship, secure that his death will not leave humankind unprotected.

Wand [F] A tool which causes metamorphoses and endows beings or objects with supernatural powers. In fairy lore, a wand has a star on one end and draws its strength from the sun. Using a bloodied knife, the wand is cut at sunrise to tap fresh solar power and is blessed in a highly secretive rite. If it is to be used to cause transformations, the wand is whittled from hazelwood; if for satanic ends, cypress is used. Often, a magnetic tip will be affixed to the wand to focus magnetic energy to work illusions. In medieval times, one of the most practical applications of the magic wand was its ability to paralyze game, specifically rabbits. It is for this reason that contemporary magicians wave a wand to cause hares to appear. The potency of the wand also gave rise to the scepter as a symbol of authority, and the walking stick as representative of power or importance. Because the wand is most effective—and destructive—when aimed directly at an object, society has deemed it rude and threatening to point even a finger at another person.

Whether the wand spawned or was spawned by the *caduceus,* a herald's staff and symbol of importance, is unknown. see: **Magician.**

Wandering Jew [F] The racist saga of a man who mocked Jesus on his way to Calvary. As punishment for his bad taste, the offender was given the name

Buttadeus and made to live through the years, roaming among all people until the day of judgment. At the end of each century Buttadeus falls into a coma from which he awakens a man of thirty—the age of Jesus at the time of his death. However, the lot of the Wandering Jew is not without its good points. He has been gifted with awesome learning and, during his travels, counsels others against sin, cruelty, and poking fun at those who are about to be executed. In different countries the Wandering Jew has an assortment of identities. In Spain he is Juan Espera-en-Dios, in Belgium he is Isaac Laquedem, in France he is Boutedieu, and in Germany he is Ahasuerus the cobbler. Some accounts say that at the time of the crucifixion, he was a servant named Kartaphilos in the employ of Pontius Pilate.

Waterbull [F] A powerful animal who protects the innocent in Wales. The waterbull is born a normal calf. Upon the advice of an old woman, it is locked in a farmer's barn for seven years and fed only the milk of three cows. One day, the farmer's daughter takes the other cattle to the lake to drink. Suddenly, there rises from the waters a handsome young man who asks the girl to comb his hair. As she does so, green weed begins falling from his locks. She runs, and in an instant he has set out after her—in the form of a horse. The steed gains quickly on the girl and before long they are near the farm. The old woman sees what is transpiring and orders the farmer to release the bull. He does so, and the large black beast meets the horse in battle. The next day, the bull is found bloodied and weak on the lakeshore; the horse has vanished. The wounded animal is cared for by the girl's lover and, when its health has returned, it crushes another suitor who has been annoying the farmer's daughter. As a reward for his services, the bull is set free. Today,

the waterbull is said to live in and around Llyn Cowlyd. Waterhorses have been sighted in many lakes throughout the United Kingdom.

Watersprite [FT] A lake fairy in the Grimm Brothers fairy tale which bears its name. When a young brother and sister tumble into a well, they are enslaved by a fairy who dwells in local pools. Fortunately, when Sunday arrives the fairy goes to church and the siblings are able to escape. Pursued by their captor, the girl tosses her hairbrush behind her. In a moment it has become a mountain covered with prickles. The fairy wastes a great deal of time climbing over it, but is soon hot on their trail. So the boy throws his comb between them and it grows into a mountain spoked with teeth. To delay the fairy a third time, the girl heaves her looking-glass at their taskmaster. It explodes into a mountain of glass, too slippery to climb. By the time the fairy returns home, grabs an axe, and shatters the peak, the children have disappeared. This story is most unusual in that fairies are avidly anti-Christian, yet this sprite attends church! see: **Fairies; Grimm, Jakob and Wilhelm.**

Water Wraith [O] A female water demon of Scottish legend. Garbed in green, her skin incredibly withered, the tall, slender Wraith sloshes from a river whenever anyone comes by. She points toward the person, nearly entrancing them with her tormented, perpetual scowl, and orders the victim to move toward the water. If the traveler refuses, the surprisingly powerful Wraith drags them in bodily. The Water Wraith usually appears to those who are on their way home from a pub.

Weird Tales [L] The foremost magazine of fantasy fiction. First published in March 1923 by Jacob Clark Henneberger, it featured most of the field's great names within its pages: H. P. Lovecraft, Ray Bradbury, Clark Ashton Smith, Robert E. Howard, Robert Bloch, August Derleth, Hannes Bok, and many others. *Weird Tales'* first editor was Edwin Baird, who was succeeded after a few issues by Farnsworth Wright. Wright was replaced in 1938 by Dorothy McIlwraith when the magazine was sold, the new editor remaining until *Weird Tales* folded in September 1954. It was revived briefly in 1973 with Sam Moskowitz at the helm. From its inception, *Weird Tales* lost money. But it was kept afloat as a labor of love and offered the finest run of fantastic literature in the history of the genre. see: **Bloch, Robert; Bradbury, Ray; Bok, Hannes; Derleth, August; Howard, Robert E.; Lovecraft, H. P.; Smith, Clark Ashton.**

Wells, H. G. [L] A renowned science fiction author whose fantasy is laced with humanity. Born in Bromley, Kent, in England in 1866, the son of a shopkeeper, Herbert George Wells held positions as a teacher, journalist, and draper's apprentice before publishing a work of philosophy in 1891. His debut as an author of fiction came four years later with the appearance of his novella *The Time Machine.* It was followed by such works as *The Island of Dr. Moreau* (1896), *The Invisible Man* (1897), *War of the Worlds* (1898), *First Men in the Moon* (1901), and his future history *The Shape of Things to Come* (1934). A fan of the novels *Gulliver's Travels* and *Frankenstein,* Wells distinguished himself from his contemporary, Jules Verne, by stating that his writings were not technology-oriented "possibilities of invention and discovery," but "exercises of the imagination." And so they were, placing ordinary people in incredible situations, sprinkling them with his Socialist dogma, and reporting their reactions.

Wells married his second wife Amy Catherine Jane Robbins in 1895 (his first wife was named Isobel) and fa-

thered two sons, Frank and George. His last novel was *Mind at the End of its Tether* published in 1945; he died one year later. see: **Eloi; Griffin, Dr.; Moreau, Dr.; Morlocks; Selenites.**

Werewolf [F] A person who becomes a wolf. For centuries, wolves have been identified with the occult. Why the wolf? Because early civilizations were largely agricultural, and wolves regularly massacred livestock and sheep. They were both feared and respected; the Romans made love charms from their fur—the tail section being especially potent—while later peoples felt that a wolf's head hung from a door protected the house from evil, or that one could become brave by eating the animal's heart. The notion of a person actually becoming a wolf had a twofold origin: in poor diets spawned by wolf predation, resulting in delusions and madness among farmers and peas-

Werewolf

ants; and in religious rites where people dressed in the creature's skin and were mistaken for the bonafide article by casual observers. The mythos of the werewolf became more polished when people recognized that, as the moon controls the ocean's tides, it might also influence the fluids of the human body. Thus, folklorists decided that the full moon perverts the stability of susceptible humans and makes shaggy beasts of them. Some people, such as witches, actually sought the curse of werewolfery—also known as lycanthropy—to better perpetrate evil deeds.

Because the werewolf is so feral and so deeply rooted in the superstitions of most cultures, its presence in fantastic literature has been extremely limited. Too, its habit of rending to pieces humans and animals alike is not the stuff of which light, leisure reading is made. The only classic werewolf novel remains Guy Endore's *The Werewolf of Paris*, published in 1933 and brilliantly filmed in 1962 as *Curse of the Werewolf* starring Oliver Reed in the title role. The werewolf has been far more successful on the movie screen, Henry Hull starring as the first celluloid lycanthrope in *The Werewolf of London* in 1935. He was succeeded by Lon Chaney, Jr., as *The Wolfman* (1941), a creature which appeared in four film sequels. Other hirsute histrionics surfaced in *Werewolf in a Girl's Dormitory* (1961) and *The Boy Who Cried Werewolf* (1973). A 1967 comic book entitled *Werewolf* added a new color to the character, recounting the adventures of black-garbed CIA agent Wiley Wolf—code name Werewolf. see: **Talbot, Lawrence.**

West Drayton Church [O] A London house of worship which has long been haunted by a giant black bird. Originally, the feathered fiend was thought to be the spirit of a vulture. It would hover about the tombs, pecking at them as though trying to nibble on their contents and screeching whenever accosted. However, no one was ever able to lay a hand on the creature without causing it to vanish. Only later was it realized that the bird is probably the ghost of a thief or murderer who was accidentally buried in holy ground, rather than in an unconsecrated grave.

Whale, James [MP] A noted director of horror films. Born July 22, 1896, in Dudley, Staffordshire, England, Whale had an elementary education after which he became a cartoonist for the London periodical *The Bystander.* During World War I he served as a lieutenant in the famous Seventh Worcester Infantry Regiment, later returning to England where he made his first professional stage appearance with the Birmingham Repertory Company in *Abraham Lincoln.* Whale was among the cast members in subsequent productions. Traveling to Hollywood in 1930 to appear in the film version of *Journey's End*—one of the Birmingham plays—he ended up co-directing *Hell's Angels* that same year. Among the genre pictures which followed were *Frankenstein* (1931), *The Old Dark House* (1932), *The Invisible Man* (1933), and *The Bride of Frankenstein* (1935). Whale's film career slowed during World War II, and he died in 1957. His nonhorror screen credits include *Remember Last Night* (1936), *Show Boat* (1937), *The Great Garrick* (1937), *The Man in the Iron Mask* (1939), and *Green Hell* (1940). see: **Karloff, Boris.**

White Apes [L] Powerful denizens of Edgar Rice Burroughs' Mars. Something of a giant albino gorilla, the White Ape is hairless save for a plume of fur on its head. Having the capacity to speak, the ten-to-fifteen-foot-tall brutes have four arms and wear leatherlike harnesses—these, more for decoration than function. The White

Apes inhabit deserted towns over much of the face of Mars. see: **Barsoom; Burroughs, Edgar Rice.**

White Pongo [MP] A white gorilla seen in the 1945 motion picture *White Pongo*. Its black face and paws framed by shaggy white fur, White Pongo possesses what borders on human intelligence. Because of this, the jungle dweller is thought to be the missing link between humankind and the apes, and is hotly pursued by scientists. After snatching one of the female members of the party, and becoming embroiled in a subplot involving secret service agents and a gold mine, White Pongo is finally captured.

White Rabbit [L] A pink-eyed, articulate rabbit featured in Lewis Carroll's *Alice in Wonderland*. The White Rabbit first appears to Alice in a field outside Wonderland. The hare is "splendidly dressed, with a pair of white kid gloves in one hand. . . ." Taking a watch from its waistcoat pocket, it complains, "Oh dear! I shall be too late!" and leaps into a hole beneath a hedge. Alice follows and falls for a very long time. When the girl finally lands, she finds a potion which reduces her to ten inches in height. During Alice's journey through Wonderland, the White Rabbit keeps popping up, hurrying to his unspecified engagement. Eventually, he reaches his destination and serves as a trumpet-tooting herald at the trial of a knave who stole some tarts from the Queen of Hearts. see: **Alice.**

Who, Dr. [TV] A flute-playing time traveler in the British "Dr. Who" television series. Dr. Who is a renegade from the sophisticated alien race called the Time Lords. It is the job of these beings to observe the goings-on throughout the universe. But Dr. Who wants to do more, to right all wrongs. Thus, stealing the time-hopping TARDIS—Time and Relative Dimen-

sion in Space—Dr. Who comes to earth. From this base he battles monsters of many worlds, from the robotic Daleks to the metal-skinned Cybermen to the bulb-headed Sensorites to the grotesque Krotons. Able to renew his body whenever it is struck by sickness or crippled with age, and possessing two hearts plus a body temperature of 60°, Dr. Who is 745 years old. His program is also rather long-lived, thriving since its November 23, 1963 debut and enduring four changes in lead player. The current Dr. Who is Tom Baker; his predecessors were William Hartnell, Patrick Troughton, and Jon Pertwee. In the motion pictures *Dr. Who and the Daleks* (1965) and *Daleks: Invasion Earth 2150 A.D.* (1966), the peacelord was played by Peter Cushing. Dr. Who is the hero of nearly fifty science fiction novels. see; **Cushing, Peter; Cybermen; Daleks; Koura.**

Wieroo [L] A terrible race in Edgar Rice Burroughs' *Out of Time's Abyss*, the concluding volume of his Caprona trilogy. The Wieroo are beings who live on a large island located in the Inland Sea of Caspak. A tainted offshoot of human evolution, the Wieroo enjoy tormenting all other creatures. Completely hairless, these five-to-six-foot-tall people have huge wings, strong talonlike claws, spindly legs, and wear fine togalike robes. Their faces are ever without expression, their features flat, their ears small and flush against the skull, and their heads quite round. It is Burrough's grim opinion that the heartless Wieroo are entities into which we will one day evolve. see: **Burroughs, Edgar Rice; Caprona.**

Wights [F] Ancient protector spirits of Germanic origin. Invisible, save to the eyes of those few mortals whom they trust, the wights live beneath mounds, inside trees, and behind waterfalls. They expect offerings of food to be left beside these places, in exchange for which they venture out and frighten away strangers. If offerings are not received, the wights depart and leave the land to be plundered. The only drawback to their guardianship is that the wights are terrified of ships' mastheads, and are unwilling to meet any vessels on which they are displayed. With the coming of Christianity, illogic deemed the wights pawns of the Devil and they were driven into hiding by sprinklings of holy water.

Will O' the Wisp [F] A flame-carrying spirit who guides people to their demise. Also known as Ignis Fatuus, "the Foolish Fire," Will O' the Wisp is vernacular for Willy and the Wisp, a soul with a magic light. In life, he had been a smith named Will. Will led such a debauched existence that the Devil punished him by condemning the smith to spend eternity on earth with but a coal from his forge to warm him. Greeting lost travelers, he leads them to their death in swamps, although he has also been known to draw them from clifftops. Some legends make Will a bogie with a lan-

Will O' the Wisp

tern, invented to keep children from venturing out at night. Among his other names are Peg-a-Lantern, Dead-candle, and Kitty Candlestick. Today, Will O' the Wisp means any person or thing that misleads us.

Wilson, William [L] A pseudonym for the abrasive narrator of Edgar Allan Poe's frantic short story "William Wilson." When we first meet Wilson—shortly after the events he relates in his chronicle—he lays dying. Domineering and capricious, Wilson is quite young when he first meets a boy who looks exactly like him, dresses in the same clothes, and was even born on the same day in January 1813. Whenever Wilson tries to cheat, bully, or deceive, his double appears to humiliate him and put him in his place. Wilson becomes wealthy as an adult, but no matter where he travels his twin is there to torment him. Finally, at a masked ball in Rome, the narrator encounters his doppelgänger and drags him into a small antechamber. The two men duel with swords, and the eerie duplicate is slain. However, his dying words to Wilson are "In me didst thou exist—and in my death . . . thou has murdered thyself." Poe's moral: lose your conscience and die! see: **Doppelgänger; Poe, Edgar Allan.**

Wind Demon [F] A frightful creature of Russian legend. A dwarfish, ugly man, the Wind Demon delights in whistling, a pastime which produces such strong winds that no one can travel the roads by which he sits. In the Russian motion picture *The Sword and the Dragon* (1956), a Wind Demon is captured by hero Ilya Murometz, who hurls his sword and fells the tree limb on which the hairy imp is sitting. Bringing his prisoner to the halls of Prince Vanda, Murometz commands him to demonstrate his unique talent by whistling at half-strength. Even this soft tune is nearly powerful enough to bring down the palace. see: **Murometz, Ilya.**

Windigo

RF

Windigo [F] Giants of Indian legend. Located primarily in the Northern Great Lakes region, windigos are tall but incredibly thin beings, a state dictated by their bottomless hunger for mortal flesh. They have hearts made of ice and twisted mouths which issue rattling bellows and whistles. A person is changed into a windigo when he or she consumes the meat of a fellow human or becomes lost in the woods. Both circumstances are detested by Indians, and the threat of metamorphosis turned tribe members from cannibalism during winter famine, and forced them to pay attention to where they were wandering when out on a hunt. Nocturnal visits from a windigo and the curse of a shaman are also thought to effect the change. Vomiting was once considered a sign of transformation, at which point a variety of cures was attempted. If these failed, the Indian was immediately hacked to pieces.

Winkle, Rip Van [L] One of the great nappers of all time, and the protago-

nist of Washington Irving's classic short story. Living in a Dutch settlement at the foot of the Catskill Mountains in New York, the good natured Rip is described as a kind neighbor and an obedient if henpecked husband. "The great error in Rip's composition was an insuperable aversion to all kinds of profitable labor." With his farm failing, he spends his time telling ghost stories to local children and playing with his dog, Wolf. One day he goes squirrel-hunting in the mountains and meets a short man "with thick bushy hair and a grizzled beard. His dress was of the antique Dutch fashion." The dwarfish man asks Rip to help him carry some liquor to where his fellows are playing ninepins. Rip does so, and while the little men play Rip drinks from a flagon and falls asleep. He awakens twenty years later, his gun decayed, Wolf gone, and a foot-long beard grown from his chin. Returning to the village, he finds his daughter wed, his wife dead—she expired screaming at a peddler—and the Revolutionary War come and gone. Though his house is in ruins, Rip's contemporaries recognize him and he resettles in the larger, much-changed village. As for the game playing hill people, they are assumed to be either an Indian manitou or the crew of Henry Hudson keeping an eye on their New York valley. see: **Irving, Washington; Manitou.**

Witchcraft [O] A practioner of *witchcraft*. In its first and broadest definition, witchcraft is a celebration of nature and the oldest of all religions. In its more traditional form, it is the use of supernatural powers for personal gain, to bend the will of others, or to honor the Devil. These deeds are done through ritual, and its practitioners are *witches*, a term which derives from the Anglo-Saxon *wicca*. It embraces both men and women, although male witches are sometimes referred to as warlocks.

Originally, witchcraft was merely

an extravagant fertility rite. It was run almost exclusively by women, whose menstrual link with the moon and reproduction gave them a nearly mystical tie with nature. Who better to pray for a good harvest and healthy livestock? However, the boundaries of witchcraft hazed when it occurred to ancient tribes to use these ceremonies to try and disable enemies, communicate with spirits, and influence the course of nature. In time, the witch became identified with evil. Less powerful than magicians, and far less effective than wizards, witches were and remain able to cast potent spells. The power of witchcraft in fairy tales is far greater, the witch being able to change shape and fly. This latter feat is accomplished via broomstick, a domestic article that came to symbolize evil when the home-and-hearth witches themselves made the segue. The notion of riding it is a holdover from the way witches used to straddle it on their way to a coven.

Among the most famous witches in literature are the hags in William Shakespeare's *Macbeth* (1606), the witches in L. Frank Baum's *Oz* novels, and the sundry dark ladies of Grimm fairy tales. see: **Coven; Devil; Familiars; Hansel and Gretel; Magician; Oz; Wizard.**

Witch Balls [O] Round, foul-smelling spheres used by witches to injure people. The size of a chestnut, they are made on Friday the thirteenth with the following delightful ingredients: two legs from a dead spider, the intestines and bladder of a black cat, the toenails of a dead infant, a buzzard's eggs, blood squeezed from a weasel, the tail of a rat, the eye of a fat sow, a wildcat's whiskers, the udder of a cow, the brain of a bat, a toad's foot, hair from the wig of a murdered man, dried dog excrement, and hair from a pig. These items are all smoothed together with human grease and covered with hair from the head of the

Witch

witch making the balls. When the mass is formed, it is flung at an enemy of the witch, causing severe bodily harm. If a witch ball is ever stolen from its maker, the Devil appears and lashes the witch with a whip made from rose thorns. see: **Devil; Witchcraft.**

Witch of Berkley [O] A woman of the Middle Ages who became rich after selling her soul to the Devil. However, the witch soon comes to fear for her comfort in the hereafter. Thus, as she lays dying, she asks some friends to dispose of her in a way calculated to save her soul. They are to place her body within the skin of a stag, lock it in a tomb of stone, seal the door with chains and molten lead, and for three days thereafter have 100 priests chant and pray. This is done, and for the first two nights the ceremony keeps Satan's demons at bay. On the third night, fed up with this double-dealing, the Devil himself appears. Immune to the priests' words, he punches down the door of the church, tears up the lid of the tomb, and makes off with the poor lady's soul. see: **Devil; Witch.**

Wizard [O] A person who has agreed to serve the Devil in exchange for being given demon slaves. The most powerful of all occult mortals, wizards can serve either good (behind the Devil's back) or evil. However, after tasting power, few are the wizards who do not use it for personal gain. Able to alter their shapes, wizards can order fairies as well as demons to do their bidding and read the future by eating certain foods. Though they are on-call for whenever the Devil needs an emissary on earth, most wizards find this a small price to pay for magical abilities that don't require the sacrifice of their souls. see: **Devil; Magician; Witch.**

Wizard Of Id [C] A comic strip character created by artist Brant Parker and writer Johnny Hart (creator of the popular prehistoric strip "B.C." in 1958). "The Wizard of Id" premiered in 1964 with one of the zaniest dramatis personae in the history of the medium. The Wizard himself is a bearded student of evil who is more conned than conjurer. The spirits he summons talk back to him, his articulate mirror is a cynic, and his dragons are sorry specimens indeed. His wife, Blanch, is a big girl who used to be in the army; his ruler, King Id, is a diminutive egomaniac; and the kingdom's foremost knight, Sir Rodney, is a coward. Though the wizard's huge wooden vat is always bubbling, rarely does anything wicked come his way.

Wonder Woman [C] A comic book character who first appeared in *All Star* #8, December 1941. Created by Charles Moulton—the pen name of psychologist William Moulton Marston, who designed the character to showcase his theories of male-female relationships—Wonder Woman is an Amazonian princess. Born to Queen Hippolyte on Paradise Island, a land where men are not permitted, Wonder Woman comes to America to help fight World War II. Abetting her natural super strength and great speed are an invisible robot plane, a golden lasso which compels its prisoner to speak the truth, and bracelets which repel bullets or, if welded together by a male, make a slave of our heroine. Disguised as Diana Prince, Wonder Woman is the best friend of Major Steve Trevor—whose plane crashing on Paradise Island first awakened her to the dire world situation.

Lynda Carter played Wonder Woman in the extremely popular CBS TV series which ran from 1975-1979. see: **Amazons.**

Wonka, Willy [L] The candy manufacturer created by Roald Dahl for his novel *Charlie and the Chocolate Factory*. The Charlie of the title is Charlie Bucket, a poor boy who gets to compete with four other youngsters for ownership of the Chocolate Factory once Wonka retires. His opponents are compulsive eater Augustus Gloop, the bratty Veruca Salt, the gum-chewing Violet Beauregarde, and

Willy Wonka

Mike Teavee whose name says it all. As for Wonka, he is a clever man with bottle green pants, pearly gray gloves, a gold-topped walking stick, a black top hat, and a tail coat of plum-colored velvet. After conducting a lengthy tour of the establishment, the goateed Wonka selects Charlie above the others and gives him the factory —along with its staff of dwarfish Oompa-Loompas from Loompa-land. In the 1971 film *Willy Wonka and the Chocolate Factory*, Wonka was superbly played by Gene Wilder.

Woodengown, Kari [FT] The daughter of a king and the heroine of the Scandinavian fairy tale that bears her name. When the widower king marries, his new queen and her wicked daughter make life miserable for Kari. She is fed little and forced to do all of the dirty work. One day, while she is tending the cattle, a blue bull steps from the herd and says, "In my left ear there lies a cloth." Kari takes the fabric, spreads it, and food appears. When the princess stops losing weight, the queen becomes suspicious. She spies on her stepdaughter and orders the bull to be slain. Kari and the animal flee. Soon they reach a castle. The bull tells her to go to the pigsty, don the wooden gown she will find in the mud, and introduce herself to the prince as Kari Woodengown. She is also to flay the bull, roll its skin into a ball, find a silver leaf, a copper leaf, and a golden apple in the forest, and bury them all beneath a rock. This she does, then enters the castle. Kari gets a job in the kitchen. However, when she wants to impress the prince she sneaks to the rock and taps it. A man crawls from beneath, turns the copper leaf into a dress, whistles up a horse, and presents them to Kari. The prince falls in love with her, and she leaves him with a glove before departing. To no avail the lovesick young man scours his kingdom in search of the glove's mysterious

owner—all the while treating servant Kari like dirt. The second time Kari visits the rock she is given a silver gown, and leaves the prince with her riding whip. Again he is unable to find his beloved. The third time Kari gets a gown of gold and, before departing, leaves her shoe. The prince invites all the maidens in his kingdom to try it on. The daughter of the evil queen slices off her toe to make for a perfect fit—but at their wedding the blood pumping from her foot is a dead giveaway. Finally, Kari tries on the shoe, wears it well, and becomes the prince's bride. see: **Cinderella; Magic Tablecloth.**

Worm of Lambton [F] An English monster. Centuries ago, the young Lambton heir decided to skip church and go fishing. For his indiscretion, the lad is made to hook a small snakelike lizard with nine holes around its mouth. Tossing it in a well, the young man goes off to fight in the Crusades. Over the years the creature becomes a giant which slithers about the countryside

Worm of Lambton

killing livestock with its poison breath. It even turns on Lambton Hall, where it is kept at arm's length by being fed the milk of nine cows daily. Knights come from afar to slay the Worm—but each time they hack it to pieces the segments inexplicably reseal. Finally, the Lambton who hooked it returns home. When he consults a witch, she tells him to attach sharp metal prongs to his armor, lure the monster to the center of a river, slay it, and then kill the next living thing he sees. Failing to do the last will blight his family for nine generations.

The creature is drawn to the middle of the river, is prevented from constricting the lad by the spikes on his armor, and is summarily cut to pieces. Alas, anxious to see how his son has fared, the young man's father hurries to the shore. The hero is unable to murder the elder Lambton, and the worm returns to life—utterly invulnerable for nine generations.

In the lore of Great Britain and Scandinavia, worms are closely allied to dragons and, indeed, the Loch Ness Monster is often described as a worm. It was the job of most monster worms to guard buried treasure. see: **Dragon; Loch Ness Monster.**

Wulver [F] A fearsome looking but surprisingly kind creature of Scottish folklore. Built like a human, it has a wolf's head and sports brown fur all about its body. Dwelling in a cave which it claws in the side of a cliff, the wulver emerges only to fish. Sitting on a rock in the deepest part of a stream or lake, it reaches down and paws its meal from the water. If someone living nearby is especially poor, the beast-being will not hesitate to leave a fish or two on that person's windowsill. Given the bad press enjoyed by most wolves, this creature was doubtless invented to calm blind fear of roaming packs of canines. see: **Werewolf.**

XY

Xenomorph [MP] The protoplasmic alien in the 1953 film version of Ray Bradbury's tale *It Came from Outer Space*, directed by Jack Arnold. When a spaceship crashes on earth, its extraterrestrial passengers impersonate local humans—this to unobtrusively procure the materials needed for the craft's repair. To do so, of course, necessitates imprisoning the originals—a circumstance which eventually comes to the attention of the citizens in the besieged Arizona town. They storm the ship and an intergalactic incident is averted only by the intervention of astronomy buff John Putnam (Richard Carlson) who has deduced just what is going on. Putnam detains the crowd long enough to allow the spaceworthy ship to take off and the missing persons to be returned. In their natural form, the Xenomorphs are horrendous looking, with a small body, an enormous bulbed head, and a single giant eye. see: **Bradbury, Ray.**

X-Men [C] A group of superheroes created by writer Stan Lee and artist Jack Kirby. As originally conceived in September 1963, the X-Men were a group of mutant teenagers. Led by the wheelchair bound Charles Xavier—Professor X—they were Cyclops, whose eyes emit a destructive beam; the Angel, who boasts a majestic pair of wings; Iceman, who can both radiate ice and freeze objects in his vicinity; the Beast, a brutish and powerful man with huge feet; and Marvel Girl, a lass with telekinetic abilities. The roster of X-Men has changed dramatically over the years, and of the original group only Cyclops remains. His coheroes are now the clawed Wolverine, the blue-skinned teleporter Nightcrawler, the sonic-screamer Banshee, the weather-mistress Storm, and the mighty Colossus. see: **Lee, Stan; Kirby, Jack.**

Yallery Brown [F] A fanciful being of English legend. Raising a huge stone one day, farmer Tom Tiver discovers a man the size of an infant. His name is Yallery Brown, and he has incredibly wrinkled skin, golden hair, and a long golden beard. For freeing him, the little man promises to do all of Tom's chores ever after. Yallery Brown cautions that the only time he'll desist is if Tom ever embarrasses him by thanking him. Tom is thrilled with this stroke of good fortune, and his farm prospers. Unfortunately, Tom's huge success causes his neigh-

Yallery Brown

bors to lose business and go broke. Not wishing to make any enemies, Tom thanks Yallery Brown, sacrificing prosperity for fellowship. But the gesture is more costly than Tom could have imagined. Brown accepts the humiliation with a barb of his own: "If I can't help then I'll hinder." Soon thereafter the Tiver farm fails. None of Tom's neighbors offer to assist him and he dies a poor man, plagued by Yallery Brown unto death.

Yara [F] A spirit who murders young men. Taking the form of a beautiful maiden, Yara sits beside a lake and sings an irresistible song. Any young male who hears it and walks toward the siren dies. There is no way to kill Yara, and the only means of avoiding her is to carry a seashell into which the man's lover has crooned a melody. When he sees the she-demon, the would-be victim must clap the shell to his ear or perish. see: **Siren.**

Yellow Bird [FT] In the fairy tale "The Yellow Bird" by the Comte de Caylus, a fairy is punished for malicious mischief by the High Court of Fairyland. Her sentence is to become an animal, and the fairy selects a yellow bird with shining golden feathers. Before long she is captured, put on sale, and purchased by Badi-al-Zaman, a wealthy man from Baghdad, who is intrigued by a legend written under her wings: "He who eats my head will become a king, and he who eats my heart will find one hundred gold pieces under his pillow every morning." Ordering a poor woman to cook the bird, Badi-al-Zaman returns to find that she has innocently fed the heart and head to her two sons, "since these morsels are not generally much esteemed." Badi-al-Zaman dies of frustration. As for the two boys, the one who becomes wealthy is slain by robbers, while his brother proves such a bad ruler that he is assassinated. The expressed moral: "Simple things are more likely to bring you happiness than many things that seem more desirable."

Yena [F] A demon that lives in tombs or tears up graves to feed on corpses. When struck by the mood, it also lures living mortals to it by calling for help in a nearly human voice—after which it eats them. Able to change its sex at will, the yena personifies the inconsistencies in nature. Afraid of dogs, it has the power to quiet and paralyze the animal by running twice around it. Instead of eyes, the yena has a pair of stones set in its head. If these are removed and put in a human's mouth, that person will be able to see into the future. It is thought that the cold eyes and deceptive voice of the hyena first gave rise to the twelfth century tales of the yena.

Yena

Yen-lo-Wang [M] The Chinese god of the dead and the lord of hell. One of a group of mighty deities called the Ten Kings, Yen-lo-Wang decides when and through what means mortals shall die, as well as what fate awaits their souls in the afterlife. Though feared by humans, Wang is not nearly as powerful as many other Chinese gods—such as Sun Hou-Tzu, the king of the monkeys. In a tilt for supremacy, Wang once had Sun kidnapped and brought to hell. Furious, the ape-lord liberated not only himself but the souls of all his followers—Wang's powers proving insufficient to deter him. see: **Hell.**

Yeti [U] A shaggy humanoid said to live in the Himalaya Mountains. The Yeti first became news beyond the range in 1951. At that time, a party scouting routes for the conquest of Mt. Everest by Sir Edmund P. Hillary in 1953 photographed monstrous footprints. Located 18,000 feet up the slope, they were large and five-toed. Was it a set of human tracks that had melted and refrozen? Many scientists said it was—ignoring similar sightings in 1887, 1921, and 1937 among others. The Sherpa natives attributed the prints to a creature they called Yeh-Teh—*yeh* meaning "a rocky place" and *Teh* meaning this animal in particular. Actually, there are two breeds of Teh: the relatively tame Mih-Teh and the larger, predatory Dzu-Teh. Yeh-Teh is the former, Dzu-Teh being described as an enormous bear.

Yeh-Teh—or Yeti, as it became colloquialized—has been seen by many Himalayan expeditions. In general, it is pictured as nearly six feet tall with reddish brown fur. Its head is pointed, it possesses a high voice, and it walks erect except when in a rush. The Yeti's diet consists primarily of rodents and other tiny mountain animals. Few in number and rootless by nature, they are thought to be an offshoot of human evolution ideally adapted for cold mountain life. If they actually exist, these "Abominable Snowmen," as they were nicknamed in the fifties, are probably related to the North America, Sasquatch. see: **Sasquatch.**

Ymir [M/MP] In Norse mythology, the first giant. Ymir is quite an ancient being, having lived in Utgard (also known as Jötunheim) long before the formation of the earth. This evil father of the equally nefarious Frost Giants came into existence shortly after creation itself. From the void there arose the endless depths called Ginungagap, and the land of mist named Niflheim. From Niflheim the twelve frozen rivers flowed; to the south lay Muspelheim, the land of fires and home of warm air. The heated breezes eventually reached and melted the river ice, and from its vapors rose the Frost Maidens, the cow Audhumbla, and Ymir, who suckled on Audhumbla. The steamy waters then produced Odin, Vili, and Ve who slew Ymir after a tremendous battle. The gods used the giant's body to make the earth, his blood the seas, his bones the mountains, his hair the trees, his skull the heavens, and his brain the clouds. From the sweat Ymir produced during his struggle with the gods rose the Frost Giants. All save two were drowned in his spilled blood: a son, Bergelmir, and a daughter, both of whom settled at the end of the world and bred a race of giants.

Ymir is also the name of the Venusian come to earth in Ray Harryhausen's 1957 motion picture *Twenty Million Miles to Earth.* Less than one foot tall when he first arrives, the monster becomes a rampaging giant due to earth's alien atmosphere. The sulfur-eating beast razes much of Rome before being shot from atop the Colosseum. see: **Giants; Harryhausen, Ray; Odin.**

Yorga, Count [MP] A vampire played by Robert Quarry in *Count Yorga, Vampire* (1970) and *The Return of Count Yorga* (1971). A modern-day bloodsucker, Yorga leaves Transylvania and travels via freighter to Los Angeles. There he sets up shop on a large estate. Aided by the hulking Brudah, the pasty-faced seance-conducting Yorga pursues both young men and women to sate his infernal lust. In the first film, Yorga is destroyed by a stake in the heart. In the sequel, set in San Francisco, he perishes after falling from a balcony. see: **Vampire.**

Young, Mighty Joe [MP] A giant gorilla animated by Willis O'Brien and Ray Harryhausen for the 1949 special effects Oscar-winner *Mighty Joe Young.*

When we first meet Joe he is a baby, bought for a flashlight from a pair of natives by youthful Jill Young. The gorilla is raised on her father's African plantation, and obeys Jill (Terry Moore) implicitly. When she whistles the tune "Beautiful Dreamer" he is especially calm. Meanwhile, entrepreneur Max O'Hara (Robert Armstrong) comes to Africa to capture animals for his new Hollywood nightspot, The Golden Safari. He convinces Jill to bring Joe to America, where they perform a variety of acts at the dinner club. Alas, after four months on the stage Joe becomes disheartened. He is kept in a cage and his spirit quickly pales. Thus, when a trio of drunks feed him liquor and touch a match to his hand, the inebriated Joe bashes from his prison, levels the nightclub, and is sentenced to be shot. Feeling guilty, O'Hara bribes a sea captain to sail Joe quietly back to Africa. However, while sneaking the gorilla by truck to the pier, Jill passes a burning orphanage. The ape climbs to the top, rescues a trapped baby, and is severely injured in the process. Joe recovers, and for his bravery is pardoned and allowed to return to Africa in style. A sequel, *Joe Meets Tarzan*, was planned but never filmed.

Z

Zacherle, John K. [TV] A popular host of horror programs. Born in Philadelphia in 1918, Zacherle was an English major at the University of Pennsylvania. After serving in World War II, he turned to acting. One of his early assignments was playing a cabinet and coffin maker in a live western show seen locally in Philadelphia. The black-garbed character proved popular with the public, and in 1958 the executives at WCAU decided to give him his own show. The result was Roland, the Cool Ghoul, who hosted broadcasts of horror movies. Preceding the feature, Roland would instruct the would-be mad scientists in his audience on how to transplant brains (although he used a cauliflower), do-it-yourself embalming, dealing with girl friends like his own grim Isobel, and the like. During the film he would interrupt to poke fun at the often hokey storyline.

The success of Roland brought an offer from WOR-TV for Zacherle to host a similar show in New York. He accepted, and adopted the guise of Zacherley. In both incarnations, he was an emaciated figure with slick black hair and a white brow. During the height of his fame, Zacherle edited several horror-filled short story collections such as *Zacherley's Vulture Stew* (1960) and *Zacherley's Midnight Snacks* (1960), and recorded the album *Dinner with Dracula.* In 1967 he took a job hosting a teenage dance program on a New Jersey UHF station, but is currently enjoying a renaissance as a popular radio disc jockey.

Zantis [TV] Extraterrestrials featured in the "Outer Limits" episode "The Zanti Misfits." Foot-long, articulate, antlike creatures, the Zantis have six legs, a large mouth, a bush of golden hair on their heads, twin antennae, and a pair of big eyes. Arriving on earth in a small spaceship, they begin attacking everyone in sight. Eventually, the Zantis are destroyed in a battle which consists of guns and stomping human feet. As the Zantis back home later explain, these creatures were criminals. Since the Zantis are unable to execute their own kind, they sent the felons to our world— knowing that we are not contrite about killing and would do the dirty work for them. see: **Outer Limits, The.**

Zarkon [L] A contemporary hero created in 1975 by author Lin Carter. Headquartered in a block-long building in Knickerbocker City, Zarkon works with a group of five men called the Omega Crew. Individually they are boxer Aloysius Murphy "Scorchy" Muldoon, a magician Nick Naldini, pilot Francis "Ace" Harrigan, Theophilus "Doc" Jenkins who is something of a human computer, and electrical genius Mendel Lowell "Menlo" Parker. As for Zarkon himself, the Lord of the Unknown is thirty years old and a few inches over six feet. He has tawny skin, hypnotic eyes, a superbly muscled physique, and a brilliant mind. An artificially bred superhuman, he hails from the future, traveled backward in time to try and undo disasters that may threaten the world of tomorrow. The first three adventures in the continuing Zarkon saga are *The Nemesis of Evil* (1978), *Invisible Death* (1978), and *The Volcano Ogre* (1979). see: **Carter, Lin; Savage, Doc.**

Zemis [F] Idols worshiped by the

Arawak Indians of the Caribbean. These zemis were fashioned to represent the guardian spirits of each tribe. Actually, every Indian had a spiritual protector. But its powers were determined by the relative wealth and authority of the person it represented. Naturally, the Indians wanted the most potent spirit to look after the tribe as a whole, so the guardian of the chief was automatically named the mascot of all the people. The zemis were carved in both human and animal form, and all of them boasted traditional three-pointed rocks etched with complex decorations. These figures were said to possess the same abilities as the spirits they represented. Generally housed in temples, the zemis were brought forth for tribal rites, which the Indians held on monolithic platforms and in caves. see: **Mascot; Totem.**

Zeus [M] The king of the Greek gods, known as Jupiter or Jove to the Romans. The son of Cronus and Rhea, Zeus was born on Crete. Here he was suckled by the goat Amalthea and looked after by demigods known as Curetes. He'd rather have been in the heavens, but he was safe on Crete— away from the father who had eaten

Zeus

his brothers and sisters, fearful that they might one day overthrow him. Needless to say it is Zeus who returns to unseat Cronus, setting himself up as god of gods. Zeus' first wife is Metis, the daughter of Oceanus and Tethys. However, to forestall being dethroned by one of her children, as prophesied, Zeus eats his spouse. Zeus' second wife is his sister, Hera, who, though she avoids her predecessor's dire lot, in no way has her husband's fidelity.

By Hera, Zeus is the father of Ares, Hephaestus, and Hebe. As for the god's other families, his celestial concubines and offspring are Leto, who bears him Apollo and Artemis; Dione, who mothers Aphrodite; Mala, a daughter of Atlas and mother of Hermes; Themis, by whom he has the Hours; Eurynome, who bears the Graces; Demeter, who presents him with Persephone; and Mnemosyne, with whom he parents the Muses. Zeus' mortal lovers and children are Semele, to whom he appears as lightning and fathers Dionysos; Leda, to whom he comes as a swan and sires Pollux and Helen; Danaë, whom he blesses as a shower of gold and produces Perseus; Alcmene, whom he deceives by masquerading as her husband and brings forth Hercules; Europa, for whom he takes the form of a bull and makes possible Minos, Rhadamanthys, and Sarpedon; Io, by whom he fathers Epaphus; Callisto, to whom he gives Arcas; and Antiope, by whom he sires Zethus and Amphion.

Zeus was held in the highest regard by the Greeks. The Olympics, the great athletic festival, were held in his honor, and the third drink at every meal was downed in his honor. He was feared for his awful temper, and for the rain and lightning he sent, and was beloved for his great rewards and climate moods and weather. If people were good, Zeus was not averse to visiting them and telling them the future through signs, oracles, and lesser gods; if wicked, his wrath knew no bounds.

The king of the gods was constantly within reach of two jars, one containing good things and the other bad, which he was forever passing out to mortals.

Zeus is the youngest or eldest of Cronus' children, depending upon the legend. His brothers are Poseidon and Hades, and his sisters Demeter, Hera, and Hestia. see: **Aphrodite; Apollo; Ares; Artemis; Atlas; Cronus; Demeter; Dionysos; Graces; Hades; Hephaestus; Hera; Hercules; Hermes; Muses; Olympus; Perseus; Poseidon; Rhea; Titans.**

Ziz [F] A gigantic bird of Hebrew lore. The king of birds, Ziz is so large that when its feet are planted on the ground its head pierces the clouds; its wingspan is so great that where the animal flies the ground is darkened from horizon to horizon. It will take an axe seven years to sink to the bottom of a lake which barely covers the feet of this titan! Born on the Fifth Day of Creation, the giant bird uses its wings to protect the earth from strong winds. On the negative side, when its egg hatches, the fluid is sufficient to flood sixty cities, each piece of falling shell crushing 300 trees. Ziz is also known as Sekwi and as Renanim, whose song is heard as the whistling of the wind. see: **Roc; Simurgh.**

Zombie [O] The reanimated corpse of the newly dead. The term zombie comes from the West African *zumbi* which means "god." Revived through voodoo ritual, the zombie obeys the unspoken commands of its master. Though it is most often used to labor in mines or on plantations, the living dead can also be a tool of vengeance. As such, they are the perfect engines of destruction. Extremely powerful, zombies never speak nor do they utter a cry when maimed or wounded. Hacking a zombie to bits may stop the corpse, but each piece will live on; fire will leave a pile of pulsing ashes. Only by feeding salt to a zombie can it be destroyed. A secondary form of zombie is a living person whose soul has been stolen by an occultist.

Although literature has found few plots to hang on a zombie, motion picture makers have found them a most profitable subject. Among the many films in which zombies have been featured are *White Zombie* (1932), *Revolt of the Zombies* (1936), *King of the Zombies* (1941), *Revenge of the Zombies* (1943), *I Walked with a Zombie* (1943), *Zombies on Broadway* (1945), *Zombies of Mora-Tau* (1957), *War of the Zombies* (1963), and *Plague of the Zombies* (1965). see: **Voodoo.**

Zothique [L] A huge land mass of future earth and the setting for many tales by Clark Ashton Smith. Zothique is the sole continent in a great world ocean. Tiny islands float upon the sea which surrounds it including Naat, the Isle of Necromancers; Uccastrog, the Isle of the Torturers; Irobos, the Isle of the Crabs; and the Ilozian Sea archipelagoes where griffins, vampires, and other monsters dwell. A land of deserts, great cities surrounded by even greater walls, and wicked monarchs, the awesome Zothique is located in the spot presently occupied by Asia and Africa. see: **Smith, Clark Ashton.**

SELECTED BIBLIOGRAPHY

Literally hundreds of books, journals, newspapers, and interviews were consulted to produce the more than 1,000 entries contained in this volume. A partial listing follows. It is not complete. This bibliography does not list novels or redundant references. However, it does offer a cross section of volumes ranging from general in scope to very specific—but ever interesting and worth your attention!

Ashley, Mike. *Who's Who in Horror and Fantasy Fiction.* New York: Taplinger, 1978.

Barber, Dulan. *Monsters Who's-Who.* New York: Crescent, 1974.

Beck, Calvin. *Heroes of the Horrors.* New York: Collier, 1975.

Botkin, B.A. *A Treasury of Western Folklore.* New York: Crown, 1975.

Briggs, Katharine. *The Encyclopedia of Fairies.* New York: Pantheon, 1976.

Brombert, Victor. *The Hero in Literature.* New York: Fawcett, 1969.

Campbell, Joseph. *Myths to Live By.* New York: Bantam, 1973.

Cohen, Daniel. *The Greatest Monsters in the World.* New York: Pocket Books, 1977.

Coxe, A.D.H. *Haunted Britain.* London: Pan, 1973.

Daniels, Les. *Living in Fear.* New York: Scribners, 1975.

Dinsdale, Tim. *Monster Hunt.* Washington, D.C.: Acropolis, 1972.

Foster, Robert. *A Guide to Middle Earth.* New York: Ballantine, 1971.

Garden, Nancy. *Vampires.* Philadelphia: Lippincott, 1973.

Gerani, Gary. *Fantastic Television.* New York: Harmony, 1977.

Goulart, Ron. *An Informal History of the Pulp Magazine.* New York: Ace, 1972.

Gray, Louis H. *Mythology of All Races* (thirteen volumes). Boston: Marshall Jones, 1916.

Haining, Peter. *Witchcraft and Black Magic.* New York: Bantam, 1973.

Hall, Edwin S. Jr. *The Eskimo Storyteller.* Tennessee: University of Tennessee, 1975.

Hole, Christina. *English Folk Heroes.* London: B.T. Batsford, 1948.

Horn, Maurice. *The World Encyclopedia of Comics.* New York: Avon, 1976.

Jacobs, Gertrude. *Dictionary of Mythology, Folklore, and Symbols* (two volumes). New York: Scarecrow, 1962.

Josephy, Alvin M. Jr. *The Indian Heritage of America.* New York: Bantam, 1969.

Landsburg, Alan. *In Search of Myths and Monsters.* New York: Bantam, 1977.

Lang, Andrew. *The Brown Fairy Book.* New York: Dover, 1965.

Lang, Andrew. *The Green Fairy Book.* New York: Airmont, 1969.

Lang, Andrew. *The Rainbow Fairy Book.* New York: Schocken, 1977.

Lang, Andrew. *The Red Fairy Book.* New York: Dover, 1965.

Lee, Walt. *Reference Guide to Fantastic Films* (three volumes). Los Angeles: Chelsea-Lee, 1974.

Lord, Glenn. *The Last Celt.* New York: Berkley, 1977.

Lupoff, Richard. *Edgar Rice Burroughs: Master of Adventure.* New York: Ace, 1968.

Maltin, Leonard. *The Disney Films.* New York: Popular Library, 1978.

O'Hanlon, Rev. John. *Irish Local Legends.* Dublin: James Duffy, 1896.

Ransome, Arthur. *Old Peter's Russian Tales.* Middlesex, England: Puffin, 1974.

Robinson, H.S., and Wilson, Knox. *Myths and Legends of All Nations.* Totowa, New Jersey: Littlefield-Adams, 1976.

Rottensteiner, Franz. *The Fantasy Book.* New York: Collier, 1978.

Roy, John Flint. *A Guide to Barsoom.* New York: Ballantine, 1976.

Santesson, Hans. *Understanding Mu.* New York: Warner, 1970.

Stanford, Barbara. *Myths and Modern Man.* New York: Pocket Books, 1972.

Steiner, Rudolf. *Dictionary of the Psychic, Mystic, Occult.* New York: Blauvelt, 1973.

Terrace, Vincent. *The Complete Encyclopedia of Television Programs* (two volumes). Cranbury, New Jersey: A.S. Barnes, 1977.

Trimble, Bjo. *The Star Trek Concordance.* New York: Ballantine, 1976.

Wolf, Leonard. *Monsters.* San Francisco: Straight Arrow, 1974.

Current magazines which provided helpful information and are excellent, ongoing windows into the world of the fantastic are:

For fantasy films and merchandise:

Famous Monsters of Filmland, Warren Publishing Company, 145 E. 32 St., New York, NY 10016.

Cinefantastique, P.O.B. 270, Oak Park, IL 60303.

For science fiction literature:
  Omni, 909 Third Ave., New York, NY 10022.
  Analog, 304 E. 45th St., New York, NY 10017.

For comic books:

The Comic Reader, Street Enterprises, P.O.B. 255, Menomonee Falls, WI 53051.

ABOUT THE AUTHOR

JEFF ROVIN, science fiction consultant and former comic book editor, is the author of *A Pictorial History of Science Fiction Films*, *The Fabulous Fantasy Films*, *From the Land Beyond Beyond*, *The UFO Movie Quizbook*, and *The Superhero Quizbook*, among many other books.